D0850337

The History of US-Japan Relations

Makoto Iokibe
Editor

Tosh Minohara
English translation editor

The History of
US-Japan Relations

From Perry to the Present

palgrave
macmillan

Editor:
Makoto Iokibe
Prefectural University of Kumamoto
Kumamoto-ken, Japan

English translation Editor:
Tosh Minohara
Kobe University
Kobe, Japan

ISBN 978-981-10-3183-0   ISBN 978-981-10-3184-7   (eBook)
DOI 10.1007/978-981-10-3184-7

Library of Congress Control Number: 2017930259

Cover illustration: J. F. Woodruff / Alamy Stock Photo

Printed on acid-free paper

This Palgrave Macmillan imprint is published by Springer Nature
The registered company is Springer Nature Singapore Pte Ltd.
The registered company address is: 152 Beach Road, #21-01/04 Gateway East, Singapore 189721, Singapore

PREFACE

In 1853, an American fleet led by Commodore Matthew C. Perry steamed into Edo Bay with the mission of bringing an end to Tokugawa Japan's policy of more than 200 years of seclusion. This contact marked the very beginning of a rich relationship that was maintained for nearly 90 years until the outbreak of the Pacific War in 1941, after which it was quickly resumed upon the end of American occupation in 1952 and has strengthened for nearly 65 years.

When America and Japan first encountered each other, they were both on the fringes of the great-power politics still very much centered in Europe. At the same time, however, both nations were just at the dawn of significant transformations that would eventually allow them to attain their status as great powers. As history shows us, America's pivotal role in the two global wars of the twentieth century transformed it into the most powerful and prosperous nation that the world has seen in modern times, allowing it to forge what is now known as the "American Century." It was also during this time that Japan gradually ascended in importance among the family of nations once it abandoned the policy of seclusion and quickly turned to embracing the path toward rapid modernization. The effort paid off handsomely as Japan was able to pull off stunning victories over both China and Russia which, in turn, catapulted Japan to the status of not only the first nation state in Asia to successfully modernize, but also as a mighty imperial power in its own right.

But rapid change also had ramifications. The tremendous pace of Japan's progress also impacted the very foundation of US–Japan relations. Early on, this bilateral relationship was based on primarily on mutual friendship, with America acting as the wise and benevolent mentor, astutely guiding Japan in its quest to enter the global system and survive. But such a relationship was far from permanent. As both countries entered the twentieth century, the intricate relationship between these two emerging powers on opposite sides of the Pacific transformed itself into one that possessed elements of *both* cooperation and rivalry. After time, feelings of rivalry and the ensuing perception of threat began to gradually supplant the spirit of cooperation in the aftermath of First World War. US–Japan relations hastily deteriorated even further during the "dark valley" of the 1930s as Japan increasingly leaned more toward militarism and sent its army into Manchuria in September 1931. The Japanese policy of expansionism now redefined the relationship to one that was based on friction and tension; it would ultimately reach its breaking point and completely collapse in December 1941.

But as soon as the vicious and bitterly fought conflict in the Pacific came to an end with Japan's surrender and acceptance of the terms of the Potsdam Declaration, the two countries wasted no time in returning to their original state of mutual friendship and cooperation with the start of the postwar occupation period. In hindsight, the reforms implemented during the occupation and the reconstruction of Japan were actually a joint venture based on cooperation between the two countries. Japan was determined and fully committed to embark on the postwar path to a peaceful return to international society, while the United States—which in the meantime had become the most influential nation in the world as well as the leader of the West—enthusiastically supported Japan's democratization process, along with its quest of economic recovery. Friendship once again became the backbone of the relationship, which reached its zenith with the reversion of Okinawa to Japan in May 1972. But once reversion had been achieved, US–Japan relations entered a new phase that was marked by intense economic friction. Japan's rapid economic rise and the resulting industrial prowess of the country began to be perceived by many Americans as a real threat to US national interests. This feeling was further exacerbated by the fact that the United States was entering into a period of relative decline while also struggling to cope with the deep wounds that the Vietnam War had inflicted upon its society. It was almost as if history would repeat itself as America and Japan encountered a difficult period, with elements of both cooperation and conflict coexisting within their bilateral relationship. For some, the two nations seemed to be once again heading for a cataclysmic clash.

However, despite a few superficial similarities to the prewar period, hostilities never ensued and instead a strong alliance remained throughout the Cold War. This also marked the stage where the relationship finally attained a level of maturity. The postwar US–Japan alliance began in 1952 and remained intact even during the era of bitter economic friction from the 1970s to the 1990s. Mike Mansfield, then US ambassador to Japan—a position that he held for 12 years, longer than any other US ambassador to Japan to this day—aptly described the US–Japan relationship during the 1980s as "the most important bilateral relationship in the world, bar none."

But drastic changes to the international environment would bring about new challenges to this formidable relationship. When the Cold War came to an abrupt end with the collapse of the Soviet Union, both America and Japan lost a common threat that had made alliance not only pertinent, but ever stronger. Thus, there were a few who predicted a demise of the US–Japan alliance—after all, it had outlived its purpose—or at least the scaling back of military support to levels such that US armed forces would only be present in Japan during times of national crisis. As history shows us, however, this never materialized. Even without a common foe, the mutual understanding and affinity between the two peoples only deepened further as both nations shared the common core values of democracy, human rights, the rule of law, and a free market economy. The relationship today has become even closer in the face of the threats posed by North Korea's repeated attempts to develop nuclear capability and conduct missile tests as well as China's blatant disregard for international law and aggressive expansion into the surrounding oceans, which are also claimed by other nations. Thus, in the postwar period spanning just over 70 years, the US–Japan relationship has been further strengthened by a firm and deep bond; it has indeed become one of the most formidable and mutually empowering relationships that exists on this planet.

Before we delve into our examination of the history of US–Japan relations in the following chapters, it will be convenient it to keep in mind the respective periodization of the prewar and postwar periods:

Prewar Period:

1. Early friendship (1853–1905): From the "Black Ships" to the Treaty of Portsmouth.

2. Cooperation and rivalry (1905–1930): Game of realpolitik between the two powers.
3. Collapse of relations (1931–1945): From the Manchurian Incident to the end of the Pacific War.

Postwar Period:

1. Early friendship (1945–1972): From the Occupation period to the reversion of Okinawa.
2. Cooperation and rivalry (1972–1995): Economic friction and security cooperation.
3. Maturing of relations (1995–present): Maturing of the partnership and facing new global challenges.

* * *

The Japanese edition of this book was first published in 2008. The purpose of the original version was to provide a comprehensive yet easily comprehensible overview of the historical changes and developments in the diplomatic and political relationship between these two nations, from the arrival of Perry to the present day. The Japanese edition was born out of the close collaboration of 18 leading scholars of history and international politics who all possess deep knowledge and insight into the politics and diplomacy of America and Japan. This team of experts labored closely with one another to create a consistent and structured account of the rich history that the US–Japan relationship provides. The initial research and writing phase lasted for over three years, and the contributors were all meticulous in their efforts to thoroughly review each other's work and provide helpful comments to one another. As a result, the book possesses a solid consistency and fluidity that is seldom seen in edited volumes. Perhaps this is one reason why this book has been widely acclaimed in Japan; it has now attained the position of becoming the standard textbook on the subject matter throughout Japan's major universities. It has also been widely read by the general reader, as attested by the fact that the Japanese edition is now in its tenth printing which is a remarkable feat for any work of history.

The catalyst for producing the English edition of the book was provided by the Japan Library initiative that was launched in 2014 by the Japan Publishing Industry Foundation for Culture (JPIC). This ambitious project set out to translate and publish 100 works of non-fiction—

published in Japan within the past decade—that best represent Japanese history, culture, and society with the aim of ensuring that a global audience can also enjoy these standard works that until now have been accessible only to those who can read Japanese. It was our good fortune that this book was recognized and selected by a panel of experts of the Japan Library selection committee as an "outstanding work" that met the Japan Library criteria and was chosen to be among the first fourteen books to be translated into English and then published by the leading publishers throughout world.

In preparation for this English edition, not only has the original text been thoroughly edited, but an entirely new final chapter has also been added which traces US–Japan relations from the beginning of the twenty-first century until 2015. Therefore, the English version covers much more contemporary ground than the Japanese edition. At the same time, however, supplementary sections in the original edition that provided further insight into key terms and events have been omitted in order to keep the English edition more fluid and focused on the main text. Photos, diagrams, tables, and lists of references originally included with the Japanese reader in mind have also been removed from this edition. While these multiple changes to the English edition make it an altogether different book than the original Japanese edition in many aspects, the reader of this volume can rest assured that the spirit and the quality of the original book remains very much alive and intact within the pages.

Finally, some words of acknowledgement. I am profoundly grateful to Professor Tosh Minohara, the English translation editor, for his time and effort in adroitly guiding this book to its publication. He not only secured a publisher, but he also took immense care and attention in editing as well as adapting the original Japanese edition so that it would be better suited for a non-Japanese audience. Furthermore, he worked very closely with the original contributors to ensure that no translation errors remained in the final text. And last but not least, I would like to extend my sincere gratitude to Palgrave Macmillan for recognizing the value of this work and embracing our mission of making this volume much more accessible to readers beyond Japan.

Makoto Iokibe, editor
January 2017

CONTENTS

EDITORS

Makoto Iokibe, Ph.D. (Editor). Chancellor, Prefectural University of Kumamoto; President, Hyogo Earthquake Memorial 21st Century Research Institute; Former President, National Defense Academy of Japan; Professor Emeritus of Japanese political and diplomatic history, Kobe University.

Tosh Minohara, Ph.D. (English translation editor). Professor of US–Japan relations and international history, Graduate School of Law, Kobe University; Fellow, St. Antony's College, University of Oxford; Advisory Board Member, US–Japan Council, Fellow and Former Executive Committee Member, US–Japan Foundation Leadership Program.

CONTRIBUTORS

Robert D. Eldridge, Ph.D., President, The Eldridge Think Tank.

Ryūji Hattori, Ph.D., Professor of East Asian international political history, Faculty of Policy Studies, Chuo University.

Satoshi Hattori, Ph.D., Adjunct Lecturer of Japanese political and diplomatic history, School of Foreign Studies, Osaka University.

Kaoru Iokibe, Ph.D., Professor of Japanese political and diplomatic history, Graduate Schools for Law and Politics, University of Tokyo.

Fumiaki Kubo, Ph.D., Professor of American political and diplomatic history, Graduate Schools for Law and Politics, University of Tokyo.

Ayako Kusunoki, Ph.D., Associate Professor of Japanese political and diplomatic history, International Research Center for Japanese Studies.

Ryōta Murai, Ph.D., Professor of Japanese political and diplomatic history, Faculty of Law, Komazawa University.

Kōji Murata, Ph.D., Professor of international relations, Faculty of Law, Doshisha University; Former President, Doshisha University.

Hiroshi Nakanishi, M.A., Professor of international politics, School of Government, Kyoto University.

Takuya Sasaki, Ph.D., Professor of American political and diplomatic history, College of Law and Politics, Rikkyo University.

Futoshi Shibayama, Ph.D., Professor of American diplomatic history and military history, School of Policy Studies, Kwansei Gakuin University.

Yoshihide Soeya, Ph.D., Professor of international politics and international relations of East Asia, Faculty of Law, Keio University.

Masayuki Tadokoro, Ph.D., Professor of international relations, Faculty of Law, Keio University.

Shūsuke Takahara, Ph.D., Professor of American diplomatic history, Faculty of Foreign Studies, Kyoto Sangyo University.

Akihiko Tanaka, Ph.D., Professor of international politics, Institute for Advanced Studies on Asia, University of Tokyo; Former President, Japan International Cooperation Agency.

Yasutoshi Teramoto, Ph.D., Vice President, Hiroshima University; Professor of Japanese diplomatic history and international relations, Graduate School of Social Sciences, Hiroshima University.

PART I

CHAPTER 1

America Encounters Japan, 1836–94

Tosh Minohara and Kaoru Iokibe

Ending Japan's Policy of Seclusion

Japan's northerly neighbor was the first country to show a strong interest in opening Japan to trade and commerce. In the late seventeenth century Russian trappers traveling eastward through Siberia began to venture south through the Kamchatka Peninsula. By the mid-eighteenth century they had also begun to set foot in Ezo (Hokkaido) via the Kurile Islands and Sakhalin, areas that were inhabited by the Ainu at that time. This prompted the Shogunate (Bakufu) to send a number of survey expeditions to Ezo in order to strengthen its administrative control of the region. Around this time Russia sent its first official mission to Japan, led by Lieutenant Adam Laxman, who traveled to the city of Hakodate in 1793 in what became the first of several attempts by Russia to establish trade relations with Japan.

American sailors also began to edge closer to Japan in the 1820s as the growth of the prosperous whaling industry sent whalers further into the Western Pacific. In 1825, the Bakufu responded to the rapid increase in

T. Minohara
Graduate School of Law, Kobe University, Kobe, Japan

K. Iokibe
Graduate Schools for Law and Politics, University of Tokyo, Tokyo, Japan

© The Author(s) 2017
M. Iokibe (ed.), T. Minohara (trans. ed.), *The History of US–Japan Relations*, DOI 10.1007/978-981-10-3184-7_1

3

the appearance of foreign ships around Japanese waters by passing a law—the Edict to Repel Foreign Vessels (*Ikokusen uchiharairei*)—that stipulated that all foreign ships approaching Japan would be subject to shelling without any prior warning.

By this time American interest had grown substantially in establishing relations with the mystic nation across the Pacific. In 1836, President Andrew Jackson sent Edmund Roberts as a special envoy to convince Japan to end its policy of isolation and open the nation to trade. Unfortunately, the expedition was cut short when Roberts suddenly passed away in Macao en route to Japan due to an illness. The following year an undeterred Jackson sent a second expedition to Japan led by Charles W. King, on the merchant ship *Morrison*. However, King was forced to terminate his mission when the first official encounter between the United States and Japan near the coast of Uraga led to a one-sided use of force by the Japanese. At this point, the United States had yet to extend its territory to the Pacific coast but it would soon make a push westward in order to fulfill its "Manifest Destiny."

From 1845 to 1848, America's push to expand westward gained further momentum as it annexed the Republic of Texas and the southern portion of the Oregon territory, and further seized vast amounts of territory, especially in the aftermath of its victory in the Mexican–American War (1846–48). The newly acquired lands were soon occupied as the gold rush in California drew in huge numbers of Americans from the East and Midwest to settle on the West Coast.

Just a decade after King's unsuccessful mission to Japan in 1837, the United States had been transformed into a Pacific nation. Naturally, the United States began to look across the ocean seeking trade relations with Japan. The whaling industry was of particular importance and thus it made practical economic sense to secure an agreement from Japan that it would provide coal, food, and drinking water to American whalers, as well as docking privileges to allow them to conduct ship repairs.

While the Bakufu had decided to respond to the growing numbers of foreign ships around Japan by brute force, on the other hand it did very little to strengthen its coastal defense fortifications. This began to change, however, when the Opium War broke out in neighboring China in 1840. The Qing dynasty was soundly defeated by the British, leaving it with no recourse but to accept an unequal treaty which forced it to cede Hong Kong, open Shanghai and four other ports, pay a large reparation, and consent to consular jurisdiction as well as renouncing the right to tariff autonomy to the British. This humiliating defeat demonstrated to the Bakufu that even China, a nation that Japan had looked up to and tried to emulate for many years, was utterly helpless when faced with the might of a modern Western power.

Although isolated, Japan was alert to the Western encroachment, and fearing a similar fate to that of the Qing dynasty, the Bakufu prudently changed its policy to one that would avoid a direct conflict with the Western powers. This was done by repealing the Edict to Repel Foreign Vessels and issuing a new proclamation in 1842, the Edict for the Provision of Fuel and Water (*Shinsui kyūyorei*), which permitted fuel, food, and water to be provided to foreign ships as necessary. This coincided with Washington's third attempt to establish relations with Japan.

Keen to avoid a repeat of the failure of the *Morrison* mission, President James K. Polk next chose an active duty naval officer, Commodore James Biddle of the Pacific Squadron (there was no "fleet" in the US Navy until 1907 during the presidency of Theodore Roosevelt). He had previously successfully concluded America's first treaty with China, and was confident that he could accomplish the same feat with Japan. However, this mission was cut short when the Bakufu adamantly refused to negotiate and instead ordered him to sail to Nagasaki. But when Biddle was forced to temporarily retreat due to the outbreak of the Mexican–American War, the Bakufu misread his sudden departure as capitulation as a result of its uncompromising position.

Almost three years later, in April 1849, Commander James Glynn sailed to Nagasaki on the warship USS *Preble* and was able to retrieve the shipwrecked American crew of the whaler *Lagoda*, who had been detained by the Japanese authorities two years earlier. Returning to America as a hero, Glynn advised President Millard Fillmore that America should work toward establishing trade relations with Japan without further delay, and suggested that future US missions be willing to display a show of force if necessary. Fillmore's Secretary of State, Daniel Webster, who was anxious to establish relations with Japan, tasked Captain John H. Aulick, commander of the East Asia Squadron, with the mission of opening up Japan once and for all. Once preparations had been completed in June 1851, Aulick set sail with three warships. The mission did not even reach Japan, however, as President Fillmore was forced to relieve Aulick of his command due to reports of his constant bickering with his captains, which was seen to be undermining the entire mission.

Commodore Perry and the Treaty of Kanagawa

After this setback, the goal of opening Japan fell upon the shoulders of Commodore Matthew C. Perry. As a senior naval officer, Perry already had an impressive career that ranged from enforcing the slave trade ban along the coast of Africa to the recent Mexican–American War. Thus, his initial reaction was that the appointment was not suitable for someone of his stature and he only accepted the position on the condition that there would be a doubling in number of ships attached to the East Asia Squadron. Believing that Perry was the most capable individual up to the task, President Fillmore granted the request and Perry was given the appointment of commander of the East Asia Squadron in March 1852.

Born to a prominent naval family, Perry felt a strong sense of responsibility to succeed in whatever mission he was given, and this would be no exception. For eight months, he painstakingly planned his mission by conducting meticulous research on Japan, not only carefully examining the past missions to Japan, but also traveling to the port of Nantucket to personally speak with the whaling captains who possessed vast amounts of firsthand knowledge of the winds and currents around Japan. He also purchased a large collection of books on Japan from the Netherlands, at that time the only Western country that had direct contact with Japan. After a thorough study and deliberation, he reached the conclusion that it would be necessary to take a firm stance in negotiating with the Bakufu and be prepared to utilize force if necessary.

Perry also made sure that there were clear mission objectives. Whereas Glynn and Aulick had focused on the establishment of trade relations, Perry felt that the opening of Japanese ports to American ships for resupplying, fueling, and repairs should take priority. In his mind, protecting the lives of American sailors shipwrecked in Japanese coastal waters was of utmost importance. His was also keen on establishing a string of coaling stations along Japan's coast, since the steamships of the day were very limited in their range. Perry's prioritization was based on the desire to find the best methods to further support and develop the whaling industry which was the backbone of the American economy at the time.

Having decided early on that it would be necessary to take a firm stance in his negotiations with Japan, Perry realized that he needed to make a strong impression upon the Japanese. Therefore, he gathered the best examples of American industrial prowess at the time, such as a quarter-size working steam locomotive, an electric telegraph, a telescope, and even spectacles. As Secretary of State Daniel Webster had complete trust in his commander, he provided unwavering support as Perry made his preparations; he even allowed him to draft his own orders while at sea. Webster's support was crucial in ensuring the success of the mission as Congress was becoming increasingly skeptical over the rising costs of the mission.

On November 24, 1852, Perry boarded the USS *Mississippi*, a side-wheel steam frigate, and set course due east, crossing the Indian Ocean and stopping at several ports along the way to refuel before casting anchor in Hong Kong on April 7, 1853. Upon his arrival, Perry was disappointed to learn that the sidewheel steam frigate USS *Susquehanna*, the largest and most powerful warship in the squadron, had not yet arrived; Perry believed that this ship would play in a key role in the upcoming negotiations with the Japanese. Unbeknownst to Perry, the *Susquehanna* had been urgently dispatched to Shanghai on the orders of the US commissioner to China, Humphrey Marshall, shortly before his arrival. This event highlighted the clear division among American officials about whether its Asia policy should prioritize Japan or China. Marshall favored a stronger American commitment toward China and as a result felt that it was entirely consistent with America's national interests to take advantage of the ongoing domestic chaos in China as way to gain concessions alongside the other powers. However, Webster did not share this view and thus the *Susquehanna* was promptly ordered to revert to Perry's command.

Perry's reinforced squadron arrived in Naha Bay on May 26, 1853, where he met the regent of the Ryukyu Kingdom. He then headed for the Ogasawara Islands (also known as the Bonin Islands), which turned out to possess a good natural harbor that would be suitable for mooring steamships as well setting up a coaling station. Thus claim was immediately laid upon Ogasawara as American territory in accordance with the international practice of the day (surprisingly, some of the residents of Ogasawara were American castaways from New England).

On July 8, Perry finally reached the coast of Uraga and requested that the Bakufu receive a personal letter from President Fillmore that requested the opening of Japanese ports to American ships. The Bakufu responded in its usual manner by redirecting foreign envoys to Nagasaki, but Perry flatly refused and instead threatened to push deeper into Edo Bay, threatening, if necessary, to send a landing party up to Edo Castle to deliver the letter personally. Unbeknownst to the Japanese, Perry was merely bluffing as he was under orders from the president not to take any action that could lead to war.

Perry's imposing "black ships" (*kurofune*)—named by the Japanese after the colour of the hulls which were covered in tar—imposingly sailed into Edo Bay and began surveying the surrounding area. Shaken by this unprecedented and brazen conduct, the Bakufu officials grudgingly consented in accepting the president's letter, hoping that this would satisfy Perry's demands. To their disappointment, however, Perry informed them that he would only be withdrawing temporarily to give the Bakufu time to deliberate over President Fillmore's request. This move, initially unplanned, was Perry's clever response to counter the Bakufu's procrastination. Since his ships were becoming low on both fresh water and food— he had refused the Japanese offer of fresh supplies lest his position would be undermined—it made tactical sense to withdraw to Hong Kong to resupply while not revealing their vulnerability.

However, by the time Perry reached Hong Kong via Naha on August 7, the American position had changed as the incoming president Franklin Pierce and his secretary of state William L. Marcy considered the mission to be futile. Moreover, Pierce was concerned that Perry's belligerent approach towards Japan might lead to conflict between the two countries. Thus, the president reiterated to Perry that his mission was to conduct peaceful negotiations and the use of force for was only permitted for self-defense; he went as far as to remind the commander that the final authority to declare war rested with Congress. Pierce was also critical of the additional financial burden incurred by Perry's decision to postpone the conclusion of a treaty until the following spring. Therefore, he subsequently overruled the decision by the previous administration to dispatch the USS *Vermont* to further bolster Perry's squadron. But the strongest message conveyed to Perry was the refusal to approve the American annexation of the Ogasawara Islands on the grounds that Perry had overstepped his authority (after Pierce renounced America's possession of the Ogasawara Islands, they were later claimed by the Meiji government and officially incorporated as Japanese territory in 1876).

Since Perry was confident that his approach would eventually succeed, he decided to disregard Pierce's orders and persist in confronting the Bakufu in a firm manner. Perry not only felt that it was in American national interests to pry open Japan, but it was also in their utmost interest to accomplish this before the great European powers of Britain, France, and Russia did so. Thus when he learned that the Russian envoy Admiral Yevfimy Putyatin was sailing toward Japan, he hastily departed Hong Kong for Edo in February 1854, nearly six months earlier than planned. His revamped squadron would be an impressive display of naval force, consisting of seven vessels, including the *Susquehanna* and the *Mississippi* and the new flagship, the USS *Powhatan*, a state-of-the-art sidewheel steam frigate.

The formidable East Asia Squadron arrived in Japan on February 13, 1854, and proceeded up the coast to Kanagawa (near Yokohama, which was at that time a small and remote fishing village), the site that had been decided earlier. The negotiations began on March 8 and lasted nearly three weeks. The Bakufu was fully aware that it could not resist the pressure from the Western powers indefinitely. The Bakufu's chief negotiator, scholar-diplomat Hayashi Fukusai, and a number of other Bakufu officials accepted Perry's request to shelter American castaways since it was a purely humanitarian issue. Hayashi wisely suggested that because the issue of trade relations was less pressing it should be discussed in depth at a later date. Perry concurred, and on March 31, 1854, a 12-article treaty entitled the Treaty of Peace and Amity between the United States and the Empire of Japan (*Nichibeiwashin jōyaku*) was drafted. This treaty, known more commonly as the Treaty of Kanagawa, marked the official beginning of relations between the US and Japan (see Table 1.1).

Although still an emerging power itself, the United States had succeeded in becoming the first nation to open Japan, even ahead of Britain, the most powerful nation at that time. As a result, Japan was able to obtain much more favorable terms than Qing China had received when it had been forced open by Britain. Thus Japan was fortunate that its doors had been

Table 1.1   Main points of the Treaty of Peace and Amity (Treaty of Kanagawa)

1.	Opening of Shimoda and Hakodate, supplying wood, water, provisions, and coal at both ports, and the establishment of zones where American sailors have the freedom to move about
2.	Permission for US consuls or agents to reside in Shimoda (the interpretation of this point would later be contested by the Americans and the Japanese)
3.	Rescue of shipwrecked sailors
4.	Permission for American ships to purchase necessary commodities
5.	Inclusion of a most-favored-nation clause (such that all future concessions granted by Japan to other foreign powers would also be granted to the US)

opened to the world by the United States rather than by a European power with more imperialistic ambitions.

Townsend Harris and the Opening of Japan to Commerce

Once Perry had achieved the goal of opening Japan, America soon began to seek out trade relations. This important task was entrusted to Townsend Harris, an obscure individual at the time whose appointment was a result of his personal relationship with the secretary of state in addition to his persistent requests to the president. As a bachelor who was deeply interested in and knowledgeable about affairs in Asia, Harris emerged as the ideal candidate for this rather unpopular position. As no one else showed an interest, he was promptly sent to Japan as the first US consul general (later minister) to that country, as had been stipulated by Article 11 of the Treaty of Kanagawa. In contrast with Perry's mighty warships, Harris arrived lacking any military support, accompanied only by his Dutch American interpreter and secretary, Henry Heusken. This left a clear impression upon the Bakufu that the United States was a vastly different nation than the other European powers.

Harris, an Anglophobe, had been critical of the injustices inflicted upon Qing China by the British, particularly during the Opium War, and felt that it would be his personal mission to protect Japan from the hostile intentions of the imperialist powers. Harris's first task was to meet with Shogun Tokugawa Iesada to deliver a letter from the president requesting the conclusion of a treaty of trade and commerce. However, a few senior Bakufu officials acted to prevent direct negotiations with the Shogun by intentionally making the entire process painfully slow. But a breakthrough was reached when the Shimoda magistrate Inoue Kiyonao agreed to negotiate revisions to the Treaty of Kanagawa in exchange for Harris delaying his meeting with the shogun.

Seizing this opportunity, Harris accepted the proposal and this led to the conclusion of the Shimoda Convention in June 1857. This convention had two important points. First, it fixed the rate of exchange between the dollar and the Japanese currency (set at 1 dollar to 4800 *mon*), which established the ground rules necessary to incorporate Japan into the global trade system. Second, it granted American consular jurisdiction (extraterritorial rights) that allowed American criminals to be tried by the American Consul General in accordance with US domestic law. It was not until October that Harris was finally allowed to proceed to Edo for his first meeting with Iesada that paved the way for official negotiations to take place in concluding a commerce treaty with Japan.

During the negotiations, Harris persuaded the Bakufu that it was in Japan's best interests to conclude a treaty with the United States, emphasizing the peaceful and amicable intentions of America in contrast with the military-backed imperialism displayed by the other Western powers. A case in point was the ongoing conflict engulfing neighboring China in the Second Opium War (1856–60). Bakufu officials were fully aware that America was not as innocent as Harris had claimed it to be since it possessed knowledge that the United States had seized territory through its victory in the Mexican–American War and that there were many American merchants involved in the opium trade. However, given the current predicament, the Bakufu leaders reached the decision that it was in Japan's best interests to accept Harris' proposals. The ensuing negotiations led to the US–Japan Treaty of Amity and Commerce (*Nichibei shūkotsūshō jōyaku*), or, more commonly, the Harris Treaty of July 29, 1858 (see Table 1.2).

It is worthwhile to keep in mind that while the Harris Treaty would be presented as a prime example of an "unequal treaty" afterwards, at the time of its signing the Bakufu was quite satisfied with its content. Both Japan and Qing China looked favorably upon extraterritoriality from the standpoint that it extricated themselves from the responsibility of having to deal with foreigners. Likewise, both nations found the unilateral most-favored-nation clause an expedient way to encourage competition amongst the foreign powers. Furthermore, due to Harris's good intentions, the customs duties were set relatively high at nearly 20%, and unlike China, Japan was able to oppose a clause that allowed foreigners to engage in direct commerce within its borders.

Table 1.2   Main points of the Treaty of Amity and Commerce (Harris Treaty)

1. Opening of four new ports, including Kanagawa and Hyogo; the right to reside and lease land in these areas
2. Opening of the cities of Edo and Osaka; right to reside and lease land for commercial purposes
3. Granting of consular jurisdiction
4. Continuing negotiations regarding customs duties
5. Permitting the exchange between domestic and foreign currency; foreign currency to be accepted where ports are open and unrestricted export of currency including gold and silver
6. Approving a unilateral most-favored-nation clause

Although the Imperial Court refused to approve the treaty, the Bakufu was committed to taking the first big step toward modernization. Japan's doors were now open and over the following weeks, the Bakufu entered into similar agreements with the Netherlands, Britain, France, and Russia. Along with the Harris Treaty, these are collectively referred to as the Ansei treaties, being signed during the era of Ansei (1854–60).

THE TREATY REVISION AND THE FIRST SINO-JAPANESE WAR

While Harris was successful in establishing a special relationship between America and Japan, the Bakufu was also able to quickly capitalize on this new relationship. Towards the end of Harris's tenure as minister, the United States came to Japan's rescue on a number of occasions. The signing of the Harris Treaty in the face of strong opposition from the Imperial Court led to a surge in the xenophobic movement to expel foreigners from Japan (*jōi*). The substantial disruption caused by supporters of the *jōi* movement made it impossible to open the ports of Hyogo (Kobe) and Niigata as well as the cities of Edo and Osaka prior to the deadline stipulated by the Ansei treaties. Realizing that it was domestic turmoil that was hindering the implementation of the treaty, Harris quickly stepped in to mediate on behalf of the Bakufu to convince Britain and France to allow delaying the opening these ports and cities until mid-1862 (Ishii 1966). This effectively removed any excuse for these powers to intervene in Japan.

Despite some difficulties dealing with the Bakufu, America continued to demonstrate its unwavering friendship toward Japan, something that the European nations had no interest in doing. But US–Japan relations would be tested in January 1861 when Heusken was assassinated by a group of *jōi* samurai. Although this assassination was but one of several attacks on foreign nationals in the final chaotic years of the Bakufu, it had a particularly adverse impact on Japan's image. In a show of protest toward the Bakufu the contingent of foreign ministers and consuls, with the notable exception of Harris, withdrew to Yokohama. Despite his deep personal loss, however, Harris not only remained in Edo but also supported the Bakufu by helping to deflect the criticism by the European powers who insisted that the Bakufu should be held accountable.

Despite the special relationship, America's presence in Japan showed a marked decrease during the early 1860s due to the outbreak of the American Civil War (1861–65), but this did not alter Japan's perception of America as a trusted and dependable partner. Minister Resident Robert

H. Pruyn, who was appointed by President Abraham Lincoln, succeeded Harris in 1862, and he continued the policy of supporting the Bakufu. At times, however, this was not easy—as when the American legation in Edo was burned to the ground in May 1863. Pruyn took refuge in Yokohama amid rumors of a possible attack on himself, but he still refused to lay blame on the Bakufu.

But Pruyn refused to support the Bakufu when American interests were threatened. For example, when the Bakufu, under unrelenting pressure from the Imperial Court, suggested the closing of the port of Yokohama, Pruyn promptly joined the European ministers and refused to comply. Furthermore, Pruyn took a similar course following a military clash in the Shimonoseki Straits in June 1864. The Chōshū clan, which was at the center of the *jōi* movement, had shelled unarmed foreign merchants ships from their forts ashore. America joined with the British, French, and the Dutch to retaliate. The forts were quickly overrun in September and in the following year the diplomatic representatives of the four nations sent their warships to the shores of Hyogo to send a message to the Imperial Court in nearby Kyoto. This show of force finally led the Imperial Court to cease resisting the Ansei treaties. But the Bakufu was also penalized and it had to relent to a revision of customs duty rates. In June 1866, the Bakufu consented to a new harsher convention that drastically reduced duties down to 5% on most items. Despite this, Pruyn still continued to play the role of mediator between the European powers and the Bakufu, and due to this position, US–Japan relations never became as tense as they did between Japan and Europe.

The Meiji Restoration and the Birth of Modern Japan

The anti-Bakufu movement led by the Satsuma and Chōshū clans gained more steam, and in January 1868 the Imperial Court declared a return to Imperial rule. A civil war, known as the Boshin War (1868–69), soon pitted the forces of the new government against the supporters of the Bakufu. The domestic chaos in Japan also affected the United States. When Pruyn's successor as minister resident, the former New York State congressman Robert B. Van Valkenburgh, visited Kobe in February to attend the opening ceremony of Hyogo port, samurai from the Bizen province (present-day Okayama) opened fire upon a group of foreigners. But the new government was able to quickly seize control of the situation—the leader of the incident, Taki Zenzaburō, was quickly arrested and forced to commit seppuku—which led the United States to have more faith in the Meiji government.

The center of Bakufu power, Edo Castle, was surrendered to the new government in May 1868. At this juncture, Van Valkenburgh believed that the Bakufu could still return to power. However, Washington's stance was more ambiguous so Valkenburgh used utmost caution to remain neutral. For instance, when the ironclad American warship *Stonewall* that was sold to the Bakufu arrived in Japan, Van Valkenburgh, on consultation with the other foreign powers, refused to relinquish the ship to the Bakufu under the pretext of neutrality. When it was finally released, it was to the new government. The formidable *Stonewall*, renamed *Azuma*, was the warship that delivered the coup de grâce to the Bakufu naval forces led by Admiral Enomoto Takeaki. But Van Valkenburgh persisted in dealing firmly with the Meiji government. When it detained the *Peiho* in May 1869—a former Bakufu ship purchased by an American merchant—and tore off the Stars and Stripes, Van Valkenburgh promptly issued a stern protest and even hinted of a military retaliation.

But American policy was to remain neutral and not to get involved in Japan's domestic affairs. This was in stark contrast to the stances of both Britain and France, who were eager to influence Japanese politics and take sides; Britain favored the Satsuma and Chōshū while France supported the Bakufu. Given that the political situation was very fluid at the time, American policy was a logical one considering that it was nearly impossible to devise a coherent strategy toward Japan.

Charles E. De Long, who assumed the post of US minister to Japan in 1869, took pains to rebuild the special friendship between America and Japan once it was clear that the Meiji government was here to stay. Therefore, he was eager provide advice to the new government and cooperated wherever possible in order to promote trust. He also attempted to reduce the strain of the unequal treaties upon Japan by proclaiming that, wherever appropriate and practical, American residents would respect Japanese laws and regulations. However, the Japanese leadership had larger goals in mind. Upon restoring imperial rule, the new government had set the revision of the unequal treaties as a top priority as a way to placate the supporters of the *jōi* movement.

In November 1871, the Meiji government sent the Iwakura Mission to America and Europe to learn from the West. But a hidden objective was to feel out the powers to see if they were willing to engage in treaty revision negotiations. As it sought to distinguish itself from the imperialistic European powers, Washington was committed to its magnanimous approach to Japan and thus it did not object to discussing treaty revisions when the Iwakura delegation brought up the matter with Secretary of State Hamilton Fish in March 1872. The United States was also the only nation that decided to unilaterally return its portion of the indemnity that it had received in compensation for the attacks by the Chōshū clan during the Shimonoseki Strait incident in 1864; any amount remaining after taking out costs for the actual damages incurred was returned to Japan in April 1883.

But De Long was critical of any move to revise the treaties; he felt strongly that American residents in Japan should not be forced to adhere to Japan's backward laws and regulations. De Long was taking a much more conservative stance than that of the State Department, which had already proclaimed as early as 1871 that it was prepared to accept the applicability of Japanese laws and rules to its own residents (Shimomura 1948, 1962). While negotiations between America and Japan continued, the European nations began to insist on being included in the treaty revision talks. To the delight of De Long, this fact—as well the lack of any real progress—led the US–Japan bilateral negotiations to be terminated in July 1872.

Following the abolition of feudal domains and establishment of prefectures in 1871, Japan emerged as unified nation state with a strong desire to preserve its national sovereignty. A number of Americans played key roles in Japan's development during this period, such as Minister De Long, and E. Peshine Smith, who was also employed by the Japanese government as a foreign advisor. The New York–born Smith had served in the State Department for a number of years as a specialist of international law and was a trusted assistant to Secretary Fish.

Unlike Smith, however, De Long was a very political individual and liked to delve into Japanese policy decisions. The State Department attempted to limit his involvement with the Meiji government as he was venturing well beyond his authority and also occasionally deviating from the official US policy. During a horrific incident that took place in Taiwan in December 1871, where aborigines slaughtered 54 shipwrecked Ryukyuan sailors, De Long assisted Japan by recommending Charles Le Gendre, a French-born American diplomat who had a strong command of Taiwanese affairs, as an advisor to the Foreign Ministry (*Gaimukyō*). However, contrary to De Long's expectations, Le Gendre proposed a quick punitive military operation which the Meiji promptly followed through by sending troops to Taiwan in May 1874.

De Long's successor, John A. Bingham, was not only opposed to the Japanese government's decision to dispatch troops to Taiwan; he also did not support the involvement of American advisors (implying Le Gendre) for this expedition on the grounds that America had a treaty obligation with China to remain neutral. In this way, American policy toward Japan was often inconsistent. This was because, at a time when it took 30–60 days for a letter to reach Tokyo (formerly Edo) from Washington, a large degree of policy formulation was left to the individual minister.

The Quest for Treaty Revisions under Terashima Munenori

Former congressman from Ohio Bingham, who had made a name for himself as a judge advocate in the Lincoln assassination trials, took up his new post in 1873 and would remain in Japan for the next 12 years. During his time in Japan, he became the first American minister to Japan to conduct a comprehensive review of the special rights enjoyed by Americans residing in Japan. His conclusion was that American citizens should be bound by Japanese laws and regulations without first having to wait for the authorization of the minister. But any punishment would be meted out in accordance with American law and the actual trial would be conducted by an American consul. Bingham argued that this conformed to Article 6 of the Harris Treaty, which stipulated that Americans should only be "punished, and not tried" according to American law.

Bingham's unconventional approach was not embraced by all American representatives in Japan, and the various American consuls at the open port cities frequently frustrated him by blatantly disregarding Japanese laws. However, the State Department's support for Bingham's position on this issued was unwavering.

The members of the Iwakura Mission returned to Japan with a strong realization of the difficulties that stood in the way of treaty revisions. Thus with Ōkubo Toshimichi taking a leading role, the government decided to tackle domestic reform first. However, this clashed head on with Saigō Takamori's faction that called for a military expedition to Korea (*seikanron*). When the government refused to budge, Saigō and his followers, including the foreign minister, resigned from their government positions in 1873.

Terashima Munenori, who was highly knowledgeable in terms of both international law and public finance, was appointed as the new foreign minister. Based on advice from Bingham, he promptly set out to restore Japan's tariff autonomy as he felt that this was standing in the way of Japan's path toward industrialization. The Japanese minister in Washington, Yoshida Kiyonari, was tasked with the negotiation that led to a tariff convention with Secretary of State William M. Evarts in July 1878. Under the agreement, America acknowledged Japan's sovereignty over tariffs as well as its right to regulate trade. In return, Japan promised to open more ports and to abolish existing export duties. There was very little American opposition to Japan raising its import duties, as US trade to Japan at that time was largely based on the import of raw silk and tea rather than exports (Ishii 1977). The conclusion of this convention marked the highpoint in US–Japan relations on the matter of treaty revision until 1894.

On the other hand, stronger US–Japan ties led to discord in their relations with the European powers. Britain took affront at the fact that US–Japan negotiations had been concluded first, and retaliated by declining Terashima's request for the restoration of autonomy over taxation. Germany and France also followed suit. As a result, the US–Japan convention—which, according to its Article 11, would only take effect when other treaty nations concluded a similar convention—never took effect and Terashima's efforts came to naught. This development prompted some Japanese to become disillusioned with America. It was felt that while the United States espoused friendship, it lacked the will and the ability to actually support Japan.

The Quest for Treaty Revisions under Inoue Kaoru

In September 1879, Foreign Minister Terashima was succeeded by Inoue Kaoru, who steered Japan toward a new course of winning over the European powers. The primary target was Britain and with its consent a preliminary conference was held in Tokyo from January to July 1882. This event symbolized Japan's departure from the nurture and protection of America as it began to pursue a more balanced foreign policy. During the ninth meeting, which was held on April 5, Inoue proposed opening Japan's interior for trade in exchange for abolishing consular jurisdiction. This clearly signified Inoue's willingness to compromise on the current foreign settlement arrangement that had been established by Harris.

In December 1885, the cabinet system was established in Japan and Inoue became the first foreign minister (*Gaimudaijin*) under the new system. In May 1886, he initiated another round of meetings to negotiate a treaty revision. Based on a draft proposal by Britain and Germany, the representatives of both countries finally reached an agreement in April 1887 according to which Japan would open its interior in exchange for the restoration of judicial authority. But Japan was still required to employ foreign judges and prosecutors as well as to compile a Western-style legal code which needed to be approved by the two nations prior to promulgation.

Although the United States had supported the restoration of Japan's judicial authority from the beginning, it was now forced to concede its leading role in the treaty revision negotiations to Britain and Germany. Former Texas governor Richard B. Hubbard, who became the American minister to Japan the year before the negotiations, was staunchly opposed to the increasing influence of Germany, and thus he resolutely objected to certain points of the agreement claiming that it was unfair toward the United States.

Hubbard's strength was not in handling complex diplomatic negotiations, but in cultivating a pro-American public opinion in Japan by effectively utilizing his close personal relationships with individuals such as the prominent intellectual Fukuzawa Yukichi. Hubbard was tested in March 1887, however, when the American warship USS *Omaha* conducted a shelling exercise toward the island of Ikeshima in Nagasaki Prefecture, which resulted in 11 casualties. This act was in clear violation of international law as well as Japanese regulations that prohibited weapons from being fired within 3 nautical miles of the coast without prior authorization. In the end, *Omaha*'s captain was cleared of any wrongdoing by a US military tribunal. However, the US government did agree to pay a substantial sum as compensation for the victims. Such an act helped in maintaining friendship between the two countries. But this did not help Inoue as his draft treaty revision proposal never saw the light of day as it was fiercely opposed by those who could not accept the humiliating compromises that Japan needed to undertake (Iokibe 2010).

The Quest for Treaty Revisions under Ōkuma Shigenobu

In February 1888, Ōkuma Shigenobu succeeded Inoue as foreign minister. In contrast with the approach of his predecessor, Ōkuma pursued a policy of holding negotiations with each country individually. Seeing this as an opportunity to overcome the setbacks that US–Japan relations had endured while Inoue was at the helm, Hubbard cooperated enthusiastically with Ōkuma and was the first to support the new treaty proposal.

However, Hubbard's actions failed to restore the privileged relationship that America had once enjoyed with Japan. Concerned that the European powers would become resentful if negotiations with the United States were to proceed ahead of their own discussions with Japan, Ōkuma intentionally reduced the pace of the US–Japan treaty negotiations. This, in turn, frustrated the Americans. This coincided with a new Republican president, Benjamin Harrison, entering the White House. US policy toward Japan began to shift again as Harrison, a committed protectionist, pushed to assert the economic interests of America with Japan being no exception. With this in mind, in March 1889 Harrison appointed former congressman from California John F. Swift as the new minister to Japan. Cognizant of his mandate, Swift quickly proceeded to adopt a less cooperative approach.

Quest Partially Fulfilled: The Abolishment of Extraterritoriality

After Ōkuma, succeeding Japanese foreign ministers reverted to once again placing emphasis on negotiations with Britain. Under Foreign Minister Mutsu Munemitsu, the negotiations for treaty revision finally reached fruition in the form of the Anglo–Japanese Treaty of Commerce and Navigation (*Nichiei tsūshōkōkai jōyaku*), which was negotiated by the Japanese Minister to Great Britain Aoki Shīzō and signed in July 1894. This was a sad day for America, given that it had long played a leading role in the treaty revision negotiations with Japan.

During this time, tensions were growing between Japan and China over the control of Korea. While the State Department transmitted its wish to both governments that the two parties should work together in avoiding war, it also felt that Japan was being too provocative. Thus, the secretary of state delivered a stern message to Japanese Minister to the United States, Tateno Gōzō. Britain and Russia also made independent attempts to ameliorate the situation in cooperation with the United States, because it had amicable relations with both China and Japan. However, Washington refused to go along and thus it had no influence upon Japan's decision to go to war against China. Hostilities erupted on July 25, 1894 with the Battle of Pungdo; war was officially declared on August 1.

After the outbreak of war, Japan began to push again for treaty revision negotiations with the United States. However, the negotiations hit a stumbling block over the issue of mutual free movement of US and Japanese citizens between both countries—a key provision that formed the basis for "amity"—as it raised fears in America over an influx of immigrant laborers. Desirous to improve Japan's international position, Mutsu decided to concede to the United States on this point. This cleared the way to a new treaty that was signed on November 22, 1894 by Secretary of State Walter Q. Gresham and Ambassador Kurino Shinichirō.

The new treaty required the collection of a customs duty to be applied across the board to all vessels importing goods, regardless of the national origin of the ship. In order to make the treaty more attractive to the Senate, a clause was also added that allowed it to be annulled at any time with an advance notice of twelve months. Nevertheless, as a result of this treaty, Japan successfully freed itself from the shackles of extraterritoriality.

Concluding the First Sino-Japanese War

At the outset of the Sino-Japanese War, the majority view in America and Europe was that China would emerge victorious in the conflict. However, after securing decisive victories both on land and at sea early in the war, by summer 1894 the Imperial Japanese Army (IJA) was on the verge of taking control of the entire Korean Peninsula and the Imperial Japanese Navy (IJN) had complete control of the sea following the Battle of the Yellow Sea in September. In the following month, the IJA made its first thrust into China. Fearing an imminent collapse of the Qing government, Britain urged both Japan and China to come to the peace table. Acting independently, the United States also offered to mediate in the following month. Although Mutsu declined the American offer of mediation, he did acquiesce in allowing the China's peace offer to be transmitted through Washington. Thus, Japan and China initiated their peace talks with the United States as the unofficial mediator (Dorwart 1975).

But difficulties soon surfaced when the Qing government demanded that all five great powers—Britain, France, Germany, Russia, and America—needed to be present at the negotiations. It was the American Minister Charles Denby who finally persuaded the Chinese to proceed with the talks based on the original agreement. After some haggling, the diplomat Li Hongzhang was sent to Japan with the authority to sign a treaty on behalf of his government (Tabohashi 1951).

During the peace talks, Japan repeatedly sought the assistance of the United States to gain information on the movements of the European powers. Although Washington was wary of getting too involved in the peace talks, as it did not trust the intentions of the European powers, it did occasionally provide crucial pieces of information to Japan. One such piece of information was that Russia had designs on Manchuria, and that it would act accordingly if Japan were to cede any territory from the Chinese mainland.

However, Japan chose to conveniently disregard this advice when it finalized the terms of the peace treaty with China. The treaty, signed in Shimonoseki on April 17, 1895, required the Chinese to affirm Korean independence, pay 200 million *taels* in indemnity, provide equal trade privileges to Japan with Europe and the United States, and to cede Formosa (Taiwan) as well as the Penghu Islands (Pescadores Islands). Most importantly, China was forced to cede the Liaodong Peninsula on the mainland. As the United States had forewarned, this led to prompt action by several European powers. On April 23, the Russian, German, and French ministers visited the Japanese Foreign Ministry and tersely demanded the return of Liaodong Peninsula to China; this became the so-called Triple Intervention.

Tokyo initially attempted counter this move by enlisting the support of Britain, Italy, and the United States in opposing the intervention. Although the United States was not willing to get itself directly involved in the affairs of European power politics, it did, however, apply increased pressure on Qing China to promptly ratify the peace treaty upon the return of the Liaodong peninsula.

In the immediate aftermath of the Sino-Japanese War, Japan struggled to maintain an amicable relationship with the European nations in contrast to its friendly relationship with the United States. America had refused to cooperate with the European powers while it helped Japan by pressuring the Qing government in ratifying the treaty. In this way, the Japanese realized that it could work in a partnership with the Americans. Meanwhile, the United States too was making advances into the Pacific—the Philippines, Guam, Samoa, and Hawaii—following the Spanish–American War of 1898. With the United States and Japan both expanding their respective spheres of influence near the end of the nineteenth century, the Pacific Ocean was becoming a much smaller place. However, as we will see in the ensuing chapters, the very moment that their interests began to overlap, the nature of their relationship would be fundamentally transformed.

BIBLIOGRAPHY

Dorwart, Jeffrey M. 1975. *The Pigtail War*. Amherst, MA: University of Massachusetts Press.

Iokibe, Kaoru. 2010. *Jōyaku kaisei-shi* [Meiji Treaty Revision]. Tokyo: Yūhikaku Publishing.

Ishii, Takashi. 1966. *Meiji ishin no kokusaiteki kankyō* [The International Environment of the Meiji Restoration]. Tokyo: Yoshikawa-kōbunkan.

———. 1977. *Meiji shoki no kokusai kankei* [International Relations in Early Meiji]. Tokyo: Yoshikawa-kōbunkan.

Shimomura, Fujio. 1948. *Meiji ishin no gaikō* [The Diplomacy of the Meiji Restoration]. Tokyo: Ōyashima Shuppan.

———. 1962. *Meiji shonen jyōyaku kaisei-shi no kenkyū*. Tokyo: Yoshikawa-kōbunkan. Studies in the History of Early Meiji Treaty Revision.

Tabohashi, Kiyoshi. 1951. *Nisshin seneki gaikō-shi no kenkyū* [Study of the Diplomatic History of the Sino-Japanese War]. Tokyo: Tōe Shoin.

CHAPTER 2

The Emergence of Japan on the Global Stage, 1895–1908

Yasutoshi Teramoto and Tosh Minohara

East Asia and the Pacific in the Late 1800s

The transition between the nineteenth and the twentieth centuries was a significant turning point in global politics. After decades of post–Civil War reconstruction, the United States emerged as a global power with its victory over Spain in 1898. Japan also became the first Asian nation to enter the ranks of the major powers when it defeated both China (1895) and Russia (1905). Through their military victories, both the United States and Japan were able to join the European powers at the center stage of international politics by the early twentieth century. Invariably, such changes also impacted US-Japan relations. In addition to their bilateral relationship, they also began to realize that their interests in Asia increasingly overlapped. This meant that there was now room for greater strategic cooperation but this also came with a greater risk of confrontation.

A year before Japan went to war with China, the United States was struck by a severe economic depression known as the "Panic of 1893." A succession of railroad company bankruptcies led to the failure of a string of

Y. Teramoto
Graduate School of Social Sciences, Hiroshima University, Hiroshima, Japan

T. Minohara
Graduate School of Law, Kobe University, Kobe, Japan

© The Author(s) 2017
M. Iokibe (ed.), T. Minohara (trans. ed.), *The History of US–Japan Relations*, DOI 10.1007/978-981-10-3184-7_2

23

other major enterprises. The financial damage spread because at that time the United States did not have a central bank that could have contained it. Due to its preoccupation with this domestic economic crisis, the United States had only a limited interest in the Sino-Japanese War or the geopolitical shift that the war would bring about in East Asia. As mentioned in the previous chapter, although the United States had consented to abolishing its extraterritoriality in Japan under a Treaty of Commerce and Navigation (*Nichibei tsūshōsōkai jōyaku*) signed in November 1894 (effective from July 1899), it really did not have the leeway to pay attention to Japan's affairs until the American economy recovered in 1898.

The year 1898 was also an important turning point in US strategy toward East Asia as a result of two key events: the Spanish–American War and the annexation of Hawaii. America had delivered a crushing blow to Spain and as a result it acquired the territories of Cuba, Puerto Rico, Guam, and the Philippines. This transformed the United States into a nation with a direct stake in the Pacific, but it was the country's possession of the Philippines that had the greatest impact on its East Asia policy. Since America could not disregard its traditional position of anti-imperialism, the question of how to deal with the Philippines, a distant territory with a large population, became a highly controversial and sensitive subject. A political and public debate ensued, but ultimately this was ended by President William McKinley's decision to take outright possession of the Philippines after compensating Spain for the cessation of the land.

In the same year, McKinley also annexed Hawaii as the Spanish–American War had highlighted to American military strategists the geostrategic importance of the island chain in the center of the Pacific. The United States had nurtured its political and economic relations with the Kingdom of Hawaii from the late nineteenth century, and, under a new Hawaiian Constitution in 1887, Pearl Harbor was leased to America for the establishment of a naval base. However, when Queen Liliuokalani ascended the throne several years later, she sought to regain monarchial authority, prompting American residents in Hawaii to oust the queen and seize power in a coup d'état in 1893. A new republic was established the following year with the hope of being annexed by the United States.

Grover Cleveland, the president at that time, was a supporter of isolationism and was therefore opposed to the takeover of Hawaii. However, after McKinley succeeded Cleveland in 1897, he took advantage of the pro-expansion jingoistic sentiment in America and promptly took steps to annex the islands. The unfounded rumor that Japan was secretly plan-ning to invade Hawaii—Japanese immigrants outnumbered American residents by a whopping 100 to 1—also provided a sense of urgency in taking action.

There were several factors that encouraged America to reverse its previ-ous policy of anti-colonialism. Toward the end of the nineteenth century America was keen to secure new markets, prompted by historian Frederick Jackson Turner's theory of the end of the American frontier. Influential Republicans such as Theodore Roosevelt and Henry Cabot Lodge, who sought to establish a more powerful America, were spurred on by naval strategist Alfred Thayer Mahan's theory that control of the seas was essen-tial for national prosperity.

American missionaries also pressured the government to secure new markets where they could propagate their faith. An equally significant motivation during this period was the threat of German expansion in East Asia. Germany's influence was rapidly growing not only in China, but also across the Western Pacific. The question of Samoan sovereignty even led to a diplomatic crisis between the United States and Germany. The rise of German imperialism prompted Britain to urge America to take outright possession of the Philippines in order to keep a check on Germany and maintain the status quo.

The United States was initially hesitant to make a deeper thrust into Asia, but once it did so, it became difficult to stop this inertia. Acquiring the Philippines as a colony had a significant impact on America's policy toward the entire region. It could no longer remain aloof as the world powers scrambled to grab whatever concessions they could obtain from China, which by this time was ridiculed as the "sick man of Asia." But the United States also did not attempt to extend its territories any further. It was still reluctant to make a complete break with its anti-imperialist and anti-colonialist ideals. Instead it sought to secure its national interests by espousing its ideals in a set of principles based on the equal opportunity for trade and commerce in China known as the Open Door policy.

In a note issued by Secretary of State John M. Hay in September 1899, the Open Door policy was unilaterally proclaimed to the other major powers that possessed interests in China. The aim was to ensure that the United States would not be excluded from the Chinese market, even though it did not possess any territory or concessions in China. This approach ultimately became the cornerstone of America's strategy in Asia for the next half-century. Foreign Minister Aoki Shūzō consented to Hay's call for the maintenance of the status quo and the equal opportunity for trade in Qing China under two conditions. First, trade and navigation by the foreign powers in each country's sphere of influence had to be respected. Second, the remaining powers also needed to agree to respect Hay's declaration.

In July 1900, Hay supplemented his initial Open Door policy note with a second one that called for the respect of China's territorial and administrative integrity. Although the American intention was to prevent China from being further divided up by the major powers, this was difficult to enforce as the United States did not possess the military capability to back up its proclamation. What was clear, however, was that through the acquisition Hawaii and the Philippines, the United States had matured into a maritime state with vital interests in the Asia Pacific. Following McKinley's assassination in September 1901, the new president Theodore Roosevelt would pursue an even more proactive role for the United States on the international stage.

Repercussions of the Triple Intervention

In the late nineteenth century, Russia attempted to expand southward toward the Mediterranean through the Balkans and Crimea. After this ambition failed, it next advanced into Afghanistan in the 1880s, which provoked another confrontation with Britain. With nowhere to expand but eastward, by the end of the century Russia began to show a greater interest in East Asia. Meanwhile, Japan was pushing ahead with its own expansion into Asia which focused primarily on the Korean Peninsula, or, as Foreign Minister Komura Jutarō would exclaim, the "sharp dagger" (*rijin*) protruding from the continent toward Japan (*Nihon gaikō monjo* [Documents on Japanese Foreign Policy]). As a result of victory in the Sino-Japanese War, Japan was able to release Korea from its subordination to China, but it soon encountered increased tensions with Russia who had their own designs on the peninsula.

Japan had achieved its victory over China through a combined diplomatic and military strategy. However, even before the ink on Japan's peace accord with China was dry, Japan was delivered a devastating blow when the combined powers of Russia, Germany, and France demanded a change to the terms treaty through the so-called Triple Intervention. Faced with this crisis, Vice Foreign Minister Hayashi Tadasu, who was directly involved in negotiations, considered the possibility of an alliance with the other powers as a way of preventing international isolation as well as to counter the intervention. The resulting conclusion was that an agreement with Britain would be most ideal. Tokyo also hastened its military buildup program which was carried out under the slogan *Gashin shōtan* (Enduring hardship now for the sake of later revenge).

In the end, Japan was forced to cede the Liaodong Peninsula to Russia. The latter then proceeded to obtain the right to establish the Chinese Eastern Railway through a secret treaty with China in 1896. Two years later, Russia also leased Port Arthur and Dairen at the tip of the Liaodong Peninsula and secured the right to construct a new southern branch line of the Chinese Eastern Railway. As these developments were in clear violation with its agreement with Japan, tensions quickly increased between the two countries.

Japan's relationship with the United States also became tense in 1899 when Tokyo surreptitiously attempted to provide weapons, ammunition, and military advisors to the Filipino independence movement led by General Emilio Aguinaldo. Although adroit diplomacy by Foreign Minister Aoki averted a deterioration of US–Japan relations, this incident clearly showed that the United States would not regard with indifference any action that would undermine its interests in the Philippines.

The Boxer Rebellion and the Anglo-Japanese Alliance

The conclusion of the Sino-Japanese War prompted a rush by the great powers to establish their respective spheres of influence in China in the final days of the Qing dynasty. This blatant intervention led to a violent uprising in June 1900, when a group of anti-imperialist martial arts fighters from a society called "The Fists of Righteous Harmony" (*Yihetuan*)—dubbed the "Boxers" by the West—converged on Beijing under the rallying cry "Support the Qing, destroy the outsiders!" (*Fu Qing mie yang*) and laid siege to the foreign legations and settlements. At the behest of Britain, which was engulfed in its own war with the Boers in South Africa, Japan sent troops to suppress the uprising. This earned Japan praise and recognition as the "military police of the Far East," due to its geographical proximity and the exemplary behavior displayed by the disciplined Japanese army.

Threatened by Russia's policy of southward expansion, Japan embraced Hay's Open Door policy as a means of securing diplomatic support from both the United States and Britain. Russia's increasingly aggressive actions quickly reignited tensions with Japan as Russia refused to complete the withdrawal of its troops from Manchuria even after the conclusion of the Boxer Rebellion. This was in spite of an agreement with China in 1902 according to which Russia promised to remove its soldiers deployed in Manchuria in three stages. To the consternation of Japan, the Russians followed through on only the first stage. Furthermore, it soon became apparent that Russia had designs on Korea when it demanded the leasing of Yongamp'o.

Britain and Germany also quickly voiced their support for Hay's Open Door policy in October 1900 by committing to the maintenance of Chinese territorial integrity through the Yangtze Agreement. On the pretext of reducing the enormous reparations that were being demanded from Qing China over the Boxer Rebellion, the United States inquired to Japan whether it could lease land in Sansha'ao. Foreign Minister Katō Takaaki rejected this request outright, pointing out that it went against the April 1898 agreement between Japan and China that stipulated the non-partition of any land in Fujian province. Furthermore, it conflicted with the principle of maintaining Chinese territorial integrity, something that America itself had espoused through the Open Door declarations. Realizing that its position was untenable, the United States never again raised the issue of territorial concessions in China.

The increasing wariness toward Russia's unabated appetite for expansion in East Asia was felt not only in Japan, but also in Britain. This shared sense of a common threat culminated into the Anglo-Japanese alliance (*Nichi-ei dōmei kyōyaku*) in January 1902 that ended Britain's policy of "splendid isolation."

THE RUSSO-JAPANESE WAR AND AMERICA'S SUPPORT

Prior to the Russo-Japanese War the Japanese leadership was divided between two contrasting approaches on how to deal with Russia over Korea and Manchuria. When Prime Minister Katsura Tarō formed his cabinet in June 1901, he was determined to establish an alliance with Britain, a move that was supported by Foreign Minister Komura Jutarō. They had both reached the conclusion that war with Russia was inevitable, and while they did not view Russian occupation of Manchuria necessarily as a casus belli, they were willing to resort to war in order to prevent Russian expansion into the Korea Peninsula. With the Anglo-Japanese alliance in place, war with Russia now had a place on the list of Japan's policy options.

On the contrary, Itō Hirobumi, a key elder statesman (*genrō*) hoped to appease Russia in order avoid war. He was not opposed to an alliance with Britain per se, but he felt strongly that considering Japan's limited military and economic strength, it was more prudent to resolve the issues over Manchuria and Korea through diplomacy with Russia. Itō also wished to preserve Japanese national interests, but he was driven by a pragmatic fear that war with such a powerful nation like Russia would spell disaster for Japan.

Japan had learned the importance of diplomacy from the bitter lessons of the Triple Intervention. Thus, as the clouds of war began to loom with Russia, Japan acted to form a diplomatic support network that would prevent it from being isolated as it fought Russia. Ultimately, lack of mutual trust on both sides stood in the way of resolving their differences at the negotiating table (Chiba 1996). Russia's uncompromising stance over Korea became the chief issue that led to the war in February 1904.

Japan realized that it needed the support of the United States in successfully waging this war. Therefore, Itō dispatched Kaneko Kentarō, a graduate of Roosevelt's alma mater Harvard University, to America to secure his personal support. Kaneko played a pivotal role in obtaining Roosevelt's backing of the war, and through his public diplomacy he successfully won over American public opinion as well.

War is always a terribly costly venture, and Japan needed to secure vast amounts of funds before it could even consider fighting Russia. This proved to be difficult as even Japan's staunch ally Britain felt that the odds were stacked against Japan. As a result, the London financial market was reluctant to provide the necessary financing. Japan therefore had no choice but to seek funds from the fledgling New York market that did not yet have any experience in initiating a financing operation of this magnitude. The vice president of the Bank of Japan, Takahashi Korekiyo, was sent to the United States as a special envoy to deal with financial matters and with the assistance of Jacob Schiff, a Jewish investment banker at Kuhn, Loeb & Co., Japan was successful in raising more than 800 million yen in loans throughout the war, most of it coming from Wall Street. Schiff had a personal reason for helping Japan; he was outraged against the repeated anti-Jewish pogroms in Russia and thus wanted the Tsar to be defeated.

In many ways, the Russo-Japanese War was a proxy war among the great powers. Russia was supported by Germany, which had urged war to counter the "yellow peril" in the first place, as well as by France, which had a formal alliance with Russia. In Japan's corner were the United States and Britain, who perceived Japan to be a champion of the Open Door policy.

Ending the War: The Portsmouth Peace Conference

Once war commenced, the Japanese military quickly secured a succession of key victories against Russia. But the Japanese leadership fully realized that a prolonged war of attrition would be to their disadvantage. Japan was not only low on soldiers and munitions, but was also faced with a dire shortage of funds. Therefore, after the decisive Battle of Mukden in March 1905, *genrō* Yamagata Aritomo began to call for more "balance in political and military strategy," and persuaded Katsura and Komura to begin considering a diplomatic resolution to the war.

Amid such voices, Tokyo carefully executed its plan to get President Roosevelt involved in mediating the war. Despite the huge victories at Mukden and the Tsushima Strait, its rapidly dwindling resources would not allow it to fight a protracted war. Thus ending the war, albeit in terms favorable to Japan, was critical. To this end, Japan was fortunate when Roosevelt agreed to mediate a peace treaty between Japan and Russia. In planning the peace conference, Roosevelt asked his friend, New Hampshire Governor John R. McLane, to recommend a venue where the Japanese and Russian representatives could engage in thorough deliberations. McLane suggested two locations: Portsmouth on the coast, and Bretton Woods in the mountains. Ultimately, Portsmouth was chosen as the stage for the Russo-Japanese peace negotiations because it possessed a naval base that could provide easy access from the water as well as security.

Roosevelt's main motivation in getting involved in the dispute between Japan and Russia was born out of his desire to maintain the balance of power in East Asia. To be sure, the president did also have sympathy toward Japan and wanted to ensure that it would gain a fair concession that would reflect its overwhelming victory on the battlefield.

After repeated prodding by Roosevelt, Tsar Nicholas II finally agreed to a peace conference, to be held from August 1905. Komura was sent to Portsmouth as head of Japan's peace delegation. He was instructed by Itō, Yamagata, and the other *genrō* to negotiate an end to the war with the condition that Japan be given the rights to the South Manchuria Railway (SMR) and the Liaodong Peninsula. However, reparations were considered unnecessary, as well as any claims to Sakhalin (*Gaimushō kiroku* [Ministry of Foreign Affairs Records]) which Japan had occupied near the end of the war.

Although Japan had high hopes for Roosevelt as a supporter of Japan over Russia, the president's priority was naturally to resolve the conflict in a manner that would be acceptable to both sides. This required that both Japan and Russia compromise over several key issues. Roosevelt advised Japan that as a member of the family of civilized nations, it had a moral obligation to seek peace now that it had successfully acquired the Korean Peninsula and southern Manchuria. In his dealings with Russia, Roosevelt persuaded the Tsar to cede Sakhalin to Japan, arguing that Sakhalin had been a Russian territory for only around three decades. Eventually the Tsar grudgingly agreed to cede the lower half of Sakhalin but without any payment of an indemnity. Given these critical concessions by each of the parties, peace was now possible. For his efforts, in 1906 Roosevelt became the first American to be awarded the Nobel Peace Prize.

Public opinion had a role in swaying diplomacy during the peace conference. High-profile groups such as the Anti-Russian Association (*Tairodōshikai*) and a group of University of Tokyo academics known as the "Seven Professors" (*Shichi hakase*) called for a continuation of the war with Russia. On the other hand, a few newspapers, such as the *Heimin Shimbun*, were outspoken proponents for peace. As the Japanese public knew only about the huge victories attained by Japan's military, however, they were inclined to possess an overblown expectation of the final peace treaty with Russia. Thus, once it was learned that Japan would not receive an indemnity, public indignation led to a massive riot in Hibiya Park in Tokyo on September 5, 1905. Individuals such as the former Minister of Agriculture and Commerce Tani Tateki were appalled by this public reaction as it completely disregarded Japan's inability to continue fighting. He was resolute in his call for an immediate end to the conflict. In his mind, it was "impossible to secure international support" in continuing the war to gain reparations (Tani 1976).

Since the control of Korea had been the primary reason for going to war, Japan quickly entered into agreements with the United States and Britain to secure its position on this issue. In July 1905, Secretary of War William H. Taft and Prime Minister Katsura agreed to that in exchange for America recognizing Japan's control of Korea, Japan would respect

US control of the Philippines. This also became the first step in a series of treaties that would change the political landscape of Asia. The world needed to accommodate Japan's rise in status as a new power and its accompanying expanded sphere of influence. This was clearly reflected in the Franco-Japanese agreement and the Russo-Japanese agreement. The 1902 Anglo-Japanese alliance was also revised in August 1905 so that Britain now also recognized Japan's control of Korea.

In aftermath of the Portsmouth Peace Conference, Japan's new international status allowed it to gain recognition over the exclusive control of the Korean Peninsula as well as newly acquired rights in southern Manchuria, such as Port Arthur, Dairen, and the SMR. Japan had successfully made its entry onto the global stage as a great power in its own right.

JAPAN'S ROLE IN SHAPING US POLICY TOWARD EAST ASIA

The chief outcome of the Portsmouth Peace Treaty was that Japan and Russia now recognized each other's established spheres of influence. Russia acknowledged Japan's exclusive control of the Korean Peninsula and its dominance in southern Manchuria. From Japan's perspective, this outcome alone more than justified the decision to go to war. Until this time, the Asian continent had been the stage of a battle for supremacy centered on the European powers of Britain, France, Germany, and Russia. However, the defeat of Russia led to a major change in the geopolitical dynamics of the region as it necessitated a readjustment in the balance of power to incorporate Japan.

The Russo-Japanese War also marked the moment when America and Japan began to directly face each other across the Pacific as two young and powerful nations. Japan's rise to prominence transformed its relationship with the United States from a more manageable student–mentor relationship to one that was much more complex and reflective of geostrategic realities. One event that epitomized this shifting relationship was the creation of a military operation plan by the US Joint Army and Navy Board, known as War Plan Orange. (Orange was the designated color for Japan.) Ironically, the war plan toward Japan revealed that the United States lacked the naval capability to defend its interests in Asia. This highlighted the importance of partnering with Japan as a way to defend the Philippines, which Roosevelt aptly described in 1907 as "America's Achilles heel." In contrast to China, which was falling into an abyss of chaos, Japan was perceived as a stabilizing force in the region. Roosevelt therefore had no qualms over Japan establishing its own sphere of influence as long as it adhered to the Open Door policy and respected American interests in the region.

The United States had integrated Latin America into its own sphere of influence by opposing intervention by the European powers as well as by advocating the exclusive right to intervene in the Caribbean under the Roosevelt Corollary of 1904. As a realist, Roosevelt felt that a great power such as Japan was also entitled to its own sphere of influence. This understanding was clearly reflected in the Taft–Katsura agreement of July 1905. Roosevelt and his secretary of state, Elihu Root, aimed to further strengthen the ties between the United States and Japan by ensuring that each nation was allowed to maintain its respective rights and interests.

Japan's Postwar Diplomacy

In a policy paper on the conditions for peace with Russia dated July 1904, Komura wrote that Japan had entered war with the aim of securing the "independence of Korea" and the "preservation of Manchuria." Prior to that, then Prime Minister Yamagata had defined the Japanese mainland as the "line delineating Japanese sovereignty" and the Korean Peninsula as the "line delineating Japanese interests" when addressing the first session of the Imperial Diet in 1890. However, after the war, Komura now perceived Korea as "within the scope of sovereignty" and Manchuria as "within the scope of interests." Japan's victory had prompted a change in what it viewed as vital interests and therefore expanding its rights and interests in Manchuria became a high priority objective from the perspective of Japanese national interests (*Nihon gaikō monjo* [Documents on Japanese Foreign Policy]).

Although Japan was given the southern branch line of the Chinese Eastern Railway (i.e., the SMR) under the terms of the Portsmouth Peace Treaty, operating the railway and the coal mines owned by the railway company posed an enormous financial hardship. At this time Japan was still repaying its huge war debt as well as the loan to rebuild the railway. In late August 1905, just as Tokyo was deliberating over how to handle the situation, the railway magnate Edward H. Harriman visited Japan at the urging of the US Minister to Japan, Lloyd C. Griscom. Harriman wanted to fulfill his grand ambition of building a global railway network. With this goal in mind, he proposed to Prime Minister Katsura a joint Japanese-American syndicate to manage to operations of the SMR. Seeing this as an opportunity to reduce Japan's financial burden, Katsura reached an

agreement with Harriman, which they signed in October. This was enthusiastically greeted by influential figures such as the *genrō* Inoue Kaoru and
the business leader Shibusawa Eiichi.

However, as soon as Foreign Minister Komura learned of this agreement
upon his return to Tokyo from Portsmouth, he was enraged. Japan had
fought a bitter war with Russia to obtain the rights over the SMR and he was
not about to let the United States have a stake quite so easily. Thus, Komura
moved to reject agreement on the legal basis that Article 6 of the peace treaty
stipulated that former Russian rights and interests could not be ceded to any
third party without China's prior consent. Komura felt that the SMR, with
its tremendous potential for development, was an important resource that
Japan had acquired from the peace conference. Komura's position was also
motivated by the fact that the Morgan financial group, a rival to Harriman,
offered to provide financial assistance on more favorable terms (Matsumura
1987). Komura was also wary about the reaction of the Japanese public,
especially in the light of the Hibiya Riots, once they learned of Japan's concession to the United States. Regardless of the reasons for his objections, by
annulling the Harriman-Katsura agreement, Komura was able to effectively
put a check on any American attempt to expand its influence into Manchuria.

Japan's Three Approaches to Diplomacy

After the Russo-Japanese War, the Japanese government pursued two fundamental goals. First, it sought to secure the rights and interests that it
had gained through war with Russia as a way of firmly establishing its
sphere of influence in the region. Second, it took the necessary steps to
ensure that other nations approved of and supported its new status. To
this end Japan's leaders adopted the following three contrasting, but at
times complementary, approaches to foreign policy:

- Strengthening military control over southern Manchuria (supported
  by the army).
- Securing new rights and interests for Japan and expanding the empire
  (supported by Komura Jutarō).
- Pursuing pragmatic diplomacy focused on maintaining the status
  quo (supported by Hayashi Tadasu).

Placing southern Manchuria under firm military control was a policy that was promoted by the Imperial Japanese Army (IJA) which had
wrested Manchuria from the Russians after fierce fighting. Thus, the IJA

obstinately remained in southern Manchuria even after the signing of the peace treaty. It also refused to relinquish military administration over the area. These actions, however, were in direct conflict with the Open Door policy. Considering that one reason that both the United States and Britain had supported Japan in the Russo-Japanese War was the hope that Japan would remove Russia's steadfast grip over Manchuria, it was only natural that both nations were alarmed by the IJA's actions which simply replaced Russian occupation with that of the Japanese.

Despite repeated demands from Japanese Prime Minister Saionji Kinmochi, the IJA refused to cease its military administration over Manchuria. On May 22, 1906, Itō convened a joint council of the cabinet and *genrōs* to discuss the Manchurian problem, at which he tersely reprimanded the army leadership, stating that Manchuria was a "legitimate territory of China," and that the IJA was making a "fundamental error" in judgment. Faced with outright hostility from the senior political establishment, the IJA grudgingly agreed to end its military control over Manchuria. The tense domestic situation over Manchuria following the Russo-Japanese War offered a clear indication of the weakness of the government during the Meiji period; clearly it could only restrain the military with the support of the *genrōs*. This was a worrying sign because the *genrōs* could not live forever.

The Diplomatic Approach of Komura and Hayashi

When Komura annulled Katsura's agreement with Harriman over the joint operation of the railway, he felt that Japan could independently fund and manage the SMR as soon as it became profitable. Komura firmly believed that the SMR would eventually become a trunk route that would be the backbone for future economic development on the continent.

In November 1905 Komura visited China, where he secured China's consent to the terms of the Portsmouth Conference through the Peking Treaty in December 1905. Three years later, Komura was reappointed as foreign minister in the second Katsura cabinet where he successfully resolved the issue of ceasing the construction of the Hsinmintun–Fakumen Railway in September 1909 under the Sino-Japanese agreement concerning Manchuria (*Manshū go-anken ni kansuru nisshinjōyaku*). This was an exclusively Chinese-controlled line financially supported by the United States but Tokyo viewed this as a direct threat to its interests because it ran nearly parallel to Japan's SMR.

During the first decade of the twentieth century, Katsura and Saionji alternated as prime minister, but while Komura was the preferred foreign minister for Katsura, Saionji clearly favored Hayashi Tadasu. Hayashi favored a pragmatic approach to issues and he also believed in the art of compromise. His skills shone through during the negotiations leading to the Anglo-Japanese alliance and after the Russo-Japanese War he sought to increase the respectability of Japan by pursuing a moderate policy that served to maintain the status quo. On the contrary, Komura's focus was on seizing the initiative and taking bold but calculated steps in order to expand Japan's empire. In this way, at first glance Komura and Hayashi's approaches to diplomacy differed considerably. However, in actuality they only differed in terms of where they placed emphasis, and at times their positions were almost indistinguishable. For example, both Komura and Hayashi spared no effort in strengthening Japan's relationship with America after the war. In addition, they were both actively in involved pushing out the boundaries of the Japanese empire by taking steps to annex Korea.

For Japanese diplomacy, 1907 was to be a watershed year. First, Japan successfully concluded treaties with its former enemies, Russia and France. This was crucial in that it allowed Japan to prevent another clash with Russia while also obtaining a treaty that would augment its alliance with Britain. Second, Japan was able to maneuver a position that allowed it to be seen as a stabilizing force for maintaining the status quo in Europe. This ran counter to Germany, which was increasingly being viewed as a force that was challenging the existing order. This new threat brought Russia and France into an alliance against Germany. Britain later joined the two nations to form a new alliance known as the Triple Entente. Because Japan had treaties with all three nations of the Triple Entente, it too became an indirect became a member of the alliance. After the Russo-Japanese War, the European powers were now relying more on Japan as a stabilizing force in the international system.

THE PROBLEM OF RACE AND IMMIGRATION

While Japan's international status rose in the aftermath of the war with Russia, this also drastically changed Japan's image as more and more Americans began to view Japan as a potential threat. Mixed with the existing racial prejudices of the time, a serious row emerged between the Untied States and Japan over the discrimination experienced by Japanese immigrants in California.

In October 1906, the San Francisco Board of Education acted to segregate Japanese students from their American counterparts and had them transferred to the Oriental School, which had been established for children of Chinese and Korean nationalities. Ostensibly, this was done because the schools had been damaged in wake of the Great San Francisco Earthquake and the subsequent fire that had devastated the city in April of that year. However, this argument was hard to support in light of the fact that were just 93 Japanese children enrolled in the schools at the time. Moreover, these schools had suffered very little actual damage.

In reality, the school board's decision was the result of several factors (Minohara 2016). Firstly, after Chinese immigrants had been excluded from the United States following the Immigration Act of 1882, many Japanese immigrants began to arrive in San Francisco, the "Gateway of the West," where they began to quickly settle. After Hawaii was annexed in 1898, Japanese immigrants began to flow out from this new territory to California which also contributed to a dramatic increase in the Japanese population.

Secondly, local politics were a factor. Since 1900, the Union Labor Party had held sway over San Francisco and as the party's support base was overwhelmingly the white working class. Japanese immigrants, who worked for lower wages and were not union members, were naturally seen as a threat as they took available jobs. Thirdly, the existence of a local press served to further fuel the fire of the anti-Japanese movement by inciting fear among whites. When American public opinion toward Japan plummeted in the aftermath of the Hibiya Riots, newspapers across the state published a flurry of anti-Japanese articles that helped influence public opinion. In particular, the newspapers owned by newspaper tycoon William R. Hearst played a major role in propagating negative sentiment against the Japanese immigrants.

Finally, Japan's surprising defeat of Russia had altered the perception of Japan from a distant friend across the Pacific to a potential adversary. Japan's rapid rise worried many Americans who now feared that Japan could very well pose a threat to US interests in East Asia. This perception was further reinforced by the popular image of hordes of Asians taking over the world, or the so-called "yellow peril." This made Japan's new presence as a major great power all the more unsettling.

These were all-important factors that led to the school board's decision to segregate Japanese children. They had miscalculated on one point, however: the Japanese had found a new sense of pride in having achieved the status of a first-rate power. Therefore, the Japanese government could not tolerate their nationals being treated as though they were second-class citizens. Hence Tokyo acted quickly to resolve the problem lest its prestige would be injured. On learning of the situation in San Francisco, Foreign Minister Hayashi immediately instructed the Japanese ambassador to lodge a formal protest with Secretary of State Elihu Root. Of course, Japan had no intention of clashing with the United States over an issue that was more a matter of national pride rather than affecting real national interests. That being said, as the only non-white nation among the global powers, Japan also needed to save face and preserve its dignity. This was particularly important for Japan since memories of past unequal treaties still lingered. But Tokyo's decisive diplomatic action merely reinforced the perception that Japanese immigrants were indeed dangerous, as it showed that they had the backing of their own government.

President Roosevelt Diffuses the Crisis

As a pragmatic realist, President Roosevelt clearly saw the utter foolishness of allowing such a minor issue over 93 Japanese schoolchildren damage America's relationship with Japan. But Roosevelt had to act fast before tensions in California escalated any further; rumors were rampant that war was imminent with Japan. Even though this claim could not be further from the truth, nevertheless, the segregation imbroglio still managed to lead to the first crisis in US–Japan relations.

Committed to resolving the issue quickly and decisively, Roosevelt sent Commerce and Labor Secretary Victor H. Metcalf, a native Californian, to San Francisco to bring the "infernal fools in California" back to their senses. In private, Roosevelt even spoke about the need to send Federal troops to the state to protect Japanese immigrants in the event of a riot. But while he brandished his hallmark "big stick," Roosevelt did not forget to offer a carrot. To placate the Californians, he pushed through a new immigration bill that would prohibit all future Japanese immigration to the mainland from the territory of Hawaii. He also invited the members of the San Francisco School Board, many of whom had never visited the nation's capital before, to the White House with expenses paid by the Federal government. This was a gratifying gesture which went a long way in getting the group to cooperate.

When the schoolboard returned to San Francisco, it quickly rescinded its decision to segregate the Japanese school children. With this move, an incident that had precipitated a diplomatic crisis was finally brought under control and US–Japanese relations had been preserved. On the other hand, the manner in which the issue was resolved gave the Japanese the false impression that the federal government would always be willing to act decisively on the immigration problem. They were not aware that in many ways Roosevelt was an exception. Not only did he highly value US–Japan relations from a strategic standpoint, he also happened to care very little about states' rights.

Roosevelt also acted to prevent any future problems with Japan over immigration. He therefore requested a bilateral meeting with Japan to address the issue. These secret discussions between 1907 and 1908 led to the so-called Gentlemen's Agreement that consisted of 11 official notes exchanged between Foreign Minister Hayashi and the American Ambassador to Japan Thomas J. O'Brien. The agreement prohibited the Japanese, except for children aged 20 and under, from entering America as laborers. Since Japan's leaders wanted to avoid the stigma of being forced into an unequal treaty—Japan could not take similar measures since there were no immigrant laborers from the United States to Japan—Tokyo insisted that the unilateral agreement be made into a voluntary one. Roosevelt felt this was a reasonable request and thus the agreement became an executive order rather than a treaty. As such, it was never ratified by Congress and this general lack of understanding over the agreement would lead to dire consequences for US–Japan relations in the future. But in the meantime, Japan was content that it was able to avoid a repeat of the humiliation suffered by the Chinese government through the enactment of the Chinese Exclusion Act.

The White Fleet and the Return of Amicable Relations

On March 13, 1908, Roosevelt announced his grand plan for the US Navy to make a round-the-world training cruise with stops at Hawaii, New Zealand, Australia, and the Philippines during the Pacific leg of their journey. Consisting of all of America's 16 battleships, one aim of this unprecedented tour—which was initially opposed by most admirals on the ground that it posed too many risks—was to subdue the call for war in America and Japan over the school board incident. In other words, Roosevelt wanted to demonstrate to the jingoes in Japan the might of American naval power, which had become the second most powerful in the world (compared with Japan's fifth), while also sending a message to American jingoes that the United States had not backed down to Japan. As Tokyo was keen to improve relations with the United States as soon as it learned of the impending visit to nearby waters by the US fleet, an invitation was sent to the State Department requesting the fleet make a port call in Yokohama. Roosevelt embraced this offer and a press release exalted the visit as a contribution to increased international friendship and the cultivation of trust between Japan and America.

The impressive American armada was called the "White Fleet" since the typical grey color had been repainted to make it more visible and prominent. When the feet finally arrived in Yokohama in October, it received the warmest and by far the most enthusiastic welcome that it had encountered throughout the entire cruise up to this time. When this story broke to the public, a strong sense of friendship began to emanate from the both sides of the Pacific. The tensions of the immigration issue had completely vanished as America and Japan once again returned to their original state of amicable relations. Taking advantage of this sentiment, in November 1908, Japanese Ambassador in Washington Takahira Kogorō and Secretary of State Root reached an important agreement that was based on three fundamental points: maintaining the status quo in the Asia Pacific; preserving China's territorial integrity; and upholding the principle of the Open Door policy for economic opportunities.

In combination with the Gentlemen's Agreement, the so-called Root–Takahira Agreement formed the cornerstone of Roosevelt's diplomacy toward East Asia. He would give tacit approval of Japan's sphere of influence in Manchuria and Korea, as long as Japan compromised on the immigration issue. In this way, under the statesmanship of Roosevelt, US–Japan relations had once again returned to their former state.

BIBLIOGRAPHY

Chiba, Isao. 1996. Nichiro kōshō [Russo-Japanese Negotiations]. In *Nenpō Kindai Nihon kenkyū* [Annual Bulletin of Research on Modern Japan], vol. 18, ed. Kindai nihon kenkyū-kai. Tokyo: Yamakawa Shuppansha.

Gaimushō, ed. 1957, 1958, 1960. *Nihon gaikō monjo* [Documents on Japanese Foreign Policy]. 36-1, Nichiro V, 38-1, 41-1.

Gaimushō Chōsa-bu Dai 1-ka. 1939. Kaneko Kentarō Hakushaku jutsu [Statements of Count Kaneko Kentarō]. In *Gaimushō kiroku* [Ministry of Foreign Affairs Records] No. 2.1.0. 4-1.

Matsumura, Masayoshi. 1987. *Nichiro sensō to Kaneko Kentarō, Zōho kaitei-ban* [The Russo-Japanese War and Kaneko Kentarō]. Tokyo: Shinyūdō.

Minohara, Toshihiro. 2016. *Amerika no hai-Nichi undō to Nichibei kankei* [The Anti-Japanese Movement in America and US–Japan Relations]. Tokyo: Asahi Shimbun Press.

Tani, Tateki. 1976 [1912, Seikensha]. *Tani Tateki ikō* [Unpublished Writings of Tani Tateki], ed. Shimauchi Toshie. Vol. 4. Tokyo: University of Tokyo Press.

CHAPTER 3

The Great War and Shifting Relations, 1909–19

Tosh Minohara, Shūsuke Takahara, and Ryōta Murai

Dollar Diplomacy and Ensuing Economic Rivalry

During the global transitional period when the interests of the United States and Japan started to overlap and increasingly led to friction, President Theodore Roosevelt's successor William H. Taft took office. Although Roosevelt initially naively believed that his friendship with Taft would allow him to influence foreign policy indirectly, this was not the case as Taft had his own independent agenda and the two had a falling out over their views with regard to domestic policy. Taft was a staunch conservative, whereas Roosevelt was a progressive. Because the two could not see eye to eye on many critical issues—the Republican Party would soon split among conservative and progressive lines—it was only a matter of time before Taft's foreign policy began to diverge from the course set by his predecessor.

T. Minohara
Graduate School of Law, Kobe University, Kobe, Japan

S. Takahara
Faculty of Foreign Studies, Kyoto Sangyo University, Kyoto, Japan

R. Murai
Faculty of Law, Komazawa University, Tokyo, Japan

© The Author(s) 2017
M. Iokibe (ed.), T. Minohara (trans. ed.), *The History of US–Japan Relations*, DOI 10.1007/978-981-10-3184-7_3

43

Much more than Roosevelt, Taft and his Secretary of State Philander C. Knox placed priority on keeping the interests of major American corporations in mind while pursuing their East Asia policy. Therefore, it became important to secure a foothold so that companies could freely invest and conduct business in China and Manchuria. This would later be referred to as "Dollar Diplomacy," a term that was used in Taft's final State of the Union Address to Congress in December 1912. Looking back on his term in office, Taft commented that his foreign policy had been about "substituting dollars for bullets" as an effective way to "respond to modern ideas of commercial intercourse."

This fundamental shift in foreign policy was based on expanding American economic interests in Manchuria. This naturally required a revising of the existing sphere of influence that Roosevelt had agreed upon with Japan. Considering the enormous sacrifices that Japan had made during the Russo-Japanese War in seizing control of southern Manchuria, it was not prepared to stand idly by as the United States attempted to unilaterally change the status quo. On the other hand, the United States was not willing to forgo the potentially huge economic profits that could be reaped from Manchuria. Therefore, Taft brought in a large American railroad corporation so that it could obtain a share of the railroad concessions in Manchuria. However, this attempt ultimately failed as the result of vehement opposition from Tokyo and the untimely death of the key proponent of this endeavor, the railroad magnate Edward H. Harriman. Knox then proposed that all nations with a vested stake in the region contribute loans to China while supporting a neutralization policy of the railroads in Manchuria as a last-ditch measure.

But this proposal also collapsed due to strong objections not only from Japan, but also from Britain and Russia. However, in 1911 Knox was able to arrange for US participation in the Currency Reform Loan to augment the existing three-power consortium of foreign loans from France, Germany, and Britain. The timing of this new four-power consortium was far from ideal, however, as the Xinhai Revolution erupted shortly after the agreement had come into force. As a result, American capital never materialized in the region.

In contrast to Roosevelt's realist diplomacy, which placed an emphasis on the concept of balance of power and national interest, Taft's Dollar Diplomacy was rooted more in "idealistic humanitarian sentiments," meaning that his policy can therefore be viewed as a forerunner to Wilsonian idealism. This idealism was also reflected in Taft's rhetoric, which espoused such ideas as the commitment to "keeping in mind China's future and striving to preserve its administrative and territorial integrity." Of course, one must not read too much into this statement as the papers left by Taft do not suggest a president who was genuinely sympathetic toward China's plight. Rather, Taft's comments on humanitarianism and idealism should be interpreted as a way to provide moral justification to his aggressive pursuit of America's commercial interests in China.

The State Department's Shifting East Asian Policy

In taking over the helm of the Department of State from his predecessor Elihu Root, Knox felt that it was necessary to reorganize the State Department in order to keep pace with the rapidly changing international environment. He wanted to transform the department from an organization that dealt mostly with administrative matters into a professional organization that could play an active role in creating policy. Thus, Knox replaced the traditional approach to hiring staff that was largely based on nepotism to a new one based more on merit and abilities. As part of the reforms, the Division of Far Eastern Affairs established by Root in 1908 was further expanded, while the Division of Latin American Affairs, the Division of Western European Affairs, and the Division of Near Eastern Affairs were newly created. To support the administration's Dollar Diplomacy, the Bureau of Trade Relations was also vastly expanded so that it could manage the various issues relating to trade and overseas investment.

The Division of Far Eastern Affairs, which oversaw Japan, was tasked with formulating US policy toward the whole of East Asia. But the succession of division chiefs appointed by Knox—first William Phillips, followed by Francis M. Huntington-Wilson, and, finally, Willard D. Straight—all favored a pro-China policy. This policy was based in part on a nostalgic attachment to China and its long history, which, in their eyes, made it far superior to Japan. They also believed that China's large national territory offered much more potential for the United States in terms of economic benefits. Furthermore, Straight and Huntington-Wilson firmly believed that the Root–Takahira Agreement, which they saw as an agreement sacrificing American interests in China in favor of recognizing Japan's sphere of influence in Manchuria, epitomized the many failings of the previous administration. Wanting to correct the Roosevelt–Root Japan-leaning policy, the Taft–Knox policy shifted America toward China. In this new atmosphere, the so-called China hands would go on to exert an ever-increasing influence upon American policy toward East Asia.

Shifting Bilateral Relations

As American policy began to encroach upon Japan's sphere of influence in Manchuria, Dollar Diplomacy became a serious point of contention between the two nations. However, excluding Manchuria, Taft realized the importance of maintaining a framework of cooperation between the United States and Japan and thus he placed priority in concluding the new Treaty of Commerce and Navigation with Japan in February 1911. This finally restored tariff autonomy to Japan, marking the moment that Japan finally achieved treaty equality with the Untied States. This treaty led to economic relations between America and Japan blossoming during this period as Japan's economy grew steadily while America's trade with Japan also increased markedly. Despite Taft's fascination over "China's limitless market," in reality the volume of America's trade and investment in Japan was more than three times of that in China.

But Taft's mark upon US foreign policy would be limited to one term. Roosevelt's departure from the Republican Party to form the Progressive Party (the so-called Bull Moose Party) allowed the Democrats to return to power in the 1912 presidential elections after a 16-year hiatus. With this, America's diplomacy toward East Asia was now in the hands of the new president, Woodrow Wilson.

Reemergence of the Race Issue: 1913 California Alien Land Law

Although the 1908 Gentlemen's Agreement limited the number of Japanese who could immigrate to America to 500 people per year, the Japanese immigrant community on the West Coast grew steadily. As they tended to concentrate in the same area and were viewed by whites as being incapable of assimilating with American mainstream society, many Californians began to fear the increasing Japanese population. During the state elections of 1910, state politicians seized on this as a key political issue that would lead to votes. While Republican state assembly members avoided politicizing the issue, since they knew the federal government had no sympathy with the anti-Japanese movement, their Democratic counterparts had no such qualms as the current president, Taft, was not from their own party. By widely appealing to the anti-Japanese sentiment in the state with campaign slogans such as "Keep California White!" and creating an image that the Republicans were soft on the "Japs," the Democrats were able to increase their seats in the California State Legislature (Minohara 2016).

Following the San Francisco Board of Education Incident in 1906, Tokyo had become sensitive to the anti-Japanese movement in California as it injured Japan's pride and its sense of national prestige. Therefore, when in 1911 the state legislative session a new bill appeared that placed limits on land ownership by "aliens ineligible for citizenship"—namely, Japanese and other immigrants from Asia—the Japanese ambassador promptly urged the State Department to intervene in order to prevent the bill from being passed.

The timing of the bill could not have come at a worse time as both countries were engaged in delicate negotiations over the US–Japan Treaty of Commerce and Navigation before it expired. Taft was strongly opposed to the anti-Japanese movement in California and he was not amused by the state's reckless action that would injure US–Japan relations.

Taft wasted no time in dealing with this issue. He sent off an urgent telegram to the governor of California, fellow Republican Hiram W. Johnson, requesting his cooperation in killing off the offensive bill. If this request had come from Johnson's trusted friend Roosevelt, surely this alone would have been enough to secure his support. But Taft needed to provide a carrot to secure Johnson's assistance. During this time, a national debate was underway to determine which city would host the 1915 World Fair—officially known as the Panama-Pacific International Exposition—to celebrate the completion of the Panama Canal.

San Francisco and St. Louis remained as the final two candidate cities. Taft seized on this and gave Johnson a gentle reminder that it surely would not lead to a positive image of California if an anti-Japanese bill were to be passed. Johnson understood this hint; he acted decisively to get the bill thrown out and consequently San Francisco was selected as the host city. Accordingly, Taft had successfully averted a diplomatic crisis with Japan. As this incident indicates, on the issue of Japanese immigration, Taft was guided by realism. He was not going to allow the anti-Japanese movement to adversely affect US–Japan relations. But this pragmatic approach would not continue under President Wilson.

The return of a Democrat president to the White House was received with enthusiasm by the Democratic assembly members in California who had been repeatedly frustrated by Republican intervention into the affairs of their state. They were now eager to push through an anti-Japanese bill as even Wilson himself had voiced support for the anti-Japanese movement during the presidential election campaign.

Encouraged by Wilson's election, a new alien land bill was submitted on the first day of the state legislative session. When news of the impending bill reached Tokyo, the Japanese ambassador was instructed to bring it to attention of the US government. Wilson was startled by this news; he had been completely in the dark about what had been transpiring in California as neither his predecessor Taft nor California's Republican governor Johnson felt that it was necessary to inform the president.

Although Wilson had capitalized on anti-Japanese sentiments to improve his election chances, he quickly realized the folly of allowing relations with Japan to deteriorate over the issue. However, he was still reluctant to intervene as he had presented himself as a strong supporter of states' rights. Compounding the problem was his poor relationship with Governor Johnson. Since Johnson despised Wilson and the Democrats, he did not hesitate to exploit the anti-Japanese movement for his own political gain. Johnson made his position on the issue quite clear when he divulged to his assistant that this was the perfect opportunity to expose Wilson's hypocrisy to the American public.

Lacking the cooperation of the governor, there was nothing more that Wilson could do. In May 1913, the California legislature passed the 1913 Alien Land Law—known in Japan as the "first anti-Japanese land law" (*Daiichiji hainichi tochihō*)—which prevented "aliens ineligible for citizenship" from owning outright any farmland as well as limiting the length of land leases to a maximum of three years. Wilson would later describe this incident as a "most dangerous and difficult problem" as it led to a war scare that gripped both sides of the Pacific.

Both governments worked quickly to contain the damage. In July 1913, two months after the enactment of the Alien Land Law, Japanese Ambassador to the United States Chinda Sutemi and Secretary of State William Jennings Bryan agreed to official negotiations that would seek to prevent any such anti-Japanese legislation in the future through a mutual treaty. The talks got off to a good start, but were abruptly broken off the following year by Katō Takaaki who had been appointed to foreign minister in the second Ōkuma Shigenobu cabinet that was established on April 16, 1914.

Katō attached great importance to upholding Japan's national prestige and international status. Thus, he flatly refused to endorse any negotiation that affirmed the 1913 Alien Land Law as a starting point. Although the immigration problem could have reignited at this point, the outbreak of the First World War in July helped to remove the immigration problem from the forefront of US–Japan relations. But the problem had not been resolved and, as will see in the next chapter, it would resurface again with a vengeance after the end of the war.

THE REVOLUTION IN CHINA AND THE GREAT WAR

In the aftermath of the Russo-Japanese War, Japan had entered into various agreements that allowed it to enter the club of great powers. Everything seemed to be going well for Japan, but instability was approaching from unforeseen developments both at home and abroad. These challenges to Japan's diplomacy began externally with the Wuchang Uprising in October 1911, which led to a period of chaos in China. Japan was concerned about the unraveling situation but it struggled to respond as the Imperial Japanese Army (IJA) was getting itself more involved in diplomacy toward China, to the great consternation of the foreign ministry.

In his second term, Prime Minister Saionji Kinmochi's goal was to simply maintain the status quo in Manchuria while expanding Japanese influence in central China with the cooperation of the other powers, in particular the British. In January 1912, Sun Yat-sen was sworn in as the provisional president in Nanjing where he declared the creation of the Republic of China, Asia's very first republic. Despite all the fanfare, however, the new Chinese government lacked the ability to unite the entire nation. In March, Sun was soon replaced by Yuan Shikai, leader of the Beiyang Army. With events taking place so quickly, Tokyo was in a conundrum as to how to proceed. The *genrō* Yamagata Aritomo supported the plan of sending an army division to Manchuria, and the IJA was eager to oblige. But instead Saionji elected to work closely with Admiral Yamamoto Gonnohyōe who advocated a "wait-and-see" attitude until Japan could discern the exact path that China was heading toward.

Thus, Saionji halted a plan by army leaders that called for the intervention in China as a way to secure the independence of Manchuria and Mongolia. Although Saionji made certain that Japanese rights in southern Manchuria would remain undisturbed, in the spirit of international cooperation he advocated joining the existing four-power consortium of Britain, France, Germany, and America. Tokyo also signed the third Russo-Japanese agreement in response to the independence movement taking place in Outer

Mongolia following the revolution in China. Although a sound move, the government's restraint toward taking unilateral action led to fierce criticism from within Japan (Hatano 1995; Usui 1972).

Furthermore, a change to Japan's domestic political structure also contributed to the instability. While the government had been relatively stable as it alternated between the leadership of Katsura and Saionji during the 1910s, the prime minister's seat changed hands on six different occasions. Along with the spread of mass culture and democracy that represented the Taisho Period (1912–26), public opinion also began to influence policy more than ever before. This in turn spurred the growth of political parties that represented various domestic views. It was Saionji's firm belief that an emerging nation such as Japan should tread cautiously. This meant that military expansion was out of the question since it would only lead to increased suspicions by the other great powers. He was forced to resign as prime minister in December 1912, however, due to his refusal to support the IJA's demand to increase its troop presence in Korea, annexed in 1910 by two divisions (Itō 1981).

But the army's insistent meddling in politics led to a popular movement to protect the constitutional government (*goken undō*). Saionji was succeeded by Katsura, who set out to implement diplomatic reform, but he too was forced to resign after two months after receiving a vote of no-confidence in the Diet in face of mounting public unrest. Before leaving office, however, Katsura established a new party, the Rikken Dōshikai (Constitutional Association of Friends), which would later be led by Katō.

Domestic political stability was finally restored by Admiral Yamamoto Gonnohyōe, who was supported by the *Seiyūkai* party. He promptly set about to implement various reforms and abolished the system that required the appointment of active-duty generals and admirals to the positions of the army and navy ministers (*gunbu daijin geneki bukansei*). This change prevented the military from meddling in the government by refusing to appoint any minister to the cabinet.

In 1913, Sun Yat-sen's supporters launched an abortive uprising in China against Yuan Shikai, who had consolidated power after receiving loans from the six-power consortium. As Sun fled to Japan, Tokyo had no choice but to acknowledge Yuan Shikai as the leader of the Chinese Republic. Just as Japan was returning to political stability, however, Yamamoto was brought down by major scandal in March 1914 when it was revealed that a Siemens executive had bribed Japanese navy officers in landing naval contracts. After the massive political fallout, the Rikken Dōshikai came to power under the leadership of Ōkuma, who established his second cabinet with the support of the *genrōs* as well as the enthusiasm of the Japanese public who were hoped for more stability (Sakurai 1997; Kobayashi 1996).

Japan's Entry into the Great War

In his approach to China President Wilson took a quite different approach from those of the European powers and Japan. Shortly after he took office in 1913, America withdrew from the six-power consortium and tried to distance itself from the perceived financial exploitation that was believed to be detrimental to China's sovereignty. In May, Washington recognized the government of the Republic of China much sooner than the other powers. Wilson believed that America had an obligation to support the "Sister Republic" that emerged from the revolution in 1911. The president also hoped that as the most powerful and established nation in Asia, Japan would join hands with America in supporting this new China.

However, world events would take a drastic turn and bring focus back to Europe with the outbreak of the Great War in July 1914. The *genrō* Inoue Kaoru described the event as "divine intervention" (*tenyū*) that would serve as a much-needed boost to Japan's development. Although the war initially worsened Japan's economic recession, it would later lead unprecedented economic growth which would free Japan from the shackles of interest payments on its foreign loans. When the war first broke out, Japan's leaders believed that the conflict would be mostly contained to Europe. Thus, Japan's initial policy was to remain neutral.

But this changed when Britain made a formal request to Japan for assistance in searching out and destroying German raiders posing as neutral merchant cruisers. Foreign Minister Katō was adamant that Japan should join the war on the side of Britain as he placed great importance on the Anglo-Japanese alliance. He was also quite certain that this war would end in a victory for the Allies.

Tokyo officially declared war on Germany on August 23 on the grounds of its alliance with Britain. Japan's aim was to boost its international prestige by helping to eliminate German military positions throughout Asia and the Pacific. Katō, who was also the leader of the ruling party the Rikken Dōshikai, detested the continued attempts at intervention in foreign policy on the part of the *genrō* and the military. He therefore acted to consolidate foreign relations under the control of the central government, brushing aside all criticism against Japan's participation in the war voiced by the *genrō*. But Katō's overzealousness even caused concern in Britain as it began to perceive that Japan's true intention was to capitalize on the war as a way to expand its influence in China (Dickinson 1999; Sakurai 2001).

Among those in Japan who urged for more caution was the *genrō* Yamagata, who was worried about the final outcome of the war. He also viewed the Great War as a contest between the races, and feared that the war could ultimately lead to an all-out confrontation between the "white" and "non-white" races. From this standpoint, he felt that it was imperative that Japan not alienate its Asian neighbors such as China. Similarly, Hara Takashi, a member of the opposition party the *Seiyūkai*, was also reluctant to support Japan's entry into the war because he valued Japan's relationship with the United States which had declared its neutrality. After all, the United States was of critical importance to Japan's economy—vastly more so than Great Britain—and it was quite apparent that if Japan were to ever clash with America, its alliance with Britain would have no meaning whatsoever (Mitani 1995).

Japan's Diplomatic Blunder: The Twenty-One Demands

By October 1914, Japan had gained complete control of the German Pacific islands north of the equator, and by the following month it had also secured the territory leased by Germany on the Shandong Peninsula. Wilson was gravely concerned by Japan's rapid expansion and his worries were exacerbated by the fear that Japan may also have designs on the Philippines.

In January 1915, the Japanese minister in Beijing, Hioki Eki, issued a list of requests to Yuan Shikai with the intention of addressing the outstanding points between Japan and China. This would eventually become known as the infamous Twenty-One Demands. The points were divided into five groups. Groups 1 and 2 sought recognition of Japan's newly acquired interests in Shandong province as well as the further expansion of its rights in both southern Manchuria (i.e., Port Arthur, Dairen, and the South Manchuria Railway) and eastern Inner Mongolia. Group 3 asked for Chinese acknowledgment of Japan's interests in the Han-Ye-Ping Iron and Coal Company. Group 4 requested China from ceding or leasing any harbors or islands near the coast to other powers. But by far the most controversial was Group 5, which included Japan's various "desires" such as the appointment of Japanese advisors to the Chinese government and the joint administration of the local police force. Katō had the wherewithal to secure prior approval by British Foreign Secretary Edward Grey on the most critical issue, the extension of Japan's leases in China. However, Katō had no idea that Group 5 would create a firestorm of backlash with the Americans.

Although Japan's requests had actually been conveyed to China as "requests" rather than "demands," China nevertheless felt that Japan was taking advantage of China's weak position. Japan actually never perceived it in this manner and was merely trying to secure similar rights that were already possessed by the European powers in China. Japan also realized that Group 5 was not realistically attainable. Thus it planned to use it as a bargaining chip whereby Japan would forgo them altogether in exchange for China accepting the remaining four groups.

While the negotiations between Japan and China were to remain absolutely confidential, the Yuan government cleverly leaked an exaggerated version of Japan's demands to the United States and Europe. The Chinese knew what the Japanese were intending all along, but they decided to turn Japan's card into a weapon against it by revealing the unreasonable "demands" to the world in order to turn international public opinion against Japan.

As a result, the negotiations soon reached an impasse, excluding those that dealt with the request to prohibit any nation from constructing military facilities along the coast of Fujian province. However, Katō steadfastly persisted in his goal of obtaining Chinese approval of the remaining items in the first four groups. This led to heavy anti-Japanese lobbying by English-speaking Chinese in the United States as well as a boycott of Japanese goods in China.

Upon learning the contents of Group 5, Washington was antagonistic over Japan's blatant disregard for Chinese sovereignty. But Wilson initially adopted Secretary of State Bryan's policy of appeasing Japan by acknowledging that a special relationship existed between Japan and China and by showing understanding toward the nature of Group 5 as being nothing more than mere "wishes." In a memorandum to the Japanese Ambassador on March 13, 1915, Bryan gave support for Japan's special interests in southern Manchuria and eastern Inner Mongolia. But Wilson did have his misgivings over this policy and was becoming increasingly wary over Japan's actions.

Japan interpreted Bryan's response as a sign of tacit American support and began to apply even greater pressure on China. In an attempt to send a clear message, Japan took steps to reinforce its troops in the area. This move alarmed Paul Reinsch, the US minister in China, as well as Edward Williams, the chief of the Division of Far Eastern Affairs, who were both sympathetic to China. A strong call for the United States to fulfill its duty as China's guardian also came from American missionary circles in China. Wilson was infuriated by Japan's actions and promptly instructed Bryan to issue a second memorandum. The May 11 memorandum proclaimed that the US government would not dismiss any Japanese actions that infringed upon Chinese sovereignty. Wilson felt that it was America's obligation protect China. This would naturally lead to increased tensions between the United States and Japan over China; Wilson's deep mistrust of Tokyo's intentions would subsequently be the prime shaper of his policies toward Japan.

In order to break the impasse with China, Katō decided to resort to an even stronger tactic of issuing an ultimatum. This required the approval of the *genrō* council, but the council would hear none of it as they felt that Katō's policies were misguided. For example, Yamagata firmly believed that in order for Japan to maintain its rights and interests in China, it was crucial to obtain China's trust above all else. In the end, on May 7, 1915, Katō issued an ultimatum to China but dispensed with Group 5. Two days later, Yuan accepted the terms; May 9 would be etched in the minds of many Chinese as the "day of national humiliation."

Wilson's strong response to the Twenty-One Demands was based on his desire to preserve the Open Door policy that sought preservation of China's administrative and territorial integrity. The occasion marked the first time that America and Japan openly clashed over this principle. However, as the Untied States was embroiled in a diplomatic row with Mexico and was also occupied over how to deal with the unrestricted submarine warfare unleashed by Germany, Washington was reluctant to precipitate a diplomatic crisis with Japan over China. Memories of how low US–Japan relations had sunk during the passage of the 1913 California Alien Land Law were still vivid within Wilson, and thus with war ranging in Europe, he decided it would be prudent not to press Japan too hard on issues regarding China.

WILSON'S VISION FOR A POSTWAR INTERNATIONAL ORDER

After the outbreak of World War I, President Wilson pursued a policy of maintaining American neutrality while also seeking a way to achieve peace. As the war raged on in Europe, Wilson addressed the Senate in January 1917 and called for the creation of a new international organization that would ensure lasting peace based on the principle of justice and without being swayed by the victor's desire for revenge. He felt that such an organization could serve to solve international disputes through negotiation rather than by the use of force. However, the United States was not strictly neutral; it was forging closer ties with the Allies by exporting weapons and providing funding as Germany and the Austro-Hungarian Empire were increasingly seen as a threat to Wilson's vision of freedom and democracy.

After the sinking of a US passenger liner by a German U-boat as well as the revelation of a German plot to coax Mexico into war with the United States, Wilson received the support of Congress in April 1917 to enter the war as an "associated power" on the side of the Allies with the aim of making the world "safe for democracy." In November, a socialist revolution in Russia toppled Alexander Kerensky's government and brought the Bolsheviks to power. The new government, led by Vladimir Lenin, issued a "Decree on Peace" that called for peace without annexation or indemnities, the guarantee of the right of every nation to self-determination, and the abolition of secret diplomacy.

Wilson now had to worry about the ideological threat posed by the Bolshevik government. Thus, Wilson asked his trusted advisor, Colonel Edward M. House, to set up a committee of experts, known as "The Inquiry," to consider the possible global scenarios in the aftermath of the war. In his role as secretary, Walter Lippmann, who would later become one of America's most prominent columnists and political commentators, put together the report that would become the basis for Wilson's peace terms. The findings, referred to as the "Fourteen Points," were presented to Congress by the president on January 8, 1918.

The peace terms encompassed a number of key proposals, including the abolition of secret diplomacy, freedom of navigation on the open seas, removal of economic barriers, reduction of armaments, impartial solution of colonial issues, and the establishment of a general association of nations, the precursor to the League of Nations. The Fourteen Points led to a sense of solidarity among the Allies in their quest to defeat Germany. It also became the rallying cry for world peace. By bringing out a completely new concept of collective security in the realm of international politics, Wilson had prompted a diplomatic paradigm shift in the existing international order. This would allow him to play a central role at the Paris Peace Conference held in Versailles in 1919. And it would be this conference that would ultimately shape the postwar world order.

The Ishii–Lansing Agreement and the Siberian Intervention

While US–Japan relations remained strained after the Twenty-One Demands, Japan's relations with China were entering a new phase. Ōkuma tried to convince Yuan Shikai to not revive imperial rule, but when it became clear that he would not heed this request, Japan moved to oust him from power. As this was transpiring, a third revolution erupted in China which reinvigorated the independence movements in both Manchuria and Mongolia. Adding to this general level of confusion was Yuan's sudden death in June 1916.

In October, a new Japanese cabinet was formed under General Terauchi Masatake, who had been critical of Ōkuma's policy toward China. As prime minister, Terauchi adopted a new policy of non-intervention in Chinese domestic affairs and supported the Duan Qirui government as a means of obtaining greater economic cooperation from China. At the core of his economic policy was a series of loans arranged by Finance Minister Shōda Kazue and businessman Nishihara Kamezō, Terauchi's close friend.

With America's entry into the war in April 1917, the US and Japan became allies. This presented an opportune moment to patch up relations. Thus, Wilson decided to temporarily shelve the outstanding issues over China and form a security agreement with Japan that espoused cooperation in the Pacific. Secretary of State Robert Lansing was appointed as the chief American delegate in the negotiation; Ishii Kikujirō was to be his Japanese counterpart.

After some intense discussions, an agreement was finally reached on November 17, 1917, whereby the United States recognized Japan's special interests in China, and, in turn, Japan respected the Open Door policy in China. Notwithstanding the inherently paradoxical nature of the agreement, there was also ambiguity as to the precise meaning of "special interests." The United States saw these as interests derived merely from "geographical proximity," while the Japanese interpreted them as also including "political" interests. In Japan, the *genrō* Yamagata was elated by the Ishii–Lansing agreement as it put US–Japan relations back on the same page. However, Wilson was quite discontent over the agreement and had accepted it as way to appease Japan during the ongoing war.

Despite its shortcomings, the Ishii–Lansing agreement did help to improve US–Japan relations. Even before the ink could dry, however, Russia was now emerging as the new point of friction between the two countries. After the Russian Revolution, the country made a separate

peace with Germany and quickly left the war. This action was in contravention to the London Declaration of October 1915, an agreement
whereby the Allies had committed themselves not to make a separate
peace with the Central Powers. An alarmed Britain and France urged
Japan to quickly deploy troops to the Eastern frontier of Siberia to maintain a second front.

This led to a heated debate within the ad hoc Advisory Council for
Foreign Affairs (*Rinji gaikō chōsaiinkai*), a policy formulating body established by the Terauchi cabinet. Most vocal in the council were Hara Takashi
and Makino Nobuaki, representatives of the lower house of the Diet and
the House of Peers, respectively, who were both staunchly opposed to any
independent actions taken by Japan. Terauchi and Yamagata supported
this view and thus the decision was made not to send any troops to Siberia.
However, as soon as the United States proposed a joint operation in Siberia
to rescue the stranded Czechoslovak Legion that was fighting on the side
of the Allies, Japan reconsidered as it saw it to be an opportunity for the
two nations to work together. The first soldiers arrived in August 1918.

However, US–Japan friction quickly arose when the IJA ignored
the agreed limit of 12,000 troops and deployed 73,000 men instead.
Washington interpreted this as Japan's intent to gain exclusive control of
northern Manchuria as well as Siberia. It was not until the Hara cabinet
came to power in September 1918 that the troop levels were reduced to
prevent an escalation of tensions with the United States. To express its
displeasure, however, once the Czechoslovak Legion had been liberated,
the United States unilaterally withdrew its forces from Siberia on January
1920 without any prior notice to the Japanese. Tokyo was taken aback.
But as it moved to withdraw troops, a horrific massacre of Japanese civilians by Russian partisans took place in the town of Nikolayevsk-on-Amur
in the Russian Far East. This halted all plans to remove the remaining
Japanese forces from Siberia; they would remain until October 1922.

AMERICAN AND JAPANESE OBJECTIVES AT THE
PARIS PEACE CONFERENCE

In November 1918, the armistice with Germany brought the war that had
engulfed Europe for more than four years to an end. A peace conference
to discuss the postwar period began in Versailles in January 1919. From
Japan, Saionji Kinmochi and Makino Nobuaki were sent to the conference to represent Japan. A pressing matter was how to deal with Wilson's

Fourteen Points that were anticipated to become the new standard in the conduct of foreign affairs. In the end, Tokyo adopted a policy of working closely with Britain as a way to inherit Germany's former interests in the Asia-Pacific. Also a decision was made that Japan would only intervene in issues that directly involved Japanese interests; it would keep a watchful eye toward the "tendencies of the majority" to see how Wilson's proposal for the creation of a League of Nations would be accepted by the other powers (Hattori 2001).

Although Japan participated in the conference as one of the five great powers—the so-called Big Five—it still clung to a policy of only engaging in issues that were directly related to its own national interests. As a result, Japan gradually sidelined itself in the talks while the other powers delved into the task of reshaping postwar Europe. For this behavior, Japan was ridiculed as a "Silent Partner," but the Japanese became quite vocal when it came to the following three objectives:

The first was to ensure that Japan would inherit Germany's former interests in Shandong province, and, in particular, to secure rights and interests in railroads and mines as well as establishing a settlement in Qingdao. The second was to take control of the former German Pacific islands north of the equator. Britain, France, Russia, and Italy had all acquiesced to these two demands during the war. The final goal was the inclusion of a racial equality clause in the League of Nations covenant.

This seemed to be a reasonable request considering that it was already agreed upon that the covenant would include a clause that stipulated equality among all religions. The Japanese government wanted to expand this so that it would encompass race as well. The motive behind this was to preserve Japan's national prestige by ensuring that it would not have to endure discrimination from the white powers. Of course, a hidden agenda was to prevent any future anti-Japanese legislation from being enacted in California and other US states. In other words, Japan was attempting to use international law as a shield against the anti-Japanese movement that would surely resurface after the peace conference.

America, by contrast, participated in the Paris Peace Conference with the purpose of proposing fundamental solutions to the pressing issues facing Europe. This was the first time in US history that a sitting president had crossed the Atlantic in order to join a conference with the European powers. The torch of being the world's preeminent global leader had been passed on to America; the United States would henceforth be given the center stage in international relations.

The United States had been preparing for the peace conference chiefly through three organizations: the Inquiry, the State Department, and the military. As this meant that there were three policy options, Washington struggled to devise a unified policy as well as an effective strategy. Despite Wilson's repeated calls for "New Diplomacy," the true direction of the president's own policy was often unclear and inconsistent. For example, on many occasions Wilson had to subordinate his principled approach in favor of meeting Japan's demands lest it leave the conference and doom the creation of the League of Nations.

Wilson's initial approach to the question of the Shandong territory, an issue that was of vital interest to Japan, was to support China's demands that the territory be directly returned from Germany. However, faced with stiff Japanese objections, Wilson was forced to reconsider when he came to realize that it was legally impossible to nullify the diplomatic notes exchanged between Japan and China regarding the Shandong railway following China's declaration of war on Germany in September 1918.

In this way, Wilson's support of China began to gradually fade in favor of fulfilling his ambition of creating the League. However, Japan did agree to receive only economic interests and rights that had been possessed by Germany. It also promised not to further infringe upon Chinese sovereignty when establishing a settlement in Qingdao. But by this time the Chinese plenipotentiaries became completely disillusioned by Wilson's reversal.

On the issue of Japan's annexation of the former German Pacific islands, Wilson saw this as undermining his "New Diplomacy." Thus, he labored to reject annexation and instead recommended the territories in question be placed under the control of League of Nations. However, this encountered severe opposition from Australia and New Zealand, two nations in particular that wanted outright annexation of the former German possessions.

The deadlock was finally broken by the chief delegate of South Africa, Jan C. Smuts, who proposed a compromise plan whereby Germany's colonies would be classified into three classes of mandates and accordingly be either governed or annexed depending on their economic, demographic, and geographic characteristics. As a result, the Pacific Islands were classified as Class C mandates (not at all ready for independence), and those located north of the equator were to be governed, but not annexed, by Japan. Of course, for all practical purposes, there really was no significant difference between the two. Although Wilson had stood up for the cause of anti-colonialism, in the end compromises were made in order to successfully conclude the peace conference (Takahara 2006).

The Reemergence of the Race Issue

Wilson agonized over the issue of abolishing racial discrimination. Since he felt a moral obligation to uphold the universal concept of racial equality, he was initially supportive of Japan's proposal and even included, in the original draft of the League Covenant, a text that called for the "equal treatment" of all races and ethnicities. However, this clause met with strong opposition from Australia, supported by Britain, which had in place a White Australia policy at the time. Wilson's enthusiasm was also deflated by his realization of the domestic political ramifications of pushing for a racial equality as many Americans resented the fact that state laws—no matter how racist—could be overruled by an international agreement (Minohara 2016).

Japan ultimately had to settle with satisfaction of the racial equality proposal being recorded in the minutes of the conference. Upset over this outcome, several members of the Japanese delegation felt that their government should not sign the final treaty. But ultimately Saionji and Makino felt that it was in Japan's interests to cooperate with the other powers rather than pushing for racial equality. As a result, Japan agreed to the terms of the Treaty of Versailles that was signed in June 1919.

Saionji was quite content at what Japan had gained by the treaty. Despite a few setbacks, Japan able to proudly join the newly founded League of Nations as a charter member as well as one of only four permanent members to the League Council (the United States did not join the League due to Congressional opposition). Japan was also rewarded by having a Japanese national, Nitobe Inazō, appointed to the post of under-secretary general.

However, the mid-level delegates from the Ministry of Foreign Affairs did not share Saionji's enthusiasm and concluded that Japan had not gained as much as it could have from the conference due to poor preparation—Saionji had actually arrived late for the start of the conference—and incompetence shown by the senior delegates such as not holding press conferences. This led, in turn, to a movement in the Foreign Ministry calling for a major overhaul of the personnel and organizational structure of the bureaucracy. As a part of this modernization scheme, the Treaty Bureau (*Jōyakukyoku*) was established soon after the conference, and in 1920 the Political Affairs Bureau (*Seimukyoku*) separated into two sections that would be devoted to Asia/Europe and to the Americas, respectively. This was followed a year later by the creation of the Intelligence Division (*Jōhōbu*). Several former members of the Japanese delegation, including Yoshida Shigeru, Shigemitsu Mamoru, Matsuoka Yōsuke, and Arita Hachirō, would later play an important role in shaping Japanese diplomacy. Another delegate, Konoe Fumimaro, who harshly criticized Wilsonianism as a faux pacifism that actually aimed to maintain the status quo of the "have" nations in his famous essay, "Rejecting the Anglo-American-Centered Pacifism" (*Eibei hon'i no heiwashugi o haisu*), became a key political leader as prime minister during the 1930s.

Dissatisfaction over the results of the Paris Peace Conference would surge in a powerful way during the 1930s when Japan's foreign policy began to increasingly diverge from the West and become more focused on returning back to Asia (*datsuō nyūa*). However, as we will see in the next chapter, Japan during the 1920s was still guided by adroit and strong leaders such as Hara, Saionji, and Makino who all pursued a policy that emphasized international cooperation among the powers.

BIBLIOGRAPHY

Dickinson, Frederick R. 1999. *War and National Reinvention*. Cambridge: Harvard University Press.

Hatano, Masaru. 1995. *Kindai Higashi Ajia no seiji hendō to Nihon no gaikō* [Political Shifts in Modern East Asia and Japanese Diplomacy]. Tokyo: Keiō Tsūshin.

Hattori, Ryūji. 2001. *Higashi Ajia kokusai kankyō no hendō to Nihon gaikō 1918–1931* [Changes in the East Asian Diplomatic Environment and Japanese Diplomacy 1918–1931]. Tokyo: Yūhikaku Publishing.

Itō, Takashi, ed. 1981. *Taishō shoki Yamagata Aritomo danwa hikki*. [Records of Conversations with Yamagata Aritomo in the Early Taisho Period]. Tokyo: Yamakawa Shuppansha.

Kobayashi, Michihiko. 1996. *Nihon no tairiku seisaku 1895–1914* [Japan's Continental Policy 1895–1914]. Tokyo: Nansōsha.

Minohara, Toshihiro. 2016. *Amerika no hai-Nichi undō to Nichibei kankei* [The Anti-Japanese Movement in America and US–Japan Relations]. Tokyo: Asahi Shimbun Press.

Mitani, Taichirō. 1995. Taishō demokurashi to washinton taisei [Taisho Democracy and the Washington Treaty System]. In *Nichibei kankei tsūshi* [A Complete

History of US–Japan Relations], ed. Hosoya Chihiro. Tokyo: University of Tokyo Press.

Sakurai, Ryōju. 1997. *Taishō seijishi no shuppatsu* [The Start of the Political History of the Taisho Period]. Tokyo: Yamakawa Shuppansha.

———. 2001. Katō Takaaki to Ei-bei-chū sangoku-kankei [Katō Takaaki and Relations Between Britain, America, and China]. In *Taishōki Nihon no Amerika ninshiki* [Japanese Views of the United States in the Taisho Era], ed. Hasegawa Yūichi, 79–121. Tokyo: Keiō University Press.

Takahara, Shūsuke. 2006. *Uiruson gaikō to Nihon* [Wilson Diplomacy and Japan]. Tokyo: Sōbunsha.

Usui, Katsumi. 1972. *Nihon to Chūgoku* [Japan and China]. Tokyo: Hara Shobō.

CHAPTER 4

The 1920s: The Washington Treaty System and the Immigration Issue

Ryūji Hattori and Tosh Minohara

FINANCIAL COOPERATION IN CHINA: THE NEW FOUR-POWER BANKING CONSORTIUM

Upon the resignation of Terauchi Masatake due to the massive rice riots of September 1918, a new cabinet was formed under Hara Takashi, president of the Constitutional Association of Political Friends (*Rikken Seiyūkai*). This became the first cabinet in Japanese history drawn up along party political lines, and it advocated four key political platforms: strengthening national defense; promoting education; stimulating industry; and expanding transportation networks. The government also adopted the single-member district electoral system, thereby ensuring that the *Seiyūkai* would acquire an absolute majority. The eligibility for governors of Japanese colonies was widened to include civilians; in the past only active service military officers could be considered. Hara also gradually withdrew the Japanese troops deployed in Siberia.

R. Hattori
Faculty of Policy Studies, Chuo University, Hachioji, Japan

T. Minohara
Graduate School of Law, Kobe University, Kobe, Japan

© The Author(s) 2017
M. Iokibe (ed.), T. Minohara (trans. ed.), *The History of US–Japan Relations*, DOI 10.1007/978-981-10-3184-7_4

Hara's foreign policy was largely focused on cooperating with both the United States and the United Kingdom, with the prime example being the New Four-Power Banking Consortium, which was established in October 1920 to provide a platform for joint investment in China by Japan, America, Britain, and France. This scheme was based on a proposal by then Secretary of State Robert Lansing to Japanese Ambassador to the United States Ishii Kikujirō at the end of the war. The major obstacle that stood in the way of forming the consortium was Japan's request that the whole of southern Manchuria as well as eastern Mongolia be excluded from discussions regarding the consortium. This clashed with the position of the American and British delegates, who insisted that only those areas in which Japanese control was clearly established should be excluded. Hara ultimately acquiesced and a final agreement was reached through an exchange of letters between Kajiwara Chūji, representing the Japanese banking group, and his American counterpart, Thomas W. Lamont (Mitani 1995).

This coincided with a transitional period in American diplomacy. Wilson was entering his final few months of office and Bainbridge Colby had succeeded Robert Lansing as Secretary of State. During this transitional phase, Wilson shifted his Japan policy on more than one occasion, and at one point he even floated the idea of forming a three-power consortium with Britain and France, excluding Japan. Wilson clearly failed to realize that as a genuine party cabinet, the Hara cabinet was actually the most ideal government yet for the United States to work with and establish a cooperative relationship. To be sure, Hara did not necessarily attach the greatest importance to the agreements made by the New Four-Power Banking Consortium, and he discreetly expanded Japanese interests by constructing railways in Si-Tao and Nanxun in northern and southern China. As a shrewd and capable leader, Hara adopted an approach that would allow him to maintain cooperation with the United States and the United Kingdom while also pursuing a plan for economic expansion. However, the consortium was met with Chinese hostility that left it incapable of providing a single loan.

In the final weeks of the Wilson administration, US policy in relation to East Asia had abandoned the pragmatic approach that Lansing had taken toward cooperating with Japan. That being said, the pro-China approach advocated by the American minister to China, Paul Reinsch, was also severely hindered by Wilson's compromise toward Japan at the Paris Peace Conference. In protest, Reinsch resigned his position in the aftermath of the May Fourth Movement in 1919. It was clear that by this stage the administration was no longer able to implement an effective policy toward East Asia.

The Washington Naval Conference and the Triple Treaties

Wilson's failure to guide the Untied States in the League of Nations was compounded by a major defeat on the domestic front. The Democratic candidate was clobbered in the November 1920 presidential elections—the first in which women were permitted to participate—and the Republicans were able to send their man to the White House in March 1921 for the first time in eight years. The Republicans also secured a solid victory in Congress, increasing their presence in the Senate by 18 seats and also securing a 42-seat majority over the Democrats in the House of Representatives. Although he had gained an overwhelming majority, the new president, Warren G. Harding, was determined not to make the same blunder as his predecessor Wilson. Harding was an incumbent senator, and his bid for the presidency had been supported by the efforts of his fellow senators who wanted a president who would respect the Senate. Thus, Harding was expected to assuage the rivalry between the executive and legislative branches that Congress had developed under Wilson, and to return to a peacetime America, which was implied by his call for a "Return to Normalcy." The president turned much of his attention toward domestic affairs as he was concerned with the high unemployment rate resulting from rapid postwar demobilization. Harding's solution was to maintain a policy of high tariffs and fiscal austerity. On the other hand, having little interest in diplomacy, Harding entrusted most foreign policy matters to his secretary of state, Charles Evans Hughes, who was one of the most influential figures in the Republican Party. Therefore, now it fell to Hughes to undo the damage that Wilson had inflicted on US–Japan relations.

Hughes believed firmly that the best means of establishing stable relations with Japan was to address the various outstanding issues within a framework for cooperation in East Asia among the major powers. He also wanted to bring a halt to the economically debilitating arms race over warship construction. In order to provide a forum for the powers to address issues, Hughes convened the Washington Naval Conference in 1921. This conference had three principal agendas: naval disarmament, the status quo in the Pacific, and the future of China. Three treaties resulted from these deliberations, each named after the number of signatories: the Five-Power Treaty, the Four-Power Treaty, and the Nine-Power Treaty. This international conference allowed the United States to demonstrate its global leadership role in the post–World War I world.

At the beginning of the conference, Hughes proposed a bold new policy that called for a ten-year moratorium on the construction of warships. He also revealed a plan that would set a cap on capital-ship tonnages at 5:5:3 ratios among the United States, Britain, and Japan. Katō Kanji, a member of the Japanese delegation representing the navy, was shocked to learn that this radical plan would place Japan in a position of numerical inferiority, and consequently he was determined to resist it. The leader of the Japanese delegation, Navy Minister Admiral Katō Tomosaburō, believed otherwise, however. He embraced the proposal as a way to reduce military spending and maintain cooperation between the United States and Japan. Thus, in February 1922, America, Britain, Japan, France, and Italy signed the Five-Power Treaty concerning the limitation of naval armament, also known as the Washington Naval Treaty. In order to make the terms more palatable for Japan, Katō Tomosaburō had secured in the treaty the promise that the United States and Britain would not establish naval bases or other fortifications in the Pacific near Japan's territory (Article XIX). As the initial naval treaty covered only capital ships, this eventually led to a race to construct auxiliary ships as well as "pocket battleships" that were not classified as capital ships under the existing terms of the treaty.

Next, the Four-Power Treaty emerged from discussions to establish a new arrangement between the United States, Britain, and Japan to replace the Anglo-Japanese Alliance. Britain initially proposed to renew the bilateral alliance, but Shidehara Kijūrō suggested adding the US to the agreement as he felt that the US would oppose any extension of the Anglo-Japanese Alliance. Hughes responded by proposing that a new agreement also include France and not apply to China. This idea became the basis of the eventual Four-Power Treaty that was signed in December 1921 (Asada 1993). Article IV of the treaty stipulated that the Anglo-Japanese Alliance would terminate upon ratification of the new treaty.

Shidehara's approach to the issue was prudent in the sense that it allowed him not only to improve relations with the United States by squarely addressing Hughes's concerns over the renewal of the Anglo-Japanese Alliance, but also to strengthen Japan's credibility with other powers, and to boost the confidence of not only himself but also that of Japan among the conference attendees. As the alliance was limited by Britain's close relationship with America and as it would not take effect in the event of conflict between the United States and Japan, in actuality Shidehara was giving up very little in return for gaining a high degree of US trust. Shidehara had clearly learned the lessons of the failures of Foreign Minister Katō Takaaki when he issued the infamous Twenty-One Demands to China (Hattori 2006).

The Chinese delegate Alfred Sao-Ke Sze, also serving as Chinese Minister to the United States, proposed his ten principles in addressing the issues in East Asia, which included guaranteeing the Open Door policy. In response, the American delegate, former Secretary of State Elihu Root, countered with four principles of his own regarding China: upholding sovereignty and territorial/administrative integrity; establishing a stable government; maintaining equal opportunities in the areas of trade and commerce; and refraining from seeking special interests in China that would infringe upon the rights of other nations.

After some deliberation, the powers agreed to accept Root's four principles, as they conveniently protected China's sovereignty while also permitting the powers to hold on to their existing interests in the country (Asada 1993). However, Root's approach, which focused on achieving cooperation with Japan while maintaining the status quo, was not supported by the whole American delegation. In fact, Hughes submitted a resolution that essentially set out to redefine the Open Door principle and recommended the establishment of a committee to look further into Root's principles. This was steadfastly opposed by Shidehara and as it never garnered much support from the other participating countries, it was allowed to lapse. In the end, Hughes had no real alternative but to acknowledge Japan's special interests in southern Manchuria by making them an exception to the final agreement.

Finally, the Nine-Power Treaty that was agreed upon in February 1922 reaffirmed the Open Door policy and the principle of equal opportunity for trade and commerce in China. These principles were not disputed by either Japan or Britain, as the vital issue was whether or not the principles would apply to the existing interests of the powers. Shidehara felt that equal opportunity was a fundamental basis for the further economic development of the continent. Root's four principles were incorporated in Article I of the Nine-Power Treaty, and, as such, the final treaty did not demand any drastic changes to the existing interests of each power. This was a pragmatic solution in Root's mind as his priority at this time was to rebuild America's relationship with Japan. In this way, the various agreements reached between the United States, Japan, and Britain during the Washington Conference were all ultimately about maintaining the status quo in China. These agreements were shaped through a tacit Anglo-Japanese understanding which was also acknowledged by Root as a way to gain the cooperation of Japan. In the end, Hughes had to accept this position in order to successfully conclude the conference.

US–Japan relations under the Washington Treaty System consisted of three main aspects: geopolitical tension concerning the Pacific; the coordination of interests in and ideals regarding the Asian continent; and social and cultural friction based on race. These three aspects manifested themselves as the naval disarmament issue, policies toward China, and the immigration problem. The Washington Treaty System succeeded in bringing the United States and Japan closer together in a feeling of mutual cooperation on the first two issues. For the third, Hughes had intentionally detached it from the basic agenda out of fear that it could derail the entire conference. The secretary of state was right in this assessment, but he would pay a huge price later on for not addressing this issue as soon as the Washington Conference had been concluded.

John V. A. MacMurray, chief of the Division of Far Eastern Affairs in the State Department, would also suffer from the consequences of the immigration problem. MacMurray was deeply involved in shaping the main issues concerning East Asia at the Washington Conference. His diplomatic skills shone through when he succeeded in forming a viable solution to the Shandong problem. As a result, the two nations signed the Shandong Treaty in February 1922, under which China promised to reimburse Japan for the loss of its railroad assets in a 15-year deferred payment of Chinese treasury notes, and both nations agreed to a joint management of the mines in the region. In this way, the Shandong problem, which had been a sore point in Sino-Japanese relations during the Paris Peace Conference, was resolved by the Japanese agreeing to return the territory to the Chinese. It should be kept in mind that MacMurray's approach was quite different from those adopted by either Hughes or Root. Hughes's approach provoked strong objections from Japan by attempting to extend the Open Door principles to existing interests of the powers, and Root invited suspicion from China by acknowledging the existing interests of the powers in his quest to preserve the status quo. MacMurray, on the other hand, attached importance to Japan's desires as well China's fears, allowing him to seek compromises from both parties by devoting himself as an impartial mediator between Japan and China.

But there is some doubt as to whether or not the United States really was committed to cooperating with Japan in the aftermath of the conference. A glimpse of America's divergence from its commitment can be found in the recollections of Eugene H. Dooman, the first secretary at the US Embassy in Japan, who suggested that by allowing China to trample over the interests of the foreign powers, the United States undermined the position of the Japanese officials who honored the Nine-Power Treaty, such as Shidehara and Wakatsuki Reijirō, making it easier for militarists to challenge them. Although Dooman placed too much emphasis on linking the rise in Chinese nationalism to America's carefree benevolence, his comments are nevertheless significant in that they clearly show the contrast between America and Japan's approach to China. In other words, Japan was wary of Chinese nationalism because it wanted to protect its existing interests in China, while the United States was generally supportive of Chinese nationalism as it converged with principles such as the Open Door policy and the right to national self-determination.

In sum, the Washington Conference signalled an end to the decline in relations between America and Japan and allowed them to revert to a policy of mutual cooperation. Japan, America, and Britain all worked together to establish a new framework for cooperative diplomacy in which China would play a subordinate role and the Soviet Union would be excluded. This framework, in other words the Washington Treaty System, would be the guiding principle for East Asian policy until the Manchurian Incident in 1931.

THE IMMIGRATION PROBLEM AND US–JAPAN RELATIONS

The immigration problem fell by the wayside during the Great War, but as soon as the war ended in 1918, the anti-Japanese movement flared up once again, partly as a result of the 1913 Alien Land Law not having the desired effect of reducing the amount of farmland owned by Japanese immigrants. Moreover, as the Japanese immigrants were used to successfully cultivating poor soil in Japan, they thrived as farmers, sparing no effort in clearing and cultivating the non-desirable land that the white farmers deemed unfit for agriculture. Fearing this new competition, white farmers once again began to call for a stronger Alien Land Law that would further tighten the restrictions on Japanese farmers. The local politicians quickly jumped on the bandwagon as many felt that this would be the ideal policy issue in the upcoming state election in 1920 (Minohara 2016).

In fact, the 1913 Alien Land Law did contain a few notable loopholes. For instance, there were no restrictions on farmland purchased in the name of a child born in America—who would therefore be an American citizen—while families without any children could possess land either through ownership in a land-holding stock company or a share-cropping contract. Although these flaws were known prior to the enactment of the land law, they were conveniently disregarded by the governor of California at that time, Hiram Johnson, as his main priority was to score a political victory over President Woodrow Wilson. Johnson also wanted to avoid introducing a law that would have severe financial repercussions on the Japanese community because he had been warned by his good friend, former President Theodore Roosevelt, that he should avoid any action that would be detrimental to American–Japanese relations.

But at the close of World War I, the glaring shortcomings of the Alien Land Law again raised the specter of the anti-Japanese movement from its wartime slumber. In the first California state elections after World War I, much attention was given to the newly implemented process whereby citizens could enact/revise a law or amend the state's constitution directly through a ballot measure. As a progressive state, California was expanding the means of democracy by giving voters the power to legislate. Any ballot initiative—or proposition—could become law without passing the state legislature and also could not be vetoed by the governor. The anti-Japanese leaders were fully aware of this new political system, and once they confirmed that the new governor, William D. Stephens, was reluctant to support any anti-Japanese legislation, they devoted their energy to introduce an initiative that would close the loopholes of the existing Alien Land Law. This became known as Proposition No. 1, which was placed on the state ballot during the 1920 elections. Japan was concerned by this turn of events as it was determined to preserve its honor as a first-class power. Therefore, it appealed directly to Washington to intervene.

The Morris–Shidehara Talks and the Road to Japanese Exclusion

After Japan's failure to secure the racial equality clause in the League Covenant at the Paris Peace Conference, Tokyo felt that the best way to resolve the issue was through a process of direct bilateral negotiation. What it had in mind was a series of informal meetings between the American Ambassador to Japan, Roland S. Morris—who had momentarily returned to Washington—and the Japanese Ambassador to the United States, Shidehara, later known as the Morris–Shidehara talks. Following the 24 meetings (including the preliminary discussions) that took place between September 1920 and January 1921, Morris drafted a comprehensive report that concluded that the most effective means of permanently resolving the anti-Japanese movement would be to allow Japanese immigrants the right to acquire full citizenship. But Morris also realized that in order for this to happen, the federal government needed to first secure the support of Congress. This, however, was unlikely considering the ongoing tensions between the president and Congress (Minohara 2006).

While the Morris–Shidehara talks were taking place, the Republicans secured a landslide victory in the November 1920 election. On the same day, votes were cast on the ballot measures and the 1920 Alien Land Law—referred to in Japan as the "Second Anti-Japanese Land Law"—was passed by an overwhelming majority of three to one. Unlike in 1913, however, this did not trigger a serious diplomatic crisis in relations between America and Japan due to the fact that both sides were anxiously looking forward to the recommendations of Morris–Shidehara talks. The anti-Japanese forces in California quickly realized that they had exhausted the last legal means of targeting the Japanese immigrants. Thus, the next logical thing to do was to expand the anti-Japanese movement in California to a national level so the tide of future Japanese immigration could be stemmed through an Act of Congress (Minohara 2006).

President Warren G. Harding would not have to deal with the ensuing US–Japan diplomatic row as he passed away suddenly in August 1923. However, his successor, the former vice-president John Calvin Coolidge, was doomed from the outset because he had very limited loyalty from the inherited Harding administration and he lacked both the presence and the leadership skills to take full control of the administration. Coolidge also had to deal with the misdeeds of the former Harding administration in the Teapot Dome scandal, which came to light shortly after he took office. This further weakened the government as it had to endure condemnation from not only the opposition Democrats, but also the progressive Republicans, and several members had to resign. Although the Republicans held the majority in Congress, the scandal left them in a vulnerable position. In addition, the progressive wing of the party was being more uncooperative to the extent that the GOP was unable to successfully nominate the chairmen for the various congressional committees, despite being in the majority.

During this time, Congress was deliberating on how to replace the stopgap Immigration Act of 1921 with a comprehensive and more permanent law. Seeing this as an opportunity, the anti-Japanese forces of California were actively lobbying Congress to pass an immigration legislation that would exclude the Japanese, which was the only Asian nation that had avoided exclusion to date. Although the House had already passed an immigration bill that contained a clause for Japanese exclusion, it was widely believed that the Senate, which placed greater importance on foreign affairs, would not do the same because doing so could hinder relations with Japan. In fact, the only senators who were openly supporting Japanese exclusion were from the West Coast. Surprisingly, the senators from the South, who were mostly intolerant toward other races, did not show much interest in the issue of Japanese exclusion. Thus at this juncture it seemed very unlikely that the Senate would pass an anti-Japanese immigration bill.

The general atmosphere in the Senate changed abruptly on April 14, 1924. A few days earlier, a letter from Japanese Ambassador to the United States Hanihara Masanao, which had been addressed to Secretary of State Hughes, had been distributed in the Senate in order to eliminate any misunderstandings over the issue of Japanese immigration. The letter had actually been drafted with the cooperation of the State Department with the aim of explaining the content of the 1908 Gentlemen's Agreement. The friendly letter also reiterated the importance of US–Japan relations. However, Henry Cabot Lodge, the chairman of the Senate Foreign Relations Committee, took issue over the phrase "grave consequences" in the final paragraph of the correspondence. On the Senate floor, he denounced this as a "veiled threat" toward the United States and urged other senators to push forward Japanese exclusion in order to demonstrate that the United States would never back down to any threats. Seemingly convinced by Lodge's arguments, many senators who had initially been against Japanese exclusion now reversed their earlier positions and expressed their support for the bill.

It is a common misunderstanding that Hanihara's letter led to the immigration bill being passed with the Japanese exclusion clause intact on May 15, 1924. In reality, however, it was a classic example of domestic political factors affecting the final decision by the Republican senators and sealing the fate of the legislation. Due to the political scandal, the many Republicans were facing an uphill battle in their respective elections. The incessant factional rivalry between the conservative and progressive wings of the party also did not help the situation; party unity was crucial in a presidential election year in which Coolidge was seeking to be elected for his first full term. This naturally increased the presence and influence of the senators from the West Coast states gaining their support was crucial if the party were to emerge victorious in the upcoming elections. Faced with this stark reality, a secret Republican caucus was hastily convened where the Republican leaders agreed to sacrifice US-Japan relations on the altar of preserving the cohesion of the party.

This unfortunate event on the heels of establishment of the Washington Treaty System injured America's moral leadership; it would also lead to Japan's disillusionment with not only American democracy, but the West as a whole. Japan felt that there was a racial divide that it could not cross even as a great power. Therefore, Japan would seek its position within the context of pan-Asianism (Minohara 2002).

THE CHINA PROBLEM AND US–JAPAN RELATIONS

During the US congressional debates over the new immigration legislation in mid-1924, the Japanese government was headed by Prime Minister Kiyoura Keigo. A former bureaucrat and protégé of Yamagata Aritomo, Kiyoura appointed most of his cabinet from members of the House of Peers, but, in particular, he filled the ranks from its largest faction, the *Kenkyūkai*, and was supported by just one political party, the *Seiyū Hontō*, which was a splinter group of the *Seiyūkai*. The remaining members of the *Seiyūkai*, along with the *Kenseikai* and the *Kakushin Kurabu*, were loud in their criticism of the Kiyoura cabinet as a relic of a bygone era. Therefore, the three main parties forged a coalition with a call to protect constitutional government (*Goken Sanpa Naikaku*). The coalition secured an overwhelming victory in the general elections and as a result it formed a new cabinet in June under the *Kenseikai* president Katō Takaaki. During his tenure as prime minister, Katō introduced the Universal Male Suffrage Act in March 1925 and established diplomatic relations with the Soviet Union. This so-called party cabinet system—the heyday of pre-war Japanese parliamentary democracy—remained in place from Prime Minister Katō until the assassination of Prime Minister Inukai Tsuyoshi on May 15, 1932.

The position of foreign minister was filled by Katō's brother-in-law, Shidehara, and he promptly declared to the Diet that his chief policy objective was to uphold the policy of nonintervention in China as a way to "establish a closer economic relationship between Japan and China under the principle of equal opportunity." Of course, this also conformed perfectly with the spirit espoused in the Washington Conference. Shidehara worked to inform American public opinion. When the *Chicago Daily News* reporter Edward P. Bell visited Japan, the two met and Shidehara shared his views about China. He also spoke frequently with the American ambassador to Tokyo, Edgar A. Bancroft, a lawyer who was keen on respecting Japan's racial sensitivities and thus distraught over the negative impact of the 1924 Immigration Act. At the same time, however, both Bancroft and Shidehara were careful not to bring any further unwanted attention to the matter and thus avoided any formal discussions of the issue. In Washington, the position of the Japanese Ambassador to the United States had passed from Hanihara to the former vice-foreign minister, Matsudaira Tsuneo.

While US–Japan relations were momentarily improving due to Tokyo's concerted effort to play down the 1924 Immigration Act, this very action contributed to an upsurge in public discontent as many felt that Japan was being weak-kneed in its approach. This resentment boiled over in China when, in early February 1925, numerous strikes broke out at Japanese-owned cotton mills throughout Shanghai and Qingdao and further led to demonstrations by Chinese workers and students. On May 30, British police fired on Chinese protestors in Shanghai, resulting in a number of fatalities. This tragedy, which became known as the May Thirtieth Incident, triggered a massive wave of nationalist demonstrations across the country and prompted the Beijing government to revisit the issue of revising the unequal treaties.

America was most sympathetic toward Chinese sensibilities and the new secretary of state, Frank B. Kellogg, immediately sent a commission to investigate the issue of extraterritoriality, whereas the American minister to China, MacMurray, took a more cautious approach in addressing China's pleas. On the other hand, Britain was firmly opposed to revising the treaties. Since there was a conflict between American and British views, Shidehara felt that he should attempt to bridge the two approaches so that all the powers could better coordinate their response.

In October 1925, the Washington Conference powers gathered in Beijing to discuss an increase to the customs tariff as well as other pertinent issues, as stipulated under the 1922 Chinese Customs Treaty. Heading into the conference, Kellogg and Nelson T. Johnson, chief of the State Department's Division of Far Eastern Affairs, were both intent on revising the unequal treaties and approving higher customs tariffs for China. However, Shidehara countered by insisting that the discussions be limited to the issue of surtaxes and that the participants focus their attention on how the extra revenue should be spent. As a result, the conference soon reached an impasse and all further meetings were postponed indefinitely in July 1926.

The failure of the three great powers to coordinate their diplomacy at the conference in Beijing should not be interpreted as representing the demise of the Washington Treaty System. Although Kellogg was overly supportive of China to the extent that he wanted the United States to act unilaterally, this did not necessarily mean that he was willing to break away from the Washington Treaty System. What Kellogg actually had in mind was to bring China into the Washington Treaty System on an equal footing with the other treaty signatory nations. In contrast, Shidehara and MacMurray wanted to keep the framework of the Washington Conference that was based on the premise that the powers would retain their existing interests in China.

The US and Japan's differing aims should be interpreted as a divergence *within* the framework of the Washington Treaty System rather than as a debate over whether or not to uphold the system itself. The outcome could have been different had Shidehara and Kellogg been able to take the time to reconsider the importance of cooperative relations between the United States and Japan. Instead, as will be discussed later in this chapter, the divergence between the two nations was spurred on by events resulting from the Northern Expedition pushed through by the Chinese National Army. The Beijing government adroitly maneuvered to drive a wedge between the United States, Japan, and Britain by approaching each nation differently. The effort finally paid off, and in January 1927 the US announced that it would fully cooperate in negotiations with China on revising the unequal treaties regardless of the position taken by the other powers.

The Nanjing Nationalist Government

Prime Minister Katō passed away in January 1926 and was succeeded by fellow *Kenseikai* member, Wakatsuki Reijirō. As a former bureaucrat from the Ministry of Finance, Wakatsuki handed the management of foreign affairs to Shidehara. In southern China the National Army, led by Chiang Kai-shek, launched their Northern Expedition in July with the objective of subduing the warlords that were standing in way of Chinese reunification. On reaching Nanjing in March 1927, however, the ill-led Chinese forces unwisely stormed the Japanese and British consulates, confiscating foreign property and assaulting foreign residents.

America and Britain promptly sought retribution, their battleships relentlessly pounding the city from the coast. On the other hand, Japan refrained from retaliating. This was because Foreign Minister Shidehara opposed any military action and instead pressed Chiang to resolve the situation quickly. Shidehara's restrained response was criticized by the

Japanese public as being weak. Ultimately, the policy of non-intervention led to the resignation of the Wakatsuki cabinet. Once Chiang launched his anti-Communist coup d'état in April and established the Nationalist Government in Nanjing, the Wuhan National Government led by Wang Jingwei joined Chiang's government in September (Etō 1968; Usui 1971).

The new Japanese cabinet was formed in April 1927 and Tanaka Giichi, a former army general and president of the *Seiyūkai*, held a joint appointment as prime minister and foreign minister. In contrast with Shidehara's economics-oriented diplomacy, which had relied on restraint, Tanaka's foreign policy toward China was less reluctant to utilize force to pursue national interests. He therefore deployed troops to Shandong Peninsula in order to separate Manchuria and Mongolia from an ever-chaotic China. When the Northern Expedition advanced through central China and approached Manchuria, Tanaka feared Chinese intrusion into the area and in May sent troops to protect Japanese residents in the region. This would be the first of three Japanese expeditions sent to Shandong. Britain was sympathetic to Japan's cause and even proposed a joint deployment operation. As this suggests, Britain's policies were much more aligned with those of Japan than with America's. Ironically, since the United States had also landed its forces in Taku during this time, on this occasion China denounced both the United States and Japan.

Despite the military intervention, Japan was striving to uphold the Open Door principles in Manchuria and even encouraged American investment in the South Manchuria Railway (SMR). Negotiations were conducted between Bank of Japan Governor Inoue Junnosuke and the Chief Executive of J.P. Morgan and Company, Thomas W. Lamont, during the autumn of 1927. The president of the SMR, Yamamoto Jōtarō, was also eager to secure American capital. However, the negotiations collapsed due to strong Chinese opposition to the negotiations which in turn led to a hostile reaction from the American public.

In April 1928, the Tanaka cabinet deployed troops to the Shandong Peninsula for the second time. The following month, Japanese troops felt the rising tide of Chinese nationalism directly when they clashed with the National Army as it entered the city of Jinan. Following this incident, America and Britain changed course and began to pursue closer relations with the Chinese Nationalist Party (Kuomintang). As a result, the US in particular became increasingly critical of Japan's military involvement in China. According to a lengthy memorandum written seven years later by MacMurray, American policymakers had viewed the incident in Jinan as "evidence of [Japanese] antagonism toward the Nationalists, whom the American public opinion continued to favor as though they were the champions of [their] own ideals."

Among the senior US officials, it was Assistant Secretary of State Johnson who was most vehemently opposed to MacMurray's views and thus pressed hard for the establishment of diplomatic relations with the Nationalist government. After Wang Zhengting took office as minister of foreign affairs in the Nationalist government in June 1928, Secretary of State Kellogg adopted Johnson's approach and on July 25 agreed to a treaty that recognized China's tariff autonomy from January 1929. The treaty became the starting point for the establishment of more formal relations between the United States and the Chinese Nationalist government. Without a doubt, this also marked a significant turning point in US–Japan relations over China.

Tanaka sought to align Japan's policies closer with Britain in responding to the issue of tariffs and export duties. However, the economic foreign policy interests of the British government under Stanley Baldwin had begun to diverge from those of Japan and thus he was no longer interested in working together with Japan. This added to Tanaka's diplomatic isolation which had been greatly exacerbated by the assassination of the Manchurian warlord Zhang Zuolin by the Japanese Kwantung Army in June of the previous year. During the final months of Tanaka's tenure as prime minister, it was becoming increasingly difficult to maintain the spirit of cooperation under the Washington Treaty System (Satō 1992; Hattori 2001; Gotō 2006).

THE 1929 SINO-SOVIET CONFLICT AND THE LONDON NAVAL CONFERENCE

In March 1929, Republican Herbert C. Hoover took office as president and Henry Stimson was appointed as secretary of state in July of the same year. In Japan, a new cabinet was formed under Hamaguchi Osachi, president of the *Rikken Minseitō*, which had been formed as a result of a merger of the *Seiyū Hontō* and the *Kenseikai* in 1927. Hamaguchi reappointed Shidehara as foreign minister, showing his commitment to return to a more cooperative foreign policy with the powers. In January 1930, Finance Minister Inoue Junnosuke returned Japan to the gold standard that it had left temporarily during World War I. While the other major powers had returned to the gold standard a few years earlier, Japan had delayed its decision due to the postwar financial crisis. But the timing could not have been worse, as the Great Depression gripped America from October 1929 and by returning to the gold standard Japan could not shield itself from the global economic downturn. This in turn contributed to growing social unrest within the country.

The major points of contention between Japan and America leading up to the Manchurian Incident in 1931 were threefold: the state of affairs in China; the issue of naval disarmament; and racial discrimination. These issues reflected the juxtaposition of friction and cooperation between the two nations. Regarding China, the issue became even further muddled when conflict arose in the latter half of 1929 between the Soviet Union and the Mukden government led by Zhang Xueliang, the oldest son of the deceased warlord Zhang Zuolin. The incident was sparked by China's attempt to seize complete control of the Chinese Eastern Railway—which was then jointly managed by China and the Soviet Union.

Shidehara mediated between the Chinese and Russians, but he felt strongly that as long as the Soviets were demanding a return to joint management of the railway, the Chinese had no choice but to comply. In contrast, Secretary of State Henry Stimson, who had a legal background, responded by calling for the establishment of a special committee to mediate the conflict, comprised of delegates from the nations that had ratified the General Treaty for the Renunciation of War (also known as the Kellogg–Briand Pact)—an agreement that had originally been signed in August 1928 by 15 nations proclaiming to resolve international disputes through peaceful means. Stimson gathered the ambassadors of Japan, Britain, France, and Italy, and the acting German ambassador, and made his sales pitch regarding this proposal. Stimson's suggestion was initially met with some opposition from State Department officials such as Assistant Secretary of State William R. Castle, who felt that it was ill-advised. Stanley Hornbeck, chief of the Division of Far Eastern Affairs, also questioned the actual effectiveness of the committee. Foreign Minister Shidehara and Japanese Ambassador to the United States Debuchi Katsuji were also naturally reluctant to support the proposal, as the last thing that they wanted was for the United States and the European powers to spread their influence in Manchuria.

Around mid-August 1929, the Soviet army advanced past Heilongjiang in northeastern China and started to rout the Nationalist army. Even as the Soviet troops were advancing, Shidehara continued to mediate between the Soviet Ambassador to Japan Alexander Troyanovsky and the Chinese Minister to Japan Wang Rongbao as he worked desperately to keep the negotiations from falling through. Yet, in mid-October the Soviet army launched a major offensive in northern Manchuria and captured the key port of Manzhouli. Startled by the sudden turn of events, Stimson received the blessing of Hoover to request Japan, Britain, France, and Italy to join the United States in issuing a joint proclamation based on the spirit of the Kellogg–Briand Pact. Shidehara flatly refused to cooperate, preferring instead to continue down the mediation route. As the other powers were also lukewarm in their support, in the end Stimson's plan never got off the ground. Even the pro-US Chinese Minister of Foreign Affairs, Wang Zhengting, did not believe Stimson's endeavor would yield any concrete results. Meanwhile, Zhang Xueliang finally accepted the Soviet terms for ceasing hostilities, including the return to a joint Sino-Soviet management of the Chinese Eastern Railway and the immediate release of the Soviet citizens who had been detained by the Manchurian authorities. As a result, the Chinese and Russian talks at Khabarovsk quickly headed toward a resolution.

The contrasting approaches of Shidehara and Stimson to the Sino-Soviet conflict clearly demonstrated the differences in American and Japanese visions toward China. Shidehara's approach itself was contradictory: on one hand, Shidehara wanted to balance the interests of Japan, China, and the Soviet Union in Manchuria through diplomatic negotiations while on the other he sought to ensure that Japan alone would play the foremost role in the affairs of China, as witnessed by his role in arranging for the repayment of foreign loans by China and his mediation of the Chinese–Russian conflict (Iriye 1965; Hattori 2001). For him, it was crucial to prevent the United States and other European powers from meddling in Manchuria and Mongolia. By quickly restoring the original status quo, it can be concluded that Shidehara had been quite successful in attaining his objectives.

On the contrary, the United States had yet to establish a policy toward East Asia that could bring about the cooperation of the powers. Although Stimson's foreign policy failed to bring forth desired results in this part of the world, he would have much more success on the issue of naval disarmament.

The London Naval Conference

After the conclusion of the Washington Conference, it was only natural that the signatory powers embarked upon a new a race to build up auxiliary vessels which were not included in the limitations set forth by the Washington Naval Treaty. Thus, a conference was convened in Geneva in the summer of 1927 with the goal of placing limits on the tonnage of auxiliary vessels, but it failed amid fierce bickering among the United States and the European powers. During 1929, the world was gripped by the Great Depression which added a true sense of urgency that had not been present during the Geneva Conference. Given that the naval race was a huge burden upon the economies of the respective nations, another conference was arranged in London from April 1930 to settle the issue.

Upon receiving the invitation to participate in the conference, Hamaguchi appointed former Prime Minister Wakatsuki Reijirō to head the Japanese delegation in London. Other senior delegates were Navy Minister Takarabe Takeshi, Ambassador to Britain Matsudaira Tsuneo, and Ambassador to Belgium Nagai Matsuzō. For Hamaguchi, the London Naval Conference was of utmost importance as it allowed the government to follow Shidehara's cooperative policy toward the United States and Britain as well as Finance Minister Inoue's policy of fiscal discipline.

Prior to the conference, Hamaguchi approved the following negotiation goals: the tonnage of auxiliary ships and heavy cruisers would be set at 70% of America's, and the number of submarines would be kept at its current level. Japan's chief objective was to have the other powers concur on these points. The Chief of the Naval General Staff Katō Kanji championed the voice of the hardliners, who felt that any compromise on these points was unacceptable. But Wakatsuki and the other delegates felt otherwise and thus they continued to negotiate with Stimson and British Prime Minister Ramsay MacDonald. In the end, Japan agreed to an average total tonnage of 69.75% of that of the United States in addition to securing the same number of submarines as the United States and Britain (Asada 1993).

Besides Katō, there were some other Japanese officials who were unhappy with the compromise, such as Vice-Chief of the Naval General Staff Suetsugu Nobumasa, who warned that the ratio of the heavy cruisers set at a mere 60% of America's and that the eventual decrease in the number of submarines by one-third of their current numbers would make Japan vulnerable in the event of a naval battle with the United States. But pragmatic minds prevailed, and thus Hamaguchi signed the 1930 Treaty for the Limitation and Reduction of Naval Armament, or the London Naval Treaty as it is more commonly known.

During the conference, Hoover had sent his trusted former Assistant Secretary of State Castle as ambassador to Japan to function as a representative of the pro-Japan hands within the State Department and also as a confidant to Hoover to directly report events in Japan. Castle and Shidehara shared a similar view toward the importance of the London Conference as well as on matters relating to China, such as extraterritoriality. In contrast, Katō and other hardliners argued vehemently that by agreeing to the naval disarmament treaty, Japan would now be subject to increased pressure from America with regard to its policies toward China. This concern was also shared by the Privy Council's committee, which was tasked to review the terms of the London Naval Treaty.

But perhaps the most unfortunate aspect of the London Naval Treaty was that it precipitated a controversy in Japan over the question of whether or not signing the treaty by the government was in contravention to the emperor's prerogative of supreme command (*tōsuiken*) over the military as written in the Meiji Constitution. Seizing this moment, Katō attempted to directly appeal to the emperor in order to block the treaty, presenting a detailed report that showed the various restrictions stipulated in the treaty and how they would be a severe hindrance to Japanese naval strategy. From a strictly legal perspective, agreeing to disarmament treaties could hardly fall under the emperor's prerogative over the military. However, the opposition party, the *Seiyūkai*, added fuel to the fire by suggesting that Hamaguchi's actions constituted a blatant violation of the emperor's prerogative; the party's motive was to undermine its political rival, but in hindsight this action served to undermine the very foundations of party politics itself.

For the time being, the successful conclusion of the naval disarmament conference helped to increase the feeling of mutual cooperation between the United States, Japan, and Britain. Sensing this new atmosphere, the Japanese ambassador Debuchi felt that this was an opportune moment to raise the issue of repealing the Japanese exclusion clause of the 1924 Immigration Act. This request was taken to heart by Secretary of State Stimson but since Congress was in no mood to reexamine what was essentially a done deal, in the end nothing ever came about. The next time this issue would be revisited would be during the 1941 US–Japan negotiations when both countries were frantically seeking a diplomatic solution to avert a military clash.

In retrospect, however, the conclusion of the London Naval Treaty marked the zenith of prewar US–Japan relations. From here on forward, there would be a stark divide within the State Department between the pro-Japanese and pro-Chinese camps that would undermine the department's effectiveness in implementing the East Asian policies of the secretary of state and president. On the other hand, while Japan remained true to its pursuit of cooperative diplomacy under leaders such as Shidehara, the future would see more instances in which the military, driven by its narrow sectional interests, sought to overstep its boundaries and meddle in Japanese foreign policy. This intervention would gather momentum with the rise of Chinese nationalism on the continent. Finally, the harsh economic climate of the 1930s would become a further impediment to the foreign policy that had been grounded in the spirit of mutual cooperation espoused by the Washington Treaty System.

BIBLIOGRAPHY

Asada, Sadao. 1993. *Ryō taisenkan no Nichi-Bei kankei* [US–Japan Relations between the Wars]. Tokyo: University of Tokyo Press.

Etō, Shinkichi. 1968. *Higashi Ajia seiji-shi kenkyū* [Studies in East Asian Political History]. Tokyo: University of Tokyo Press.

Gotō, Harumi. 2006. *Shanhai o meguru Nichi-Ei kankei 1925–1932 nen* [Partners or Competitors? Anglo-Japanese Relations over Shanghai 1925–1932]. Tokyo: University of Tokyo Press.

Hattori, Ryūji. 2001. *Higashi Ajia kokusai kankyō no hendō to Nihon gaikō 1918–1931* [Changes in the East Asian Diplomatic Environment and Japanese Diplomacy 1918–1931]. Tokyo: Yūhikaku Publishing.

———. 2006. *Shidehara Kijūrō to nijūseiki no Nihon* [Shidehara Kijūrō and 20th Century Japan]. Tokyo: Yūhikaku Publishing.

Iriye, Akira. 1965. *After Imperialism*. Cambridge: Harvard University Press.

Minohara, Toshihiro. 2002. *Hai-Nichi iminhō to nichibeikankei* [The 1924 Immigration Act and US–Japan relations]. Tokyo: Iwanami Shoten.

———. 2006. *Kaliforunia shū no hai-Nichi undō to Nichibei kankei* [The Anti-Japanese Movement in California and US–Japan Relations]. Tokyo: Yūhikaku Publishing.

———. 2016. *Amerika no hai-Nichi undō to Nichibei kankei* [The Anti-Japanese Movement in America and US–Japan Relations]. Tokyo: Asahi Shimbun Press.

Mitani, Taichirō. 1995. *Zōho Nihon seitō seiji no keisei* [The State of Japanese Party Politics]. Extended edition. Tokyo: University of Tokyo Press.

Satō, Motohide. 1992. *Shōwa shoki tai Chūgoku seisaku no kenkyū* [Study on Japanese Policies Toward China in the Early Showa Period]. Tokyo: Hara Shobō.

Usui, Katsumi. 1971. *Nitchū gaikō-shi* [History of Sino-Japanese Relations]. Tokyo: Hanawa Shobō.

CHAPTER 5

The 1930s: Japan's War with China and American Non-Recognition

Fumiaki Kubo, Ryūji Hattori, and Satoshi Hattori

JAPAN AND AMERICA'S DIFFERING APPROACHES TO CHINA

While America had recognized China's tariff autonomy in 1928 when Frank B. Kellogg was secretary of state, Japan only did so in May 1930. The next step for the powers was to address how to renounce extraterritorial rights as well as to ensure that China would repay its foreign loans. However, China was particularly reluctant to repay the Nishihara loans and other unsecured loans that Japan had provided.

Both Japan and the US participated in the conference for creditor nations held in Nanjing in November 1930 that was attended by Japanese Minister to China Shigemitsu Mamoru, and US Minister to China Nelson Johnson. When these negotiations stalled, Foreign Minister Shidehara Kijūrō leaned toward coordinating more with Britain. But since Britain's credit was secured, it was not interested in Japan's overtures. Despite this

F. Kubo
Graduate Schools for Law and Politics, University of Tokyo, Tokyo, Japan

R. Hattori
Faculty of Policy Studies, Chuo University, Hachioji, Japan

S. Hattori
School of Foreign Studies, Osaka University, Suita, Japan

© The Author(s) 2017
M. Iokibe (ed.), T. Minohara (trans. ed.), *The History of US–Japan Relations*, DOI 10.1007/978-981-10-3184-7_5

setback, Shidehara desired to work with both Europe and the United States on the questions of Chinese loans and the abolishment of extraterritoriality. As such, Shigemitsu took a conciliatory stance toward China and negotiated with his counterpart, Chinese Minister of Finance Soong Tse-ven, with the goal of decreasing the repayment amount of the Nishihara loans.

The US State Department, then headed up by Secretary of State Stimson, was divided between the pro-Japanese Assistant Secretary of State William R. Castle and the pro-Chinese Chief of the Division of Far Eastern Affairs Stanley K. Hornbeck. This schism became readily apparent in the negotiations on the abolishment of extraterritoriality. Castle adopted a stance similar to Shidehara, and was critical of the fact that the United States and China were engaged in a discussion between Hornbeck and Wu Chaoshu, Minister of the Republic of China to Washington. Castle prodded Hornbeck to get Japan and Britain involved in the negotiations, and with the approval of Shidehara, the talks were relocated to China (Iriye 1965; Hattori 2001).

Japanese Expansion into Manchuria

A single incident that began in September 1931 sparked drastic changes in the issues surrounding China. On September 18, 1931, the Kwantung Army plotted to destroy a section of the South Manchuria Railway (SMR) at Liutiaohu on the outskirts of Mukden (currently Shenyang). They planned to blame this on the Chinese and use it as a pretext to take military action that would allow them to greatly expand their area of control. Staff officer Lieutenant Colonel Ishiwara Kanji, who led the incident along with Colonel Itagaki Seishirō, was driven by the hope that the incident would instigate a "struggle for supremacy" between America, the "leader of the West," and Japan, the "master of the East."

On September 19, Shidehara reported to Prime Minister Wakatsuki Reijirō that the Gaimushō had received a telegram from the Japanese consul general at Mukden stating that the incident was staged by the Japanese military. The situation was initially contained, as War Minister Minami Jirō was unable to send reinforcements from the Japanese Army stationed in Korea (Chōsen Army), and the cabinet was against any further military operations. This gave Washington the impression that Shidehara had the situation under control. However, in a sudden position reversal just three days later, the cabinet approved the actions of Lieutenant General Hayashi Senjūrō, who had sent his troops across the border to Manchuria without any orders from Tokyo. Showing a startling lack of resolve, Wakatsuki lamely commented that he had no choice but to approve because the troops had already been moved. On October 9, Wakatsuki decided on a new policy whereby troops would be withdrawn once an agreement had been reached with China regarding the prohibition of boycotts on Japanese goods, as well as a general Sino-Japanese agreement over the railway issue. On learning this, Castle warned the Japanese Ambassador to the United States Debuchi Katsuji that such a course of action would surely incite anti-Japanese sentiment around the world and recommended that Japan immediately withdraw its troops to the area surrounding the SMR before demanding an end to the Chinese boycotts.

However, the Kwantung Army was beyond the control of the Gaimushō, and it bombed Jinzhou, a city that was located a considerable distance away from the SMR. Stunned by this new development, Stimson urged President Hoover to place economic sanctions on Japan. Although Stimson hoped that such pressure would send a stern message to the Japanese militarists, Hoover was reluctant to do so and instead supported a proposal from China that requested that the United States, Britain, and France establish a neutral zone in Jinzhou. However, this plan fell apart when Shidehara demanded that both the Chinese Army and the Zhang Xueliang administration at Jinzhou withdraw their troops to the west of the Shanhai Pass, and the Chinese government refused to do so. In mid-November, War Minister Minami was finally able to bring Shidehara and Wakatsuki around to the proposal of invading Qiqihar and establishing a puppet regime there, after which Japanese troops would be withdrawn. In this way, the military was gradually increasing its influence over Japan's China policy.

Unable to effectively respond to the developments in East Asia, Stimson's only option was to verbally check Japan. Upon learning that the further troops were sent to Jinzhou in late November, Stimson resorted to leaking a highly confidential piece of information that Shidehara had communicated to US Ambassador to Japan William Forbes, which stated that Japan planned to abort the attack on Jinzhou. This careless act of betrayal threw relations between the United States and Japan into a tailspin, particularly because it led to the impression that Japan had bowed to American pressure. But in fact, the decision had already been made independently. Moreover, the pro-US Shidehara was subjected to a bitter interrogation from the cabinet as being the most likely source of the information. His powerbase was being severely undermined as he faced criticism from all quarters. Wakatsuki was unable to control the fallout and thus the cabinet resigned en masse in December. Shidehara was also forced out of the Gaimushō and no doubt this was an important factor in the eventual demise of the Washington Treaty System (Banno 1985; Hattori 2001, 2006).

Japan's Withdrawal from the League of Nations

The new cabinet was formed by *Seiyūkai* president Inukai Tsuyoshi in December 1931. The new finance minister, Takahashi Korekiyo, promptly restored the embargo on gold exports to stem the outflow of gold and foreign currency from Japan. The government also moved Japan out of the gold standard, this time permanently. By this time Britain had already left the gold standard. Buoyed by the success of Takahashi's expansionary fiscal policy which led to economic recovery, the *Seiyūkai* secured a landslide victory in the February 1932 general elections. Yoshizawa Kenkichi was recalled from his post as ambassador to France to serve as the new foreign minister.

In the aftermath of the Japanese occupation of Jinzhou in early January 1932, Stimson informed both Japan and China that the United States would not recognize "any situation, treaty, or agreement which may be brought about by means contrary to the covenants and obligations" of the Nine-Power Treaty or the Kellogg–Briand Pact. This declaration of "non-recognition," which became known as the Stimson Doctrine, was also transmitted to the other signatory nations of the Nine-Power Treaty. Later that month Japanese and Chinese troops clashed in Shanghai, as a result of tensions that developed following an attack on Japanese monks by Chinese civilians. In actuality, however, the incident was instigated by Major Tanaka Ryūkichi, the military attaché to the Japanese legation in Shanghai, who had been requested by Colonel Itagaki to find a means of distracting the attention of the powers away from Manchuria.

When fierce fighting ensued in Shanghai between the Japanese naval landing forces and the Chinese 19th Route Army, the Inukai cabinet was forced to send in reinforcements. China responded by appealing to the League of Nations, and as a result Britain, France, Italy, and Germany formed an enquiry committee in Shanghai with American cooperation. In February, the British, American, and French ambassadors appealed to Foreign Minister Yoshizawa to bring an end to the fighting. With the British playing the key role, the fighting was finally concluded in May (Stimson and Bundy 1948; Ferrell 1957; Morison 1960; Saitō 1987; Usui 1974).

In the meantime, in December 1931 the League of Nations Council approved Japan's proposal for a commission to be sent to investigate the circumstances of Japan's intervention in Manchuria. Known as the Lytton Commission, the members visited Japan in February 1932 before continuing their investigation in Shanghai, Nanjing, Peiping (currently Beijing), and Manchuria. The United States was represented in the commission by Stimson's good friend Major General Frank R. McCoy. In response, Japanese Ambassador to China Shigemitsu hurriedly put together a report on the current status of Sino-Japanese relations, anticipating a harsh conclusion from the Lytton Commission. The Gaimushō also produced various documents which were presented to the commission by Yoshida Isaburō, Japanese ambassador to Turkey, who accompanied the commission as the Japanese representative.

In October 1932 the commission released a report of its findings in Japan and China, concluding that the actions of the Japanese Kwantung Army on September 18 could "not be regarded as measures of legitimate self-defense," and that the newly-established independent state of Manchuria—known as Manchukuo—could "not be considered to have been instituted by a genuine and spontaneous independence movement." While declaring that the actions of the Kwantung Army were unjust, the Lytton Report was also sympathetic to Japan's position with the aim of solving the issues of the Manchurian region. Therefore, it proposed establishing an autonomous government in Manchuria under the sovereignty of China, and also suggested the appointment of foreign consultants by the League of Nations to demilitarize the region (Nish 1993; Usui 1995; Hattori 2002).

However, the domestic situation in Japan took a turn for the worse. The party cabinet system collapsed following the assassination of Prime Minister Inukai in the May 15 Incident of 1932. In the interim, a bipartisan "national unity cabinet," including members of the *Seiyūkai* and *Miniseitō*, was established under Prime Minister Saitō Makoto, a former navy admiral. In August, Foreign Minister Uchida Kosai declared to the Diet that he would pursue Japan's official recognition of Manchukuo even if it meant "reducing the nation to ashes"—inspiring the term "scorched-earth diplomacy" (*shōdo gaikō*)—and the Saitō cabinet acknowledged the creation of Manchukuo under the Japan–Manchukuo Protocol (*Nichiman Giteisho*) in September. Furthermore, in an act of protest to the Lytton Report, Japan left the League of Nations in March 1933. In retaliation, the United States sent an observer to the league's Far Eastern Advisory Committee and demanded sanctions against Japan, but without any success.

In May 1933, with the situation in Manchuria temporarily under control, Japan and China agreed to establish the Great Wall as the border between Manchukuo and China under the Tanggu Truce agreement. However, Washington was still suspicious of Japan's expansion into China and the establishment of a puppet government in Manchukuo.

From Hoover to FDR: The Great Depression and the New Deal

Since the 1920s, the United States had looked to Japan for assistance on East Asian affairs, given that the Soviet Union had fallen to communism, China was consumed by domestic unrest, and Britain, France, and the other European nations had never been likely to be fully cooperative with America in that field. There was also concern in Washington that a hardline approach toward Tokyo would only add momentum to Japan's military and weaken the moderate faction upon which America depended. This dilemma had significant influence on America's response to Japan's military actions in Manchuria from 1931 onward.

President Hoover took office in March 4, 1929 as the "most respected man in America" but he quickly lost his popularity once the Great Depression gripped the nation just eight months after he had entered office. It came as no surprise that he failed to be reelected and was succeeded in March 1933 by Roosevelt, whose policies differed on a number of key points. Whereas Hoover had attributed the Great Depression to external factors, Roosevelt felt that the nation's economic troubles were homegrown and he devised bold domestic measures to tackle them. Roosevelt also scaled down American cooperation in the area of foreign currency stabilization and scuttled the 1933 London Economic Conference, which Hoover had championed as a forum for solving America's economic problems.

In his approach to Japan, Roosevelt essentially continued the policies that had been formulated by Stimson during the previous administration. Just before taking the reins of the presidency, Roosevelt received Stimson at his home in Hyde Park, New York, on January 9, 1933, and declared his support for Stimson's policy of non-recognition. On January 17, Roosevelt told his advisors that he had always "had the deepest sympathy with the Chinese," and suggested that Stimson's policy was the only possible course for handling Japan. Of course, it is likely that Roosevelt simply felt that it was his moral responsibility to be critical of Japan's military aggression as he had no intention of resorting to war in East Asia. One needs to keep in mind that at the beginning of his term, Roosevelt's first priority was to deal with the ongoing domestic crisis.

A formidable figure within the new Roosevelt administration was the Secretary of State Cordell Hull, a former senator from Tennessee. Hull strongly opposed the protective tariff and advocated implementing mutual, gradual tariff decreases in order to establish a free trade system which he believed would lead to global peace. As such, he was highly critical of the 1930 Smoot–Hawley Tariff Act, which had lifted America's tariffs to the highest levels ever.

Roosevelt initially chose to pursue a course of domestic reform and economic nationalism. However, Hull's ideas had long been popular among the southern Democratic congressmen, and, in turn, he garnered significant support in a Democratic Party–controlled Congress. In 1934, Congress finally established the Reciprocal Trade Agreements Act, granting the president the right to decrease tariffs by up to 50% on the basis of negotiations and agreement with the respective nation concerned, and, under the act, the United States gradually began to decrease its tariff rates.

The Ideals Behind the Neutrality Act

From the 1920s into the 1930s there was a growing sense of disillusionment toward America's participation in foreign conflicts, led in particular by pacifist movements, women's groups, members of the church, and student groups. This sentiment was further bolstered by Engelbrecht and Hanighen's exposé on the armaments industry, *Merchants of Death*, which was selected to the Book of the Month Club in April 1934. The Senate established a special committee to investigate the munitions industry, largely under the initiative of North Dakota Senator Gerald P. Nye, who was appointed committee chairman despite being a member of the Republican minority. The committee's findings closely echoed Engelbrecht and Hanighen's suggestions, implying that America had entered the war due to a conspiracy by financiers and arms dealers and other figures in the munitions industry. Its report did not prove the link outright, but nevertheless Congress and the public embraced its findings, which generated an even stronger opposition to US involvement in military action overseas.

Such public sentiment led to the establishment of an act to prohibit the export of "arms, ammunition, and implements of war" from America to any foreign nations officially declared by the president as at war, including banning the use of American vessels to transport such items. The first Neutrality Act, rammed through by the Republican opposition in August 1935, was amended the following year to include a ban on loans to belligerent nations and was further tightened in 1937 through additional amendments that made it applicable to civil wars. Britain was vehemently opposed to the Neutrality Act as it felt that it only encouraged aggression around the world.

The Neutrality Act reflects the powerful pacifist and isolationist ideals influenced by the American people as well as Congress from the mid-1930s. This sentiment severely restricted Roosevelt's policy options until Japan's attack on Pearl Harbor. In February 1934, facing the likelihood that Japan would allow the Washington Naval Treaty to lapse in 1936 unless it could gain naval parity with the United States and United Kingdom, Roosevelt proposed that both nations coordinate their approach toward disarmament negotiations. He recommended an extension of the treaty for an additional ten years with a 20% decrease in the total tonnage by each signatory. If this were to fail, he was also prepared to accept a five-year extension. In the event that Japan withdrew from the treaty, the United States and the United Kingdom would both observe the treaty while being flexible regarding the overall tonnage based on Japan's actions. Although Roosevelt was wary of Japan, he also needed to be mindful of the pacifists and isolationists at home who had the support of Congress.

The Quarantine Speech

When all-out war erupted between Japan and China in July 1937, American pacifist organizations and an isolationist Congress called for a complete withdrawal from China, including the removal of the approximately 2,300 America soldiers who were stationed in Shanghai and other locations throughout China to protect American lives and property. Roosevelt initially dispatched a contingent of 1,200 Marines to China but was also mindful to declare that they would be withdrawn as soon as the situation was under control. The US Navy requested further reinforcements in the repatriation of American citizens, but the president flatly refused on the grounds that it would provoke both Japan and domestic pacifist groups.

Roosevelt also faced the even more challenging dilemma of whether or not to enforce the Neutrality Act toward the conflict. This would satisfy the isolationists, but at the same time it would hinder China, which needed both armaments and funds from the United States to continue the fight. Based on the proposal of Secretary of State Hull and other senior officials, Roosevelt decided to combat the growing isolationist sentiment in America by giving a speech advocating more cooperation in international affairs. While visiting Chicago on October 5, 1937, he delivered an address that became known as the "Quarantine Speech," in which he reproached aggression, warning the American public of the risk that America itself might be attacked. Furthermore, he called on the "peace-loving nations" to cooperate in order to "quarantine" the aggressors. The speech did not specifically name any "aggressor nations," and was intended more as a caution than a direct threat. In the conclusion of his speech—"America actively engages in the search for peace"—Roosevelt's desire to draw the public opinion away from isolationism could be clearly discerned. His statement that "war is a contagion, whether it be declared or undeclared" is also noteworthy as it implied that although the Sino-Japanese conflict had not been declared a "war," it was still a contagion to be contained.

THE OUTBREAK OF SECOND SINO-JAPANESE WAR AND THE "NEW ORDER IN EAST ASIA"

While the establishment of the Tanggu Truce had temporarily resolved the conflict in Manchuria, the international environment became more fragile as the Great Depression and the subsequent trade war had broken down global trade. Since the First World War Japan had been counted among the five great powers and ranked only behind the United States and the United Kingdom as a naval power. That being said, its industrial capacity was still underdeveloped and was based predominantly on agriculture and the textile industry. This lack of development allowed Japan to recover quickly from the Great Depression by expanding the export of cotton products, which was supported by a weak yen. This influx of cheap Japanese products led to retaliation and a boycott of Japanese cotton goods spread around the world beginning with the British Commonwealth territories such as India and Australia, and by 1937 Japan's overseas markets had been narrowed by a barrage of import quotas and high customs tariffs. This was a serious threat to Japan given its reliance on exports in supporting its economy and would later form the basis of Japan's assertion that the possession of colonies made the difference between the "have nations" and the "have-not nations" as it now sought to resolve the "inequity" by challenging the existing international order.

Japan's domestic political situation was also unstable. Support for militarism had been growing since the collapse of the party politics system in 1932. Within the Imperial Japanese Navy (IJN), the 1930 London Naval Treaty ignited an internal conflict between supporters and foes of the Washington Treaty System, who were known as the Treaty Faction (*Jōyaku-ha*) and the Fleet Faction (*Kantai-ha*), respectively. The Fleet Faction took control of the navy through a series of personnel purges in 1933–34, and as a consequence Japan declared its withdrawal from disarmament negotiations at the second London Naval Conference (December 1935–March 1936). At the end of the following year, both the Washington and the London Naval Treaty expired; there was little left of the Washington Treaty System and the framework that it had provided for international cooperation in East Asia.

The Imperial Japanese Army (IJA) was also divided by a fierce internal struggle between the reactionary Imperial Way Faction (*Kōdōha*) and the totalitarian Control Faction (*Tōseiha*) which was resolved by a failed coup d'état on February 26, 1936, by young officers of the Imperial Way Faction, which was dissolved afterwards. After the coup, the army's intervention in politics and diplomacy escalated to the point that it became the norm. The IJA's advance through Asia did not end with the 1933 Tanggu Truce, and from 1935 onward it actively sought to control northern China as a way to establish a protective buffer zone for Manchukuo (*Kahoku bunri kōsaku*). This was made state policy by the new Hirota Kōki cabinet, which took office in March 1936.

This was strenuously opposed by China and it also led to acts of terrorism against Japanese officials and citizens residing in China. The Northern Separation Policy was subsequently halted by Satō Naotake, who became foreign minister when the Hayashi Senjūrō cabinet was formed in February 1937. The policy was reinstated, however, by Konoe Fumimaro after Hayashi was forced to resign after just four months in office. In the meantime, the Kuomintang and the Chinese Communist Party had agreed to a truce as a result of the Xi'an Incident in December 1936, and consequently a united front was formed to oppose Japanese aggression.

The situation took a drastic turn on July 7, 1937, when Japanese and Chinese troops training in the vicinity of the Marco Polo Bridge skirmished over a minor misunderstanding. The resulting exchange of gunfire escalated into full-scale military conflict between Japan and China. Both nations avoided declaring the conflict as a war as they feared US application of the Neutrality Act; in reality, they were engulfed in what would become the Second Sino-Japanese War (1937–45). The IJA was keen to quickly carry out a large military operation to force Chiang Kai-shek to accept the new status quo in northern China. However, instead of meeting the Japanese troops head-on, the Chinese army quickly withdrew to the interior to avoid a decisive battle. This forced the IJA to overextend their battlefronts across China and it was never able to pin down the Chinese army to provide the crushing blow to end the war.

On December 12, 1937, the eve of the fall of Nanjing, the gunboat USS *Panay* on the Yangtze River was accidently bombed and sunk by Japanese planes. Washington vigorously protested and the president considered stern measures such as freezing Japanese assets in the United States, imposing economic sanctions, and establishing a maritime blockade. Fearing a meltdown in relations with the United States, Tokyo assuaged American sentiment by quickly issuing an apology and offering full compensation. The *Panay* incident is noteworthy in that it led to calls from the American public to withdraw all US vessels from the conflict area in order to avoid similar incidents in the future. One senator even declared that there was surely not a single person in the Senate who would vote in favor of going to war against Japan. Although ultimately thrown out, a bill to amend the constitution such that the American people would have the final decision on declaring war—requiring all declarations passed by Congress to be approved by a nationwide referendum—gained significant support in Congress. In early 1938, the American press was notably more supportive of Japan than it was toward China.

Emboldened by such movements, in January 1938 Prime Minister Konoe unilaterally broke off diplomatic relations with China through his infamous declaration that the Japanese Imperial government would "no longer deal with the Nanking Nationalist government" (*teikoku seifu wa jigo kokumin seifu o aite to sezu*). Using this as a cue, the IJA successfully launched its invasion of Guangdong Province in October 1938, quickly capturing the city of Guangzhou (Canton). Within a month, the army occupied an expansive territory that spanned from northern to southern China. Spurred on by the situation on the ground, the Konoe cabinet declared its commitment to establishing a "New Order in East Asia" (*Tōa shinchitsujo*) in November. Tokyo framed its military action in Manchuria and the establishment of Manchukuo as a revision of the Washington

Treaty System. Its aim was clear in its declaration that it would establish a new independent regional order in the region amongst Japan, Manchukuo, and China. However, by changing the status quo through the use of military force, Japan was playing a dangerous game of chicken with the United States.

War in Europe and Japan's Southward Advance

The Konoe cabinet resigned en masse in January 1939 over his inability to contain the situation in China and was succeeded by the Hiranuma Kiichirō cabinet. The IJA was bent on pursuing military expansion in Manchuria and northern China as it was motivated by a combination of anticommunism and a desire to secure a geopolitical position that would better prepare it for a conflict with the Soviet Union. There were also those in the IJA who hoped that the events in Manchuria would lead to a war with the United States. Tokyo also sought to secure alliances with other nations who wanted to change the status quo, and thus it entered into the Anti-Comintern Pact with Germany in November 1936, which was later joined by Italy a year later.

An increasing number of Japanese believed that Britain's assistance to China was stiffening the Chinese resolve not to capitulate, and this led to an assumption that the submission of Britain was necessary in order to settle the conflict with China. By fall 1938, this was incorporated in the proposal to transform the Anti-Comintern Pact into a military alliance against Britain. However, this concept was quickly discarded once Germany signed the Treaty of Non-Aggression (Molotov–Ribbentrop Pact) with the Soviet Union on August 1939 as it amounted to an act of betrayal toward Japan. Japan also applied direct pressure on Britain, and it did succeed in securing British consent toward its "New Order in East Asia" under an agreement signed by Foreign Minister Arita Hachirō and Robert Craigie, the British ambassador to Japan in July 1939.

While Japan had secured Britain's support, it now found the United States standing in its way. The long and ever-escalating conflict in China had led to a formation of a wartime Japanese economy that increased Japan's imports and decreased its foreign currency reserves. Although Konoe had declared that the "New Order in East Asia" would lead to economic self-sufficiency, Japan was in fact becoming increasingly dependent on the United States for machinery and natural resources. This was also the reason why Tokyo was keen on keeping the conflict with China an "incident" (*jihen*)—concealing the fact that in reality it was a war—as it prevented the Neutrality Act from being enforced. But Washington took advantage of this Japanese vulnerability and issued a notification of its intent to abrogate the US–Japan Treaty of Commerce and Navigation, paving the way for economic sanctions against Japan.

In the face of stiff opposition from the US, Tokyo now found it necessary to reconsider the benefits of clinging to the "New Order in East Asia." After Hiranuma left office in late August 1939 following the signing of the Molotov–Ribbentrop Pact—with his famous words that the situation in Europe had become "complicated and inscrutable" (*fukuzatsu kaiki*)—the succeeding cabinets of Abe Nobuyuki and the Yonai Mitsumasa that followed in January 1940 both reflected Japan's move away from the Axis powers and toward cooperation with the United States. However, neither of these cabinets had the wherewithal to consider the possibility of abandoning the "New Order in East Asia." Quite the contrary, both the Abe cabinet—with the prime minister initially serving in conjunction as foreign minister until the appointment of former Admiral Nomura Kichisaburō—and the Yonai cabinet, in which Arita was foreign minister, were more focused on lessening Japan's economic dependence on the United States by attempting to strengthen economic ties with Southeast Asia.

Amid this flurry of short-lived cabinets, World War II had broken out in Europe in September 1939. Germany stunned Europe with its blitzkrieg on the western front in spring 1940, and by the end of June it had seized most of Central and Western Europe with the notable exception of Britain. This in turn meant that the European powers that had colonized Southeast Asia—namely the Netherlands, France, and Britain—were now tied down in a conflict with Nazi Germany. A power vacuum had emerged in Asia, and Japan saw this as an opportunity to pursue a policy of southward advance (*nanshin-ron*) by siding with Germany and Italy.

Foreign Minister Matsuoka's Diplomacy

The second Konoe cabinet was formed in July 1940, and the fate of the southward advance policy was now placed in the hands of the new foreign minister Matsuoka Yōsuke. Appealing to the calls by the Japanese public, Matsuoka strove to increase Japan's political clout and economic independence by incorporating the natural-resource-rich Southeast Asian region into the former "New Order in East Asia," to create a "Greater East Asian Co-Prosperity Sphere" (*Daitōa Kyōeiken*) which amounted to a culmination of the aspirations that Japan had held since 1931. Matsuoka was prepared to use foreign policy aggressively to achieve this aim and thus he supported the military occupation of northern French Indochina in September 1940 as the first step to realizing the new sphere. He also oversaw the conclusion of the Tripartite Pact with Germany and Italy during the same month. The new military alliance forced the Soviet Union to enter into a non-aggression pact with Germany. Matsuoka had initially intended to coordinate with Germany to form a united front with the Soviet Union, but when he arrived in Europe for a one-month visit in March 1941, he realized that Germany planned to momentarily suspend its war on Britain and open up a new front against the Soviet Union. This had been decided four months before, but was kept hidden from the Japanese. Despite this new knowledge of German bad faith, Matsuoka visited Moscow and negotiated the Japan-Soviet Neutrality Pact in April 1941. With its back now protected, Matsuoka felt that the conditions had been established for Japan to pursue its southward advance policy.

In June 1940, one month before the formation of the second Konoe cabinet, the United States adopted military and economic measures to contain Japan's southward thrust. The Pacific Fleet was stationed in Hawaii, and Congress enacted several bills to authorize the construction of warships, such as the Two-Ocean Navy bill sponsored by Congressman Carl Vinson and Admiral Harold Stark. Export of key resources to Japan was also controlled by new legislation that made it necessary for US exporters to first obtain a license to export items such as armaments, ammunition, and other strategic war materials. When the second Konoe cabinet initiated the southward advance, Washington further ramped up the pressure on Tokyo, and placed an embargo on the export of scrap iron to Japan. Further items were added to the embargo list over the next few months to prod Japan's leaders to consider a new path.

However, the sanctions had exactly the opposite effect, making the Japanese military more determined than ever to advance southward in order to secure vital resources. A plan was hatched where by the military would gain control of French Indochina by mediating a conflict that had escalated from a border skirmish with Thailand in November 1940. But Matsuoka prudently intervened in this plan as it was sure to provoke a strong backlash from the United States.

Upon the conclusion of the Tripartite Pact, Matsuoka's approach was to refrain from any actions that would provoke Washington, as he knew that US economic sanctions could strangle the Japanese economy.

Although Matsuoka had wanted to dismantle the British Empire in Asia, in 1941 he was more focused on not alienating the United States, and ensuring that US economic resources would be supplied to Japan. The initial tensions between Japan and Britain over China had evolved into a confrontation with America over Japan's southward advance policy. The Tripartite Pact had ensured that the United States would now intervene in issues in Asia as Germany was at war in Europe. Matsuoka was cognizant of this, and as he was determined to prevent a war with the United States, he now sought to abandon the southward advance policy and appease Washington. Thus when Germany invaded the Soviet Union, Matsuoka now advocated a northward advance policy (*hokushin seisaku*) and urged the military to launch a strike against the Soviets. This was not supported by the military because there were no natural resources to be gained by going north, and the Red Army posed a formidable force.

Konoe, who was seeking a compromise with the United States, was now caught in the middle between the military, which sought to push Japan south, and Matsuoka, who called for going north. In the end, the weakest link had to give. The northward advance policy was rejected outright and Matsuoka was sacked as foreign minister in a sudden cabinet reshuffle in July that was orchestrated so that he could be dismissed. Although Matsuoka had wanted to create a Greater East Asia Co-Prosperity Sphere while simultaneously avoiding a clash with the United States, his grand strategy of a four-power alliance ultimately collapsed due to the actions taken by Germany.

Once Matsuoka had left, the third Konoe cabinet hurriedly set out to seek an understanding with the United States but, powerless to contain the military, it allowed it to go forward with the plan to occupy southern French Indochina. This fateful decision would eventually bring about a fatal consequence not only in the context of US–Japan relations, but also in global history.

The German and Japanese Threat to America

Despite Japanese transgressions, Roosevelt was in fact far more concerned with the threat of Hitler's Germany than that of Japan from the late 1930s; Japan was clearly of secondary importance compared to the conflict engulfing Europe.

In July 1939 Secretary of State Hull notified Japan that the US–Japan Treaty of Commerce and Navigation would be allowed to lapse in January of the following year. Roosevelt ignored warnings from his advisor that this move ran the risk of driving Japan to Hitler's side. The president's calculation was that Japan would realize its impotence and decide on an alternate course of cooperation with the United States. At the same time, Roosevelt's hands were tied due to a strong pro-isolationist sentiment within Congress. He had secured Congress' approval in rebuilding US airpower, but a bill in September 1940 that introduced the first peacetime military draft in American history passed by only a narrow margin. When the act was renewed the following year, it was approved in the House by a mere single vote.

The Tripartite Pact in September 1940 was a severe setback for the Roosevelt administration, as it now presented the real possibility that Japan and Germany may join forces and engage the United States in a global war. This posed a grave problem because the United States did not possess the military capacity to engage with both nations on two separate fronts. Roosevelt adroitly used the pretext of national self-defense to pursue a gradual buildup of the military, but it was not enough. Hence, providing assistance to Britain so that it would remain in the fight against Germany became the president's utmost priority. In September 1940, Roosevelt pushed for 50 obsolete destroyers to be provided to Britain under the "Destroyers for Bases" agreement. Shortly after Roosevelt's "great arsenal of democracy" speech, Congress finally came around to passing the Act to Promote the Defense of the United States, also known as the Lend-Lease Act, in March 1941. This permitted not only the sale but also the loaning—in which payment could be waived as necessary—of war materials to countries that the president deemed "vital for the defense of the United States," which essentially meant Britain.

Roosevelt also supported China as a means of countering Japan. In December 1940, the United States agreed on a $100 million loan to the Chinese government. Roosevelt was also quick to affirm the inclusion of China in the terms of the Lend-Lease Act, and he also permitted American military airmen to enlist in a volunteer corps affiliated with the Chinese Air Force. The president also pursued diplomacy with Japan, and from April 1941 began talks with the intent of averting war between the two nations.

Roosevelt also made a huge effort to stress the importance of supporting Britain to the American public. In his State of the Union address to Congress in January 1941, Roosevelt declared his "Four Freedoms" speech: "freedom of speech and expression," "freedom of every person to worship God in his own way," "freedom from want," and "freedom from fear." With this as a backdrop, in his first meeting with the British Prime

Minister Winston Churchill in August, Roosevelt affirmed his commitment to supporting Britain by establishing the Atlantic Charter. This document called for the self-determination of peoples, freedom of trade and commerce, and freedom of navigation. It also declared that upon "the final destruction of Nazi tyranny," the United States and the United Kingdom would work toward the establishment of a peace that would "afford to all nations the means of dwelling in safety within their own boundaries," and guarantee that all people could live "in freedom from fear and want."

While the Charter encompassed a few principles that served to unite America and Britain in their fight against Nazi Germany, it also revealed a conflict of interest since the United States was also hoping to dismantle the British colonial empire. With Britain desperate to secure American support, Roosevelt had been able to force Churchill to agree to the inclusion of such commitments as ensuring "access, on equal terms, to the trade and to the raw materials of the world" and respecting "the right of all peoples to choose the form of Government under which they will live."

Although public opinion polls of this period may not be entirely reliable, data from summer 1941 indicate that at around 75% of the American public felt the need to support Britain, while 45% supported Roosevelt's diplomacy. In comparison, support from Congress at the same time was a dismal 25%. In a personal letter to Churchill in August 1941, Roosevelt complained bitterly that he was struggling in his efforts to control the isolationist forces in Congress. But Roosevelt was also upbeat, suggesting that he would "become more and more provocative," and would make every effort to make any "incident" a way to enter into the hostilities. His position was clear; although he had publicly announced that the United States had no intent of protecting British transport ships, in reality he agreed to provide escort vessels. By November 1941, US military ships were directly transporting munitions to Britain, and in the following month, when three American warships came under the attack by the German Navy in the North Atlantic—resulting in the sinking of one ship and causing 172 deaths, Roosevelt saw this as an opportunity to repeal the Neutrality Act.

The Oil Embargo and the Path to the War in the Pacific

Oil had been intentionally excluded from the sanctions that Washington had been gradually introducing against Japan since June 1940 out of fear that stopping the outflow of oil would merely serve to push Japan toward a southern advance. However, when Japan advanced troops to southern

French Indochina in July 1941, Roosevelt acted quickly to freeze Japanese assets in the United States and also enforced a complete embargo on oil exports to Japan. Britain and the Netherlands also followed in step, making it nearly impossible for Japan to conduct trade. It was now faced with the choice of either giving up the southward advance to release Japanese assets, or pursuing a military option into Southeast Asia as a way to secure oil and other natural resources. Prior to this, the Japanese military high command had grossly miscalculated, believing that neither the United States nor Britain would put up a strong opposition to the occupation of southern French Indochina as long as it remained peaceful.

Neither the Japanese government nor the military felt that Japan's chance of victory in a war with the United States was particularly good. Matsuoka's successor, Toyoda Teijirō, continued in his attempt to reach a compromise with Washington over its demands that Japan withdraw its troops from French Indochina and China, and that it withdraw from the Tripartite Pact. However, Japan was also up against time. It was clear that Japan's oil reserves would be depleted in less than a year, and if war with the United States was to be contemplated, the decision to do so needed to be made quickly, lest Japan lose the ability to fight. Japan was also conscious of the US's military prowess. Although in late 1941 the US Pacific Fleet was slightly smaller than the IJN, the tables could easily be turned due to the overwhelming disparity in economic production. A simple comparison of the production capacity of both nations in 1941 shows that the United States was capable of producing 9.3 times more coal, 12 times more pig iron and steel, 74 times more iron ore, and a whopping 527.9 times more oil than Japan. On average, US production capacity was 77.9 times greater than that of Japan.

Faced with this stark reality, Konoe sought to negotiate directly with Roosevelt in Juneau, Alaska in August as a way to reduce tensions. However, Hull was staunchly opposed to the summit meeting and as a result it never got off the ground. Reacting to this, on September 6, the Japanese government redrew its bottom line and decided to abandon negotiations in early October if no agreement could be reached. As the deadline approached rapidly, Tokyo received a memorandum from Washington on October 2 that reemphasized the principles that the United States had been asserting on the basis of the Washington Treaty System: "respect for the territorial integrity and the sovereignty of each and all nations," "support of the principle of non-interference in the internal affairs of other countries," "support of the principle of equality including equality of commercial opportunity," and "non-disturbance of the status quo in the Pacific except as the status quo may be altered by peaceful means." The Japanese military interpreted this memorandum as proof that the United States was not serious about reaching an agreement with Japan and voiced its opinion that war was the only viable option. Konoe disagreed and advocated for the negotiations to continue, but he was forced to resign due to this position and was succeeded by War Minister Tōjō Hideki on October 18, 1941.

Tōjō's basic position was to continue the negotiations with the United States as he had been instructed by the Emperor Hirohito to "wipe the slate clean" (*hakushi kangen*) and work afresh in the quest to attain peace. The new foreign minister, Tōgō Shigenori, was tasked to counter the military hardliners who were still calling for an early decision to go to war. On November 5, the government adopted a two-pronged approach of preparing for war while also continuing the negotiations until the end of the month. If an agreement had not been reached, then Japan would pursue war by early December. Frantic efforts were made to reach a compromise between the two nations on the basis of a tentative agreement of returning to the status quo prior to the occupation of French Indochina. However, on November 26, the United States submitted to Japan the infamous "Hull Note," which left no room for any compromises. After receiving this note, even moderate Japanese such as Tōgō abandoned their attempts to achieve peace and became committed to a path of war.

US isolationism had lessened its grip in the wake of the developments in Europe, but still remained an obstacle that Roosevelt desperately needed to overcome in order to get America involved in the conflict abroad. However, this isolationism was quickly cast aside the moment IJN launched its surprise attack on Pearl Harbor on December 7, 1941. Fortunately for Roosevelt, both Germany and Italy declared war on America just four days later. America was now at war in both Europe and Asia.

BIBLIOGRAPHY

Banno, Junji. 1985. *Kindai Nihon no gaikō to seiji* [Diplomacy and Politics in Modern Japan]. Tokyo: Kenbun Shuppan.

Ferrell, Robert H. 1957. *American Diplomacy in the Great Depression*. New Haven: Yale University Press.

Hattori, Ryūji. 2001. *Higashi Ajia kokusai kankyō no hendō to Nihon gaikō 1918–1931* [Changes in the East Asian Diplomatic Environment and Japanese Diplomacy, 1918–1931]. Tokyo: Yūhikaku Publishing.

————. 2002. *Manshū jihen to Shigemitsu chūka kōshi hōkokusho* [The Manchurian Incident and the Reports of Japan's Minister to China, Shigemitsu]. Tokyo: Nihon Tosho Center.

————. 2006. *Shidehara Kijūrō to nijūseiki no Nihon* [Shidehara Kijūrō and 20th Century Japan]. Tokyo: Yūhikaku Publishing.

Iriye, Akira. 1965. *After Imperialism*. Cambridge, MA: Harvard University Press.

Morison, Elting E. 1960. *Turmoil and Tradition*. Boston: Houghton Mifflin Company.

Nish, Ian. 1993. *Japan's Struggle with Internationalism*. London: Kegan Paul International.

Saitō, Takashi. 1987. Bei-Ei-Kokusai renmei no dōkō, 1931–1933 [The Trend of America, Britain, and the League of Nations, 1931–1933]. In *Taiheiyō sensō e no michi: Kaisen gaikō shi 2* [The Road to the Pacific War: A Diplomatic History of the Origins of the War, vol. 2], ed. Nihon Kokusai Seiji Gakkai Taiheiyō Sensō Genin Kenkyūbu. Tokyo: Asahi Shimbunsha.

Stimson, Henry L., and McGeorge Bundy. 1948. *On Active Service in Peace and War*. New York: Harper and Brothers.

Usui, Katsumi. 1974. *Manshū jihen* [Manchurian Incident]. Tokyo: Chūōkōronsha.

————. 1995. *Manshūkoku to Kokusai Renmei* [Manchukuo and the League of Nations]. Tokyo: Yoshikawa-kōbunkan.

PART II

CHAPTER 6

The Pacific War and the Occupation of Japan, 1941–52

Futoshi Shibayama and Ayako Kusunoki

PEARL HARBOR: THE WAR IN THE PACIFIC BEGINS

The Imperial Japanese Navy's (IJN) surprise attack on Pearl Harbor delivered a massive blow to the US Pacific Fleet. With the US Navy temporarily knocked out of the fight, the IJN proceeded to take command of the seas of Southeast Asia by sinking two key British battleships. The Imperial Japanese Army (IJA) also quickly overcame the US Army in the Philippines as well as the British army in Singapore and the Malay Peninsula. General Douglas MacArthur, commander of the US forces in the Far East, was forced to flee to Australia. The United States had to deploy a task force of its remaining aircraft carriers to prevent the IJA from invading Australia and to protect the maritime link between America and Australia. During this initial period when Germany and Japan possessed the advantage, the United States was busy trying to prevent the defeat of the other Allied nations. Under the Lend-Lease Act, President Roosevelt desired to provide ample military and economic assistance to both Britain and the Soviet Union before they capitulated to the enemy.

F. Shibayama
School of Policy Studies, Kwansei Gakuin University, Nishinomiya, Japan

A. Kusunoki
International Research Center for Japanese Studies, Kyoto, Japan

© The Author(s) 2017
M. Iokibe (ed.), T. Minohara (trans. ed.), *The History of US–Japan Relations*, DOI 10.1007/978-981-10-3184-7_6

The United States also expanded the Atlantic Charter with Britain into a United Nations Declaration on January 1, 1942. Under the declaration, 26 nations, including Britain, the Soviet Union, and China, committed themselves to fighting the Tripartite Pact to the end and all pledged not to enter into any individual peace agreements. In a proposal to Soviet Foreign Minister Viacheslav Molotov on May 29, 1942, Roosevelt advocated that America, Britain, the Soviet Union, and China act as "four policemen" who would be responsible for maintaining order in the postwar world, thereby providing the practical means of maintaining the international order that the League of Nations could not. The Soviets supported this proposal and the Grand Alliance between America, Britain, and the Soviet Union was formalized in June. The alliance consisted of a series of treaties and declarations, such as the British–Soviet Mutual Assistance Agreement of May 26 and the US–Soviet Mutual Aid Agreement of June 11.

The war frenzy forced the United States to take some extreme measures. For instance, Washington became excessively fearful of an invasion or espionage by the Japanese and forcibly interned around 120,000 Japanese Americans living on the West Coast to camps located inland. It also successfully pressured several Latin American governments to deport a significant number of immigrants of Japanese descent to America to be detained despite not having committed any crime.

The Change in the Tide of the War

In early summer 1942, the Allies began to gain the advantage in the war. The Axis lost all hope of defeating the Soviet Union after the Stalingrad offensive faltered in late January 1943. As the Soviet Union was still valiantly holding off the German forces it was eager to see the American and British forces land in France as soon as possible and open the second front that would force Germany to divert its troops to Western Europe. Partly as a means of appeasing Stalin, the American and British leaders issued a declaration at the Casablanca Conference in January 1943 that they would not compromise nor would they agree to an individual peace with the Axis Powers and would only accept an "unconditional surrender."

In the Pacific, the United States began to halt the Japanese momentum after launching their first air raid on Tokyo in April 1942. This was followed by the sinking of four Japanese navy aircraft carriers at the Battle of Midway in June. Having worn down the Japanese forces in the Solomon Islands through a campaign of attrition in 1943, the United States was gradually setting the stage for a final victory over Japan; its enormous industrial production rate could not be matched by Japan.

From late November through early December 1943, Roosevelt, British Prime Minister Winston Churchill, and Soviet leader Joseph Stalin met for the first time at the Tehran Conference, and discussed their commitment to cooperation and future strategies for the war, as well as their visions for the postwar world and how Japan and Germany should be dealt with after their defeat. Shortly before the conference, Roosevelt and Churchill had also met with Chinese President Chiang Kai-shek at the Cairo Conference and came out with a declaration signed on November 27, 1943. The declaration called for an unconditional surrender; seizure of all Japan's overseas colonies and the relinquishing of Manchuria, Taiwan, and the Penghu Islands to China; abandonment of all islands that it had seized in the Pacific after 1914; and the independence of Korea.

A second front in Europe was finally opened in June 1944. At the Bretton Woods Conference the following month, America and Britain led the participating powers in establishing the foundations for the free trade system that would ensure stability in international finance and currency in the aftermath of the war. Moreover, this system would also support economic development and recovery from the destruction inflicted upon the world economy by the current war by establishing the International Monetary Fund (IMF) and the International Bank for Reconstruction and Development (IBRD).

THE OCCUPATION AND RECONSTRUCTION POLICY OF JAPAN

During the war, Washington began to look into not only the general issues concerning the postwar international order but also potential means of rebuilding Germany and Japan. The State Department's Division of Special Research, a newly established division tasked with formulating postwar policy, included a Far Eastern group consisting of Japan experts and sympathizers from with in and outside the department, such as Clark University professor George H. Blakeslee, Columbia University associate professor Hugh Borton, and Robert A. Fearey, who had served as personal secretary to former US ambassador to Japan Joseph C. Grew. While critical of Japanese militarism, these experts also gave praise to Japan's modernization and the establishment of democratic principles in the prewar period. Their fundamental vision for postwar Japan was to maintain the traditional system of the emperor as head of state (*tennō-sei*) as a general framework under which the Japanese would be encouraged to engage in liberalist and democratic reform, with the ultimate goal of having Japan return to international society as a peaceful member.

However, there was scant support for this approach among the American public as well as most government officials during the war. At the 1944 Post-War Programs Committee (PWC), Secretary of State Cordell Hull and his senior staff advocated that the main aim should be to prevent Japan from posing any future threat to international society and recommended the adoption of strict measures that emphasized demilitarization and democratization. Ultimately, these State Department officials and pro-Japan sympathizers reached a compromise and developed an approach that would incorporate both goals while also restoring the political independence and economic opportunities that Japan would need to eventually return to international society. The occupation forces would possess supreme authority, and while they could dismantle large parts of the Japanese government, they would keep and utilize the lower bureaucratic institutions.

The question surrounding the future role of the emperor led to numerous heated debates. The Japan hands argued that the emperor could be a convenient tool in bringing the war to an end and reestablishing democracy in Japan. On the other hand, the senior State Department officials believed that the imperial system was at the very root of Japan's militarism and should be abolished. As there was no sign of them reaching a compromise, a final decision on this issue was put aside. At this juncture, there was still the choice of stripping the emperor of his political powers but retaining him as a symbol head while governing through Japanese administrative organizations that would, in that case, be more cooperative in carrying out the reforms. These contrasting policies were also reflected in the document "US Initial Post-Surrender Policy Relating to Japan" (SWNCC-150) finalized by the State–War–Navy Coordinating Committee (SWNCC) in June 1945 which would form the basis of Washington's policies toward Japan until up to the end of the war (Iokibe 1985; Hellegers 2002).

Japan's Postwar Scenario

Japan's own formulation of postwar policies was naturally less comprehensive. The Greater East Asia Joint Declaration (*Daitōa kyōdō sengen*)— developed under the initiative of Foreign Minister Shigemitsu Mamoru and issued at the Greater East Asia Conference (*Daitōa kaigi*) in Tokyo, November 1943—also espoused similar principles to those of the Atlantic Charter, such as mutual respect for sovereignty, economic cooperation, and the equal use of resources among the nations of East Asia. However, in the eyes of the military and the Ministry of Greater East Asia (*Daitōashō*) the declaration was a means of bringing the people of Asia together under Japan to establish a cooperative system for the mobilization of the human and material resources needed to resist the Allied invasion of Japan (Iriye 1978; Hatano 1996).

In fact, the Japanese forces quickly began to lose ground soon after the Greater East Asia Joint Declaration was unveiled. At the Battle of the Philippine Sea in June 1944, Japan lost most of its remaining aircraft carriers, and the fall of Saipan in July placed the mainland within the reach of long-range bombers. As Japan's impending defeat became self-evident, the foreign ministry turned its attention toward analyzing the Allied plans for a postwar Japan. But the debates over the future of the emperor represented the source of Japan's utmost concern. Japanese officials were wary about how Britain, America, and the Soviet Union would seek to pursue their national interests while also cooperating with each other and how this would impact the occupation of Japan.

The United Nations project was observed as an alliance against the Axis, and Japanese officials were carefully considering how to convey its proposals for revising the Allied vision for the organization in a joint communiqué to be announced during the Second Greater East Asia Conference in April 1945. The communiqué recommended that when establishing the fundamental principles for the postwar international order it would be necessary to ensure the elimination of racial discrimination and the freedom of trade, as well as promoting equality between sovereign nations and peaceful reform of the present international order. It is important to realize that by the time the war was approaching its end, Japan had come to accept most of the postwar vision and ideals set forth by the Allies.

THE END OF THE PACIFIC WAR AND ROOSEVELT'S VISION FOR A POSTWAR WORLD

Between summer 1944 and spring 1945, Japan and Germany both faced imminent defeat. At the same time, the cooperation among the United States, Britain, and the Soviet Union was also beginning to show signs of strain. The United Nations was eventually established after a compromise was reached during the Yalta Conference (February 1945) and the San Francisco Conference (April–June 1945). In October 1944, Churchill and Stalin agreed to each other's spheres of influence in Eastern Europe under a "percentages agreement" that Roosevelt had no choice but to tacitly approve, as his utmost priority was to secure the Soviet Union's entry into the war against Japan.

In East Asia, Roosevelt was concerned that China may not be able to fulfill the role that he had expected it to play as one of the four policemen, given its disappointing military showing. In contrast, the US forces inflicted the final blow to the IJN in the Philippine Sea in June 1944, and from late November launched a full-scale B-29 strategic bombing campaign of the Japanese mainland by establishing airstrips on Saipan, Guam, and Tinian Island. However, the strategic bombing campaign did not immediately shatter Japan's resistance, and as the atomic bomb had not yet been completed, the United States was eager for the Soviets to join the fight.

During the Yalta Conference, Roosevelt was forced to concede to Stalin's persistent demands for a stake in East Asia in return for Soviet entry into the war against Japan. In a supplementary secret agreement at the conference, Roosevelt, Churchill, and Stalin agreed on the maintenance of Soviet influence in Outer Mongolia, the joint Sino-Soviet management of the Chinese Eastern Railway and the South Manchuria Railway, the development of Dairen into an international port, the development of Port Arthur into a major Soviet naval base, and, finally, the return of southern Sakhalin as well as the cession of the Kurile Islands from Japan to the Soviet Union. Stalin was eager to establish a Soviet sphere of influence in East Asia and his adamant position on this issue forced Roosevelt to make some serious concessions on his own vision of an ideal postwar world.

However, the American military situation greatly improved following Yalta. The massive firebombing of Tokyo on the night of March 9–10 wrought havoc upon Japan's largest metropolis and Washington felt that it no longer required a strategic air base in Soviet territory to defeat Japan. On March 17, US troops successfully completed the campaign to gain control of Iwo Jima (Iwoto in Japanese), which now allowed fighters to escort the B-29 bombers to their targets over Japan, making the air defenses in place almost useless. On April 1, the first American troops landed on Okinawa, the main island of the Ryukyus. However, Roosevelt passed away suddenly just 11 days later and Vice President Harry S. Truman was sworn in to the presidency just as the United States was reaching the final stage of bringing about the surrender of Japan and Germany.

The Truman Administration and the Path to Japan's Surrender

Germany was the first to surrender in May 1945 and thereafter Washington's main challenge was to defeat Japan without incurring a severe military cost. Between May and June, the US government began to consider various ways of forcing Japan to surrender. Firebombing missions were increased and by mid-June most of Japan's large cities had turned to ash, while the unrestricted marine warfare granted the US forces total control of Japanese waters and transportation routes. By this time, it was simply a question of when Japan would capitulate. But with the hardliners still in power, Washington felt that a full-scale invasion of the mainland would be required to secure Japan's defeat, which would entail huge casualties in terms of US lives. Nevertheless, on June 18 Truman approved the plan to land troops in southern Kyushu—codename Operation Olympic—to be initiated on November 1.

It was at this time that a number of US and British government and military officials began to express strong reservations regarding the potentially huge cost of invading Japan, especially when considering the large losses suffered by US Marines in Saipan, Iwo Jima, and Okinawa. In a meeting with Truman on May 28, 1945, former Japanese ambassador Joseph C. Grew, then undersecretary of state, urged the president to issue a statement to Japan to offer a guarantee that the emperor system would remain so as to bring about an early surrender via a diplomatic route. On the following day, Secretary of the Army Henry L. Stimson and other senior officers expressed their support for Grew's proposal but also suggested that it was too early to provide such a guarantee. The British government also supported the proposal. The new Secretary of State James F. Byrnes, who had taken office in early July, opposed such assurances and showed determination, along with his new assistant secretaries Archibald MacLeish and Dean Acheson, to accept nothing but an unconditional surrender from Japan.

Truman began to place his hopes on a new revolutionary weapon, the atomic bomb, which would deliver the final blow that would push Japan to surrender without the need of an invasion. By the time Germany surrendered in May 1945, the United States had successfully developed the atomic bomb and therefore the question became whether it should be used against Japan. On July 16, Stimson, who was at the Potsdam Conference, received a top-secret telegram informing him that the first atomic bomb had been detonated and that its destructive power had "exceeded expectations." Ultimately, Truman supported Stimson's proposal to force Japan into early surrender with a combination of the Potsdam Declaration and the use of the atomic bomb. Beyond the conventional reasoning behind the decision to drop the atomic bomb, recent academic debate has centered on the interpretation that the use of the atomic bomb had less to do with the war against Japan and more to do with drawing concessions from the Soviet Union in preparation for the anticipated Cold War.

Hirohito's "Sacred Decision" to Surrender

As Japan's ability to wage war began to erode, a number of prominent Japanese government officials began to call for an end to hostilities. After the fall of Saipan in July 1944, Okada Keisuke and a number of other senior statesmen joined hands with individuals such as Kido Kōichi, lord keeper of the privy seal, to force Prime Minister Tōjō to resign.

However, the new cabinet formed under Koiso Kuniaki on July 22 lacked the strength to put an end to the war, particularly given that the Allies were demanding an unconditional surrender. The Japanese military was inevitably opposed to demands for disarmament, the punishment of war criminals, and changes to Japan's system of government. Even those who argued for peace could not accept surrender without the guarantee that the emperor would remain at the center of Japan's fundamental national polity (*kokutai goji*). It was Japan's strong hope that the Soviet Union would honor the Japan–Soviet Neutrality Pact and help to mediate a peace that would allow Japan to avoid a humiliating unconditional surrender.

As the Yalta Conference had reaffirmed the alliance between the United States, Britain, and the Soviet Union, on April 5, 1945, the Soviets unilaterally notified Japan that they would not be extending the Japan–Soviet Neutrality Pact which was to expire the following year. This news reached Japan just as it was struggling to deal with the firebombing of its cities and the invasion of Okinawa. Hirohito wished the war to be brought to an end as quickly as possible, as the daily air raids and the naval blockade had a devastating impact on Japan's capacity for industrial output, and ordinary citizens were struggling to survive. There was also genuine concern among Japan's ruling elite that defeat would spark social unrest that could lead to a communist revolution. This threat was highlighted by former Prime Minister Konoe Fumimaro in his conversation with Hirohito in February 1945 which he had prepared with the help of Yoshida Shigeru and other former officials.

However, in mid-May, the Supreme Council for Directing the War (*Saikō sensō shidō kaigi*) decided that Japan should persist in negotiations with the Soviet Union with the aim of securing Stalin's support in mediating a more palatable peace agreement, and, at the very least, to ensure that the Soviets would not enter the fight against Japan. But any attempt to negotiate with the Soviet Union was an exercise in futility. Moscow was keen to remain a participant in the war to ensure that it could enjoy the spoils alongside the other victors, and thus it conducted negotiations with the sole purpose of postponing Japan's collapse until it was prepared to enter the war. Once this was completed, Molotov issued the Soviet declaration of war on Japan to the Japanese ambassador Satō Naotake on August 8, 1945 (Slavinsky 1995; Hasegawa 2006).

With the Soviets unwilling to mediate, accepting the Potsdam Declaration became Tokyo's only remaining path toward surrendering. At 11:00 a.m. on August 9, the Supreme Council for the Direction of War met in the wake of the dropping of the atomic bomb on Hiroshima three days earlier and the Soviet invasion of Manchukuo that had been launched at dawn that day. The council was divided, with Foreign Minister Tōgō Shigenori and Navy Minister Yonai Mitsumasa advocating the acceptance of the Potsdam Declaration with the condition that Japan's national polity be retained, and Army Minister Anami Korechika, Chief of the Army General Staff Umezu Yoshijirō, and Chief of the Naval General Staff Toyoda Soemu adamant in their position that Japan should also be exempt from the punishment of war criminals and military disarmament, as well as having a say in the extent of the occupation. As the council was struggling to reach a consensus, they received news that a second atomic bomb had been dropped on Nagasaki.

Later that night, Prime Minister Suzuki requested the emperor to make the final decision given that the council was evenly divided: three in favor, three against. Hirohito chose to support Tōgō's proposal, describing his decision as a way to "save the people from catastrophe and protect the happiness of all humankind, by enduring the unendurable and suffering what is insufferable." After Hirohito's "sacred decision (*seidan*)," Tokyo accepted the Potsdam Declaration, but still insisted on the emperor's unchallenged authority. The US response received on August 11 did not specifically offer such a guarantee, but instead stated that the "authority of the Emperor and Japanese Government to rule the state" would be "subject to the Supreme Commander for the Allied Powers (SCAP)" and that the form of the Japanese government would ultimately be decided in accordance with the "freely expressed will of the Japanese people," as determined in the Potsdam Declaration.

Had Japan failed to accept the Potsdam Declaration at this juncture, it certainly would have suffered a catastrophic invasion by American, Russian, and other Allied troops. There is also little doubt that the occupation of the Japanese mainland would have been conducted under two spheres, one led by the United States and the other by the Soviet Union. In the end, it was external pressure provided by the atomic bombings of Hiroshima and Nagasaki and the Soviet entry into the war that prompted Hirohito to take a highly unprecedented step in making the decision to ensure that Japan would accept the Potsdam Declaration.

THE BEGINNING OF AMERICAN OCCUPATION OF JAPAN

By 1945 the Soviet Union had not only expanded its control over Poland and other eastern European nations, but it also began to issue demands to Britain's ally Turkey for the cession of territory, rights to freedom of navigation in the Turkish Straits, and the establishment of Soviet naval bases. Following heated discussions with the Soviet representatives at Potsdam, Truman became increasingly wary of Soviet ambitions in Europe and East Asia, and thus tried to limit the area occupied by the Russians in China and the Korean peninsula as far as possible. The president made it clear that the United States considered the Japanese mainland to be within its sphere of influence, and would seek to exclude any Russian influence from Japan. On August 18, Washington rejected the military's proposal for dividing the occupation of Japan, and instead adopted a policy for a unified occupation by the Allied nations with MacArthur acting as supreme commander, giving the United States administrative control of Japan as a whole. It was on this day that Truman rejected Stalin's demand of August 16 that the Soviet Union should be entrusted with the duty of occupying northeastern Hokkaido. The Soviet Union continued its military actions in Japan until early September, occupying Sakhalin, the Kuriles, and the islands of Habomai and Shikotan.

However, in response to Stalin's demands for Soviet involvement in the occupation of Japan, an international framework for supporting the occupation of Japan was laid out: the Washington-based Far Eastern

Commission (comprised of 11 nations), which was the supreme body for formulating policies relating to Japan, and the Tokyo-based Allied Council for Japan (comprised of the "Big Four"), which was tasked to act as an advisory body for MacArthur.

In reality, the real power was held by MacArthur's General Headquarters (GHQ). MacArthur was a talented but highly authoritarian general who was known for his impressive performance in World War I and the Pacific War where he had been in charge of defending the Philippines and operating successful attacks against Japan by using an "island hopping" strategy. As supreme commander of the occupation forces in Japan, MacArthur made it his personal mission to put Japan back on its feet, which he pursued by wielding authority that exceeded not only that of the prime minister but also the emperor.

Indirect Administration through the Emperor and Japanese Government

After the formal signing of the Instrument of Surrender aboard the USS *Missouri* on September 2, MacArthur sent Tokyo into a panic when he gave it notice that he was planning to announce "three proclamations" the following day that would show the occupation authorities' intention to establish a direct military government with English as the official language, conduct trials against those who violated GHQ orders, and to issue occupation currency. Perhaps in the absence of any specific plans for indirect government, MacArthur's announcement was based on a plan that had been created in May of the same year under the codename Operation Blacklist. However, MacArthur agreed to withdraw the proclamations when Foreign Minister Shigemitsu Mamoru, who had taken office as part of the new cabinet formed by Prince Higashikuni Naruhiko on August 17, promised the Japanese government's full cooperation with occupation policy and thus requested indirect rule by the GHQ.

Washington's true intent on the occupation of Japan was based on the Initial Post-Surrender Policy for Japan (SWNCC-150/4) that President Truman had approved on August 23. However, partly in response to the Soviet Union, Australia, and other Allied nations, the United States began to take a more severe stance toward Japan and sought to "use, but not support" the emperor and Japanese government. But in Tokyo, MacArthur now attached greater importance to the role of the emperor as he was aware that his presence assured the demilitarization of Japan without any major resistance. After first meeting with Hirohito on September 27, MacArthur declared that he would protect the emperor's position as a means of ensuring that the occupation would proceed smoothly. In essence this meant that MacArthur would subscribe to a policy of indirect rule during the occupation (Iokibe 2007).

On October 2, 1945, the General Headquarters of the Supreme Commander of the Allied Powers (SCAP/GHQ) was established. Directly under the chief of staff were a general staff section and special staff section consisting of various sections, including the Government Section, the Economic & Scientific Section, the Natural Resources Section, the Civil Information and Educational Section, and the Civil Intelligence Section. The various organizations within the special staff section each jostled for influence as they developed their own occupation reform policies. The office of MacArthur's political staff, the Government Section (GS), led by MacArthur's confidant Courtney Whitney as chief from December 1945, exercised a particularly high level of input in pushing through the demilitarization and democratization of Japan during the early stages of the occupation. MacArthur was also keen to eliminate intervention from Washington and to solidify his own authority in Japan as he wanted to play a key role in the historic undertaking of rebuilding Japan (Sodei 1974).

Initial Occupation Policy: Demilitarization and Democratization

The GHQ began the initial stage of the occupation by aggressively pursuing demilitarization. In the first six months alone, it implemented a succession of measures to break apart and punish the former regime and leadership, the most prominent being the arrest of Tōjō Hideki and other suspected war criminals. These measures had a direct impact on the Japanese political system and society. The Civil Liberties Directive of October 4, 1945, and the directive for the removal of undesirable personnel from public office of January 4, 1946, purged as many as 210,000 officials as "wartime leaders," which made the Higashikuni cabinet resign en masse while the Shidehara cabinet was significantly reshuffled. In addition, these measures included disarmament and demobilization, the dissolution of the military organization, and the abolition of the secret police. The International Military Tribunal for the Far East, commonly known as the Tokyo Trials, was convened on May 3, 1946, to try the leaders who had overseen Japan's aggressive expansion from 1931 to 1945. When the trials were finally concluded in November 1948, Tōjō Hideki and six of the 28 accused were sentenced to death, although Hirohito was not held accountable for his role in the war.

In the beginning, the GHQ did not receive any instructions from Washington on democratization reforms other than the basic principles laid out in the Potsdam Declaration and the aforementioned SWNCC-150/4. On October 11, 1945, MacArthur issued Prime Minister Shidehara directives for five major areas of democratization reforms and encouraged the government to take an active role in promoting democracy in line with these basic policies. Shidehara sought in earnest to implement these reforms, and, in many instances, the government was actually using this opportunity to implement reforms that they had already been contemplating both before and during the war. Of the reforms the Japanese government proposed, the Labor Union Act and the amendment to the House of Representatives Election Act (both promulgated in December 1945) were approved and implemented by the GHQ without any changes.

However, between late 1945 and early 1946, the GS and other sections of the GHQ began to pursue far more radical reform measures, sometimes drafting their own proposals and pushing the government to accept them, including the proposals for constitutional revisions that were reflected in the Japanese government's publication of the "Outline of a Draft for a Revised Constitution" (*Kenpō kaisei sōan yōkō*) in March 1946. Shidehara's government was ordered to draft more comprehensive reforms, such as a revised plan for agricultural land reform (October 1946). Many of the reforms were neither conceived nor anticipated by the Japanese, such as the dissolution of the industrial and financial conglomerates (*zaibatsu*; November 1945), the Antimonopoly Act (*Dokusen-kinshi-hō*; April 1947), and the founding of the municipal police in December 1947.

Shidehara and other conservative leaders such as Yoshida Shigeru, who was appointed prime minister in May 1946, believed that restoring and strengthening Japan's prewar liberalist and democratic movements was sufficient. Although he voiced his concern regarding the harsher occupation policies, he adhered to the directions stipulated by the GHQ. These reform policies were often seen as a "product of radical idealism," out of touch with the unique circumstances of Japan (Yoshida 1957-58), but resistance was virtually impossible.

The proposal to revise the constitution was a cause for alarm. The Japanese government had dithered on this issue and in February 1946 the GHQ came to the end of its patience and applied pressure on Japan to accept a proposal drafted by the GS on the basis of MacArthur's "Three Principles," which advocated retention of the emperor system, the complete renunciation of both aggressive and self-defensive war, and the abolition of the feudal system. Shidehara had no choice but to accept this under GHQ's assurances that it would guarantee preservation of a symbolic emperor, which was the issue of utmost concern.

Furthermore, the provisions of Article 9, which renounced war, placed extreme constraints on Japan's postwar national security policy. Within the GHQ it was agreed that Japan would still be allowed to engage in military action for the purpose of self-defense. However, the Japanese government interpreted the proposal as renouncing both aggressive and defensive wars, even after the "Ashida Revision," an amendment to Article 9 passed by the Diet in fall 1946 that allowed Japan to exercise the right to self-defense. It was not until 1950, during Yoshida's second term in office, that Japan finally adopted this interpretation of Article 9, and it was not until 1955, under the Hatoyama Ichirō cabinet, that this became officially recognized.

These and other reforms introduced in the occupation period formed the political and social foundations of postwar Japan. By improving the efficiency and productivity of farming the agricultural land reforms generated surplus labor force and increased farmers' purchasing power, which led, in turn, to Japan's rapid economic growth. The groups of entrepreneurs and economic bodies that replaced the *zaibatsu* played a crucial role in Japan's postwar economic development as well as supporting conservative governments. On the other hand, workers became increasingly organized and this became the main support base for the progressive parties.

US–Japan Relations During the Occupation Period

The occupation was the only time in the history of US–Japan relations that the two countries were not interacting as mutually independent nations that maintained diplomatic relations, but rather as occupier and the occupied. Three main types of relationships developed between the Japanese government and the GHQ. The leaders who failed to establish a cooperative relationship with GHQ struggled to maintain their power; the Higashikuni cabinet was not necessarily able to understand GHQ's policy, while Hatoyama Ichirō, the president of the Liberal Party, was purged just prior to forming his cabinet as he was branded too conservative by the GS Deputy Chief Charles Kades.

On the other hand, cabinets led by former diplomats-turned-prime ministers Shidehara Kijurō and Yoshida Shigeru developed a solid relationship with the GHQ which made it easier to run the government. Both Shidehara and Yoshida encouraged MacArthur to wield his authority to address issues that threatened the survival of Japan, such as relief of food shortages and the prohibition of general strikes. Yoshida, who met frequently with MacArthur, successfully deflected attempts by Kades and his cohort to oust him as prime minister. Shirasu Jirō, a close confidant to Yoshida, and other officials cooperated closely with anti-communist conservative Charles A. Willoughby, who headed G2 Section (the intelligence apparatus of the GHQ), and firmly opposed the actions of the New Deal reformist Kades.

Lastly, Prime Minister Tetsuya Katayama, who headed the Socialist Party (*Shakaitō*), and his successor Ashida Hitoshi, who led the Democratic Party (*Minshutō*), were the two prime ministers to cooperate most closely with Kades. Keen to promote a more progressive political movement in Japan, Kades played an important role in shaping occupation reforms, and Katayama and Ashida permitted themselves to be much more influenced by him than Shidehara and Yoshida ever allowed MacArthur. As a result, both cabinets lost their ability to conduct independent action in accordance with public opinion and to govern effectively, as Kades intervened on each and every key issue.

Upon the resignation en masse of the Ashida cabinet following a bribery scandal in fall 1948, Kades was determined not to allow Yoshida to return to office as the leader of the popular Democratic Liberal Party (*Minshu-Jiyūtō*) by working behind the scenes to appoint Secretary General Yamazaki Takeshi to become the party leader. However, Yoshida adroitly defeated Yamazaki by using the support of MacArthur and Willoughby. Having been defeated in this political battle, Kades lost his power base for involvement in the Japanese government and thus returned to the United States just as Yoshida began his second tenure in office.

With the internal power struggle resolved, the occupation was now focused on two main issues: reconstructing the Japanese economy to ensure its viability in a global market and restoring Japan's independence under a peace treaty. Yoshida was committed to overcoming these challenges with the assistance of two special GHQ envoys, Detroit Bank Chairman Joseph M. Dodge and John Foster Dulles, advisor to the secretary of state, who respectively played key roles in the promotion of economic development and the peace negotiations.

The Cold War and the End of Occupation

The immediate postwar tensions between the United States and the Soviet Union and their allies also had significant policy implications for occupied Japan because Washington's policy was not consistent, but was instead based on the use of trial and error to find the appropriate response to the Soviet Union. Secretary of State Byrnes placed an emphasis on coordinating relations with the Soviet Union and other Allies and involving them in the occupation of Japan, which led to the establishment of the aforementioned Far Eastern Commission and the Allied Council for Japan. As a part of this initiative, in February 1946 he also proposed that the Allied nations monitor Japan's disarmament and demilitarization for a period of 25 years.

However, as tensions grew between the two superpowers, Byrnes's approach lost domestic support and the US Cold War strategy began to be guided instead by George F. Kennan's theory of "containing" further military expansion by the Soviet Union rather than naïvely hoping to establish a cooperative relationship. Given that the East–West rivalry was anticipated to continue for a considerable period, Kennan argued that the United States, Western Europe, and Japan all needed to ensure their superiority over the Soviet Union by strengthening and uniting their economic and political powers. The Marshall Plan, announced in June 1947, was meant to put Western Europe back on track.

Kennan felt that his theory should also be applied to Japan, arguing that it was necessary to rebuild Japan as a staunch member of the West. He was critical of the proposals that the State Department had developed based on MacArthur's proposal, suggesting that Allied monitoring of Japan for a quarter-century and other such measures were based on an outmoded approach that sought to weaken defeated nations. The National Security Council "Recommendations with respect to US Policy toward Japan" (NSC-13/2), approved by President Truman in October 1948, incorporated Kennan's suggestions with plans for the United States to establish a thriving economy in Japan.

Special envoy Dodge first arrived in Japan in early February 1949 to help Japan break away from the occupation-led economy in which it was completely dependent on aid and subsidies. Dodge's basic idea for reviving Japan's economy through sound market competition, which required the drastic approach of adopting an ultra-austere fiscal policy, was fully imple-mented by Prime Minister Yoshida and Finance Minister Ikeda Hayato. In the short term, this led to a severe economic recession—contributing to social unrest in 1949—but the economy recovered rapidly the following year with the outbreak of the Korean War.

MacArthur's perspective on demilitarization and democratization was that it should be aimed at demonstrating the common ideals of human-ity, as opposed to punishing the defeated. On this basis he successfully pushed through the revision of the constitution and the implementation of comprehensive reforms by 1948 while adamantly refusing the requests of the top brass in Washington for a limited rearmament of Japan. He also rejected the stationing of US forces on the Japanese mainland, on the grounds that the US forces could defend Japan from Okinawa. In the NSC-13/2 recommendations, Truman had taken into consideration the fact that Kennan, MacArthur, and American taxpayers held the view that the costs of Japan's economic recovery should be kept down.

The friction between the GHQ, the US military, and the State Department on the approach toward attaining a peace treaty and whether or not US troops should be stationed in Japan after it regained its indepen-dence complicated Truman's efforts to formulate a unified national security policy toward Japan. Recognizing that the Cold War had developed into a serious geopolitical confrontation, the Katayama cabinet developed its own proposal for the president that Japan be provided with a military security guarantee by the United States in the event that the United Nations was unable or unwilling to assist Japan. This attempt by Katayama to engage in independent diplomacy was frowned upon by the GHQ, which felt that this action was an unwanted intrusion upon its authority over Japan.

Cold War Tensions and the Path to Japanese Rearmament

In 1949, Cold War tensions mounted even further. The Soviet Union con-tinued to enforce the blockade that it had imposed upon Berlin in June of the previous year, and as a response the United States formed the North Atlantic Treaty Organization (NATO) in April 1949. The United States also lost its monopoly on nuclear weapons when the Soviet Union successfully conducted its first nuclear test in August 1949. The political map of East Asia was significantly revised as well, following the Communists' defeat of the Nationalists in China in the same year. Ever more aware of the strategic importance of Japan, Truman wanted to ensure that Japan would remain part of the Western camp following its independence, and thus he pursued a peace treaty with Japan without the participation of the Soviet Union.

In view of the above developments, Truman slowly began to lose faith in Kennan's economic approach to the problem. Instead, he turned an ear to calls from Kennan's successor, Paul H. Nitze, to shift the emphasis to military "containment," which would entail military buildup and substantial increases in the US defense budget, as outlined in NSC-68, completed in April 1950. Despite his commitment to maintain sound public finances, Truman acquiesced to such military expenditures, and the Nitze plan was implemented due to the outbreak of the Korean War in June 1950.

Two months prior to the Korean War, Yoshida had sent his confidant Ikeda to Washington with a message for Truman that the Japanese government was prepared to allow US forces to remain in Japan even after the end of occupation. As the bases in Japan were regarded as an essential component of the US Cold War strategy, the Japanese government decision harmonized the previously antagonizing views that existed between the US military and GHQ regarding the peace deal. With the consolidated support for reaching a peace treaty with Japan, Truman was encouraged to take the necessary steps and Dulles was sent to Japan to begin the preliminary negotiations.

The Korean War broke out while Dulles was in Tokyo, but Truman allowed Dulles to continue with the negotiations. With the drastic decline in US forces stationed in Japan due to the Korean War, MacArthur ordered the establishment of a 75,000-strong National Police Reserve (*Keisatsu Yobitai*) in July 1950 to boost domestic public security as well as to function as the foundation for a future Japanese military. When the Chinese forces entered the Korean War in October 1950 and began to drive the US and South Korean troops back, the equipment and organization of the Police Reserve Force was revamped in order to ensure that it could also operate as a military force if necessary.

Yoshida's ideas were grounded in a three-pronged security policy that the Japanese government had put together in early 1951 in preparation for the peace treaty negotiations. First, Japan, lacking even the most basic of supplies, and utterly incapable of defending itself, would secure the guarantee of protection from the United States by forming a security agreement and allowing the use of bases in Japan, particularly given the formation of the Sino-Soviet alliance in February 1950. Second, Japan would not rearm before a peace treaty was attained, and third, Japan would seek to retain sovereignty of the Ryukyu and Ogasawara Islands while also taking into account American strategic requirements.

Given the situation in Korea, a number of Yoshida's advisors had strongly advocated a policy of rearmament. While Yoshida supported the idea of Japan later developing a self-defense force placed under civilian control, he feared that giving rearmament priority within Japan's process of regaining independence could unwittingly lead to a revival of Japanese militarism. He was also concerned that the economic demands of rearmament could lead to social unrest which would, in turn, strengthen communist sentiment in Japan. Thus Yoshida firmly believed that Japan should embark on rearmament only after it had gained independence, created a stable economy and society, and developed a sound domestic political system. He also believed that allying Japan with the United States and its allies was the best way of ensuring Japan's eventual return to international society. Therefore, he stood firm in this approach despite calls by left-wing progressives for a more neutral, non-military agreement incorporating all the Allied nations.

The Road to the Peace and Security Treaties

The peace negotiations reached their apex during the Yoshida–Dulles talks in January and February 1951. The Treaty of Peace with Japan (*Tai-nichi heiwa jōyaku*) and the US–Japan Mutual Security Treaty (*Nichibei anzen hoshō jōyaku*)—which were both signed in San Francisco on September 8, 1951—allowed the United States to welcome Japan to the Free World and accord it an important place within the nascent security framework strategy for East Asia.

The US–Japan Security Treaty became the legal basis for stationing US troops in Japan, and it also permitted their use for maintaining peace and security in the Far East. In the official notes exchanged between Yoshida and Secretary of State Acheson as a supplement to the treaty, Tokyo committed itself to supporting the activities of the UN forces on the Korean peninsula, and to continue providing Japanese facilities and services.

The US–Japan Security Treaty was perceived by Japan to be a solid guarantee that the United States would defend Japan, although there was no explicit clause to this effect. While the clauses pertaining to Japanese territory were somewhat ambiguous, the peace treaty was on the whole generous. The restrictions on Japan's sovereignty, economy, and military were largely deleted, and Japan was exempted from reparations, although the reparations in service to Southeast Asian nations were to be dealt through bilateral agreements after the establishment of the peace treaty. In sum, the purpose of the treaty was to assure the economic recovery of Japan while welcoming it as an equal member of international society; there would be no repeat of Versailles.

The American delegation wanted Japan to willingly accept the terms of the treaty and was ready to seize the pro-American sentiment Yoshida represented; otherwise they could lose all of Japan—a concern that was echoed by MacArthur as well as his successor Mathew B. Ridgeway and Dean Rusk, who were tasked with negotiating the Administrative Agreement (Rusk would later become secretary of state in the Kennedy administration). Although keen to ensure Japan's potential contribution to the Free World, Dulles was also ultimately prepared to respect the Japan hands' intrinsic understanding of Japan. However, the American delegates were disappointed with Yoshida's reluctant attitude toward rearmament, and the two nations would continue to clash throughout the early 1950s over the scale and speed at which rearmament should proceed.

While Yoshida was generally satisfied with the Security Treaty, at the same time a number of issues still remained unaddressed. For example, the treaty did not conform sufficiently to the Charter of the United Nations and it did not explicitly refer to America's obligation to defend Japan. He also felt that the treaty did not fully possess an element of reciprocity between the two nations due to the inclusion of the so-called "civil unrest clause," and its lack of a set term and provisions for prior consultation. These concerns later became the significant motivation for Japan in pursuing treaty revisions (Nishimura 1999). Furthermore, Japan was not successful in seeing Okinawa returned to Japanese sovereignty. While Article 3 of the peace treaty recognized that the Japanese government had "residual sovereignty" over the Ryukyu and Ogasawara Islands, it was unclear where the United States actually stood on Okinawan reversion. Another issue that remained ambiguous was the question over relations with China. When the US Senate approved the ratification of the treaties, Dulles asked that Japan establish formal relations with the Nationalist government in Taiwan. To honor this request, Yoshida sent a correspondence to Dulles in December 1951 expressing his intention to form a peace treaty with the Nationalist government, known as the "Yoshida letter." However, as can be witnessed in the following chapters, the question of *what kind* of relationship Japan would establish with mainland China or Taiwan became a pertinent and delicate issue of Japanese diplomacy for the next two decades.

BIBLIOGRAPHY

Hasegawa, Tsuyoshi. 2006. *Antō* [Racing the Enemy]. Tokyo: Chūōkōron-shinsha.

Hatano, Sumio. 1996. *Taiheiyō sensō to Ajia gaikō* [The Pacific War and Asian Diplomacy]. Tokyo: University of Tokyo Press.

Hellegers, Dale M. 2002. *We, the Japanese People*. Palo Alto: Stanford University Press.

Iokibe, Makoto. 1985. *Beikoku no Nihon senryō seisaku* [America's Occupation Policy Toward Japan]. 2 vols. Tokyo: Chūōkōronsha.

———. 2007. *Senryōki* [Occupation Period]. Tokyo: Kōdansha.

Iriye, Akira. 1978. *Nichibei senso* [The War Between Japan and the United States]. Tokyo: Chūōkōronsha.

Nishimura, Kumao. 1999. *San Furanshisuko Heiwa jōyaku, Nichibei anpo jōyaku* [The San Francisco Peace Treaty and Japan–US Security Treaty]. Tokyo: Chūōkōron-shinsha.

Slavinsky, Boris N. 1995. *The USSR–Japan Treaty and Stalin's Diplomacy*. Moscow: TOO Novina.

Sodei, Rinjirō. 1974. *Makkasa no Nisennichi* [MacArthur's Two Thousand Days]. Tokyo: Chūōkōronsha.

Yoshida, Shigeru. 1957–58. *Kaisō jūnen* [Memoir of the Ten Years]. Vols. 1–4. Tokyo: Shinchōsha.

CHAPTER 7

The 1950s: Pax Americana and Japan's Postwar Resurgence

Takuya Sasaki and Hiroshi Nakanishi

JAPAN'S POSTWAR ROLE WITHIN AMERICA'S GLOBAL STRATEGY

During the 1950s, the United States was at the zenith of its power. By the end of the decade, its GNP was six to seven times that of the United Kingdom and West Germany and as much as 11 times that of Japan. America relied upon its overwhelming economic strength to pursue containment policies toward the Communist bloc, while maintaining and developing a free and multilateral trade system through the General Agreement on Tariffs and Trade (GATT) in the West; as the leader of the Free World, the United States had extended the "dollar and nuclear umbrella" to its allies (Ishii 1995).

Emerging victorious from the 1952 US presidential election was the former Supreme Allied Commander of Europe and national hero Dwight D. Eisenhower, who brought the Republican Party back to power for the first time in twenty years. Eisenhower advocated a more cost-effective containment strategy, conscious that a security strategy that was based on

T. Sasaki
College of Law and Politics, Rikkyo University, Toshima, Japan

H. Nakanishi
School of Government, Kyoto University, Kyoto, Japan

© The Author(s) 2017
M. Iokibe (ed.), T. Minohara (trans. ed.), *The History of US–Japan Relations*, DOI 10.1007/978-981-10-3184-7_7

127

NSC 68 would contribute to a large fiscal deficit. The US involvement in the Korean War had already forced its annual defense expenditure to triple to $50 billion, and this level of expenditure was unlikely to be reduced in the immediate future. With the fiscal deficit placing a significant burden on the economy, Eisenhower was firm in his belief that the United States needed to establish a new long-term security strategy for the Cold War that would not undermine the liberal and democratic institutions at home (Sasaki 2008).

In August 1952—and just after the conclusion of the Japanese occupation—Truman had approved NSC 135/1 to replace NSC 68. This document confirmed the strategic importance of West Germany and Japan, advancing the basic idea that the strength of the Free World rested upon closer cooperation in Western Europe and that a "strong and friendly" Japan would serve as a "natural anchor" for the defense of the West in the Pacific.

Eisenhower himself was fully aware of the strategic significance of Japan and his position was shared by his new secretary of state, John Foster Dulles, who prided himself as being the "father" of the US–Japan Security Treaty. NSC 162/2, the basic national security statement of massive retaliation approved by Eisenhower in October 1953, argued for the reduction of the US national defense expenditure by increasing the reliance on nuclear weapons and cutting the number of army troops as a way to establish a "great equation" between military and economic strength. This security strategy, known as the "New Look," led to a significant decrease in America's conventional forces, which meant that allies were to make up for any shortages of land forces (Lee 1996). Consequently, the United States pursued the policy of strengthening Japan by rebuilding its economic and military power.

Expectations and Concerns toward a Post-Occupation Japan

The Truman administration had laid out his vision for post-occupation Japan in NSC 125/2, adopted in August 1952, which called for the reinforcement of Japan's defense and an increase of its presence in the arena of international relations. However, NSC 125/2 also revealed US pessimism about the future of US–Japan relations; the document showed anxiety not only that Japan might eventually drift away from the United States and opt for a path that tended toward neutralism, but also that Japan might attempt to "take advantage of the United States–USSR conflict," seeking closer relations with China and the Soviet Union as it increasingly sought to "achieve an independent role in Far Eastern affairs." NSC 125/2 anticipated that Japan would pursue rapprochement with communists Asia in order to serve Japanese interests by allowing it to restore its influence on the continent of Asia and regain the advantages that came from trade with China. The main points from this document were inherited by Eisenhower, who approved NSC 125/6 the following June and reemphasized the importance of Japan's defense enhancement, but he was also more conscious than his predecessor that this should be "consistent with" Japan's economic capabilities.

By early October 1953, Eisenhower had become more insistent that Japan should bolster its ground forces, asserting that while Japan's constitution denied it the right to possess any military capabilities, the time had come "when they must become responsible for their own internal defense, even though to avoid frightening our other friends in the Pacific." In December, Dulles's dissatisfaction with the lag in the Japanese rearmament program turned to outright anger when Tokyo indicated their hope that the recently concluded US–Japan agreement on the reversion of the Amami Islands was going to lead Washington to return Okinawa to Japan. Dulles complained bitterly that the Japanese were "constantly asking more and more from the US, without feeling any obligation" to promote the security of Asia, emphasizing that he was "frankly disappointed" with Japan's lack of interest in contributing to its own security, particularly in comparison with Germany. The Mutual Security Assistance (MSA) agreement concluded in March 1954 was Washington's leverage to encourage the rearmament of Japan, but still Japan's defense forces were not regarded to have attained an adequate level.

NSC 125/6 recognized that Japan's ongoing economic survival was an issue of critical importance for the security of America in the long term, although its assessment of Japan's potential to reverse its economic fortunes was pessimistic. As a means of supporting the development of Japan's economy, the United States sought to assure Japanese accession to the GATT, to negotiate with Japan for tariff reductions "as soon as developments with respect to the Reciprocal Trade Agreements Act permit," as well as to refrain from placing restrictions on Japanese exports to the United States, encourage more investment flows into Japan, and support the funding of Japan through the World Bank and the Export–Import Bank. Washington had already advocated for Japan's membership to the World Bank and the IMF, and in April 1953 it extended most-favored-nation (MFN) status to the country.

During this period the United States also eagerly opened its markets to Japan. At a time when America was overseeing strict controls on exports to the Communist bloc nations through the Coordinating Committee for Multilateral Export Controls (COCOM) and the China Committee (CHINCOM), Eisenhower made statements approving of Japan engaging in limited trade with China as long as the country did not become economically dependent on its regional neighbor. The United States encouraged Japan to tap into the Southeast Asian market through reparation treaties, but as it was still too early to expect much from that market, the most reliable way of rebuilding Japan's economy was to allow it access to the US market (Shimizu 2001).

The Declining Leadership of Prime Minister Yoshida

On April 28, 1952, the San Francisco Peace Treaty came into effect, the Allied occupation came to an end, and Japan officially regained its independence. At first glance, this seemed to bring about few changes since Yoshida Shigeru remained in power and US troops were still stationed in Japan. However, in reality Japan immediately became painfully aware of the weighty responsibilities of independence as it faced challenges on numerous fronts: domestic politics, the economy, and foreign relations.

Within the realm of domestic politics, the power base of the Yoshida government had dwindled. Conservative politicians who had been purged from public life during the occupation period had begun to reenter politics, and many of them opted not to support Yoshida. In the Liberal Party, veteran politicians such as Hatoyama Ichirō, Ishibashi Tanzan, Kōno Ichirō, and Miki Bukichi all supported the anti-Yoshida movement, a stance that led to severe internal party struggles. Outside the Liberal Party, Ashida Hitoshi led the National Democratic Party to greater prominence and later formed the Reform Party (RP) with fellow former diplomat Shigemitsu Mamoru. Until the Liberal Democratic Party (LDP) was created in November 1955, a process of alignment and realignment occurred constantly within the conservative camp. Through two general elections in October 1952 and April 1953, Yoshida's political base diminished further and he ended up leading a minority government.

In addition to the domestic political turmoil, a sense of unease among the Japanese was heightened by concerns regarding the future prospects for the economy. The huge orders for supplies and services to Japan from forces fighting in the Korean War, the so-called "special procurements," which had been a boon for the Japanese economy, were set to end following the signing of the armistice agreement in July 1953. This led to a national debate about how to tackle the trade deficit that these special procurements had temporarily alleviated.

With regard to the issue of foreign policy, Japan was facing the difficult challenge of making its reentry back into international society. The United States pressed for Japan to resume its presence in the international arena, keen to make Japan a dependable ally of the West. However, most of the world was still wary of Japan, and while America acted as a mediator for negotiations between Japan and its former possessions and enemies following the conclusion of the peace treaty, it refrained from applying pressure to facilitate these negotiations. A case in point is the negotiations between Japan and South Korea begun in February 1952 under the urging of the United States, but that were soon suspended in October 1953 after just three rounds of meetings. Korea's right to claim war reparations had derailed the delicate negotiations, and contrary to American wishes Japan similarly struggled to make headway with negotiations with the nations of Southeast Asia. Negotiations over joining GATT also hit a roadblock.

Ultimately, Yoshida's basic policy regarding Japan's independence was to rely on the country's bilateral relationship with the United States. Therefore, the MSA agreement issue became a key litmus test for this diplomatic line. Supporters of Yoshida sought to adopt a policy of fiscal austerity while securing MSA in the form of economic assistance. The government, which was supported by the interests of mainstream business circles, also placed priority on entering the markets of advanced nations by joining the GATT while simultaneously delaying rearmament as long as possible. In response, there were calls urging proactive rearmament, led by figures such as Shigemitsu and Ashida of the Reform Party, the former declaring in July 1953 that Japan should "establish a self-defense force and accept MSA." In contrast, the RP and LDP were both more or less opposed to any MSA; the former sought economic aid from the United States, while the latter called for an independent economy centered on trade with China (Nakakita 2002). While Yoshida's political base was shrinking, he still managed to maintain leadership by manipulating the factions opposing it and securing the support of the United States by slowly conceding to American demands.

From summer 1953 into the following year, Yoshida also made the effort to secure MSA by negotiating with the Reform Party and gaining its approval in reorganizing the National Security Force into a Self-Defense Force (*Jieitai*) and adopting policies that would enhance Japan's self-defense capacity. In addition to these efforts, Yoshida sent his trusted lieutenant Ikeda to the United States in October 1953 as a special envoy to engage in talks with Assistant Secretary of State Water S. Robertson. Washington was dissatisfied with the size of rearmament proposed by the Japanese, but felt that it had little choice but to accept these terms in order to establish Japan as an independent nation while also further strengthening its relations with the United States. In this context both parties signed the MSA agreement in March 1954 and in fall of the same year, Washington arranged funding from the US Export–Import Bank and the World Bank.

Despite this, the international balance of payments deficit brought on by the end of the Korean special procurements had led to a recession. In March 1954, a Japanese fishing vessel and its crew were exposed to high levels of radiation near the atomic test site at Bikini Atoll. This episode, known as the "Lucky Dragon incident," was the subject of sensational reporting by the Japanese media, which labeled it the "third atomic bombing of Japan." In August, Ikeda, then the Liberal Party secretary-general, declared America's rollback policy a "failure" with reference to the cessation in the hostilities in Vietnam. This also tacitly implied Japanese willingness to recognize the Beijing government. Such incidents led to a sense that Japan was drifting away from the United States and shifting more toward a position of neutrality; no doubt a sign of Yoshida's waning political leadership.

The sense of crisis surrounding this series of events was exacerbated by the opinions of the US ambassador to Japan at that time, John Moore Allison. Prior to this, he had assuaged Dulles's frustration regarding Japan's lack of progress in developing its defense capabilities; at the end of August, however, he wrote a telegram to the State Department expressing his increasing disenchantment with the Yoshida government. In his view Yoshida had merely "given lip service" to Washington's belief that Japan was "potentially a strong ally" and that Japan possessed "no basic convictions for or against the free world or communism."

With confidence in the Yoshida government also diminishing within Japan, the business leaders called for the conservative forces to rally together in order to establish a new political party. In the end, the anti-Yoshida forces such as Hatoyama, Shigemitsu, Miki, Kōno, Kishi, and Ishibashi came together to oust Yoshida from power. Seemingly unconcerned with these developments, Yoshida traveled to Europe and the United States, proposing his own vision of a world in which the

United States, Britain, and Japan would cooperate together to implement anti-communist movements in Southeast Asia and to draw China away from the Soviets. However, the Western nations were indifferent toward Yoshida as by this time he had lost his domestic power base and was also struggling to normalize relations with South Korea and other Southeast Asian nations (Chen 2000). Meanwhile, the anti-Yoshida faction established the Japan Democratic Party, and, upon his return to Japan, he came under immense pressure to step down. Yoshida stubbornly attempted to hold on to power, attempting to turn the situation around by dissolving the Diet. Finally, in December he succumbed to severe criticism from his own party and resigned the premiership as well as his position as the president of the Liberal Party. Hatoyama Ichirō, the president of the Democratic Party, was promptly appointed as prime minister.

EXPANDING JAPAN'S DIPLOMATIC HORIZON: EMERGENCE OF A NEW STRATEGY TOWARD JAPAN

Washington did not exhibit any particular response to Yoshida's resignation; it was, however, unable to conceal its concern over the appointment of Hatoyama, who was bent on improving relations with China and the Soviet Union, with a strong accent on trade. Deputy Assistant Secretary of State for Far Eastern Affairs William J. Sebald predicted the "brevity" of Hatoyama's time in office, going on to say that "unlike Yoshida he is not regarded as 'pro-American' or 'reactionary.'" He added that the United States could expect Hatoyama's diplomacy to have greater focus on improving relations with the communist orbit than with the Free World. Ambassador Allison's assessment was even harsher, and he made no attempt to conceal his distrust of Hatoyama's diplomacy. In his report to the State Department in late March 1955, Allison pointed to the Hatoyama government's constant neglect of US interest in resolving pending bilateral issues while it "made continued concessions to [the] Commie orbit" such as issuing visas to the China trade mission.

The changing nature of the Cold War had become increasingly apparent by the mid-1950s with the military balance that had effectively been established between the United States and the Soviet Union. It was also highly significant that the new Soviet leadership that took power after Stalin's death in 1953 had embarked on a diplomatic offensive to improve relations with the West. Moreover, armistice agreements had been reached in both Korea and Vietnam. As global tensions eased, the focus of the Cold War shifted from military to non-military areas, and consequently the importance of economic competition became increasingly apparent. The Geneva Summit in summer 1955 epitomized this new trend, as participating political leaders pledged to address outstanding issues through discussion, rather than force. This shift was reflected in America's "New Look" strategy, which advocated limiting military expenditure as well as maintaining a sound economy.

These changes encouraged Allison to urge Washington to reexamine its policy toward Japan with a more long-term perspective, as expressed in his policy paper, an effort at "a local 'new look' at our policies and tactics in Japan." In early January 1955 he recommended that the United States would need to shift the emphasis of its policy over the immediate period from "defense" to one of "economics and internal security," and it was only through this that "a stronger and, very possibly, a more cooperative Japan" would emerge. He contended that the order of priorities should be: political stability brought by the "unified conservative force" that could maintain a strong government; economic stability achieved through their effective handling of economic issues; and, finally, the rebuilding of Japan's military capability. In the initial period, he sought for Japan to maintain a military capacity commensurate with its economic strength. It was proposed that the United States should progressively take measures such as the phased withdrawal of American troops from Japan so as to increase Japan's awareness of its responsibility to defend itself. Allison proposed treating Japan as a "potential first-class power" and an "equal partner," as Japan was becoming increasingly sensitive to the fact that America was treating it as a "second-class" nation. Dulles, receptive of Allison's recommendations, admitted that Japan was a "desperately poor country" and should not be "pressed too hard to reestablish a large military force until its economy had grown more healthy."

In the same vein as Allison's recommendations, William Leonhart, the first secretary at the Tokyo embassy, acknowledged that Washington's hopes that Japan could simultaneously pursue political and economic stabilization and defense enhancement had produced only limited success. The new thinking was that it was more crucial for the conservative forces to come together to create a "strong and stable Japanese government" and generate economic stability than it was to build defensive strength. Leonhart also suggested a revision of the US–Japan Security Treaty so that it would become a "reciprocal and mutual" arrangement.

The review of US policies toward Japan led by the American embassy in Japan came to fruition in the form of NSC 5516/1, which was adopted in April 1955. The document pointed out that although Japan was heavily dependent on the United States—economically, militarily, and diplomatically—it would seek to reduce such reliance and pursue a more independent course of action in the future, including expanding relations with the communist regimes. With Japan's increased strength, US–Japan relations would need to be redefined in terms of their "common purpose, mutual interests, and working partnership." A strong Japan was a highly desirable goal that was to be attained through "the development of an effective, moderate conservative government" and the United States should "refrain from applying pressure upon Japan to increase its military strength to the prejudice of political and economic stability."

Hatoyama's Diplomatic Initiatives

Hatoyama criticized Yoshida's policy of "following in the footsteps of America" and advocated "autonomous diplomacy" (*jishu gaikō*). Thus, Hatoyama approached a number of countries, including both the Soviet Union and China. However, the conservative politicians supporting the Hatoyama government soon realized the difficulty of ignoring the wishes of Washington in pursuing its "autonomous diplomacy," and behind closed doors it was agreed that policies needed to be adjusted to realign better with the United States. Thus, the new government announced its policy of focusing on improving relations with the Communist bloc domestically, but set forth an anti-communist stance externally. Hatoyama also repeatedly emphasized to Allison his "strong personal intention to firmly maintain the close relationship between Japan and America that had been established by the Yoshida cabinet" (Chen 2000).

The litmus test of the delicate balance between "autonomous diplomacy" and "cooperation with the US" was the Bandung Conference, which convened in Indonesia in April 1955. Hatoyama was eager to participate from the perspective of pursuing a more autonomous diplomacy, while Foreign Minister Shigemitsu Mamoru and other senior bureaucrats of the foreign ministry were hesitant about Japan's attendance from the perspective of US–Japan relations. Tokyo informed Washington that it wished to consult with the United States over this issue and that it had no intention of using the conference as an opportunity for seeking closer relations with Communist China. The United States adopted a policy of supporting its allies' participation from the point of view of opposing the "peaceful offensive" of the communist forces, and thus it did not object to Japan's participation. At the meeting, Japan avoided getting involved in political issues, and instead placed emphasis on economic matters, resulting in a somewhat restrained counterattack to the Soviet "peaceful offensive."

The limit to Japan's autonomous diplomacy was clearly demonstrated by its difficulty in attaining membership in international organizations. Even though backed by the United States, it was not until September 1955 that Japan was given membership in the GATT, and 14 countries invoked GATT Article 35, thereby withholding most-favored-nation status from Japan (Akaneya 1992). Japan's effort to join the United Nations was also fraught with obstacles. As US–Soviet relations had improved, reflected by the convening of the Geneva Summit, 16 nations were newly admitted to the UN in one sweep during the 1955 General Assembly session. Although initially listed as a country to be admitted during this period, Japan's accession to the UN was postponed that year as the Republic of China opposed the membership of Mongolia and the Soviet Union retaliated by opposing Japan's entry.

Hatoyama unilaterally declared initiatives to build up Japan's defense capacity, but this was to be accomplished by maintaining the current levels of defense expenditures, an approach that made many in Washington skeptical of the Hatoyama cabinet. This also implied that Japan would decrease its share of the cost of maintaining US troops stationed in Japan. While Washington ultimately granted Japan a 17.8 billion yen reduction in its defense contributions, the negotiations were difficult. Issues arose regarding the deployment of nuclear weapons in US bases across Japan. Shigemitsu, wishing to avoid an attack from the opposition, claimed untruthfully that the US troops in Japan possessed no nuclear weapons and that Japan had an agreement with the United States that no nuclear weapons would be brought into the country without Japan's consent (Sakamoto 2000).

The lack of unity within the Japanese government was reflected when Hatoyama sent Kōno Ichirō and Kishi Nobusuke to keep a watchful eye on Shigemitsu during his visit to the United States in late August 1955. One purpose of his visit was to propose the revision of the US–Japan Security Treaty. The exact content of his proposal has still not been completely disclosed, but it is very likely that he suggested changing the nature of the treaty so that it would become more of a bilateral mutual defense agreement. Moreover, it is probable that he requested a withdrawal of the

US armed forces within a period of six years, limitation on the use of the American bases only for the purpose of mutual defense, and the elimination of the share of defense expenses (Sakamoto 2000).

The United States turned a cold shoulder to this restrictive proposal as it would lose the ability to use its bases in Japan. While US forces in Korea were stationed exclusively for activities in the Korean peninsula, America was keen to maintain the US forces in Japan with a more global role in mind. Dulles warned Japan that if it wanted the bases to be used only in cases of mutual defense, then it would be necessary for Japan to dispatch its own Self Defense Forces overseas, which would require a revision of Japan's constitution. Shigemitsu responded by implying that mutual defense would be possible even under the current constitution, contradicting the position of his own government.

A general election under the Hatoyama government was held in February of that year, and while the conservatives continued to hold a dominant position over the progressives, it was clear that it would not be an easy feat to attain the two-thirds majority in the Diet required to revise the constitution. The Japanese political landscape was also changing as the Japan Communist Party recanted its policy of violent revolution, and in October the formerly divided socialist party agreed to reunite. On the conservative side, the Democratic Party and the Liberal Party merged to form the Liberal Democratic Party (LDP) in November.

Japan's Diplomacy toward the Communist Bloc

Eisenhower's skepticism about Hatoyama continued as the latter tried to negotiate the Soviet Union over the normalization of ties. Because the United States itself had diplomatic relations with the Soviet Union, it could not make any outward objection to Japan resuming relations with the Soviet Union, but it did urge Japan not to make any hasty concessions over territorial claims in an attempt to smooth the process.

However, when the negotiations started in Moscow in late July 1956, Shigemitsu suggested a peace treaty with the Soviet Union whereby Japan would "receive" only the Habomai Islands and Shikotan. An infuriated Dulles put a check on these developments and during talks with Shigemitsu in London in August, he warned that if the Soviet Union had sovereignty over the disputed islands, then this would imply that the United States had sovereignty over the Ryukyu Islands. In September, Dulles also handed an aide-mémoire to Japanese Ambassador to the

United States, Tani Masayuki, warning Japan not to make any imprudent compromises regarding territorial issues.

The aide-mémoire stated that "the San Francisco Peace Treaty—which conferred no rights upon the Soviet Union because it refused to sign—did not determine the sovereignty of the territories renounced by Japan," and left the question to be resolved by an international settlement. It also warned that by virtue of the San Francisco Peace Treaty, Japan did not "have the right to transfer sovereignty over the territories renounced by it therein." At the same time, it also stated that "after careful examination of the historical facts," the United States had concluded that the "islands of Etorofu and Kunashiri (along with the Habomai Islands and Shikotan which are a part of Hokkaido)" had "always been part of Japan proper and should in justice be acknowledged as under Japanese sovereignty" (Hosoya 2001).

Most likely, Shigemitsu's attempt to depart from the Japanese government's intentions during the negotiations with the Soviets would not have been accepted domestically, even if the United States had not intervened. At the same time, Washington's undivided support for the territorial claims that Japan had always asserted helped to deflect the force of Japanese nationalism away from the United States and toward the Soviet Union, empowering the receding Yoshida faction. When Hatoyama visited the Soviet Union in October, both parties set aside the territorial issue and signed a joint communiqué that resumed diplomatic relations between the two nations, to which the United States did not object. As a consequence, the Soviet Union withdrew its opposition to Japan joining the United Nations, and Japan was admitted as a member on December 1956; this event also benefited the United States.

In addition to resuming relations with the Soviet Union, Hatoyama initially hoped to build ties with Communist China as well. However, while Washington's basic policy toward Japan's relations with the Soviet Union was to refrain from objections so long as they did not harm the Free World, the United States openly voiced its disapproval of Japan's potential recognition of Communist China and rapprochement between Japan and China, as outlined in NSC 5516/1. These concerns played a large role in swaying Hatoyama to revise his position on China. Although he had stated directly after becoming prime minister that "both Communist and Nationalist China should be recognized as independent countries in their own right," Shigemitsu explained to the Diet that the government did not intend to recognize both governments as independent nations, and

Hatoyama reiterated that he had not used the term "recognize" in regards to the People's Republic of China.

However, Hatoyama also understood that resolving relations with China, a policy popular in both left-wing and business circles, would do more to create appeal for "independent diplomacy" than any approach to the Soviet Union, for which the Ministry of Foreign Affairs (MOFA) was also unenthusiastic. When ambassadorial-level talks between the United States and China began in August 1955, there was growing concern in Tokyo that a sudden change in America's policy toward China would place the Japanese government in an awkward position. To mitigate these fears, the United States reaffirmed the ongoing relevance of its "containment" policy toward China. Unpersuaded, as both the nationalist government and the communist government claimed to be the legitimate government of China—the United States recognized the former and the United Kingdom the latter—Japan tried to avoid the risk by seeking American affirmation in taking steps toward a "two Chinas" policy in order to protect the interests of both Japan and the United States.

Following on the heels of the joint communiqué between Japan and the Soviet Union, Japan became even keener to establish closer relations with China. The new government led by Ishibashi Tanzan—who achieved a surprise victory against Kishi Nobusuke, the most notable candidate in the LDP presidential election in the aftermath of Hatoyama's resignation in December 1956—was particularly eager to improve relations with China. However, Ishibashi was also careful not to allow Japan's policy toward China to destabilize relations with the United States. He therefore took the position that for the time being, Japan would merely seek the expansion of trade with China and resumption of diplomatic relations under "coordination with the United Nations and America and the other nations of the Free World" (Chen 2000). In the following year, the United States also shifted to a policy of compromise and tacitly approved the abolishment of the difference between COCOM's export controls to the Soviet Union and Eastern Europe, and CHINCOM's more severe export controls to China—the so-called "China differential"—which the Western allies, particularly the United Kingdom and Japan, had protested. A mere two months later, in February 1957, Ishibashi resigned due to ill health and was succeeded by Kishi.

Drifting Relations with Japan

Dulles' decision to reject Shigemitsu's proposal for revising the security treaty in summer 1955 was partially due to the fact that the United States still saw Japan as an undependable ally. The report on the progress of implementation of NSC 5516/1 approved in November 1955 noted that in the goals for Japan regarding "political stability and effective government, development of economic strength, and adequate defense capability" there had been "some progress although slower" than preferred. By this time Japan's economy had finally recovered from the recession following the end of Korean special procurements and was now well back on the path of recovery.

However, the NSC 5516/1 progress report of June 1956 warned that the ties between Japan and America were "wearing thin," and observed signs of decreased Japanese dependence on the United States and of more independent Japanese policies that were reflected in the resurgence of nationalism, a comfortable foreign exchange situation, and "drift" toward the communist continent. Washington entrusted Allison in Tokyo with the task of proposing the remedy for this issue. In September Allison drew up a report titled "A Fresh Start with Japan," in which he highlighted that while Japan's national strength was growing, the "sense of mutuality" that had been called for in NSC 5516/1 was not developing sufficiently, and that Japan was becoming increasingly dissatisfied over not being treated by the United States as an "equal partner with sovereignty." Allison identified a number of key areas of concern, including the revision of the Security Treaty, Asian economic development, US–Japan trade relations, Sino-Japan relations, and the release of Tokyo Tribunal war criminals.

In the first months of 1957, high officials in Washington pointed out the necessity of responding to Japan's dissatisfaction with the lack of mutuality and equality in its relations vis-à-vis the United States. Assistant Secretary of State for Far Eastern Affairs Robertson drew on Allison's report and advised that Washington should make "readjustments, including certain concessions, on a timely basis" in order "to increase the prestige of the Conservative government and reverse the Socialist trend," which was "essentially neutralist and to an extent anti-American." Among the issues, he emphasized the importance of revising "the present unmutual [*sic*] 'Security Treaty.'" Furthermore, Deputy Assistant Secretary of State for Far Eastern Affairs William J. Sebald agreed on these measures that would allow for the United States to maintain Japan as a "firm ally" in the Pacific. Special Assistant to the President for National Security Affairs Robert Cutler urged the US government to commit itself to improving US–Japan relations, which had seen a "steady deterioration" over the previous year. In late January, the situation became worse when an American soldier stationed in Japan shot and fatally wounded a wife of a Japanese farmer. This tragedy, which became known as the "Girard incident," further exacerbated the concerns of the Japanese conservatives and the American officials responsible for policy toward Japan (Ikeda 2004).

Treaty Revisions and the Beginning of a "New Era" in US–Japan Relations

With the policy debates on Japan gaining vigor, the United States embraced the formation of the new Kishi government in February 1957. Eisenhower had high praises for the political capability and strong anti-communist stance of Kishi. It was no longer of any concern that Kishi had once been a cabinet minister in the Tōjō war cabinet. The new US Ambassador to Tokyo Douglas MacArthur II—the nephew of the general—anticipated that Kishi would be "easier to work with than Ishibashi," and introduced him as "at last an able leader of Japan," while Secretary of State Dulles informed President Eisenhower that he considered Kishi to be the "strongest Government leader to emerge in postwar Japan."

Shortly after becoming prime minister, Kishi met with MacArthur and expressed his view that the recent rise in anti-American sentiment among the Japanese public was grounded in Japan's aversion to war as well as the country's "subordinate position" under the existing security treaty. He thus proposed both countries work together to reconfirm the purpose of the treaty and that a mutual agreement be reached regarding the deployment and use of US troops stationed in Japan. Kishi felt that this would form the core of the revised treaty as it would also clarify the relationship between the treaty and the United Nations Charter. He also suggested that Japan would bolster its defense capacity so that the number of US troops could be reduced much further. Kishi was envisaging the complete withdrawal of US land forces and the return of several US bases to Japanese administrative control. In regard to territorial issues, he proposed the return of Okinawa and the Ogasawara Islands within ten years.

After the meeting, MacArthur wrote to Dulles that the United States had reached a "turning point" in its relations with Japan and that it was necessary to put those relations "on the same basis of equal partnership" that it had with other allies. Although Dulles's response was cautious, he acknowledged that the period of "drift[ing]" was over, and, with Kishi in power, the time was ripe for Washington to take the initiative and set to work toward a "mutually satisfactory security arrangement" that would replace the current security treaty. It was clear to Dulles that a "strong, cooperative Japan" was "fundamental and essential" in maintaining US interests in East Asia. In order to do this, however, it was first necessary to carry out a "most careful study and preparation" that would ensure that the present security relationship with Japan would not be jeopardized. Dulles was also careful to note that the return of Okinawa and the Ogasawara Islands would be infeasible as long as there remained "threat and tension" in the region.

Making America the Cornerstone of Japanese Diplomacy

Kishi sought to follow the pro-US course initiated by Yoshida, but at the same time sought to appear to the domestic public that he made the choice independently, unlike Yoshida. For this purpose Kishi took a staunch anti-communist stance. On his visit to the United States in June 1957, Kishi set forth several key issues that would need to be addressed in the new security treaty. Although Kishi's requests were not completely consistent with what Washington deemed desirable, it adhered to the position that it would honor the request for a treaty revision and cooperate toward the achievement of that goal. Concerns that Japanese nationalistic sentiment would vector (force) Japan toward a neutralist stance had prodded the State Department to reconsider its Japan policy. This development was also demonstrated by the fact that the joint communiqué by Eisenhower and Kishi following the talks included the announcement that the US ground combat forces stationed in Japan would be withdrawn (Sakamoto 2000).

However, at this juncture, Washington was not yet ready to make any tangible proposals in responding to the issues raised by Tokyo and the joint communiqué only recognized the need for establishing a committee to study these key issues. However, the most significant outcome of the bilateral talks was that the United States now took the position that it saw Japan as a trustworthy partner, as reflected in Dulles's comments, which enthusiastically praised Kishi as a prime minister in whom the United States could "place [its] trust," who was "prepared to genuinely devote himself to the principles of the Free World" (Schaller 1997).

Recognizing the need to combine the principles of independent diplomacy with the realities of cooperation with America, Kishi also sought to clarify Japan's basic approach to foreign policy by hastening the reformulation of the "Basic Policy for National Defense" (*Kokubō no kihon hōshin*) and the First Defense Build-Up Program (*Daichi-ji bōeiryoku seibi keikaku*) prior to his trip to the United States. The "Basic Policy on National Defense" positioned the US–Japan Security Treaty system as the core of Japanese national defense, while the defense build-up program called for a 180,000-man ground SDF instead of bolstering the air force as had been strongly advocated by the pro-rearmament factions in Japan (Nakajima 2006).

In September 1957, the first edition of the MOFA diplomatic bluebook demonstrated Japan's desire to seek a foreign policy that was independent while also consistent with US–Japan interests. Japanese diplomacy relied on three basic principles: emphasis on the United Nations; cooperation with the Free World; and maintaining a firm stance as a member of Asia. All three were also embraced by Kishi. In October 1957, Japan was chosen as a non-permanent member of the UN Security Council. During the US intervention in the 1958 Lebanon crisis, Japan made a concerted effort to demonstrate its independent posture in the UN, calling for the expansion of the UN observation forces in Lebanon, while at the same time coordinating with the United States. Kishi aimed to impress upon the Asian region Japan's capacity for leadership, and before his trip to the United States, he visited several countries promoting his concept of a Southeast Asian Development Fund. Kishi's strategy for economic reentry included war reparations payments, and treaties addressing this matter were concluded with Indonesia in late 1957.

Negotiations in Revising the Security Treaty

In the late 1950s, the "missile gap" helped portray an image of the superiority of the Soviet socialist system, and in the United States there were growing calls for a large-scale buildup of armaments. While Eisenhower responded calmly and chose not to embark on a path toward an arms race, he was worried over the psychological impact on the Free World of the Soviet military and technological successes. Thus, solidarity with its allies increased in importance. In the context of policy toward Japan, this meant that the Eisenhower administration had to face up to the issue of revising the security treaty and deal with it head-on.

Dulles had been deeply concerned by growing anti-US sentiment in Okinawa since 1956. His concern was further heightened following the election of the anti-American candidate, Kaneshi Saichi, as mayor of Naha City, the prefectural capital of Okinawa, in mid-January 1958. Dulles instructed Ambassador MacArthur to make policy recommendations on Japan and Okinawa as he deemed that the US posture needed revision and should take advantage of Kishi who enjoyed a solid political base.

MacArthur's policy proposal was clear: in order to maintain close ties with Japan, the United States needed to revise the "one-sided" treaty and conclude a "truly mutual security treaty." To overcome the impossibility of concluding a mutual treaty due to Japanese constitutional constraints, MacArthur argued that if the United States were "to have Japan as a partner and thus be able to continue to use certain of her military and logistical facilities"—which were highly important for America—it was "not essential" for Japan to be committed to come to America's aid "except within a fairly limited area." It was sufficient for the treaty area to cover "all territory under the administrative control of Japan" and the "island territories in the Western Pacific" under the administration of America. In essence, MacArthur was calling for the US government to adopt a constructive and flexible position regarding the conditions of mutuality, rather than demanding an unrealistic revision of the Japanese Constitution as a prerequisite. He urged Dulles to initiate negotiations given that Kishi's political base was strong in aftermath of his victory in the recent general elections.

On July 30, 1958, MacArthur sounded out Foreign Minister Fujiyama Aichirō as to Japan's position regarding revising the security treaty, inquiring whether Japan sought "adjustments without changing the present security treaty," or rather a "new mutual security treaty for the 'Japan area.'" Kishi agreed to the latter. On September 8, upon receiving word of Kishi's response, Dulles approved the negotiations to move forward in revising the treaty. When Fujiyama visited the United States on September 11, Dulles informed him that the United States desired to enter into negotiations. The wheels were set in motion; a formal proposal was submitted to Japan and negotiations commenced in Tokyo on October 4.

Public Outrage Regarding Treaty Revision

By the time negotiations on treaty revision were in full motion, Kishi's political support was eroding rapidly. Anticipating the unrest that would follow Security Treaty revision, in October 1958 Kishi submitted a bill to the Diet for the revision of the Act on the Performance of Police Duties. However, the bill unleashed negative memories of the war, and reduced public support for Kishi, as many Japanese still viewed him to be a wartime leader, while further eroding his clout within the LDP.

Difficulties also arose in foreign relations. Kishi was careful to separate politics and economics in his China policy and thus the signing of the Fourth Sino-Japan trade agreement in March 1958 was based on the latter. But both the nationalist and communist governments became wary of Kishi's diplomacy; the former strongly opposed the establishment of a trade mission to the communist government by Japan, and the latter halted all economic relations with Japan following Kishi's visit to Taiwan and an incident involving the desecration of the Chinese flag in Nagasaki in 1957. Negotiations between Japan and Korea also hit a roadblock and broke down amid the mass repatriation scheme of sending Korean residents in Japan (*zainichi chosenjin*)—including a significant number who were originally from the South—to North Korea. Furthermore, the ratification of a war reparations agreement concluded with South Vietnam in May 1959 caused considerable tension in the Diet, which diminished Kishi's grasp on power even further.

This allowed the opposition to go on the offensive. In the May 1958 general election, the JSP had gained more than a third of the seats, enough to prevent any revision of the constitution. As the JSP was not able to increase its majority and the JCP had remained at just one seat, however, there was an attempt on the part of the JSP to expand influence in the party by ensuring that the socialists and communists would work together (Hara 2000). As such, the opposition stepped up its offensive against Kishi and gradually succeeded in linking the Security Treaty revision with other domestic political issues. Even within the LDP, Kishi's grip on power was unraveling as figures such as Ikeda Hayato, Miki Takeo, and Kōno Ichirō all became openly critical of the prime minister.

The bilateral negotiations to revise the US–Japan Security Treaty took time to conclude but it culminated finally, in January 1960, in a much more equal treaty. The wording of Clause 5 was changed from "an armed attack in the Pacific directed against the territories or areas under the administrative control of [either] Party," as MacArthur had proposed, to "an armed attack against either Party in the territories under the administration of Japan," and Clause 6 was revised so that the United States could use Japanese bases for the purpose of contributing to "the maintenance of international peace and security in the Far East." The treaty revision also included the clarification of the US obligation to defend Japan, treaty terms were stipulated (ten years), and other clauses in the former treaty that had symbolized the inequality between the two countries were all removed. Moreover, a system of prior consultation was introduced in which Washington would consult with Tokyo in advance in the event that any significant changes to the deployment and equipment, including the introduction of nuclear weapons on Japanese soil, were to be implemented with the armed forces.

However, with his domestic political power base disappearing, Kishi was forced to tackle the issue of revising the Administrative Agreement, something that Washington was hoping to avoid. The asymmetrical nature of the arrangement between the United States and Japan—Japan providing the facilities in the form of the US bases, while America provided the troops, positioning its forces in Japan to defend Japan and contribute to the interests of security in East Asia—actually became more pronounced in the new treaty. Below the surface there was friction between the Japanese, who wished to make the obligations required in maintaining the alliance as limited as possible, and the Americans, whose primary concern was to ensure that the alliance would operate smoothly in times of need. There were also a number of other sticking points such as the question of whether or not the "introduction" of nuclear weapons into Japan included ships that were docking and/or transiting Japanese ports (Hosoya 2001; Sotooka 2001; Sakamoto 2000).

Kishi's Resignation and the Formation of a New US Policy toward Japan

Kishi visited the United States in January 1960 to sign the new US–Japan Security Treaty and the Status of Forces Agreement (SOFA). It was agreed that President Eisenhower would also visit Japan, assuming that Kishi would finish the ratification process prior to the president's visit. However, the Diet deliberations on the ratification of the treaty were thrown into confusion by tough questions from members of the JSP. The JSP also became more active outside of the Diet, mobilizing labor unions and university student protests to oppose the new treaty. With the date of Eisenhower's visit approaching, Kishi took the drastic measure of ramming the treaty through the Diet in the hours just before dawn of May 20. This sparked a massive anti-treaty demonstration in which protestors attempted to storm the Diet on June 15.

With the situation becoming ever tenser, Tokyo became increasingly concerned about maintaining domestic public order during Eisenhower's visit. Thus Kishi had no recourse but to tender his resignation in exchange for the ratification of the new Security Treaty. Once the treaty had been ratified, Kishi promptly announced his intention of resigning on June 23.

Although Kishi's goal of achieving equality between the United States and Japan was supported by Washington, it failed to garner support at home.

While the opposition toward the Security Treaty was gaining momentum in Japan, a new document that outlined American policies toward Japan, NSC 6008/1, was approved in June 1960. It pointed out that on the economic front, Japan was not only the second-largest export market for the United States, but also the largest purchaser of American agricultural products, while the United States was the largest importer of Japanese products. The document expected that in the 1960s Japan would continue to maintain a solid pro-US stance while playing a more active role internationally, particularly in the area of economic development. It also opposed the decision of the United Kingdom and other countries to invoke Article 35 of the GATT against Japan, and called for further inflow of Japanese capital and technological assistance to developing countries. It was concluded that Japan's "international orientation" should allow it to "play a role of increasing importance in international affairs," and be "a constructive international force," as long it was committed to maintaining strong ties with the United States. Further, Japan's contribution to the Free World would be "principally as an economic force and as a moderating influence on the Afro-Asian area" and the availability of US logistic facilities and military bases in the country would "contribute significantly to Free World military strength in the Pacific."

While Washington was clearly shocked by the anti-security treaty riots, Ambassador MacArthur was relatively calm over the situation. He did not believe amicable US–Japan relations had been critically wounded as a result of the demonstrations. From MacArthur's perspective, the anti-security treaty movement was not so much about anti-Americanism as it was about the sheer unpopularity of Kishi. Tokyo had been so inept in its explanation of the treaty that there was still very "little understanding" by the Japanese people over the treaty's exact provisions or its real significance for Japan. "Confusion" over what the treaty was all about and Kishi's failure "to understand public opinion and his arbitrary actions combined with the fact that he had been in the Tojo cabinet" was what ultimately brought about his downfall.

BIBLIOGRAPHY

Akaneya, Tatsuo. 1992. *Nihon no Gatto kanyū mondai* [Japan's GATT Accession Problem]. Tokyo: University of Tokyo Press.

Chen, Zhao-bin. 2000. *Sengo Nihon no Chugoku seisaku* [Policy Toward China in Postwar Japan]. Tokyo: University of Tokyo Press.

Hara, Yoshihisa. 2000. *Sengo-shi no naka no Nihon Shakaitō* [The Japan Socialist Party in Postwar History]. Tokyo: Chūōkōron-shinsha.

Hosoya, Chihiro. 2001. Nichibei anpo taisei no seiritsu to Yoshida rosen [The Establishment of the Japan-US Security System and the Yoshida Course]. In *Nihon to Amerika* [Japan and America], Nichi-Bei sengo-shi henshūiinkai. Tokyo: Japan Times.

Ikeda, Shintarō. 2004. *Nichibei dōmei no seiji-shi* [Political History of the Japan–US Alliance]. Tokyo: Kokusai Shoin.

Ishii, Osamu. 1995. Nichibei pātonāshippu e no dōtei [The Road to Japan–US Partnership]. In *Nichibei kankei-tsūshi* [A Complete History of US–Japan Relations], ed. Hosoya Chihiro. Tokyo: University of Tokyo Press.

Lee, Jong Won. 1996. *Higashi Ajia reisen to Kan-Bei-Nichi kankei* [US–Korean Relations and Japan in East Asia's Cold War]. Tokyo: University of Tokyo Press.

Nakajima, Shingo. 2006. *Sengo Nihon no bōei seisaku* [Postwar Japan's Defense Policy]. Tokyo: Keio University Press.

Nakakita, Kōji. 2002. *1955-nen-taisei no seiritsu* [The Establishment of the 1955 System in Japanese Politics]. Tokyo: University of Tokyo Press.

Sakamoto, Kazuya. 2000. *Nichibei dōmei no kizuna* [The Bond of the Japan–US Alliance]. Tokyo: Yūhikaku Publishing.

Sasaki, Takuya. 2008. *Aizenhawā seiken no fūjikome seisaku* [The Containment Policy of the Eisenhower Administration]. Tokyo: Yuhikaku Publishing.

Schaller, Michael. 1997. *Altered States*. New York: Oxford University Press.

Shimizu, Sayuri. 2001. *Creating People of Plenty*. Kent: Kent State University Press.

Sotooka, Hidetoshi. 2001. Datsusenryō to reisen [The End of the Occupation and the Cold War]. In *Nichibei dōmei hanseiki* [A Half-Century of the Japan–US Alliance], ed. Sotooka Hidetoshi, Honda Masaru, and Miura Toshiaki. Tokyo: Asahi Shimbunsha.

CHAPTER 8

The 1960s: Japan's Economic Rise and the Maturing of the Partnership

Makoto Iokibe and Takuya Sasaki

The Opportunities and Realities of a New Era

The world had barely recovered from the ashes of World War II when it found itself dragged into the Cold War and its attendant rivalry. After political maneuvering in the form of major events such as the Berlin Crisis, and a direct military confrontation in Korea, the nature of the Cold War began to take on the shape of a more established and stable system, and an all-out war between the United States and the Soviet Union appeared less likely. In fact, the successful launch of Sputnik by the Soviet Union paved the way for a less dangerous way to compete over which of the two systems was superior. Under strong leadership during the 1960s, the United States rapidly rose to meet this new challenge. The beginning of the new era—aptly termed the "Golden Sixties"—brought a burst of fresh energy to America. President Kennedy's promise of a dynamic and pro-active leadership appealed to many Americans as a break from President

M. Iokibe
Prefectural University of Kumamoto, Kumamoto, Japan

Hyogo Earthquake Memorial 21st Century Research Institute, Kobe, Japan

T. Sasaki
College of Law and Politics, Rikkyo University, Tokyo, Japan

© The Author(s) 2017
M. Iokibe (ed.), T. Minohara (trans. ed.), *The History of US–Japan Relations*, DOI 10.1007/978-981-10-3184-7_8

Eisenhower, whose defensive stance toward the challenges set forth by the Soviet Union was perceived as detrimental to America's prestige.

Kennedy selected the "best and the brightest" as his core cabinet members and aides (Halberstam 1972), and appointed top intellectuals such as George F. Kennan and John Kenneth Galbraith to serve as ambassadors to key nations. Among them, Harvard professor Edwin O. Reischauer was appointed as the new ambassador to Japan. Born in Tokyo to missionary parents, Reischauer was one of the most respected Japan experts in the country. Immediately after the mass demonstrations and riots that had erupted out of fierce protest against the 1960 US–Japan Security Treaty, Reischauer had published an article entitled "The Broken Dialogue with Japan." He argued vigorously that the recent disturbances were in fact the stark reflection of a gap in understanding that existed between Americans and Japanese on many levels. After assuming his post in Tokyo, Reischauer actively pursued dialogue with influential figures in various circles, including members of the two major opposition parties, the Japan Socialist and Democratic Socialist Parties, as well as the labor unions, academic circles, and the Japanese press. The striking debut of a young president, along with the proactive engagement by Reischauer and his charming Japanese wife, who hailed from a prominent political family, instilled a sense among the people of Japan that a new era was blossoming in relations with America.

The 1960s represented a significant turning point for Japan. The unification of the Liberal Party and the Democratic Party in 1955 led to a period of sharp political division between the two main parties—the conservatives on one hand and the left-wing socialists on the other. The "1955 system," as it became known, was further exacerbated by the fact that the conservative LDP government was led by right-leaning advocates of constitutional revision and rearmament such as Hatoyama Ichirō and Kishi Nobusuke. The campaign against the security treaty had not only pointed out the treaty's defects; it had also served as a progressive spring board to the enlargement of postwar democracy as well as a rejection of the traditional nationalism apparently represented by Prime Minister Kishi, a former authoritarian bureaucrat-turned-politician and a ranking member of the Tōjō Hideki cabinet during the Pacific War. The upheaval of 1960 undermined both Kishi and the socialist forces and ushered in a very different kind of political leadership in the form of Ikeda Hayato, who succeeded Kishi as prime minister in spring 1960.

The Ikeda cabinet first urgently needed to alleviate the confrontation between the conservatives and socialists that had hitherto overshadowed

Japan's politics. This required patching up the wounds from past domestic political disputes. Ōhira Masayoshi and Miyazawa Kiichi, two of the prime minister's closest advisors, produced the slogan "tolerance and patience" (*kanyō to nintai*), and Ikeda himself launched a high-rate economic growth policy based on the "income-doubling plan" (*shotoku baizō seisaku*), which promised the Japanese electorate a doubling of national income—although not purchasing power—within the decade. The new administration attempted to bring to a halt the previous policies that were grounded in highly ideological East–West disputes, and called for a common economic goal of improving the daily lives of ordinary Japanese. This call for unity to promote economic growth was warmly embraced by a society that had grown weary of years of political disputes, and the Japanese quickly regained a positive outlook as they began to reap the benefits of the postwar economic boom that had begun in 1955.

Ikeda's policy for Japan's postwar political course was a revival of the approach taken by the former prime minister, Yoshida Shigeru, who had championed prioritizing economic recovery and depending on the United States for national security rather than seeking costly rearmament. The Ikeda administration pursued an orthodox form of the "Yoshida Doctrine," setting in motion the formation of postwar Japan as a lightly armed economy-centered state. In the mid-1950s, Ichirō Hatoyama normalized relations with the Soviet Union, and Ishibashi Tanzan adopted a very pro-Chinese posture, expanding Japan's diplomatic horizon and seeking to distance itself from the ever-dominant shadow of the United States. In contrast, Ishibashi's successor, Kishi, brought Japan's diplomacy back in line with the United States. Washington had rewarded him for this by acquiescing to the revision of the existing security treaty. However, the treaty revision had backfired and instead showed the latent strength of anti-US, pro-communist, and neutralist sentiments in Japan. The demonstrations were so fierce and powerful that a humiliated Kishi had no choice but to request that President Eisenhower—who had already arrived in Okinawa—cancel his planned visit to Tokyo. US–Japan relations had been damaged and it was readily apparent that Ikeda's main diplomatic objective was not just to rebuild but to once again forge a strong relationship with the United States.

Kennedy's Cold War Strategy and Japan

Highly critical of the Eisenhower administration's policy of massive nuclear retaliation, Kennedy adopted a measured flexible response strategy that prepared for a full range of potential military conflicts. This was achieved by not only expanding nuclear weapons capabilities, but also by strengthening conventional military forces. In a special message to Congress in March 1961, Kennedy declared his intention of doing away with the ceiling that the previous administration had effectively imposed on the defense budget, and increasing military spending (Akimoto and Kan 2003). The Kennedy administration was optimistic about generating the finances needed to support an enlarged defense budget by attaining high economic growth through massive tax cuts. Just as President Kennedy had hoped, the mid-1960s saw America's highest economic growth rate in the postwar period (Chafe 1986).

In October 1962 Congress passed President Kennedy's Trade Expansion Act, replacing the Reciprocal Trade Agreements Act that had been in force since the time of President Franklin D. Roosevelt, and granting the president the authority to negotiate significant reductions in customs duties. Kennedy saw "a vital expanding economy in the free world" as "a strong counter to the threat of the world Communist movement." This epitomizes the general mood of the American public during the 1960s, as the focus of the Cold War was shifting away from a direct military confrontation with the Soviet Union to a contest over the value of freedom and economic vitality. America's "Golden Sixties" were drawing the rest of the world into an era of prosperity as illustrated by the impressive results yielded by the Kennedy Round of the General Agreement on Tariffs and Trade (GATT) negotiations (Hara 1991).

At the same time, America's burgeoning balance of payments deficits, which had first surfaced at the end of the 1950s, were threatening to complicate Washington's relations with its allies, including Japan. Two weeks after taking office President Kennedy delivered a special message to Congress in which he declared a plan to improve the balance of payments by linking it with a number of economic and defense issues with the allies. As the speech indicated, Kennedy intended to break down the existing trade barriers in Japan and Europe that Washington had hitherto been willing to overlook until these countries were able to recover economically. Kennedy approached this issue not through import restrictions and protectionist tariffs but by pursuing an expansion of the overall volume of trade. This enlargement of the US economy provided Japan with a fertile export market that was a prerequisite for the success of Prime Minister Ikeda's "income-doubling plan" and Japan's rapid economic growth. In hindsight, Japan benefited so handsomely from the Kennedy Round that it was viewed as the "real winner" of the process (Eckes 1995).

KENNEDY'S "JAPAN POLICY" AND THE ENSUING JOHNSON ADMINISTRATIONS

In the Kennedy administration, the formulation of national security policy was largely guided by Walt W. Rostow, chairman of the State Department's Policy Planning Council. In the "Basic National Security Policy" document, which had been completed by June 1962, Rostow placed Japan as a partner on equal footing with North America and Western Europe—regions he collectively described as the "northern hard core"—to the US goal of forging a "community of free nations." Rostow emphasized that while Japan lacked the "domestic political base" to play as great a defense role as the Federal Republic of Germany, the United States should engage Japanese energies and resources within the free community, so that "this powerful nation, moving forward at an extraordinary rate" would undertake a proportional international role. This became the underlying basis of US policies toward Japan in the 1960s.

The State Department's "Guidelines of US Policy and Operations Toward Japan," formulated in the spring of 1962, advanced a set of new proposals for relations with Japan, setting out more concrete guidelines than NSC6008/1. The guidelines demonstrated America's great aspirations for Japan, highlighting the fact that Japan was not only one of its principal allies in East Asia and a host to US military facilities, but also America's second-largest trading partner. While the short-term objective of American policy was to maintain Japan's "moderate, Western-oriented government," the security goals were to firmly maintain the US–Japan Alliance through the continued presence of the US military forces and continued support of Japanese defenses. Washington should encourage Tokyo to increase its defense capabilities and further modernize its military forces, while reaffirming Japan's policy of "avoiding pressures and other actions that would hinder Japanese political and economic stability." Although there was little possibility of Japan taking on overseas military commitments, the United States could encourage Japan's cooperation in UN peacekeeping operations and seek Japan's trade liberalization. In the long-term, Washington wished to see Japan develop into a "major power center" of Asia as it possessed the technical skills and capital for a more substantial "contribution to the economic growth of non-Communist Asia," the potential to become an increasingly important "counterweight to the rise of Communist China," and more broadly, to assume an "expanded international role" in the world.

The State Department posited a similar view in its report entitled "The Future of Japan" in June 1964. At this time, Japan's economy ranked fifth among the economies of the Free World, and while its size was just one-tenth of that of the United States, it had achieved an astonishing average growth rate of 9% in the previous ten years, with 28.5% (1962) of its total export value being sent to the United States. Japan had become an Article 11 member state of the GATT and an Article 8 member state of the IMF, thereby relinquishing the special exemptions that had been initially afforded to it when joining these organizations, and it had also acceded to the Organisation for Economic Cooperation and Development (OECD). Against this backdrop, the State Department's report predicted that over the next ten years America would find itself dealing with an "increasingly strong, confident and nationalistic Japan." In this way, US policy toward Japan in the 1960s was shaped by Washington's recognition of Japan's rapid economic growth and its desire to see Japan fulfill an international role that was befitting of this progress and development.

The Ikeda–Kennedy Summit

In October 1960, in his first administrative policy speech after taking office as prime minister, Ikeda Hayato stated that despite "defense expenditure being at its lowest," Japan had "done very well to maintain peace and security and achieve remarkable economic development." Ikeda had decided to shelve the issue of constitutional revision and make no mention of defense issues, focusing instead on the economic role of the US–Japan security partnership as the foundation for progress and his "income-doubling plan." His pursuit of economic interests and efforts to improve people's standard of living as the basis for ensuring Japan's political stability and improving its international status were welcomed by most Japanese after years of exhausting political showdowns and unrest over the security treaty revision. Ironically, it was that same confrontational approach adopted by the previous government in pushing forward the revision of the security treaty that allowed Ikeda to freely pursue his economy-centered policies while avoiding national security-related issues.

Prime Minister Ikeda chose to avoid discussing the military dimension of US–Japan relations during his visit to the United States in June 1961. While Kennedy eventually acquiesced to this approach, he did so because the events of 1960 had shown Washington the risks of placing too much pressure on Japan. Another factor was that the Ikeda administration's approach fit the political and economic structure that the Cold War had shaped. Moreover, the United States had chosen to place priority on establishing a broader relationship with Japan, an approach that was partly due to the advice of Ambassador Reischauer.

It was important for Ikeda to make his meeting with Kennedy an opportunity to establish a more substantial bilateral relationship following the previous year's turmoil, which to all appearances had been an outburst against the United States. Ikeda made meticulous preparations for his upcoming US visit, holding numerous meetings with officials of the Ministry of Foreign Affairs and with close advisers such as House of Councilors member Miyazawa Kiichi, and Chief Cabinet Secretary Ōhira Masayoshi.

When Ikeda visited Washington, DC, in June 1961, President Kennedy extended a very warm and personal reception, hosting a private meeting on board the presidential yacht to foster the feeling of a cozy and amicable relationship between the two leaders. The goal of the summit meeting was to discuss a wide range of issues on the basis of "an equal partnership." President Kennedy explained that solid relations with Japan were a fundamental aspect of US national security and stated that the United States wished to work with Japan to pursue the same kind of consultations that it had with the United Kingdom and France. At a meeting between Secretary of State Dean Rusk and Foreign Minister Kosaka Zentarō, Rusk raised the possibility of US nuclear-powered submarines entering and berthing at Japanese ports. While acknowledging that it would indeed be "preferable" to invite nuclear-powered submarines to Japan, Kosaka declined to give an immediate reply on the grounds that "considerable groundwork" needed to be laid among the public first. This was achieved within a few years, and US nuclear submarines first docked at the Japanese port of Sasebo, Nagasaki, in November 1964.

Economic issues were also an important topic on the agenda. Washington embraced the proposal that Japan would repay the financial relief the United States had provided Japan in the form of the Government Appropriation for Relief in Occupied Areas (GARIOA) and the Economic Rehabilitation in Occupied Areas (EROA); the agreements were later signed in January 1962. The American representatives also expressed concerns over the increasing balance of payments deficits and Japan's protectionist policies, urging that Japan increase its pace of economic liberalization, ultimately to be achieved by the end of 1961. Ikeda responded that Japan did intend to "accelerate" its liberalization on the basis of the "Outline of the Plan for Trade and Exchange Liberalization" of June 1961, a government plan that called for "liberalization of 90% of imports by 1963."

The single greatest achievement of the summit was the agreement to establish joint committees in three areas: trade and economic affairs; cultural and educational exchanges; and scientific cooperation. Of the three, the Joint Committee on Trade and Economic Affairs (JCTEA)—which included key cabinet ministers and officials of both nations—agreed to meet each year, alternating between Japan and the United States. This was, of course, a reflection of the special consideration afforded to Japan by the United States, as the only other country with which the United States had such an arrangement was with Canada. The first JCTEF meeting took place in Hakone in November 1961, and was hailed as a "great success" by Ambassador Reischauer. Reischauer reported to Rusk that Ikeda was able to strengthen his political standing at home by demonstrating in the meeting the fruitful outcomes of his "US–Japan partnership diplomacy."

The Dollar and US-Japan Relations over Economic and Defense Issues

During his thousand days in office, the two things that most scared President Kennedy were the issues of "nuclear war and the payments deficit" (Schlesinger 1965). On several occasions, Kennedy reiterated that the American dollar was the very basis for the financial system of the West, and if it were to continue to serve that function at such uneasy times—in which the US gold outflow had reached nearly $15 billion in the previous decade alone—it would require the understanding and cooperation of all parties involved. He believed that any potential weakness in the dollar would "spell trouble" for all allies of the United States and urged them to remove trade barriers, expand aid for developing countries, and purchase American-made weapons.

In July 1963 President Kennedy proposed another cure for the balance of payments issue, an Interest Equalization Tax Plan—a tax on the purchase of foreign securities—making it less profitable for US investors to invest abroad. His successor, President Johnson, would extend this plan for another two years while adopting new measures to restrict the outflow of capital from private banks. At the same time, however, he did provide special consideration toward Japan, exempting it from Interest Equalization Tax of up to $100 million each year on American purchases of Japanese securities on the New York Stock Exchange (Hiwatari 1990).

At the second meeting of the JCTEF in December 1962, Secretary of State Rusk asked Foreign Minister Ōhira Masayoshi about the possibility of Japan bolstering its defense capacity sooner than initially planned, and sharing the costs of maintaining the US forces stationed in Japan. The Secretary of the Treasury, Clarence Douglas Dillon, bluntly stated that if Japan were to expand its defense capacity, particularly in the fields of aircraft, electrical equipment, and antiaircraft missiles, it could purchase American weapons far more cheaply than Japanese-made weapons. The Japanese scholar Nakajima Shingo notes that in US–Japan discussions on military affairs, the chief of the Bureau of Defense Policy, Kaihara Osamu, flatly rejected American demands for additional purchases of weapons and the early completion of the "Second Defense Build-Up Plan" adopted by the cabinet in 1961 (Nakajima 2006). Washington urged Japan to expand its role in international affairs, using every opportunity to point out that Japan was contributing only a moderate amount for its defense as well as foreign economic aid in comparison with NATO member nations.

The dollar problem was not the only context in which Washington was keeping tabs on Japanese defense. Washington officials raised their concerns about Japan's defense capability and expenditure. Referring to the partial withdrawal of the USAF in July 1963, Secretary of Defense Robert McNamara asserted that Japan would need to rely more on its own defense capability in the future. In January 1964, Rusk guaranteed Ōhira that the United States would provide military protection, proclaiming that "Japan's security is the security of the United States. The United States will not deploy or redeploy its military forces for balance of payments reasons." Japan's military expenditure, which was barely over 1% of its GNP, was "somewhat low," and Rusk urged a further increase. Likewise, the Joint Chiefs of Staff recommended that "Japan should be encouraged to increase its defense efforts, providing improved conventional forces for use in the common defense of Asia and providing military assistance to other nations in Asia."

A Schism in Policies toward China

One of the key pending issues between the United States and Japan in the early 1960s was a divergence in their policies toward China. While Washington saw China as its potentially most dangerous rival in the Cold War, Tokyo was seeking ways to pursue a China policy of separating politics from the economy. When Ikeda initiated steps to move forward trade relations with China—which had been halted in 1958 following an incident in Nagasaki involving defamation of the Chinese national flag—Washington made sure to put a check on this development. During an address to the America–Japan Society in September 1962, Assistant Secretary of State for Far Eastern Affairs W. Averell Harriman highlighted the fact that Japan's economic progress had effectively been achieved "without any trade with mainland China." He proceeded to give Tokyo the not-so-subtle warning that all kinds of trade with Communist nations would later be "used" for political purposes. When the Liao-Takasaki Agreement (LT Trade Agreement)—a partial trade agreement overseen by Liao Chengzhi, deputy director of the Foreign Affairs Office in the Chinese State Council, and Takasaki Tatsunosuke, former Minister for International Trade and Industry—was signed shortly after Harriman's address, President Kennedy did not conceal his displeasure. In his remarks at a luncheon meeting during the second session of the JCTEF in December 1962, Kennedy bluntly stated that China was in a "belligerent phase" of its national development and claimed that Japan and the United States should work together as "partners" to consider what could be done to prevent "the domination of Asia by a Communist movement."

The United States was gravely concerned by China's ongoing nuclear weapons program and its rapid rise in military prominence. According to National Security Advisor McGeorge Bundy, Kennedy saw China's nuclear development as "probably the most serious problem facing the world." He spoke in January 1963 of the necessity of taking "some form of action" to halt it, and suggested that the Nuclear Test Ban Treaty (NTBT) might place "pressure" on China to help deter it from developing such capabilities.

Harriman, who was promoted to Under Secretary for Political Affairs in the spring of 1963, agreed with this assessment and proposed a collective action by the United States and the Soviet Union to prevent the Chinese from possessing nuclear weapons. When Harriman raised this issue during negotiations for the NTBT in Moscow in July 1963, Khrushchev confidently responded that "it will be some years off before China is a nuclear power" and did not show any concern over the issue. During mid-September 1964, the Johnson administration made a clear decision not to conduct a preemptive attack on China's nuclear facilities, although it still continued to explore the possibility of collective military action with the Soviets. However, Soviet Ambassador Anatoly Dobrynin once again rejected the

American proposal, informing Bundy that Beijing's acquisition of nuclear arms "was taken for granted" and that China's nuclear weapons "had no importance for the Soviet Union and the US; they merely have a psychological impact" on Asia. This was despite the fact that ever since the Cuban Missile Crisis of October 1962 the Soviet Union had found itself on increasingly worsening terms with China in contrast to a thawing of relations with the United States during this period.

In October 1964, China conducted its first successful nuclear bomb test. President Johnson immediately issued a statement in which he both reaffirmed America's commitment to rush to the defense of its allies in Asia and condemned China by pointing out that other Asian nations were making efforts toward improving the lives of their citizens through economic development and the "peaceful" utilization of atomic energy. As this statement indicated, Washington was particularly concerned about the possible repercussions of the Chinese nuclear test, especially the manner in which Japan and India would react.

CONTINUITY AND CHANGE BETWEEN THE IKEDA AND SATŌ GOVERNMENTS

In November 1964, when Japan was basking in the glory of the 1964 Tokyo Olympics and coming to terms with the shock of the nuclear weapons test by the Chinese, Ikeda was forced to step down as the result of illness. He appointed Satō Eisaku to succeed him as prime minister, putting aside the rivalry that they had developed in their bitter contest during the summer 1964 election over the LDP's presidency. Like Ikeda, Satō was a former high-ranking bureaucrat and a member of the so-called "Yoshida School," protégés of former Prime Minister Yoshida Shigeru. While Ikeda's action therefore appeared as proof that ultimately Ikeda and Satō were woven from the same thread, Satō had labored hard to obtain this position through his own solid performance and achievements as a senior politician.

The relationship between Ikeda and Satō was characterized by a mixture of shared principles and diverging approaches, a combination of both cooperation and rivalry. This permeated throughout the LDP-led politics and diplomacy of the time and it also revealed itself in Satō's choice of cabinet members. On the one hand, Satō embraced in his cabinet Fukuda Takeo, who had harshly criticized Ikeda's economic policies, labeling

Ikeda's administration the "Showa-Genroku" era—a reference to the Genroku era in the seventeenth century, a period that had been marked by great affluence but ultimately ended in high inflation and financial crisis. In Satō's cabinet, Fukuda was given an important position, making him a rival of Tanaka Kakuei, who had served as finance minister under Ikeda, and indicating that Satō had shifted the direction of politics from Ikeda's liberal economics to anti-communist political conservatism.

The paramount importance accorded to US–Japan relations was the most common point shared by Ikeda and Satō. Japan's international status rose through a partnership with the United States along with an assortment of significant benefits. The effort to sign the 1965 Basic Treaty between Japan and the Republic of Korea was initiated by Ikeda and finalized by Satō as a response to repeated demands from the United States. Another culmination of efforts from both cabinets was the establishment of the Asian Development Bank (ADB) in 1966.

Commitment to economic development and stability in Southeast Asia was another crucial tenet of postwar Japanese diplomacy, beginning in the Kishi administration and continuing throughout both the Ikeda and Satō administrations, as well as with the Fukuda Doctrine of the 1970. In this regard, Japan maintained steadfast and stable relations with Indonesia by making a sustained effort to persuade the Sukarno administration to take an alternate course when it leaned toward Communist China and by providing support for its economic reconstruction. More broadly, Japan's establishment as a postwar economic powerhouse—in essence, the materialization of the Yoshida Doctrine during the Ikeda administration—had a ripple effect in Southeast and Northeast Asia from the 1960s onward. During his tour of Southeast Asia, Ikeda was clearly cognizant of this as he referred to the roles that Western Europe and the United States had in the economic development of Africa and Latin America respectively as a blueprint for Japan's role in regional development. This policy was expanded and refined during the Satō administration, as Japan shouldered the major responsibility of economic cooperation and support while the United States was embroiled in conflict in Vietnam.

There were, however, subtle yet critical differences in their approaches toward foreign policy. As a devoted disciple of economic universalism, Ikeda divided the world not in ideological terms of "East versus West," but rather in terms of "developed versus undeveloped" nations, positing a shift away from the Cold War doctrine. Ikeda's concept of the "Three Pillars"—the United States, Western Europe and Japan—as the main load-bearing structures that supported the weight of the Free World was, in fact, a concept that placed emphasis on the role played by advanced market economies. Ikeda was an advocate of Yoshida's "Counter Infiltration" Plan that called for the expansion of trade as a means of weaning China, a vehemently independent nation, from Soviet Communism and drawing it closer to the West. However, Ikeda's open-mindedness toward China began to raise a few eyebrows, particularly when the United States began to take a more rigid stance in its position against communism in the midst of escalating involvement in the Vietnam War under President Johnson.

Prime Minister Satō was different from Ikeda in this regard, as he saw the international political arena in Asia in terms of the Cold War paradigm and adopted a more hardline position toward Communism. Still, the so-called "Satō Operation"—the group of advisors headed by Kusuda Minoru, who served as chief architect behind the policies of the Satō administration—firmly believed that fully revealing Satō's conservative approach to foreign policy would neither solve the problems of the generation nor garner widespread public support. They actively sought advice from scholars who possessed a liberal international outlook and a deep appreciation of culture and civilization. Among those consulted were anthropologist Umesao Tadao, political scientists Kōsaka Masataka and Kyōgoku Junichi, and playwright and critic Yamazaki Masakazu. These experts advised Satō to present himself as a leader who was truly in tune with the voters; the medium utilized for this purpose was the popular monthly television program titled "A Conversation with the Prime Minister" (*Sōri to kataru*). Satō prudently provided attention to the balance between the domestic forces of the ideological positions of left and right, but in terms of foreign policy, he never wavered from his total commitment to grounding his diplomacy on maintaining solid relations with the United States.

From the mid-1960s the Satō administration lost its ties to China, which by then was embroiled in the chaos of the Cultural Revolution. He tacitly acknowledged and quietly supported the Johnson administration's pursuit of war in Vietnam, and decided to tour the anti-Communist nations in the region. This was based on the perception of change in the international environment which, unlike the nonideological issues of the early 1960s, led to a revitalization of the Cold War structure epitomized by the events of the late 1960s. While it is difficult to make a distinction between Ikeda and Satō in the sense that they were both firm advocates of placing the utmost importance on Japan's relationship with the United

States, they both accomplished significant achievements from quite contrasting approaches that were each appropriately suited to their own times.

The Possibility of a "Nuclear" Japan

The existence of a small rift in US–Japan relations at the beginning of the Satō administration is now apparent from official documents that have been declassified in recent years. At a meeting with Ambassador Reischauer on December 27, 1964, Prime Minister Satō, referring to China's nuclear development, expressed interest in the idea of arming Japan with nuclear weapons. He further commented that while he understood that public opinion in Japan was "not ready to accept such ideas," it would be necessary to take steps in the future to "educate the public over such matters." On another occasion he stated that nuclear weapons were "far less costly than typically perceived" and that it was possible to produce them in sufficient quantities "by relying upon Japanese science and industrial might."

Washington did share a deep concern over China's nuclear capabilities, but when it came to the subject of Japanese nuclear armament President Johnson firmly rejected the idea and reassured Satō that the United States would spare no effort in preventing the proliferation of nuclear arms as well as guaranteeing the security of Japan. In a joint statement after the meeting, Satō declared that Japan intended to "firmly maintain" the US–Japan Security Treaty. Johnson replied in a similar fashion, stating that he had "reaffirmed America's determination to abide by its treaty commitments to defend Japan against any external armed aggression." Satō clearly recognized the military security guarantee made by the United States—which in effect provided security by means of a nuclear umbrella—as a serious commitment.

At the same time, Washington felt that it was not sufficient to merely restrain Japan, whose national pride had been reinvigorated due to its breakneck pace of economic development; it was necessary to provide Japan with a different and healthy outlet for its expanding sense of nationalism in order to prevent it from going nuclear. The United States guided Tokyo's aspirations toward space development and the peaceful use of atomic energy.

Japan's economic apogee represented one such outlet for satiating its national pride. It surpassed many Western European nations from the late 1960s onwards, fueling the pride of a nation that had not expected to recover so successfully from its utter defeat in World War II and their new-found position in the world. This made the people content as it led to a rapid rise in the day-to-day quality of their standard of living, thereby creating an equitable democratic society in which the majority of Japanese perceived themselves as middle class. This, in turn, brought legitimacy to politics. Furthermore, national pride was stoked at the successful reversion of Okinawa, a political trophy of the Satō administration.

THE REVERSION OF OKINAWA AMID THE VIETNAM WAR

The United States viewed the Vietnam War as part of a larger fight against global communism and, in particular, as a way to contain the military expansion of China. Invoking the principles of the Domino Theory, Washington increased the support to the South Vietnamese government in its struggle against Communist North Vietnam to live up to "US resolution and trustworthiness" vis-à-vis Japan and other non-Communist nations in Asia. In other words, the survival of South Vietnam and the guarantee of Japanese security were two sides of the same coin.

From the early days of the Vietnam War, Satō was empathetic toward President Johnson's efforts to contribute to the "independence and freedom" of South Vietnam. He fully recognized the indispensability of US military presence in Okinawa as a contributor to the peace and stability of East Asia. In mid-July 1965, Satō informed the United States that Japan was "firmly committed" to their cause and also reiterated that Japan "harbored no doubts" regarding USAF's use of bases in Okinawa to launch strikes against Vietnamese targets. Washington was appreciative of Japan's moral support and confident that Japan's policies toward Vietnam were such that Tokyo would continue to allow the use of the bases for logistical support, albeit "without any publicity." Japan also took it on itself to provide economic assistance to South Vietnam as well as offering "modest expressions" of support for American policies in Vietnam.

An ever-expanding US intervention in Vietnam was becoming extremely unpopular with the Japanese. In spring 1965, Ambassador Reischauer expressed his concerns that the events in Vietnam were "unsettling, as opposed to stabilizing, the foothold that [the United States had] established over the last four years" (Reischauer and Reischauer 2003). He informed the State Department that there was a growing fear in Japan that the escalation of war in Vietnam would drag Japan into the conflict. Based on what he saw as Japan's "ostrich-like" pacifism in the previous two decades, Reischauer stressed that the Japanese perceived the issue in "simple terms" while believing that the "easiest way" to end the war would be for the United States to cease its aerial bombardments and other military actions. His analysis of the Japanese position was both an effort to implicitly encourage his own government to find an intelligent way of terminating American military intervention as well as to vent his frustration at the Japanese people's lack of understanding of the American perspective. Reischauer directed particular criticism toward Japan's news coverage on the state of affairs in Vietnam over the past few years, criticizing the Japanese media as being heavily biased. In September 1965, the ambassador complained to Prime Minister Satō that as a result of the negative views held by the majority of Japanese toward American policies in Vietnam, US–Japan relations had "been stagnant or deteriorating" during the preceding few months, and requested that Tokyo make a greater effort to persuade the Japanese public that a "peaceful and friendly Southeast Asia" was in fact the basic foundation of Japanese national security.

Negotiations over Okinawan Reversion

The Vietnam War served to reconfirm the strategic importance of Okinawa for the United States, prompting Prime Minister Satō to describe Okinawa as "an unsinkable aircraft carrier." As such, he expressed his understanding of Washington's position of preserving its administrative rights over Okinawa. However, it was at this juncture that Satō floated the idea to Rusk during his first visit to the United States as prime minister in January 1965 that administrative control over at least some of the other Ryukyu Islands—excluding the main island of Okinawa—that were perhaps "not so essential to national security" (what he had in mind was Iriomote) should be returned to Japan. But this elicited no response from Rusk. The joint statement following the meeting included a declaration by Satō of Japan's "desire" for a prompt reversion of the Ryukyu and Ogasawara Islands, as well as Johnson's "appreciation" of his request.

Reischauer had possessed a keen interest in the Okinawa problem for quite some time. He had been involved in advising Washington on how to manage the issue of Okinawa immediately following the end of the war, at which time his recommendation to the State–War–Navy Coordinating Committee's (SWNCC) Subcommittee for the Far East had been that the administrative rights to any territory not absolutely essential for US military purposes should be returned to Japan. After being appointed ambassador to Japan, he seized the opportunity to influence President

Kennedy through his brother, US Attorney General Robert Kennedy, to formulate a new policy toward Okinawa in March 1962 that displayed his willingness to accept the eventual possibility of the reversion of Okinawa to Japan. In July 1965 Reischauer warned that a "boil over" would probably come before 1970 and that the US–Okinawa relationship could "not be maintained on present terms for more than two years." He called for an arrangement to allow for the restoration of administrative rights to Japan while maintaining the US military presence in Okinawa (Miyazato 2000).

By fall that year, Secretary of State Rusk had embraced Reischauer's advice, which led him to agree with Secretary of Defense McNamara regarding the establishment of a working group to deal with the Ryukyu Islands issue. In March 1966, both the State Department and the Defense Department formed a high-level interdepartmental group under which a task force known as the Interregional Group for the Far East was given orders to conduct a special review into the issue. Richard Sneider, the State Department's officer in charge of Japanese Affairs, was placed in charge, while Deputy Assistant Secretary of Defense Morton Halperin supported the group's initiatives at the Defense Department. As part of this review that took place between early 1966 and early 1967, the Ryukyu working group focused its discussions on the core issue of how to restore administrative rights to Japan while ensuring a continuance of the geostrategic benefits that Okinawa offered to the US military, and discussed the multitude of political and military issues that could accompany the reversion. After due deliberation they were surprised to learn that, apart from the issue of nuclear weapons, only the bombing of Vietnam by B-52 bombers stationed in Okinawa could potentially be affected, allowing them to reach the conclusion that Okinawa should be reverted to Japan quickly rather than leaving it as a significant thorn in US–Japan relations. In other words, they concluded that it would be significantly more beneficial for the US military to cooperate with reversion and continue to use the bases under a framework of understanding with Japan. The analysis gained widespread support by senior government officials at the Defense Department by early 1967.

While unbeknownst to Japan, Washington was taking the necessary steps to address and alleviate the outstanding security concerns raised by the military before any groundwork could be laid for the return of Okinawa. However, the problem of the American balance of payments deficits, aggravated by the Vietnam War, complicated this process. Given Japan's strong economic base at the time, it made sense for Washington to consider the question of whether or not Okinawa should be returned to

Japan without any compensation. At a National Security Council (NSC) meeting on August 30, 1967, President Johnson pointed out that Japan was clearly eager to resolve the Ryukyu and Ogasawara Islands issue and this presented an opportunity to seek Japan's cooperation in various matters. The most important of these were the improvement of the balance of payments, support for the security and economic development of Asia by Japan's taking on a "greater share of regional leadership" through increased financial aid to South Vietnam, the Asian Development Bank (ADB) Special Funds and other such projects, including participation in peacekeeping operations (PKO) in the Middle East, and support for the Nuclear Nonproliferation Treaty (NPT) regime.

In November 1967, Prime Minister Satō visited the United States for his second summit meeting with the president. Satō was determined to see the reversion of Okinawa, and felt firmly that the United States had no other option but to agree. Prior to Satō's visit to Washington, the State Department reiterated that the prime minister should be given more recognition for establishing himself as a capable leader of the region, as reflected by his several official visits to nations across Asia. At the first summit meeting on November 14, President Johnson carefully avoided the issue of Okinawa, instead requesting Satō to first discuss the matter thoroughly with the secretaries of State and Defense the following day where they urged Japan to commit itself more to the security and development of Asia. At the conclusion of the meeting, the prime minister handed the president a memo which bore only the words "within a few years" scribbled in English (Satō 1998; materials provided in the appendix to Kusuda 2001).

The importance of reaching an agreement over the reversion of Okinawa before the extension of the US–Japan Security Treaty in 1970 was already well understood by Washington, but by conveying this message *literally* into the hand of the president, Satō was making an undeniable show of his decidedness. In their lengthy meeting, both Satō and the president insisted on their respective priorities, the reversion of Okinawa and Japan's engagement in economic cooperation with Asia. Eventually, each side agreed to fulfill the requirements—the United States to return the Ogasawara Islands the following year, and Okinawa within two to three years, and Japan to commit to regional development and US balance of payments improvement. In his diary entry that day, Satō wrote that he was "delighted beyond words." By successfully attaining the Okinawa reversion through painstaking negotiations, the Satō administration had succeeded in convincing postwar Japanese that it was indeed possible to maintain national pride and prestige without having to resort to nuclear development.

Japan and the United States During the Late 1960s

In 1968, the tide of the Vietnam War was turning against the United States, contrary to statements from President Johnson. The student anti-war protests gained more momentum, and public opinion began to actively support a complete withdrawal of American troops and to call for peace with North Vietnam, causing a beleaguered president to announce that he would not be running in the upcoming presidential elections. Japan for its part was experiencing ing rapid economic growth and had propelled itself to the position of the world's third-largest economic power by 1968. In 1965, Japan for the first time had recorded a trade balance surplus vis-à-vis the United States, an amount that reached $334 million. By 1969, this trade surplus had ballooned to approximately $1.4 billion.

While Satō was content with the success of his policy toward the United States, this was overshadowed by the escalation of college student riots that challenged current political authority and called for a revamping of the postwar system. The riots taking place throughout most of Western Europe and America quickly spread across Japan, enflamed by growing opposition to the war in Vietnam. Satō made a concerted effort to restore domestic stability by canceling the University of Tokyo's entrance examinations for the 1969 academic year and adopting a new law to force university administrators to control their unruly students. Having quelled domestic unrest, the Satō administration began negotiations in October with the new Nixon administration to finalize the reversion of Okinawa. President Nixon entrusted the matter to Henry Kissinger who, in moving the process forward, appointed Sneider and Halperin as the NSC staff experts on the question and instructed a complete review of the current state of Okinawa affairs. This personnel selection had the effect of maintaining policy continuity over the issue.

This process of Okinawan reversion provides a prime example of the positive contribution that track-two (both private citizens and government officials) talks can make in diplomacy. Groundwork for the return of Okinawa was laid by representatives of Japan and the United States during the 1967 conversations of the Shimoda Conference, whereas the Kyoto Conference of January 1969 saw the successful establishment of a consensus between official and civil leadership. Satō adopted the course of action recommended at the Kyoto Conference that called for an Okinawan reversion that "does not allow for nuclear weapons, and in which administration is implemented on a par with the rest of Japan (*kakunuki hondon-*

ami)." During the US–Japan summit meeting of November 1969, Nixon informed Satō that the United States would remove its Mace B nuclear missiles from Okinawa and restore the administrative rights of Okinawa to Japan in 1972.

This epitomized the fulfillment of a national goal set by Satō, who had stated, when visiting Okinawa in summer 1965, that Japan's "post-war" would not end until Okinawa was returned to the homeland. It is highly significant that this was ultimately achieved against the backdrop of the Vietnam War, and illuminates the amicable partnership that existed between the two countries. It also represented Satō's decisive victory over his domestic opposition, allowing him to secure a landslide victory in the late 1969 general elections that put a momentary halt to the continuing decline of conservative forces in Japan.

The historic achievement of peacefully restoring territory that had been lost in war helped the Japanese to have faith in the United States. This was an important factor in explaining how US–Japan relations have continued to thrive despite the level of turbulence on the international stage. Prior to the war, the 1924 Immigration Act, which excluded Japanese immigration to the United States, had sowed the seed of distrust toward America in the minds of many Japanese, and cast a long shadow upon Japan's relations with the United States in the events leading up to the Pacific War. In contrast, the reversion of Okinawa was like sunlight shining its warm rays upon the future of US–Japan relations.

However, one should not overlook the fact that this historic achievement was accompanied by an unexpected discord involving the US–Japan textile negotiations. It was later revealed that there had been a "trade-off" of reducing Japanese textile exports to the United States in return for the reversion of Okinawa. As part of his "Southern strategy" in the presidential election, Nixon demanded that Japan voluntarily restrain its textile exports to the United States so that he could bolster political support from the textile industry in the American South. Satō had agreed to this at the US–Japan summit meeting in 1969, but lost the trust of the president as the agreements were shaped through confidential discussions between Satō's secret emissary Professor Kei Wakaizumi and Kissinger, which led, in turn to Satō delaying implementation. Although the textile disputes were finally resolved in January 1972, it seems that to a certain extent Satō's breach of trust provoked President Nixon's sudden announcement in July 1971 that he would visit China the following year: a statement that marked the first of the events referred to as the "Nixon shocks," and the beginning of the unraveling of US–Japan relations during the 1970s.

BIBLIOGRAPHY

Akimoto, Eiichi, and Hideki Kan. 2003. *Amerika 20-seiki-shi* [Twentieth Century American History]. Tokyo: University of Tokyo Press.

Chafe, William H. 1986. *The Unfinished Journey.* New York: Oxford University Press.

Eckes, Alfred E. Jr. 1995. *Opening America's Market.* Chapel Hill and London: University of North Carolina Press.

Halberstam, David. 1972. *The Best and the Brightest.* New York: Random House.

Hara, Yasushi. 1991. Sengo no nichibei keizai kankei [Economic Relations between Japan and the United States after the Second World War]. In *Nichibei kankei-shi* [A History of Japan–US Relations], ed. Hosoya Chihiro and Honma Nagayo. Tokyo: Yūhikaku Publishing.

Hiwatari, Yumi. 1990. *Sengo seiji to nichibei kankei* [Postwar Politics and Japan–US Relations]. Tokyo: University of Tokyo Press.

Kusuda, Minoru. 2001. *Kusuda Minoru nikki* [The Diaries of Kusuda Minoru]. Edited and annotated by Wada Jun with introduction by Iokibe Makoto. Tokyo: Chūōkōron-shinsha.

Miyazato, Seigen. 2000. *Nichibei kankei to Okinawa 1945–1972* [Japan–US Relations and Okinawa 1945–1972]. Tokyo: Iwanami Shoten.

Nakajima, Shingo. 2006. *Sengo Nihon no bōei seisaku* [Postwar Japan's Defense Policy]. Tokyo: Keio University Press.

Reischauer, Edwin O., and Haru Reischauer. 2003. *Reischauer-taishi nichiroku* [The Daily Records of Ambassador Reischauer], ed. Iriye Akira. Tokyo: Kōdansha.

Satō, Eisaku. 1998. *Satō Eisaku nikki Showa 42-44-nen* [The Diaries of Satō Eisaku, 1967–69], ed. Itō Takashi. Tokyo: Asahi Shimbunsha.

Schlesinger, Arthur M. Jr. 1965. *A Thousand Days.* Boston: Houghton Mifflin.

CHAPTER 9

The 1970s: Stresses on the Relationship

Yoshihide Soeya and Robert D. Eldridge

Shake-Up of American Diplomacy and the Dual Nixon Shocks

When Nixon assumed the presidency in 1969, he felt that it was necessary to transform America's role in the world, while taking care not to relinquish its international standing. President Nixon and his national security advisor Henry Kissinger believed that the containment policy the United States had been pursuing across the globe had placed it on the front line of every possible international crisis and led to an impasse in American diplomacy. The Vietnam War was a prime example of this and Nixon felt that bringing an honorable end to the conflict would be an important step in reestablishing America's leadership in the world.

Nixon's first warning that he was pursuing such an approach to diplomacy—and the precursor to the shocks that he sent through relations between the United States and Japan—was his sudden announcement of a new standard in foreign intervention at a press conference in Guam in July 1969. Addressing the topic of the US role in Asia, he stated that it would keep its treaty commitments and would encourage, and be entitled to expect,

Y. Soeya
Faculty of Law, Keio University, Tokyo, Japan

R.D. Eldridge
The Eldridge Think Tank, Kawanishi, Japan

© The Author(s) 2017   171
M. Iokibe (ed.), T. Minohara (trans. ed.), *The History of US–Japan Relations*, DOI 10.1007/978-981-10-3184-7_9

the problems of military defense to be "increasingly handled by, and the responsibility for it taken by, the Asian nations themselves" (Nixon 1969).

Nixon gave a more detailed explanation of these principles, which had become known as the Nixon Doctrine, in his address to the nation on the Vietnam War that November. He emphasized three principles regarding America's future involvement in Asia. Firstly, that America would keep its treaty commitments; secondly, that America would provide a shield for its allies and other countries whose existence was considered vital for American security in the event of threat to their freedom from a nuclear power; and thirdly, that in the event of invasions using conventional weapons, America would expect nations under direct threat to fulfill their primary responsibility to provide the required military support.

Nixon highlighted the importance of this new diplomacy in his first annual report to Congress on US foreign policy, made public on February 18, 1970. In it he emphasized the need to protect national interests, explaining that "sound" foreign policy that would support US interests in the long run should be based on a "realistic assessment of our and others' interests," and the recognition that the United States' interests needed to shape its commitments, "rather than the other way around" (Nixon 1970). The president was aware that American leadership was imperative for the security of international society, but he also believed that unlimited intervention would harm US national interests. Thus, he embarked on a policy of realpolitik diplomacy that was based on seeking a balance of power, which required, in turn, an adjustment of the containment policy by engaging in détente with the Soviet Union while also seeking rapprochement with China. As a result, it was successful in utilizing the dynamics of improved relations with both China and the Soviet Union to achieve an "honorable withdrawal" from Vietnam that was concluded by the Paris Peace Accords of January 1973.

The Shift of US Policy toward China

In shifting his foreign policy toward China, it was Nixon's firm belief that "excluding a country of the magnitude of China from America's diplomatic options meant that America was operating internationally with one hand tied behind its back" (Kissinger 1994). Above all, the United States saw rapprochement with China as its strongest card for ensuring a "swing" position in which it could enjoy positive relations with both China and the Soviet Union, and therefore leverage in the balance-of-power game.

The series of military border clashes between China and the Soviet Union over the spring and summer of 1969 had a significant impact on the ensuing rapprochement between the United States and China. From then on, Washington and Beijing began to talk behind closed doors, primarily using the channels of mediation provided by Pakistan, and from July 9–11, 1971, Kissinger made a top secret visit to China. In a televised speech on July 15, Nixon delivered the news of Kissinger's visit to China as well as his own scheduled visit the following year. This sent shockwaves throughout the world, but it was felt with tremendous intensity in Japan.

Beijing approached the process of establishing rapprochement with the United States on the basis of their judgment that the difficulties in China's relationship with the Soviet Union were much greater than those in its relationship with the United States. China's approach therefore diverged fundamentally from the American strategy of simply seeking a "swing" position between China and the Soviet Union. Moreover, in this period the Chinese leadership had an accurate understanding of the international political significance of the US withdrawal from Vietnam, and helped to establish suitable circumstances for exerting its influence on North Vietnam. Ultimately, China welcomed the decrease in American presence in Asia as a shift in the strategic environment that could work to its advantage as it dealt with factors such as confrontation with the Soviet Union and the issue of the status of Taiwan. Rather than being wary of the fact that China perceived the situation in this way, the Nixon administration's policy was effectively to welcome China taking a greater role in maintaining order in Asia after the Vietnam War.

At the same time, when addressing international political strategy, Kissinger and Zhou Enlai, premier of the Chinese State Council, both expressed concern over the possibility of Japan developing its own nuclear weapons or other militarily capabilities. Both Kissinger and Zhou perceived the Japan–US security framework as the "cork in the bottle" that was preventing outward Japanese aggression. When meeting with Zhou Enlai during his second visit to China in October 1971, Kissinger stated that he had always been convinced that America was naïve to think that it could pursue the policies that it wanted to while also allowing Japan to grow stronger, and claimed he was "under no illusions about Japan" (Ishii et al. 2003).

The Textile Problem and Nixon's New Economic Policy

The relative decline in American national strength in the 1970s also resulted in economic issues playing an unprecedented role in US domestic politics, and in turn plagued bilateral relations between Japan and the United States. Japan's economic success could not have been achieved without the high standards of labor and technical skills of Japanese workers, but it was also propped up by the free trade system and the military security provided under the US–Japan Security Treaty, two international factors that Japan had assumed would remain constants.

The nagging trade problem between the United States and Japan was a factor that contributed to the Nixon administration's frustration toward Japan. When Nixon came to power, Japan was seen to be reaping all the benefits from the military security and free trade system provided by the United States, and there was growing criticism in the United States of Japan's "free riding" on security and the lack of access to the Japanese market. As noted in the previous chapter, from 1965 onward the balance of trade between America and Japan had reversed, and the United States continued to maintain an import surplus. While America's balance of trade was in a critical condition, Japan's postwar economic development had made it the second-greatest economic power among the capitalist nations. Furthermore, the products that Japan exported to the United States were also improving dramatically in quality and technical sophistication. As a result, Japan was no longer simply seen as a free-rider, but as a viable threat.

While such sentiment was developing, Nixon had made his election pledge in 1968 to pursue international negotiations to impose import quotas on textile products—a pledge which later developed into the US–Japan textile conflict. On August 15, 1971, when the US–Japan textile negotiations were at the height of confusion, Nixon announced a set of new economic policies, including levying a 10% import tax on all imported products and measures to temporarily suspend the convertibility of the dollar to gold. The "Dollar Shock," as it came to be known, sent shockwaves through the international economic system, and marked the beginning of the end of the Bretton Woods system of fixed exchange rates which was later replaced by the system of floating exchange rates.

Nixon's New Economic Policy did not shy from being openly critical of Japan. At the time, America's trade deficit with Japan had reached $3 billion, and while textiles accounted for just a small proportion of the deficit, Nixon could not conceal his frustration over the ongoing textile negotiations with Japan. At a speech to war veterans in Dallas, he even went so far as to conclude that the threat posed by such a strong economic rival was "far more serious than the challenge that we confronted even in the dark days of Pearl Harbor" (Schaller 1997). US–Japan relations in the early 1970s were therefore largely shaped by Nixon's efforts toward achieving a comprehensive shakeup of international strategy from military diplomacy to the economy, and America's strong perception of Japan as a potential threat. In its relations with the US and diplomacy as a whole Japan therefore faced the challenges of adapting to fundamental shifts in international order, and coping with the fact that America had lost the leeway to take the generous approach it had formerly adopted.

JAPANESE DIPLOMACY IN FLUX

Because it was Nixon's election promise, the resolution of the textile problem was of paramount importance to him personally. From the American perspective, Nixon's commitment to Prime Minister Satō during their meeting in November 1969 on the reversion of Okinawa to Japan by 1972 was inextricably linked to Satō's explicit promise that the textile problem would be resolved as the president desired. However, the textile problem was not mentioned in the joint communiqué issued on November 21, as it was a sensitive political issue for Japan, and it was believed Satō's promise would be criticized as selling off the textile industry for Okinawa.

Bilateral negotiations continued for another two years, but the parties failed to reach an agreement. The Japanese textile industry and the Japanese Ministry of Trade and Industry (MITI) strongly opposed restrictions on Japan's exports on the basis that there was insufficient proof that it was Japanese exports in particular that were causing damage to the American textile industry. After negotiations between Japan and the United States broke down in June 1970, Nixon and Satō reached an agreement in October to resume negotiations in San Clemente where Satō once again expressed his wish to fulfill his promise to Nixon. Nevertheless, Satō was unable to successfully establish a consensus within Japan, and sought a breakthrough by appointing Miyazawa Kiichi as the new trade minister to replace Ōhira Masayoshi. When that failed, he replaced Miyazawa with Tanaka Kakuei.

In 1971, the textile negotiations were in complete deadlock. In the absence of any positive developments over the course of ten rounds of negotiations between Washington and Tokyo, in March the Japanese textile industry declared unilateral voluntary export restrictions. When the Japanese government supported this decision, the Nixon administration was openly angered, and President Nixon himself issued a statement of protest. In September that year Washington delivered what was essentially a final ultimatum to Japan. It informed trade minister Tanaka Kakuei, who was visiting Washington to attend the eighth meeting of the US–Japan Joint Committee on Trade and Economic Affairs, that if an agreement were not reached by October 15, Nixon would unilaterally implement import quota measures. Faced with this threat, Tokyo decided to acquiesce to three years of voluntary restraints, in return for which it promised the domestic textile industry compensation, and an agreement was reached on October 15, 1971, just before the deadline. While the US–Japan textile dispute had no significant economic impact, it did set the precedent for a pattern where Japan would initially reject American demands but would eventually concede upon further pressure. This also portended the trade talks that would subsequently cause friction between Japan and the United States.

Sino-US Rapprochement and Japan's Asia Policy

Many members of Nixon's administration had known nothing of the negotiations between Washington and Beijing. Secretary of State William P. Rogers was kept completely in the dark until shortly before the announcement, and was simply given the task of notifying each ambassador. U. Alexis Johnson, the under-secretary for political affairs and former ambassador to Japan, was also stunned by the development, describing it to the then-Japanese ambassador to the United States, Ushiba Nobuhiko, as "Asakai's nightmare coming true," in reference to former Japanese ambassador Asakai Kōichirō's constant fears that the United States would unexpectedly seek rapprochement with China.

While Prime Minister Satō's political position had been weakened by America's "betrayal," he chose not to voice any criticism with regard to the United States, and resigned while still basking in the glory of having just overseen the successful reversion of Okinawa to Japan. Of course, there was still significant "resentment over the fact that the United States had gone ahead of Japan in opening up contact with China" in the Japanese government, and many were determined to move ahead of the United States in the actual normalization of relations with China (Ogata 1988). The issue of normalizing relations with China therefore became a major point for contention in the Liberal Democratic Party (LDP) election that was contested between Tanaka Kakuei, Fukuda Takeo, Ōhira Masayoshi, and Miki Takeo. In the end, Tanaka, Ōhira, and Miki joined forces and agreed to pursue the course of normalizing ties with China. This secured a victory for Tanaka, who was hugely popular because of his lack of higher education and unrestrained power for action; he provided a refreshing change given that Japanese society had become tired of the bureaucrats-turned-politicians who had dominated politics for many years.

Following the formation of the Tanaka government in July 1972, movements toward the normalization of relations between Japan and China progressed rapidly. At the press conference after his first Cabinet meeting, Tanaka declared that the government would speed up efforts to establish relations with China. Two days later, Zhou Enlai responded with a statement welcoming the new Tanaka cabinet and its policy of pursuing normalization. When Tanaka visited China on September 25, there were still a number of problems to be addressed, such as the Taiwan issue and the nagging question of war reparations, but China's flexible approach allowed for a successful conclusion to the negotiations, and a joint communiqué declaring the normalization of ties between the two countries was announced on September 29.

Although the Japanese government had to an extent been acting out of a feeling of rivalry with the United States, it did not seek a breakdown in the US–Japan security relationship as this formed the core of Japanese diplomacy. A month before Tanaka visited China, the Japan–US leaders' summit was held in Honolulu from July 31 to August 1, 1972, and it was reaffirmed that normalization of relations between Japan and China would not lead to any readjustments to the Japan–US Security Treaty.

To a certain extent, Japan also experimented with an autonomous diplomacy in its development of foreign policy toward Southeast Asia that would not conflict with its security relations with the United States. When, in the early days of the Nixon administration Washington gave signs that it was changing its policy toward the Vietnam War, the Japanese foreign ministry had embarked on an independent effort to investigate the possibility of improving relations with North Vietnam. Diplomatic relations were achieved with the Democratic Republic of Vietnam in September 1973. This Japanese action irked the Nixon administration, as it preceded the unification of Vietnam and Washington was still supporting the South Vietnamese.

Despite this, Japan continued in its efforts to pursue a proactive diplomacy in Southeast Asia, and during January 1974, Prime Minister Tanaka made a tour of Southeast Asian nations to seek new policies toward the region. However, violent anti-Japanese demonstrations that Tanaka encountered in Bangkok and Jakarta provided a shocking realization that Japan was not yet welcomed in this region. Reacting to the reality, the bureaucrats therefore set to work on a complete overhaul of Japan's diplomacy in Southeast Asia that eventually led to the Fukuda Doctrine.

The Repercussions of the Oil Crisis

Food and oil imports were of vital importance to Japan. In July 1973, President Nixon placed strict controls on certain agricultural exports, resulting in an embargo on soybean exports from the United States to Japan for two years. A few months later, Egypt's attack on Israel led to the Yom Kippur War in October 1973. The Organization of the Petroleum Exporting Countries (OPEC) voted to raise crude oil prices, and the Arab nations of the Organization of the Arab Petroleum Exporting Countries (OAPEC) decided to also reduce the production of crude oil and introduce embargos on crude oil exports to nations supporting Israel.

The international oil crisis that resulted was a fresh—and more challenging—blow to the Japanese economy just as it was making an earnest effort to respond to Nixon's New Economic Policy. Dependent on other nations for all of its energy resources, Japan saw securing crude oil as an issue of national survival, and was prepared to apply the principle of "necessity is bound by no limits." This led to severe friction with the United States, which was undeterred in its commitment to support Israel.

When Kissinger visited Japan in November 1973, Prime Minister Tanaka and Foreign Minister Ōhira sought his support for securing oil supplies, but did not set out a particular course of action. Instead, Tokyo decided to take steps to ensure that the Arab nations would recognize Japan as a "friendly" nation by expressing support for the Arab states in a statement delivered by Chief Cabinet Secretary Nikaidō Susumu in late November, and sending Deputy Prime Minister Miki Takeo to several Middle East countries in December. These efforts paid off, and a communiqué issued on December 25 after the OAPEC Ministerial Meeting included Japan among the friendly nations, and also declared that OAPEC would extend special treatment for Japan, excluding it completely from the general reduction in output.

Kissinger was not amused by Japan taking a pro-Arab stance and pursuing diplomacy based on oil, and strongly emphasized that the United States desired the developed nations to unite in opposition against the Arab nations at the energy conference for oil-consuming nations to be held in February of the following year. However, Tokyo decided to adopt an opposing position, which Chief Cabinet Secretary Nikaidō Susumu described in January 1974 as "essential to develop harmonious relations between oil producing nations and oil consuming nations in order to achieve a fundamental solution to the oil crisis" (Nikaidō 1974). Such resistance to the United States was purely motivated by the fact that securing a source of oil was a matter of survival for Japan.

The manner in which US–Japan relations developed at the time of the oil crisis made it clear that a mutual lack of trust had created a psychological barrier between the two governments. The ensuing friction not only affected the politicians and key policy decision makers, but also had a tremendous influence on public opinion, in particular the Japanese public opinion toward the United States. According to surveys taken at that time, both in 1973 and 1974, just 18% of Japanese felt a sense of affinity with the United States, by far the lowest figure in the postwar period.

In the end, however, the oil crisis did not undermine the fact that US–Japan relations were of crucial importance for the diplomatic strategies of both Japan and the United States. Consumed with the pursuit of "high politics," the Nixon administration adopted a policy toward Japan that was clearly lacking in delicacy, and Japan, which had been somewhat overprotected during its period of high economic growth, was not yet prepared to respond to America's high-handed approach.

THE DIPLOMATIC STRATEGY OF PRESIDENT FORD

After Nixon's resignation in August 1974, Vice President Ford assumed the presidency and immediately inherited a series of new strategies that had been formulated during the Nixon administration. Ford's administration faced the difficult challenges of recovering national confidence and unifying a divided nation, and also the no less important task of reviving foreign policy, which had been somewhat neglected by the Nixon administration in its final months when it was consumed by the Watergate scandal fallout.

While President Ford was inclined to essentially continue the diplomatic strategies of the Nixon administration, Kissinger's détente policies faced a significant challenge from within, particularly from Secretary of Defense Rumsfeld, one of Ford's most significant personnel appointments, as well as Chief of Staff Dick Cheney. They would later become rivals of Kissinger, who had become Secretary of State, as they were both extremely critical of Kissinger's approach of pursuing a policy of détente that was based on a traditional European approach to international politics (Mann 2004). Criticism of détente grew particularly fierce when the Soviet Union and Cuba became involved in a civil war that was triggered by Angolan independence in 1975. Both countries provided massive military support to assist the Marxist Popular Movement for the Liberation of Angola and contributed to their eventual victory in 1976.

In contrast with the Nixon administration's policy of underestimating the importance of Japan in its balance of power diplomacy, the Ford administration, faced with the growing criticism of détente and revived fear of the expansionism of the Soviet Union, played a key role in reaffirming the significance of US–Japan relations. This new stance toward Japan can be seen in the "New Pacific Doctrine" announced by President Ford in Hawaii in December 1975 on his return from a visit to China, Indonesia, and the Philippines. After emphasizing that American strength was the critical factor for maintaining the balance of power in the Pacific region, Ford went on to acknowledge the importance of the US relationship with Japan, describing it as a "pillar" of US strategy. James D. Hodgson, who served as US ambassador to Japan from July 1974 to February 1977, played a pivotal role in the process of establishing the new posture toward Japan initiated by the Ford administration.

Ford Visits Japan and the Emperor Visits America

Immediately upon taking up his post, Ambassador Hodgson set about tackling his key task of restoring trust in US–Japan relations, and used his close relationship with Ford to encourage him to visit Japan even before Ford had taken his office. As such, Ford was firmly resolved to visit Japan in November following the midterm elections in the fall, informing Hodgson that Japan would most likely be the first country he would visit as president, and noting that Japan "deserve[d] more attention" than America had given it (Hodgson 1990).

Ford's visit to Japan on November 18–22, 1974, marked the first visit of an incumbent US president to Japan. As Ford recalls, his trip was more ceremonial than substantive (Ford 1980). However, such a gesture helped to symbolize exactly the steady improvements in US–Japan relations that were needed at the time. Tokyo was also delighted with Ford's decision to make Japan his first destination for a full-scale foreign visit after taking up the presidency, and the visit contributed significantly to improving the image of the United States held by Japanese.

Between President Ford's visit to Japan and Emperor Hirohito's visit to the United States in the fall of 1975, Japan's political circles were thrown into confusion when Prime Minister Tanaka resigned unexpectedly as a result of harsh criticism over his shady financial dealings, and a new cabinet was subsequently established under Miki Takeo on December 9, 1974.

The first Japanese imperial visit to the United States began with Emperor Hirohito and Empress Nagako's arrival in Williamsburg on September 30, 1975. They travelled to the capital on October 2, where they were welcomed with an official state dinner at the White House that evening. In his toast at the dinner, Hirohito touched upon the Pacific War, describing it as "that most unfortunate war," which he "deeply deplore[d]."

Ambassador Hodgson, who was present throughout the visit, was both relieved and delighted at the dignified manner in which the emperor and empress were received, particularly since no one had been able to predict how the American public would react. In his memoirs, Hodgson suggests that the visit "probably did more to cement [the] long-term relationship between the two countries" than anything before it (Hodgson 1988). While this may be an exaggeration, it does convey the important role that the Emperor's visit played in restoring the damage that had been inflicted on the bilateral relations earlier in the decade.

Toward a Closer US–Japan Defense Cooperation Scheme

In the early 1970s the Nixon Doctrine and the realization that the United States was withdrawing from Asia had temporarily led to support within Tokyo over the policy of "autonomous defense" (*jishu bōei*), the concept of Japan's defense being provided primarily by Japan itself. Nakasone Yasuhiro, then the Director General of the Defense Agency, was a particularly prominent advocate of this policy, arguing the necessity for the United States and Japan to take equal roles in issues of defense. While emphasizing that Japan should remain a "non-nuclear middle power" (*hikaku chūkyū kokka*), Nakasone sought to expand the role of Japan within the US–Japan security relationship and establish the autonomous defense capabilities that Japan would therefore require. However,

Nakasone's strategy was not fully accepted due to political developments within and outside of Japan that did not justify the necessity for Japan to reinforce its military capabilities.

While for a significant part of the postwar period the alliance between China and the Soviet Union had posed a military threat to Japan, China was no longer an enemy following the US–China rapprochement and the restoration of diplomatic ties between Japan and China, while détente had eased tensions with the Soviet Union. In domestic politics, there were also concerns from the progressive and pacifist wings of politicians that autonomous defense was a nationalist course. Eventually the government became occupied with addressing the economic security issues created by the oil crisis, and the question of defense became a secondary issue.

When Ford took office in August and Miki succeeded Tanaka in December, Japan began to make an earnest effort to restructure its defense policies and security relations so that they would become more closely aligned with those of the United States. This developed into two key policy outcomes: the National Defense Program Outline (*Bōei kei-kaku no taikō*) of 1976, which developed out of the attempts to devise an independent response for Japan to the détente environment; and the Guidelines for Japan–US Defense Cooperation (*Nichibei bōei kyōryoku no tame no shishin*), finalized in 1978. Together, these policies helped to further institutionalize the US-Japan security relationship.

In April 1975, Sakata Michita, Defense Agency director general, set up an advisory committee of private sector intellectuals to deliberate and offer opinions on matters of defense, with the aim of providing the Japanese with a clear outline of Japan's stance. The committee's report, put together in September that year, defined the function of Japan's Self-Defense Forces as a "resisting force," or "denial capability," against sudden and limited attacks, and argued that it was not necessary for it to be a large-scale force with the capacity to prevent a wider range of attacks. These principles were in line with the concept that was being developed by Kubo Takuya, the administrative vice-minister at the Defense Agency at the time the report was finalized, and were incorporated into the "National Defense Program Outline" that was approved by the Cabinet at the end of October 1976.

The outline established that the most suitable goal for Japan's defense was to develop "the ability to cope effectively with situations up to the point of limited and small-scale aggression," an ability described as "basic defense force" (*kibanteki bōeiryoku*). It also stated that in the case of large-scale invasions that would be difficult for Japan to repel with only its own defense capacity, Japan would mobilize all its available forces to maintain a resistance "until such time" as it could receive cooperation from the United States to deal with the invasion. Namely, while the former national defense policy, the 1957 "Basic Policy on National Defense" (*Kokubō no kihon hōshin*), had stated that external aggression would be dealt with "based on the security arrangements with the United States," this was the first time in the postwar period that a clear division of responsibilities between Japan's own defense efforts and the US–Japan security framework was developed. Moreover, the plan embodied the return of Japanese politics to the rails of traditional security policies based on US–Japan relations, which contrasted with the calls to pursue autonomous defense and build up the "required defense force" (*shoyō bōeiryoku*) that had been sparked by the distanced US approach during the Nixon administration. The formulation of the outline naturally provided a good opportunity to devise US–Japan defense guidelines and further strengthen the US–Japan security relationship that was slowly progressing from crisis to cooperation.

Against the backdrop of crises in the 1970s, this policy of limiting Japan's military capacity and strengthening the US–Japan military security framework moved Japan away from the course of militarization and placed it in the direction of further military restrictions. The Miki cabinet left two extremely restrictive military guidelines to its successors: limiting the defense budget to 1% or less of GNP, and maintaining a complete ban on arms exports. Around the time when Sakata's advisory committee was beyond the critical stage of its deliberations, at meetings held in August 1975 between Prime Minister Miki and President Ford in Washington and between Sakata and Secretary of Defense James Schlesinger in Tokyo, it was agreed that a subcommittee would be established as part of the Japan–US Security Consultative Committee (SCC) in order to begin discussions on US–Japan defense cooperation. This led to the establishment of the Subcommittee for Defense Cooperation (SDC), which convened for the first time in August 1976.

Officially approved by the SCC in November 1978, the "Guidelines for Japan–US Defense Cooperation" outlined a posture for deterring aggression and actions in response to an armed attack against Japan. A third category was also included to address "Japan–US cooperation in the case of situations in the Far East outside of Japan which will have an important influence on the security of Japan," but, largely due to Japanese legal and political restrictions, this clause simply stated that Washington and Tokyo would "consult together from time to time whenever changes in the circumstances so require[d]," and it was not until the 1990s, following the end of the Cold War, that serious progress was made with discussions to define what such cooperation would entail.

CARTER'S GLOBAL STRATEGY AND THE POSITIONING OF JAPAN

In the 1976 presidential election victory went to Jimmy Carter, who was viewed as an outsider to Washington politics, little experienced in diplomacy, but at the same time seen as a man of integrity. In 1974, his participation in the Trilateral Commission between Japan, the United States, and European nations allowed him to broaden his outlook with regard to international affairs and form personal relationships with politicians who took key roles in the administration, such as Zbigniew Brzezinski, who advised him on foreign policy matters prior to his election and later took up the position of national security advisor.

On assuming office in January 1977, Carter appointed Mike Mansfield as ambassador to Japan. This was intended to mollify Congress, but it also had an impact on Japan because Mansfield had long supported Japanese interests. The appointment also conveyed the message that the United States regarded Japan as a valuable ally. During the Carter administration, confrontation arose between Brzezinski and Secretary of State Cyrus Vance on the diplomatic course to be taken with regards to the Soviet Union. While Vance adopted a dovish approach and advocated continued détente with the Soviet Union, Brzezinski sought to restructure international strategy with an underlying stance of opposition to Moscow, based on his deep concerns regarding Soviet actions such as involvement with Cuba in Angola and active support of Marxist forces in Ethiopia and South Yemen.

Implicitly, the negotiations to normalize the US diplomatic relations with China therefore involved a bitter struggle with Vance, who was trying to make a break from policies that were confrontational toward the Soviet Union. On the other hand, Brzezinski wanted to develop a strategic alliance with China as part of his policy to counter the Soviets. The conflict was eventually resolved with the victory of Brzezinski who, supported by Carter, drew up instructions declaring that Washington and Beijing shared the same long-term strategic concern: "opposition to global or regional hegemony by any single power." Given the underlying tone of confrontation with the Soviet Union in its policies, China naturally welcomed the Brzezinski policy, and the normalization of relations between China and the United States was agreed in mid-December 1978, and officially achieved on January 1, 1979.

As these negotiations were taking place, Japan and China were also engaged in negotiations to establish the Japan–China Treaty of Peace and Friendship. The focal point of negotiations was the so-called "anti-hegemony clause." While China tried to link the Japan–China Treaty of Peace and Friendship with the normalization of relations between the United States and China as part of its anti-hegemonic diplomacy toward the Soviet Union, Japan, wishing to avoid becoming embroiled in a confrontation between China and the Soviet Union, took great pains to dilute the anti-Soviet Union aspects of the treaty. Eventually, when the treaty was signed on August 12, 1978, Article II stated: "the treaty nations declare that neither nation will seek hegemony in the Asia-Pacific region or in any other region, and that they will oppose attempts by any other nation or group of nations to establish such hegemony."

A compromise between Japan and China was set out in Article IV, stating "the present Treaty shall not affect the position of either Contracting Party regarding its relations with third countries." The Fukuda cabinet's decision to establish the Japan–China Treaty of Peace and Friendship had largely been encouraged by Deng Xiaoping's show of strong leadership in China that had brought a complete end to the Cultural Revolution. Thus, it appeared that China would adopt a path of sound economic construction, in turn creating a desirable environment for Japan and Asia. Another significant factor behind the decision to establish the treaty was that—somewhat ironically—Fukuda was closely linked with the hawkish pro-Taiwan members of the LDP, and therefore he possessed the influence to convince such members to consent to the treaty.

It should not be forgotten that Moscow's foreign policy at this time facilitated the process of winding down the Cold War. In the first half of the 1970s the Soviet Union found itself in an inferior position due to the strategic move by the United States in initiating rapprochement with China and, later on, cornered by the alignments among the United States, China, and Japan. This had forced it to take consecutive aggressive actions overseas, such as the intervention in Angola in 1976, the military invasion of Afghanistan in December 1979, and support of Vietnam's military invasion of Cambodia in December 1978 that led to the perception that it was threat. The Soviet Union became the target of international sanctions, boycott, and criticism, which led to a resurgence of Cold War hostility. The series of imprudent choices in its foreign policy generated a sense of failure within the Soviet Union, and it underwent several leadership changes in rapid succession. By the time a leader capable of boldly implementing a program of reforms finally appeared with the election of Mikhail Gorbachev in 1985, it was too late.

Carter's Nuclear Nonproliferation Policy

Washington's new ambassador to Japan, Mike Mansfield, was a former Senate majority whip who was well known for his role in ensuring the passing of the Civil Rights Act of 1964 and his opposition to the Vietnam War; he had just completed a long career of 34 years in the House of Representatives and the Senate. Mansfield had also held a strong interest in Japan for many years. In September 1967, when participating in the Shimoda Conference, the first forum for non-official dialogues between Japan and the United States, he had called for the restoration of the Ogasawara and Okinawa islands to the administration of Japan, going against the wishes of the State Department, which did not want to raise the issue unless it was raised by the Japanese side. He had also met with Prime Minister Miki in 1976 during his last visit to Japan as a senator, after which he had advocated the importance of an equal relationship between Japan and the United States based on mutual benefits at the Senate Committee on Foreign Relations (Oberdorfer 2003).

Mansfield's voice played a key role in diffusing the first crisis between the Carter administration and Japan, when the Carter administration opposed the launch of operations at a nuclear reprocessing plant in Tōkaimura, Ibaraki Prefecture. This was shortly after the Japanese government had finally ratified the NPT in June 1976 following years of deliberations. From the outset, Carter had established nuclear nonproliferation as a main foreign policy objective for his administration, and deferred the reprocessing of spent nuclear fuel from the US nuclear power plants indefinitely. Seeking to make Japan a model case in an international bid to restrict the use of enriched plutonium, the Carter administration demanded that the same measures apply to the reprocessing facility in Tōkaimura, just before operations were to come online.

At the time Japan was devoted to developing a new energy strategy following the 1973 oil crisis, and it utilized the guarantee of transparency through compliance with the NPT and cooperating with inspections from the International Atomic Energy Agency (IAEA) as grounds for opposing

American demands. Brzezinski and other members of the administration recognized that energy was truly a "life or death" issue for Japan, and there was also growing concern among them that forcing Japan to accept US demands would lead to anti-American sentiments.

Mansfield's efforts were highly instrumental in encouraging the Carter administration to concede on the issue. On July 12, 1977, one month after he took up his post, he sent a letter to the president, warning that unless a compromise were sought, the issue would have serious repercussions for relations between the United States and Japan (Oberdorfer 2003). As noted by Michael Armacost, the senior staff member for East Asian affairs at the National Security Council at the time, the president made a "180-degree shift from earlier thinking" and instructed Secretary of State Vance to tell Mansfield that he intended to speed up the decision for a compromise (Oberdorfer 2003).

In September 1977, Washington gave its blessing to operate the nuclear reprocessing plant in Tōkaimura, and in December of the same year, a safeguards agreement came into effect between Japan and the IAEA. Carter also demonstrated his initiative by establishing the International Nuclear Fuel Cycle Evaluation (INFCE) committee, and the first general meeting of the committee was held in Washington in October of the same year. At the final general meeting of the INFCE in February 1980, the member nations reached an agreement that nuclear nonproliferation was compatible with the use of nuclear energy for peaceful purposes.

Although the question of Japanese nuclear armament had surfaced on numerous occasions throughout the postwar period, it was the process of reaffirming the importance of Japan–US relations in the Tōkaimura issue that firmly established Japan's final position over nuclear power, as well as its strong commitment to nuclear nonproliferation.

Fukuda and Ōhira's Approach to the United States

Despite a number of critical developments that could potentially have spelled disaster for US–Japan relations, by and large the late 1970s was a period in which the two nations could reaffirm the importance of their relationship. As witnessed in the developments of the Tōkaimura issue, the importance of bilateral relations was also reflected by Carter paying considerable heed to the strong concerns expressed by Fukuda about his election pledge of withdrawing US troops from Korea. Ultimately, Carter was unable to ignore domestic opposition to the proposal and in July 1979 he prudently decided to shelve it.

At the same time, in a speech delivered in Manila in August 1977, Fukuda announced the so-called Fukuda Doctrine, the culmination of the longstanding effort that Japan had been pursuing in Southeast Asia since Prime Minister Tanaka's marred visit to Southeast Asia in 1974. In addition to reemphasizing that Japan would never rise again as a militaristic power and would make the needed effort in consolidating relationships of mutual trust based on a "heart-to-heart" understanding in a broad range of fields, Fukuda announced that Japan would "contribute to the building of peace and prosperity throughout Southeast Asia" by cooperating closely with ASEAN and fostering relations with the countries of Indochina. From this point forward, Japan would pursue diplomacy in Southeast Asia that was based on the fundamental tenet of cultivating a relationship of mutual dependence while also contributing to the stability and prosperity of the entire Southeast Asian region. While one aspect of this new stance in Japanese diplomacy was to take advantage of America's withdrawal from Indochina and to adopt a more proactive role for Japan's foreign policy, it did not conflict with American interests.

Ōhira Masayoshi, who succeeded Fukuda as prime minister in December 1978, took the helm in pursuing new initiatives that sought to use Japan–US relations as a foundation for widening Japan's diplomatic horizon. One of these concepts was the principle of comprehensive national security, which he had made a fundamental part of his campaign for the LDP leadership election. The Study Group on Comprehensive National Security, chaired by political scientist Inoki Masamichi, published its report in July 1980 advocating the combining of efforts to strengthen Japan's own defense capability, enhancing the Japan–US security framework, and developing a favorable international environment to attain comprehensive national security. Such comprehensive security, with a traditional military security guarantee at the core, would encompass the pursuit of economic security, including energy security—the importance of which Japan had learned during the oil crisis—and domestic security, including response to major disasters such as earthquakes.

The second oil crisis, which was sparked by the Iranian Revolution of 1978–79, tested the US–Japan partnership once again. At the end of 1978, growing civil unrest against Shah Mohammad Reza Pahlavi brought a halt to Iran's crude oil production, and OPEC embarked on a policy of raising the price of crude oil. When the revolutionary forces established the

Islamic Republic of Iran in February the following year, a greater sense of impending crisis grew and many countries hurried to purchase oil, which led to a sharp rise in oil prices. At the height of the oil crisis, Japan hosted the G7 Summit for the first time at the June 1979 Tokyo Summit chaired by Prime Minister Ōhira. While the developed nations agreed to cooperate to control imports by setting oil import quotas for each country, and to pursue the development of alternative energy, Japan as chairing nation was placed in a difficult position due to the maneuvering tactics by the other participants regarding the import quotas.

The anger of the Iranian masses that had triggered the Iranian Revolution eventually turned on the United States, leading to the Iranian hostage crisis in November 1979. Washington responded by implementing economic sanctions, but Japan did not immediately follow suit because in the previous month it had just obliged to the request of the revolutionary government to recommence a joint petrochemical project. This led Secretary of State Vance to criticize Japan as "insensitive," and Ōhira agonized over how to respond before eventually buckling to US pressure and joining in sanctions against Iran as a "member of the West."

As soon as he took office, Ōhira also endeavored to pursue the principle of regional solidarity among nations along the Pacific Basin, known as the Pacific Basin Cooperation Concept. In November 1979, he appointed Ōkita Saburō, chair of a government-established research group addressing the viability of a cooperation agreement in the Pacific Basin, as Minister for Foreign Affairs, demonstrating strong determination to develop the cooperation framework. During a visit to Australia and New Zealand in January 1980, Ōhira also made an agreement with Australian Prime Minister Malcolm Fraser to pursue more in-depth review of the concept.

By the late 1970s the Japanese economy had not only adjusted to the oil crisis but had made it an impetus for a spectacular technological innovation that allowed for the development of fuel-efficient vehicles and other advanced manufactured goods. As Japan's economy took off, support for conservative policies also began to surge and thus the LDP achieved landslide victories in the June 1980 elections held in both houses of the Diet. This paved the path for the enormous prosperity of the 1980s, a period that Harvard sociologist Ezra Vogel aptly described as "Japan as Number One."

Japan also adopted a new approach to Asia during this time, epitomized in such policies as the Fukuda Doctrine, Ōhira's concept of Pacific Basin cooperation, and the launch of cultural diplomacy, led by the establishment of the Japan Foundation.

These developments continued despite Ōhira's sudden death in June 1980. The Pacific Community Seminar, which became the parent body of the later Pacific Economic Cooperation Council (PECC), was held in Canberra in September. The seeds Ōhira had sown bloomed nearly ten years later in November 1989 in the shape of the first Asia-Pacific Economic Cooperation (APEC) Ministerial Meeting, which was also held in Canberra. Although one of the key objectives of APEC was to counterbalance American unilateralism in economic matters, Japan exerted strong influence on the other nations to make sure that the United States would be included as a member.

Japan's new proactive approach allowed both the United States and Japan to rediscover the value of their relationship and created the necessary motivation to further develop the alliance. Japan was fortunate in that this coincided with a time that America was reclaiming its confidence and national prestige with the election of President Ronald Reagan in November 1980. This was a breath of fresh air after the uninspired global leadership presented by his immediate predecessors Gerald Ford and Jimmy Carter. A decade that had begun with strains in the relationship between the United States and Japan would close on a very upbeat mood based on ever-closer relations.

BIBLIOGRAPHY

Ford, Gerald R. 1980. *A Time to Heal.* New York: Berkley Books.

Hodgson, James D. 1988. Interview with Ambassador James D. Hodgson (November 25, 1988). Foreign Affairs Oral History Project, Association for Diplomatic Studies and Training.

———. 1990. *Giving Shape to a Life.* Beverly Hills: Private Publisher.

Ishii, Akira, Jianrong Zhu, Soeya Yoshihide, and Xiaoguangb Lin, eds. 2003. *Kiroku to kosho* [Records and Historical Investigation]. Tokyo: Iwanami Shoten.

Kissinger, Henry. 1979. *White House Years.* Boston, MA: Little, Brown.

———. 1994. *Diplomacy.* New York: Simon and Schuster.

Mann, James. 2004. *Rise of the Vulcans.* New York: Viking Press.

Nikaidō, Susumu. 1974. Statement by Chief Cabinet Secretary Nikaidō Susumu (January 11, 1974).

Nixon, Richard. 1969. Nixon's Informal Remarks in Guam with Newsmen, July 25, 1969. *Nixon Papers, 1969.* Washington, DC: United States Government Printing Office, 1971.

————. 1970. First Annual Report to the Congress on United States Foreign Policy for the 1970's, February 18, 1970. *Nixon Papers, 1970.* Washington, DC: United States Government Printing Office, 1971.

Oberdorfer, Don. 2003. *Senator Mansfield.* Washington, DC: Smithsonian Institution Press.

Ogata, Sadako. 1988. *Normalization with China.* Berkeley: Institute of East Asian Studies.

Schaller, Michael. 1997. *Altered States.* New York: Oxford University Press.

CHAPTER 10

The 1980s: The Decade of Neoliberalism

Akihiko Tanaka and Masayuki Tadokoro

STRENGTHENING THE ALLIANCE: THE "RON-YASU" ERA

Republican candidate Ronald Reagan's landslide victory over incumbent Jimmy Carter in the 1980 US presidential election was undoubtedly a reflection of how the public judged the Carter administration. However, for the American public the focus of the election was more about transforming America's image. In the aftermath of the defeat in Vietnam and amid rising inflation rates, America was also losing prestige as it struggled to get a handle on the ongoing Iranian hostage crisis and later faced humiliation following a botched rescue mission. The Soviet invasion of Afghanistan, which coincided with the hostage crisis, highlighted to many Americans the importance of reestablishing a "strong America." While many voters were initially wary of what they saw in Reagan's deep-rooted conservativism, ultimately the electorate chose to entrust him with reviving America.

The chief aim of Reagan's foreign policy was to confront the Soviet Union and to challenge the strategic moves it had been steadily adopting since the mid-1970s. National Security Decision Directive Number

A. Tanaka
Institute for Advanced Studies on Asia, University of Tokyo, Tokyo, Japan

M. Tadokoro
Faculty of Law, Keio University, Tokyo, Japan

© The Author(s) 2017   193
M. Iokibe (ed.), T. Minohara (trans. ed.), *The History of US–Japan Relations*, DOI 10.1007/978-981-10-3184-7_10

32 (NSDD 32), formulated in May 1982, emphasized the reality of the threat, stating that "the decade of the eighties will likely pose the greatest challenge to our survival and well-being since World War II," while also predicting that America's "response could result in a fundamentally different East–West relationship" by the end of the 1980s. Thus, Reagan felt that his utmost priority was to somehow regain the strategic advantage that America had once had in both nuclear and conventional arms. The greatest threat in Europe was the intermediate-range nuclear force (INF) that the Soviet Union had begun to deploy from the mid-1970s. In response to the revived rivalry and despite the budget deficit, Reagan, as a firm believer that a strong dollar equated to a strong America, did not hesitate to increase military expenditure.

The escalating tension with the Soviet Union led to the idea of utilizing the so-called "China Card." The importance of America's relationship with China was emphasized by officials such as Secretary of State Alexander Haig. During a visit to China in June 1981, Haig announced that America was looking into the possibility of selling non-lethal weapons to China. However, even if the United States needed to use China in its strategic tussle with the Soviet Union, it could not turn a blind eye to the core issues in Sino–US relations. This was particularly true for the question of the status of Taiwan, as Reagan himself had made a pledge during the presidential election to uphold America's security relationship with Taiwan.

The United States therefore looked to Japan to assist it in its confrontation with the Soviet Union in the East Asian region. NSDD 32 stated that "in East Asia, the Japanese should be encouraged to contribute more to their own and mutual defense efforts." Since the time of the Carter administration, America had expressed its strong desire for Japan to strengthen its defense capabilities not only through Secretary of Defense Harold Brown but also from President Carter himself, who requested that Japan take further steps in that direction. Brown also took advantage of a summit meeting on defense in December 1980 to press Japan to increase its defense spending by 9.7%. Suzuki Zenkō, who had become prime minister in July 1980 following Ōhira's sudden death, ended up disappointing Washington by only agreeing on a 7.6% increase.

This result prompted Reagan to adopt a new approach to Japan. Instead of setting numerical budget targets for Japan to fulfill, he decided to compel Japan into increasing its substantive defense capability by specifically defining the respective roles and responsibilities of each nation. When Foreign Minister Itō Masayoshi visited the United States in March 1981,

Secretary of Defense Caspar Weinberger suggested a division of duties under which the United States would continue to provide the nuclear umbrella and cover the defense of the sea lanes from the southwest Pacific to the Indian Ocean. In return, Japan would be responsible for its own territory and the surrounding air space, as well as the Northwest Pacific sea lanes north of the Philippines, and west of Guam (Weinberger 1990).

Suzuki's visit to the United States for a summit meeting with Reagan in May 1981 resulted in further commitment to develop mutual defense cooperation between the United States and Japan, but it also led to significant confusion that revealed how vastly their respective perceptions of the situation differed. The joint communiqué issued on May 8 described the relationship between the two nations as an "alliance," and stated that the president and the prime minister recognized that "the alliance between the United States and Japan is built upon their shared values of democracy and liberty." It also went on to address the US–Japan security relationship and introduce the concept of an "appropriate division of roles" between America and Japan.

Suzuki's approach at the summit was somewhat out of character, given that he did not possess a deep knowledge of military security matters and considered himself a dove in the area of defense. It is likely that he did not understand the full significance of the joint communiqué that he had just agreed to as well as his own statements afterward. When this generated controversy in Japan from those who felt that the communiqué and statements suggested that the government was seeking to strengthen the military relationship between the United States and Japan, Suzuki retorted at a press conference that the use of the term "alliance" in the communiqué "did not contain any military intentions." It is absurd to believe that an alliance would not have any military implications, but this was Suzuki's feeble attempt to repair the damage. In the end, Foreign Minister Itō resigned to take responsibility for the confusion. In fact it was not the first time that the relationship between Japan and the United States had been described as an alliance, as Prime Minister Ōhira had described the United States as an "ally" during the US–Japan summit meeting in 1979. However, it is important to keep in mind that at this time "alliance" was still a term that created a strong allergic reaction among many Japanese.

Although Japan and the United States had agreed to "an appropriate division of roles," neither Suzuki nor other senior Japanese officials immediately shared the same understanding as the United States as to what these roles entailed, such as the interpretation of "sea-lane defense." In Japan, the concept of sea-lane defense had conveniently been interpreted as the mapping of sea routes and protecting them with a convoy. In contrast, the United States believed in a far more comprehensive approach that would involve improving the overall capabilities of naval and air defenses against various threats such as those posed by submarines and aircraft. At the 13th Japan–US Security Conference for administrative-level delegates convened in Hawaii on June 10, 1981, just one month after Suzuki's visit to the United States, the US delegation requested that Japan quickly equip itself with the capability to provide naval and air defense for the shores around Japan and defense for 1,000 nautical miles of sea lanes, in particular the capability to respond to Russian submarines and bombers. Sunao Sonoda, who succeeded Itō as foreign minister, likened these demands to suddenly being asked to convert a bungalow into a ten-story building.

While Japanese security experts gradually began to share the American view, Suzuki was still reluctant to fully embrace it. The prime minister emphasized the concept of comprehensive national security, instead, by moves such as establishing the Comprehensive National Security Council. Naturally, the concept of comprehensive national security also had a military component, but Suzuki wished to place emphasis on its non-military dimension.

The Reagan administration was troubled by this development. In addition to seeking the practical application of the division of roles, the National Security Decision Directive on United States–Japanese relations Number 62 (NSDD 62), issued on October 25, 1982, stated that the United States would "accept the validity of Japan's policy of 'comprehensive national security,'" but would not "regard foreign aid as a substitute for defense" (Simpson 1995). Although the Reagan administration was advocating the concept of division of responsibilities, there were growing calls, particularly from Congress, for Japan to increase its defense expenditure further. Opinions were also divided within the administration; while George Shultz, the new secretary of state, wished to avoid placing additional pressure on Japan, there was growing support from Secretary of Defense Weinberger and other members of the administration for a more forceful approach in dealing with an obstinate Japan (Shultz 1993).

The Ron–Yasu Relationship

This atmosphere changed dramatically when Nakasone Yasuhiro was appointed Prime Minister in November 1982. Since leaving his post as a bureaucrat in the Ministry of Home Affairs in 1947, Nakasone had been a consistently active politician with ambition for the top job. As a way to survive the internal power struggle as a leader of a minor faction, Nakasone had developed a canny ability to respond at the right moment—a talent which earned him the moniker "the weathervane of Japanese politics"— and a political style that made full use of his ability to sway the general public.

At the same time, he had also constantly been devising various policy concepts since his youth, and this reflected his consistently critical stance toward the mainstream conservative approach set forth by Yoshida. Nakasone described Yoshida as a leader who "seemed like a political heavyweight but surprisingly tended to rely on subtle tricks, as if he preferred to use a dagger rather than a long sword," adding that he had not been able to swallow the fact that Yoshida had "tried to deceive the people with cheap rhetoric by suggesting that Article 9 denied Japan the right to defend itself and describing the Self Defense Forces as 'armed forces without military power.'" Nakasone believed that "if Yoshida had allowed the government to engage in serious discussions on issues such as national self-defense, measures to reduce American troops from Japan, the role of the state, the future direction of Japan, and Japan's international responsibility, Japan would not be suffering from this mess" (Nakasone 1996).

Many therefore imagined that as prime minister, Nakasone would pursue his nationalist quest to end Japan's dependence upon America, as was reflected in his call to make a "complete settlement of outstanding postwar political accounts." However, in reality, he worked quickly to resolve the various issues in Japan's relations with the United States and South Korea, which had been "at an impasse" since the time of Suzuki's government (Gotōda 1989). In January 1983, Nakasone became the first postwar Japanese prime minister to make an official visit to South Korea, and worked to iron out diplomatic sticking points, which included agreeing to South Korea's request for a loan as a way to assist in its economic recovery. These moves were vital to allowing Nakasone to improve relations with the United States, which was of paramount importance to him.

His first move for boosting relations with the United States was to exempt all defense-related expenditures from budget reductions. While the Ministry of Finance proposal was to increase defense spending by 5.1% in line with the other budgets, Nakasone ordered the director general of the Budget Bureau, Yamaguchi Mitsuhide, to increase it by 6.5%. In his diary entry of December 30, 1982, Nakasone recalled that Yamaguchi's face "twitched and became pale" on receiving the instructions. Although he understood the reluctance that he encountered, he felt that it was necessary to consistently "stick to" foreign policy fundamentals (IIPS 1995).

Nakasone's second bold action was to address the longstanding issue of exporting weapons technology to America. The "Three Principles on Arms Exports" set forth by the Satō cabinet in 1967 had banned arms exports to communist states, nations subject to United Nations arms embargoes, and nations involved in—or likely to be involved in—a dispute. In 1976, the Miki Takeo cabinet had added another layer of conditions to the policy, effectively banning the export of both weapons and weapons technology to all countries. During his administration, Suzuki had consistently refused to respond to repeated criticism from Washington over Japan's refusal to provide even weapons technology to its ally despite the fact that the United States was providing both weapons and weapons technology to Japan.

In order to bolster US–Japan relations, Nakasone felt that he would need to address the issue of exporting military technology. Thus, he informed Tsunoda Reijirō, director general of the Cabinet Legislation Bureau, who was strongly opposed to the export of military technology on the grounds that "provision of technology, if strictly controlled, would be the exchange of technical knowledge in normal operations, and not the transfer of produced weapons." If Japan were to prioritize the Security Treaty with America, Nakasone argued, providing technology to America, Japan's ally, would not pose a problem (Nakasone 1996). His cabinet settled the issue on January 14, 1983, with a statement by Chief Cabinet Secretary formally exempting the United States from export prohibition regulations of Japanese military technology.

Just after overseeing this policy revision, Prime Minister Nakasone attended a summit meeting with President Reagan in Washington from January 18–19, 1983. The new policy that the Reagan administration had chosen was outlined in NSDD 74, dated January 14. As this document indicates, Washington embraced Japan's increased defense budget and its decision to provide weapons technology to the United States. As it now stood, the only remaining item on the defense agenda was to press Japan "for a clear commitment" to implement the agreed division of labor between Japan and the United States (Simpson 1995). At the summit meeting, Nakasone turned out to be positive on this final point. As he wrote in his diary, Nakasone told Reagan that "as nations united by a common destiny, Japan and America are mutually committed to cooperating on their respective sides of the Pacific for the prosperity and stability of world peace and in particular the Asia Pacific region" (IIPS 1995). This was the meeting that marked the beginning of the so-called "Ron–Yasu relationship." According to Hasegawa Kazutoshi, Nakasone's secretary, on the morning of January 19, at a breakfast hosted by the president and his wife, Reagan suggested to Nakasone that they start addressing each other by their first names (Hasegawa 1995).

The impact of Nakasone's statements at the summit meeting itself were somewhat overshadowed by his comments at a breakfast meeting with Katharine Graham, owner of the *Washington Post*, directly before the summit. The *Washington Post* quoted Nakasone as saying that the Japanese archipelago "should be like an unsinkable aircraft carrier, putting up a tremendous bulwark of defense against infiltration of the Backfire bomber" and "should assert complete and full control of the four straits— Nakasone later stated that he had intended to say 'three straits'—through the Japanese islands in order to prevent the passage of Soviet submarines and other naval activities" (Sotooka et al. 2001). The phrase "unsinkable aircraft carrier" was not a direct translation of what Nakasone had originally said in Japanese, but according to Hasegawa, who was present at the meeting, it nevertheless accurately conveyed what Nakasone had intended to say (Hasegawa 1995). While Nakasone was pleased with the impact that the statements had in the United States, he initially denied having made them on the advice of officials from the Ministry of Foreign Affairs who wished to quell criticism from the Japanese media and the Diet. However, he changed his mind, and withdrew his denial shortly after. Aware of the intense backlash that he would face upon his return, he braced himself to deflect any challenges from the Diet, which he felt was attempting to lead the public in the direction of "utopian pacifism" (IIPS 1995).

Abolishing the 1% of GNP Ceiling on Defense Spending

Following the January summit, Nakasone actively sought to promote further cooperation with Washington in the field of security. When he participated in the 9th G7 Summit held at Williamsburg in May 1983, Nakasone used the opportunity of a face-to-face meeting with Reagan just prior to the summit to inform him that he was keen to cooperate with him in order to make the summit a huge success, suggesting that Reagan would be the "pitcher," while he would play the "catcher" (IIPS 1995). A major issue during the summit was whether or not the participating nations should issue a joint statement on the INF issue. French President François Mitterrand and Canadian Prime Minister Pierre Trudeau strongly opposed issuing a statement because they felt that the INF issue was a political matter and therefore not in line with the summit's objective of discussing economic issues.

Making an active effort to persuade Mitterrand to support the statement, Nakasone stated that although Japan was not a member of NATO, and had a "unique peace constitution and three non-nuclear principles," he still supported the statement "from the point of view of global political strategy." Nakasone argued that the statement was necessary to demonstrate solidarity, rather than "division and confusion" in the Western camp in order to prod the Soviet Union into joining in negotiations toward a solution (IIPS 1995). Nakasone was well aware that consenting to such a statement put him at the risk of facing accusations in Japan that he was embarking on exercising the right to collective self-defense. The summit ultimately issued a political declaration, which included the wording: "the security of our countries is indivisible and must be approached on a global basis." Secretary of State Shultz remarked that this statement was "the first time that Japan was officially enlisted in the security system of the Western camp" (Shultz 1993).

After clearly identifying itself as a "member of the Western bloc" at the Williamsburg summit, Japan further consolidated its position in September 1983 following the Korean Air flight 007 incident in which a Korean Air passenger jet en route from New York to Seoul via Anchorage entered Soviet airspace and was shot down by a Soviet fighter plane. Despite the initial reluctance of the Japanese Defense Agency to publicly release confidential military information, in the end the Japanese government did release the SDF-monitored records of Soviet air force communications at the United Nations Security Council and joined the United States in openly criticizing the Soviet Union.

President Reagan's visit to Japan in the fall of that year demonstrated to the Japanese people the close relationship that now existed between Reagan and Nakasone. During his visit, President Reagan also became the first US president to deliver an address to the Japanese Diet. In an attempt to further establish Japan's position as a "member of the West," Nakasone invested a significant amount of effort into repealing the 1% of GNP defense spending limit introduced by the Miki cabinet in 1976. By the early 1980s, actual defense spending was edging ever closer to 1%, and Nakasone clearly realized that sooner or later he would come up against the 1% limit. Therefore, in August 1983, Nakasone established a private advisory panel for reviewing security policy, known as the "Research Group for Peace Issues" (*Heiwa mondai kenkyūkai*), chaired by Professor Kōsaka Masataka of Kyoto University. In its report, submitted in December 1984, the group concluded that the 1% of GNP ceiling was not a suitable means of limiting defense spending. In the following year, Nakasone took action by attempting to have the 1% of GNP limitation on defense spending abolished. However, due to strong opposition—which also came from within the LDP—these developments hit an impasse.

From this experience, Nakasone decided to change his approach and use indirect means to abolish the 1% ceiling. During a diet session in September 1985, he raised the status of the midterm defense estimates, from just an internal budget within the Defense Agency to a government program called the "Midterm Defense Program" with the aim of abolishing the 1% cap when the total budget exceeded 1%. The program budget for the 1986 fiscal year was under 1%, but when the 1987 fiscal budget was formulated, the actual expenditure was expected to exceed 1%. Nakasone therefore abolished the limit of 1% of the GNP with the approval of the Cabinet on January 24, 1987. While these developments were taking place, he also approved the deployment of two squadrons (48 planes) of F-16 fighter jets to the Misawa air base in northern Honshu.

Secretary of Defense Weinberger commented that with the 1% of GNP limitation settled, a large portion of the initial objectives that the Reagan administration had in the area of Japan–US security relations had been met. Allowing for technology transfers was the only major issue that was still slow to be actually implemented (Weinberger 1990). In a statement by the Chief Cabinet Secretary in September 1986, the Japanese government agreed to participate in the Reagan administration's Strategic Defense Initiative (SDI) research, and, in 1987, the Japanese and US governments signed an agreement on SDI. However, for America, this was a prime example of how slowly Japan moved on this particular issue.

The Return of Bilateral Economic Frictions

In contrast to the impressive improvement in security relations between the two countries during the 1980s, economic relations were marred by friction. But the leaders of both countries made sure that that this did not become a hindrance for US–Japan political and security relations. The trade fiction arose in the context of a dramatic shift in economic ideologies. In a fundamental reversal of Keynesianism—the mainstream school of thought since the Second World War in both the United States and Britain—Reagan launched his "Reaganomics" that relied more on market mechanisms while reducing the role of the government. Reaganomics was said to lead to the creation of a stronger America by cutting inflation rates and strengthening the dollar, which would allow for an increase in military expenditure.

In reality, however, the Reagan administration rapidly increased its military spending while also implementing additional tax cuts. Interest rates were set high to counter inflation. As a result, the United States began to run a large "dual deficit" in both its budget and trade; exports suffered because the dollar's value remained high due to the high interest rates. On the other hand, the United States was able to bring in massive capital from abroad because of its attractive interest rates.

In contrast, Japan tried to control its fiscal deficit by privatization which was, by and large, consistent with the new economic ideology that was sweeping the across the world. Nakasone, then director of the Administrative Management Agency, established the Second ad hoc Commission on Administrative Reform (*Dainiji rinji gyōsei chōsakai*)—known as the "Dokō Rinchō" after its chair, the respected businessman Dokō Toshio—in 1981, and based on the recommendations of this commission set in motion the privatization of the three major public corporations: the Japan Tobacco and Salt Public Corporation (Nippon Senbaikōsha), Japanese National Railways (Nippon Kokuyū Tetsudō), and the Nippon Telegraph and Telephone Public Corporation (Nippon Denshin Denwa Kōsha).

Such contrasting macroeconomic management policies of the two largest economies in the world allowed the Japanese manufacturing industry to rapidly expand its exports to the United States, thus leading to record high trade imbalances between the two countries. Washington strenuously argued that this was a reflection of the closed Japanese markets, while Tokyo countered that this was merely the consequence of US macroeconomic policy and the declining competitiveness of American industry.

The most significant trade dispute in the early 1980s was centered on the automobile industry, in particular the US car manufacturers' slowness to respond to the sharp increase in oil prices, allowing fuel-efficient, small Japanese automobiles to rapidly expand their share of the US market. In June 1980, the United Automobile Workers (UAW) of America brought a case to the International Trade Commission (ITC) that asked for import restrictions on Japanese automobiles to the United States. Although the

ITC rejected the case, the situation had ballooned into a political issue involving Congress as well as the administration.

Sensitive to keep up appearances of the GATT basic principles being respected, the Reagan administration did not want to enforce import restrictions on Japanese automobiles; it did, however, try to persuade Japan to introduce some form of "voluntary" restrictions on exports (Ōkawara 2006). From early 1981 onward, the Japanese government responded by trying to persuade the Japanese automobile industry to accept these "voluntary" restrictions, which they considered to be in breach of US antimonopoly laws. When the US Department of Justice announced that this was not the case, an agreement was reached whereby Japan committed itself to implementing voluntary export restraints for the coming three years, with the first-year export quota set at 1.68 million units. Although the agreement addressed this issue, there were still matters that could potentially lead to friction in US–Japan trade relations. Congress was deliberating a local content bill that would impose a certain percentage of local production requirements on Japanese automobile manufacturers who had just stepped up production in the United States.

In addition to the issue of exports from Japan, the issue of promoting US exports to the Japanese market, which involved a complex web of Japanese domestic interests, also became a key diplomatic issue. In January 1985 Market-Oriented Sector-Selective (MOSS) talks were begun in four fields that were of vital interest to the United States: telecommunications equipment and services; electronics; forestry products; and medical equipment and pharmaceuticals. These sectors of the Japanese market posed political challenges more difficult to overcome than export restrictions and the market for agricultural products was also a particularly vexing issue. In both Japan and the United States, the agricultural sector possessed significant political influence, and negotiations over agricultural trade often escalated into serious political issues quite disproportionate to their economic significance. After a prolonged process of piecemeal concessions that sought to expand the existing import quotas, Tokyo finally relented to a complete liberalization of certain commodities such as oranges and beef in 1988.

The Plaza Accord and Japan's Presence

The repeated calls from the other industrialized nations for the United States to alter its macroeconomic policy so that it would rectify its balance of payments were long ignored. As for Japan, Washington was adamant in its position that it was Japan's responsibility to adjust its balance of payments, suggesting that the problem lay in Japan's weak domestic demand or the closed structure of Japan's financial market. Although the Reagan administration had firmly refused to intervene in foreign exchange markets during its first term on the basis that a strong dollar represented a strong America, it began to change its tune as Reagan started his second term in order to alleviate the protectionist sentiment that had built up in Congress over the years. James Baker took over from Donald Regan as Secretary of Treasury and, as a seasoned politician, he was more interested in tackling the practical political issues than economic ideology and did not hesitate to intervene in the foreign markets.

In June 1985, Finance Minister Takeshita and Treasury Secretary Baker established ground where both countries were prepared to cooperate in reducing the imbalance. Initially Japan offered joint intervention, but then accommodated the US demand for "policy coordination," which involved Japan adopting measures to stimulate its economy and decrease its trade surplus. Later in July, during the negotiations at the OECD Working Party 3 (WP3) meeting between Vice Minister of Finance for International Affairs Ōba Tomomitsu and Assistant Secretary of the Treasury for International Affairs David Mulford, Japan committed itself to the foreign exchange policies and macroeconomic policies that Mulford had proposed and acted to stimulate the economy through substantial monetary easing.

Furthermore, at a top secret meeting of the deputy finance ministers and central bank governors of the Group of Five (G5) industrialized nations—America, Japan, West Germany, France, and the United Kingdom—held in London on September 15, serious progress was made toward developing a plan that would later be known as the Plaza Accord (Funabashi 1988). Based on the Plaza Accord, the G5 nations embarked on coordinated intervention, selling huge amounts of dollars and achieving the agreed 10–12% depreciation of the dollar by the end of October 1985.

At the meeting, Finance Minister Takeshita announced that Japan would be prepared to accept yen appreciation of up to 200 yen to the dollar. The finance ministers of America and the European nations, who had been convinced that Japan was undervaluing the yen in order to promote exports, interpreted this move as being a solid resolution on Japan's part (Volcker and Gyōten 1992). As Washington applied more pressure on Japan to expand its domestic demand, the dollar depreciation was welcomed in Japan. However, when the dollar continued to depreciate even further into 1987, reaching a record low of around 150 yen, the new Finance Minister Miyazawa Kiichi was forced to make an urgent trip to Washington to request American cooperation in stopping a further appreciation of the yen (Funabashi 1988). Under the Louvre Accord of February 1987, it was agreed to stabilize the exchange rates where they stood, while the United States promised to reduce its fiscal deficit and both Japan and Germany promised to adopt measures to stimulate their economies. Of course, any sudden decline in the value of the dollar could lead to a loss of confidence in the currency and the market crash in the New York stock exchange on October 19, 1987, so-called Black Monday, clearly showed that these fears were real.

A day after the signing the Plaza Accord, on September 23, 1985, Reagan outlined a new trade policy. Under this plan, he sought to launch a new GATT round in the fields in which America was particularly competitive, such as agricultural products and services, as well as to address intellectual property issues and conduct bilateral and regional trade and commerce negotiations. A particularly worrying development for Japan was Reagan's announcement that he supported making active use of Section 301 of the Trade Act (Super 301) which granted the president the right to unilaterally identify countries as unfair trading partners and adopt punitive sanctions against those nations. By taking such measures, Washington was making it very clear that it would steadfastly pursue its national interests through bilateral and regional frameworks rather than the GATT.

As discussed earlier, the Plaza Accord generated a sharp rise in the value of the yen. Fearing a recession induced by the strong yen, Tokyo sought to expand its domestic demand by adopting economic stimulation measures which in hindsight contributed to Japan's financial bubble. Moreover, the strong yen generated by the Plaza Accord quickly increased the global presence of the yen and Japanese direct investment aroused significant attention in Europe and America.

Alongside these economic developments, Japan was also building up a greater presence in international politics. This was partially due to Nakasone's success in developing a good relationship with Reagan, combined with Japan's economic strength. He used this to his advantage as he actively played a prominent role in G7 summits and other multilateral diplomatic meetings. The G7 Summit held in Tokyo in May 1986 was the perfect stage for Nakasone to demonstrate his skills as a leader. In the elections for both houses of the Diet held in July that year, the LDP achieved a historic landslide, securing a staggering 300 seats in the Lower House and 72 seats in the Upper House. Faced with this overwhelming victory, political pundits claimed that the LDP had successfully turned the 1955 system into the 1986 system, consolidating its popularity as a "catch-all-party" that could attract a wide spectrum of supporters.

JAPAN IN THE EYES OF "REVISIONISTS" VS. A "JAPAN THAT CAN SAY 'NO'"

The global process leading up to the end of the Cold War had already begun when the Nakasone cabinet abolished the 1% of GNP defense spending limit in January 1987. In March 1985 Mikhail Gorbachev became general secretary of the Communist Party of the Soviet Union, and rapidly pushed forward with domestic policies of *perestroika* and "new thinking" in foreign affairs, which paved the way for global changes. The 1987 Intermediate Range Nuclear Forces (INF) Treaty required the United States and the Soviet Union to eliminate their immediate and shorter range missiles; the last Soviet troops were withdrawn from Afghanistan in February 1989; and the fall of the Berlin Wall prompted a rapid succession of collapses of Eastern European communist governments.

With the threat posed by the Soviet Union declining, a significant number of Americans began to perceive Japan not so much as an ally but more as an economic rival. The suggestion by the American scholar Chalmers Johnson that Japan had emerged as the winner of the Cold War was widely echoed, and it was predicted that the age of geopolitics would soon be followed by the age of geoeconomics. This was exacerbated by the fact that while in America there was constant talk of decline as it tackled social issues such as severe levels of crime and homelessness, it seemed as if nothing could go wrong for Japan as it enjoyed the immense prosperity brought about by the financial bubble in the late 1980s. The economic friction made US–Japan relations extremely tense, to the point that it even affected the Ron–Yasu relationship. In America, there was a rapid increase in the influence of theories that Japan was an intrinsically different entity from America and the other Western democratic nations, as well as suggestions that Japan was a chimera born out of a strange form of capitalism that posed a threat to America.

Journalist Theodore White's article "The Danger from Japan," a lengthy piece published in the *New York Times Magazine* in 1985, became the first in a succession of arguments posting such trends which were dubbed "revisionism." In 1989, journalist James Fallows argued that it was necessary to stop Japan's unrestrained economic expansion in his essay "Containing Japan," published in *Atlantic Monthly*. It was certainly no coincidence that in his article Fallows used the term "containment," the term used for America's policy of checking the rise of the Soviet Union during the Cold War. The high-profile book *Trading Places: How We are Giving Our Future to Japan and How to Reclaim It* by Clyde Prestowitz from the US Department of Commerce, who was involved in the trade and commerce negotiations with Japan, also asserted that the Japanese, by their nature, had very little understanding of the concept of "fair" competition.

Chalmers Johnson, who in his 1982 book *MITI and the Japanese Miracle* had suggested that, in contrast to the traditional "capitalist regulatory states" of America and Europe, Japan was a "capitalist developmental state" in which a strong interventionist bureaucracy allowed it to achieve economic success, had developed a theory that claimed that the inherent differences in Japan's system meant it would never be possible to form an economic relationship based on the principles of free trade. In his provocative book *The Enigma of Japanese Power*, Dutch journalist Karel van Wolferen argued that Japan is a repressive country controlled by a hierarchy of faceless bureaucrats where the convergence between the public and the private sectors and lack of distinction between the two meant ultimately there was no clear sense of who was accountable in Japan.

A Japan that Stands Firm

While major shifts in the global status quo were taking place, the Japanese political leadership was gradually becoming weaker. After Nakasone resigned in November 1987, the succeeding prime ministers lacked leadership skills and served only short terms in office that were plagued by their involvement in political scandals, which was the case of Takeshita Noboru and Uno Sōsuke; or they did not enjoy a strong support base within the party, as exemplified by Kaifu Toshiki, who also lacked clear direction regarding foreign policy matters.

Although US–Japan relations had weathered multiple storms created by trade disputes in the early 1980s, during the latter half of the decade the nature of the disagreements began to change as it shifted more toward fundamental issues over Japan's economic system and trade practices as a whole. This made the issue much more difficult to resolve. Furthermore, security and economic issues became closely intertwined. In the Toshiba–Kongsberg scandal in 1987, it was revealed that Japan's Toshiba Machine Company, along with Norway's Kongsberg Trading Company, had sold the Soviet Union advanced milling machinery and accompanying numerical control equipment, which was banned from being exported to Communist bloc countries under the regulations of the Coordinating Committee for Multilateral Export Controls (COCOM).

The incident fueled the fervor of "Japan bashers," and developed into a major political issue because of the rising criticism of Japan within the US administration. Despite the fact that there was significant support within the US government calling for cooler heads and gradual improvements to Japan's system of export control, somebody in the administration leaked this information to the media and the issue became politicized (Chinworth 2004).

Another point of contention was Japan's domestic development of the Fighter Support X (FSX) jet. In October 1987, Tokyo responded to America's repeated demands for Japan to purchase American-manufactured fighter jets by agreeing to co-develop a new plane with American manufacturers. However, shortly after Bush took over the presidency from Reagan, strong criticism over the agreement arose in Congress on the grounds that the joint development would allow Japanese access to key American technologies. This issue was settled in April 1989, when an agreement was reached that involved significant concessions by Japan. Despite this, severe opposition persisted over the deal from Congress and a motion was passed to seek further amendments to the bilateral agreement. Ultimately, President Bush vetoed the action by Congress and allowed for the joint development of FSX jets to finally commence in September. However, the event left behind a bitter memory for both the United States and Japan.

The United States had adopted an entirely different approach to tackle Japan's "closed-ness" in their trade and commerce negotiations, based on the understanding that it was necessary to restructure the Japanese economy as a whole to pry open the Japanese market in a truly effective way, and it began to focus on tackling the so-called "structural impediments." The Structural Impediments Initiative (SII) talks resulted in a final report in June 1990 that contained Washington's numerous demands that covered such domestic Japanese matters as improving Japan's savings and investment balance by increasing Japanese public investment, making improvements to promote land use by enhancing the taxation system, improving the distribution system by revising the Large-Scale Retail Stores Act, eliminating exclusionary business practices, and monitoring financial transactions between affiliated businesses.

Many Japanese government officials were not amused by the fact that the United States had so brazenly interfered in Japan's domestic systems. But in contrast to a time when the United States criticized Japanese "unfairness" as the root of economic friction, this time it emphasized that its demands also served the interests of the Japanese consumers. Some in the Japanese public supported America's position and questioned why their government had not taken steps to improve land use and eliminate exclusionary business practices in the first place without having to be dictated by the United States to do so.

While "structural impediments initiatives" are generally in line with free market doctrines, "Japan revisionism" suggested a "result-oriented approach" that tilted toward managed trade and thereby contravened with America's ideal of free trade. A case in point was the issue of semiconductor trade. The Japanese semiconductor industry had been rapidly grabbing the global market since the early 1980s, and many Americans began to fear that America had fallen behind in developing cutting-edge technology. The sense of this crisis, along with the revisionist theories that Japan was operating on a fundamentally different system, prompted Washington to insist that Japan allocate at least a 20% share of the Japanese market to American semiconductor products.

Eventually, when the semiconductor agreement was concluded in September 1986, Japan sent a side note stating that it would endeavor to ensure that America's market share would exceed 20% within a period of five years (Hosoya et al. 1999; Furjiwara 1988; Ōyane 2002). However, this vague compromise only made matters worse. When the actual market share did not increase, Washington implemented economic sanctions as retaliation against what they saw as a brazen breach of promise. The following administration, under President Clinton, took an even more hardline stance in the negotiations, demanding deeper concessions from Japan by brandishing the unrealized target figure.

America's heavy-handed approach generated strong resentment toward the United States within Japan. The frustration of being dependent on America in the postwar period had created a constant underlying impulse to put up a defiant response to the United States. Many Japanese also felt insulted by the fact that Japan's postwar international competitive strength, the fruits of the tremendous efforts by ordinary Japanese citizens, had been labelled "unfair." The 1989 book *The Japan That Can Say "No,"* by the conservative politician Ishihara Shintarō and Sony co-founder Morita Akio, reflected Japan's resentment. The book sent out a clearly different message to that of anti-American leftists, as it advocated that Japan was a global power in its own right and should assert its rights and not succumb to American pressure.

Political realists may argue that it was only logical that Washington started to be tougher on the second-largest economy as soon as it had won the Cold War. On the other hand, it can also be argued that it was understandable that the Japanese became more assertive when the Soviet threat began to decline. Their emotional and negative responses to American arrogance in economic areas were as intense as their strong sense of dependence on the United States during the Cold War. However, while it was satisfying to say "no" to America, Japan was not ready to lay out what it could and should do to improve the world economy and international security.

Pressures by the Press and Public Opinion

The negative perceptions that Japan and America held toward one another were amplified by the media of both countries. Japanese media had the tendency to dissect every minute item, from insignificant bills for protectionist trade laws being placed on the Congress agenda to criticisms of Japan at a public hearing. This helped to give the Japanese public the impression that all of America was consumed and obsessed with "Japan bashing." On the other hand, the interest of the American media in Japanese affairs had traditionally been limited, but through the development of Japan's financial bubble, American coverage of Japan also entered its own bubble phase as articles related to Japan written from the then-trendy revisionist standpoint rapidly increased. A notably large number of pieces adopted the portrayal of Japan not as a liberal democratic nation that stood alongside America during the Cold War, but as a strange "outsider" that was unfair, insular, bureaucrat-dominated, and the product of a confused mixture of the traditional and the ultramodern (Kimura and Tadokoro 1998; Ueno 1998).

For example, when Sony acquired Columbia Pictures Entertainment, an article published in *Newsweek* on October 9, 1989, covered this investment by one Japanese company under the front-page headline "Japan invades Hollywood!" Foreign investment in America had always been welcomed, but the article sought to incite agitation toward Japan, suggesting that acquiring a company like Columbia Pictures was like buying "a piece of America's soul." Incidentally, the fact that in the Japanese edition of *Newsweek* the title of the article was toned down to "Sony's advance" (*Sonū shingeki*) illuminates the hypocritical nature of the media (Andō 1991).

As Japan gained an increasingly high profile in American mass media, it became increasingly more common for statements by Japanese figures that would previously not have attracted the slightest interest to be picked up by the US media and to subsequently blow up into a serious issue. Nakasone himself encountered a huge backlash when, while boasting at an LDP seminar in September 1986 that Japan had become a "highly intelligent society," he stated that in America there were "many blacks, Puerto Ricans, and Mexicans," and that, on average, America's level of intelligence was "still extremely low." This was because both politicians and Japanese society in general were somewhat desensitized to the fact that racial issues were an extremely delicate topic in American society after the Civil Rights Movement of the 1960s.

However, America's rapid growth in interest toward Japan led not only to the development of revisionist theories but also to some positive developments. Around this time there was a sudden increase in the number of American university students engaging in the study of Japanese language and/or research on Japan, leading to a surge in the number of young graduates who would come to enrich US–Japan relations in the future. At the same time, in Japan the national government cooperated with the various municipalities to launch the Japan Exchange and Teaching (JET) program, which brought young native English-speakers to Japan to teach English. This developed into a highly successful initiative in "grassroots cultural exchange," allowing the participants to develop a deep understanding and affinity for Japan through their experiences during their stay.

Although it was difficult to ignore what was being touted in the American press, the American public held various opinions with regard to Japan and in the end prudent minds prevailed. Public opinion polls in America reveal that the level of trust toward Japan was relatively consistent despite the many sensationalistic headlines that appeared in the media. This was true in Japan as well, where goodwill toward America among the Japanese public remained relatively stable.

Regardless, Japan and America were allies and the democratic political systems of both nations showed no signs of weakening. Moreover, there were those in Japan who felt that the pressure America placed on Tokyo regarding economic issues was a convenient external stimulus that actually assisted in reforming the Japanese economic system, which tended to be constrained by vested interests and the dominance of the bureaucracy. It was also possible to view pressure from America as playing a key role in the Japanese political system because it offered an alternative to the Japan Socialist Party, which was becoming increasingly ineffective in fulfilling its role as the largest opposition party.

In January 1989, Emperor Hirohito passed away, bringing to an end the Showa period that had spanned more than six decades. His death also marked the zenith of Japan's unprecedented economic prosperity. In November of that year, the Berlin Wall collapsed and the Cold War ended. Soon thereafter, the United States declared Japan to be an "unfair trading partner" based on the 1988 amendments of Article 301 of the 1974 Trade Act, the so-called "Super 301" provisions. In hindsight, this marked a new stage of US–Japan relations that would eventually culminate in the "second defeat" of Japan in 1991.

BIBLIOGRAPHY

Andō, Hiroshi. 1991. *Nichibei jōhō masatsu* [US–Japan Information Friction]. Tokyo: Iwanami Shoten.

Chinworth, Michael. 2004. Tōshiba Kikai Jiken no Saikentō [Strategic Trade Management]. *Journal of International Security* 32–2 (September), 99–118.

Fujiwara, Mikio. 1988. Nichibei Handōtai Kyōtei [US-Japan Semiconductor Agreement]. *Bungei Shunjū* 66 (6), May: 124–137.

Funabashi, Yōichi. 1988. *Tsūka Retsu Retsu* [Heated Currencies]. Tokyo: Asahi Shimbunsha.

Gotōda, Masaharu. 1989. *Naikaku kanbō chōkan* [Chief Cabinet Secretary]. Tokyo: Kōdansha.

Hasegawa, Kazutoshi. 1995. Nakasone gaikō [Nakasone Diplomacy]. In *Nakasone naikakushi* [History of the Nakasone Cabinet], ed. IIPS, 175–226. Tokyo: Marunouchi Shuppan.

Hosoya, Chihiro, Aruga Tadashi, Ishii Osamu, and Sasaki Takuya, eds. 1999. *Nichibei kankei shiryōshū 1945–97* [A Documentary History of US–Japan Relations, 1945–97]. Tokyo: University of Tokyo Press.

Institute for International Policy Studies (IIPS). 1995. *Nakasone naikaku-shi shiryō-hen* [History of the Nakasone Cabinet: Documents]. Tokyo: Institute for International Policy Studies.

Kimura, Masato, and Tadokoro Masayuki. 1998. *Gaikokujin Tokuhain* [Foreign Correspondents in Tokyo]. Tokyo: Nihōn Hōsō Shuppan Kyōkai.

Nakasone, Yasuhiro. 1996. *Tenchi ujō* [The Sentient World]. Tokyo: Bungeishunjū.

Ōkawara, Yoshio. 2006. *Ōraru hisutorī: Nichibei gaikō* [Oral History: Diplomacy between Japan and the United States]. Tokyo: Japan Times.

Ōyane, Satoshi. 2002. *Nichibeikan handōtai masatsu* [Japan–US–Korean Friction over Semiconductors]. Tokyo: Yūshindō Kōbunsha.

Shultz, George P. 1993. *Turmoil and Triumph*. New York: Charles Scribner's Sons.

Simpson, Christopher. 1995. *National Security Directives of the Reagan and Bush Administrations*. Boulder, CO: Westview Press.

Sotooka, Hidetoshi, Honda Masaru, and Miura Toshiaki. 2001. *Nichibei dōmei hanseiki* [A Half-Century of the Japan–US Alliance]. Tokyo: Asahi Shimbunsha.

Ueno, Chizuko. 1998. Henken hōdō o umu nanatsu no yōin [Seven Factors Creating Prejudiced Media Coverage]. In *Warawareru Nihonjin* [The Japanese Ridiculed], ed. Zipangu. Tokyo: Zipangu.

Volcker, Paul, and Gyōten Toyoo. 1992. *Changing Fortunes*. New York: Times Books.

Weinberger, Caspar. 1990. *Fighting for Peace*. New York: Warner Books.

CHAPTER 11

The 1990s: From a Drifting Relationship to a Redefinition of the Alliance

Kōji Murata

Japan's Feeble Response to the Gulf War

By late 1989, Japan was at the peak of its bubble economy, with the Nikkei stock average reaching a record high of 38,915 yen. As the military threat from the Soviet Union receded, the United States began to perceive Japan's economic strength as its greatest threat. Strains began to appear in US–Japan relations as anxiety and resentment toward Japan surfaced in America, where it was felt that Japan had achieved economic prosperity by "free riding" on the bilateral alliance. In a public opinion poll published by the *New York Times* on July 10, 1990, for example, 58% of respondents saw economic competition from Japan as a greater threat than the military might of the Soviet Union.

Although Tokyo was already under heavy criticism for its lack of contribution to international affairs, Japan's abysmal response to the Gulf crisis of 1990–91 was not only slow but also halfhearted. This was largely a result of domestic political factors. The incumbent Liberal Democratic Party (LDP) had fallen short of a majority in the 1989 House of Councillors election and the prime minister at that time, Kaifu Toshiki, was a dovish leader with only a fragile support base within his own party.

K. Murata
Faculty of Law, Doshisha University, Kyoto, Japan

© The Author(s) 2017
M. Iokibe (ed.), T. Minohara (trans. ed.), *The History of US–Japan Relations*, DOI 10.1007/978-981-10-3184-7_11

Four weeks after Iraq's invasion of Kuwait, the Japanese government finally committed US$1 billion in aid to the coalition forces. Several Congressmen criticized Japan for this meager level of financial support, particularly given its position as the world's second-greatest economic power and one of America's principal allies, and its dependence on the Middle East for 70% of its crude oil. The US ambassador to Japan, Michael H. Armacost—who was nicknamed "Mr. Gaiatsu" ("Mr. External Pressure") due to his enthusiasm for prodding the Japanese government to contribute more internationally—appealed directly to the influential LDP Secretary General Ozawa Ichirō to step up Japan's efforts. As a result, the Japanese Ministry of Finance (MOF) gradually increased its financial contribution in stages as circumstances developed, later committing an additional US$3 billion, followed by a further US$9 billion. In the end, Tokyo had pledged a total of US$13 billion to the coalition forces, but Washington was still unimpressed, a reaction that evokes the phrase "too little, too late." Thus, Japan received no thanks when the Gulf War ended, even from the Kuwaiti government.

Reeling from this fiasco, the Kaifu cabinet sought to pass legislation that would allow Japan to contribute human resources, including dispatching the Self-Defense Forces (JSDF) to participate in logistical support. These proposals were submitted to the Diet in the United Nations Peacekeeping Operations Cooperation Bill, largely under the initiative of Ozawa, but the cabinet failed to clearly articulate to the Diet the justifications for the bill and as a result it was dropped in November 1990. Tokyo had to wait until the end of the war before it was finally able to send Maritime SDF minesweepers to the Persian Gulf. Not long after it had been seen as the "winner of the Cold War," Japan's failure to contribute promptly and sufficiently to the Gulf War relegated it to the status of the greatest diplomatic loser of the conflict. This could also have inflicted serious damage on US–Japan relations had it not been for the significant building up of the alliance in the 1980s. However, the lessons of this failure were certainly not lost upon Japanese policymakers, and when coalition forces invaded Iraq in 2003, Prime Minister Koizumi Junichirō was very quick in extending Japan's full support.

The Meandering of President Bush's Diplomacy

The American public's approval rating for George H. W. Bush reached an apex of 90% owing to strong support for the policies that he had pursued in his war against Iraq. Bolstered by this popularity, Bush concluded an agreement with Gorbachev in late July 1991 for the United States and the Soviets to further reduce their nuclear arsenals under the Strategic Arms Reduction Treaty I (START-I) that limited both countries to no more than 6,000 nuclear warheads each. This bold move toward greater reconciliation and nuclear disarmament created an impact that far exceeded the intentions of the two leaders, as it led to the dissolution of the Warsaw Treaty Organization, a failed coup d'état against Gorbachev by the conservative faction of the Soviet Communist Party, and, ultimately, the fall of the Soviet Union in late 1991, marking the definitive end of the Cold War.

The Bush administration had overstretched itself in responding in rapid succession to both the Gulf crisis and the dissolution of the Soviet Union, and Congress was less willing to give the president free rein on diplomatic issues. It quickly became evident that the Gulf War had been an exception rather than a norm for solving regional conflicts in the post–Cold War world. The Bush administration exercised realist prudence when it came to other issues that emerged after the Gulf War, such as the breakup of Yugoslavia, civil war in Bosnia, pursuing peace between Israel and Palestine, and providing support for the reconstruction of Afghanistan following the withdrawal of Soviet troops—which would come back to haunt American diplomacy in the next century. Bush began to repeatedly emphasize a need for a "new world order" in the hope of allowing America to readjust to new realities in the realm of security and preventing it from returning to an isolationist approach to its foreign policy.

However, as soon as the euphoria over the victory in Kuwait began to simmer down, the American public once again turned its attention to economic issues. With Bush's approval rating now taking a tumble, he urgently needed to engage in economic issues prior to elections in the fall. Thus, when he visited Japan in January 1992, his entourage included top executives from America's Big Three automobile producers and he repeatedly called for "jobs, jobs, and more jobs" for Americans. Unfortunately for Bush, signs of economic recovery failed to emerge as the election drew closer. However, it was ironic that despite its outward appearances, the US economy was actually growing at this time. This would manifest itself after Bill Clinton's victory in the election, in which he crushed Bush by making the economic recovery one of the key issues during the race.

Achievements of Prime Minister Miyazawa

While the 1992 presidential election was approaching in the United States, in Japan, Miyazawa Kiichi was settling into his new position, having succeeded Kaifu as prime minister in November 1991. Miyazawa was a highly experienced politician of the LDP's internationally oriented faction, and there were high hopes that his appointment would see the long-awaited advent of a powerful and determined administration representing the LDP mainstream conservative (*hoshu honryū*) faction, the Kōchikai. Miyazawa's base in the LDP was not as weak as those of Uno Sōsuke, Kaifu, and his other predecessors, as he was supported by the Takeshita faction of the LDP. Similar to Bush, Miyazawa belonged to an older generation who tended to adopt a cautious leadership style and a careful approach to the use of power.

Despite this, the Miyazawa cabinet steadily tackled the various diplomatic challenges that had been left unresolved by their predecessors. Firstly, the United Nations Peacekeeping Operations Cooperation Bill that the Kaifu cabinet had been forced to abandon was established under the agreement of the LDP, Kōmeitō, and the Democratic Socialist Party (DSP; Minshatō) in June 1992 as the Act on Cooperation for United Nations Peacekeeping Operations and Other Operations ("PKO Cooperation Act"). This made it possible for the JSDF to participate in UN peacekeeping operations. It also finally resolved the diplomatic issue that postwar Japan had wrestled with since the 1958 Lebanon crisis, which occurred not long after it had joined the UN, and provided an indirect response to the diplomatic failure of the recent Gulf War. Proposals for the JSDF to participate in peacekeeping operations also posed a risk of the JSDF becoming involved in situations in which the use of lethal force would be required, such as monitoring ceasefires and disarming combatants, but any further inquiry into this matter was shelved due to opposition from the Kōmeitō.

Other key factors that assisted the enactment of the PKO Cooperation Act were the success of the dispatch of Maritime SDF minesweepers to the Persian Gulf and the efforts of Tokyo to carefully engage in discussions and maneuvering in the Ministry of Foreign Affairs and within the LDP. The Japanese government was particularly keen to participate in peacekeeping operations in Cambodia as it wished to follow up its successful diplomatic role in reaching a peace settlement in Cambodia and also mitigate the possibility of being labelled a nation that was risk averse. Under the PKO Cooperation Act, 1,200 members of the JSDF were dispatched to take part in the United Nations Transitional Authority in Cambodia (UNTAC) peacekeeping operations over the one-year period from September 1992 to September 1993. The JSDF assisted in rebuilding social infrastructure in the relatively stable Takeo province, actions which were highly praised due to the disciplined approach of the JSDF and their diligent efforts in assisting the local populace.

Miyazawa also firmly held his ground when the Japanese public began to call for the withdrawal of the JSDF from peacekeeping operations after two Japanese—a UN volunteer worker assisting with the election and a civilian policeman—were killed in Cambodia in April and May 1993. Miyazawa recalls in his memoirs that public opinion was so vehement that he was unsure if he would be able to maintain his position if more Japanese lives were to be lost (Mikuriya and Nakamura 2005). This tug-of-war between the government and public opinion was subsequently repeated each time Japan tried to expand its security role.

The Social Democratic Party of Japan (SDPJ; Shakaitō) had attempted to prevent the PKO Cooperation Act from being passed by employing tactics such as the "ox trot" (*gyūho senjutsu*; namely, inching their way to the podium to filibuster votes) and attempting to force a resignation en masse to dissolve the lower house. However, they failed to gain the support of the majority of the Japanese public, and as Tokyo moved toward greater overseas participation, the momentum of "international cooperation" prevailed and it became a keyword to describe Japanese diplomacy in the post-Cold War era.

It was in 1992 that Japan first declared its wish to become a permanent member of the UN Security Council. While America supported Japan's permanent membership of the UNSC in principle, even to this day Washington and Tokyo have yet to make a coordinated effort in bringing this about. Beneath the surface, contentions began to develop between the two nations. Japan was dissatisfied with America's lack of understanding toward its concerns that it was not being extended a prominent position in the UN commensurate with its increased diplomatic role in the post-Cold War era, while America was disappointed with Japan's diplomatic contributions, which, although recognizably greater, were still seen as inadequate relative to its national strength.

In October 1992, Emperor Akihito made an official visit to China to mark the twentieth anniversary of the resumption of diplomatic ties between Japan and China. The visit was a response to earnest requests from Chinese officials, who were concerned about China's international isolation following the Tiananmen Square protests in 1989. Japan was the exception; it had lifted its sanctions after only a year and taken steps to bring China back into international society. In return, Beijing had restrained its criticism when Japan passed the PKO Cooperation Act, despite domestic pressures to label it "the return of Japanese militarism." There was some criticism within Japan that the emperor was being used as a political tool, but the visit demonstrated that Japan felt that stable relations with China were a necessity for ensuring the peace and prosperity of not only East Asia but also the world.

In August 1993, the Japanese Foreign Policy Bureau (*Sōgō Gaikō Seisakukyoku*) was established as part of a reorganization of the structure of the Ministry of Foreign Affairs (MOFA) in an effort to address the failure of Japan's response to the Gulf War and to create a system that would allow for the development of long-term and comprehensive strategies in Japanese foreign policy. The first director general of the Foreign Policy Bureau, Yanai Shunji, recalls that the Treaties Bureau (*Jyōyakukyoku*) had successfully played a similar role during the Cold War when international relations had been relatively static and diplomacy could be pursued through the interpretation of laws and treaties and fielding questions by the Diet. But this had ceased to be as effective after the Cold War ended and it had become necessary to pursue a more proactive role in diplomacy (Iokibe et al. 2007).

While the Miyazawa cabinet achieved a number of important developments in foreign policy, the collapse of the bubble economy and subsequent concerns regarding the increase in domestic nonperforming loans led to the sense that the postwar system had reached a dead end and was unable to tackle political reform. The LDP's one-party dominance in politics and economic management was reaching its limit, and with the end of the Cold War, the "internal Cold War," as the 1955 system was known, was on the verge of collapse. At the same time, the new economy-oriented Clinton administration and non-governmental voices throughout the media seemed to relish an atmosphere of "Japan bashing," and, in turn, the Japanese media responded by coining and popularizing the new term "*kenbei*" (contempt of America). This was the first time since the Pacific War that such sentiment was also widely felt among elite policymakers who had hitherto supported US–Japan relations.

President Bush had successfully adjusted the United States from a bipolar to a unipolar world, but he was unable to complete his "new world order" before leaving office. Likewise, Prime Minister Miyazawa expanded the horizons of Japanese diplomacy but failed to capitalize on those developments, and was forced to resign in 1993 when the LDP faced its first defeat in a national election, marking an end to the "1955 System" of LDP dominance that had begun with the party's inception.

From an Alliance "Adrift" to its "Redefinition"

Clinton's inauguration in January 1993 marked the end of 12 years of Republican rule, and partly for this reason Tokyo did not possess any strong ties with key Democratic Party leaders. Clinton, the first American president to have been born after World War II, held a very different view of Japan: that of a strong economic rival that sought to reap the post–Cold War "peace dividend," and thus not really a staunch ally on security-related issues. Clinton also lacked experience in politics at the national level and initially showed little interest in diplomacy in comparison with his predecessor Bush.

Clinton's Asian diplomacy reflected core domestic values such as freedom, democracy, and human rights, and was strongly focused on American trade interests. Shortly after taking office, he established the National Economic Council (NEC), modelled after the National Security Council (NSC). Through his diplomacy sought to secure American values and trade interests—the latter in the case of Japan, and both in the case of China. Clinton also criticized Bush's weak-kneed diplomacy toward China, declaring that America would "not coddle tyrants, from Baghdad to Beijing." However, while he sought to address the frustrations of the US trade deficit as well as the state of human rights in China, US financial circles increasingly called for the expansion of trade with China. In May 1993, the Clinton administration renewed China's most-favored-nation status and the president had his first meeting with Chinese President Jiang Zemin at the Asia-Pacific Economic Cooperation (APEC) forum in Seattle in November. It was the first summit between the leaders of the United States and China in four and a half years. Washington had already relaxed the economic sanctions that it had imposed on China following the Tiananmen Square incident and the Chinese economy had begun to grow at breakneck speed, leading to increased exchanges and consultations between both governments which in turn led to the expansion of bilateral trade.

Clinton's move to further engage with China drew criticism from within Congress, including the anticommunist hardliner camp and those who sought to promote human rights. Thus, his policy toward China would later fluctuate significantly. Assistant Secretary of State for East Asian and Pacific Affairs Winston Lord was called to the task of reconstructing a consistent Asian policy emphasizing US allies in Asia, but Clinton showed no interest in such strategic consistency. His diplomacy consequently attracted doubts from both inside and outside of the administration and from both the Pacific and the Atlantic. Asian nations became increasingly distrusting of the administration's Asia policy due its frequent shifts, whereas the European nations felt that Clinton sometimes paid too much attention to the state of affairs in Asia and was not sufficiently involved in issues surrounding Europe.

A Non-LDP Government Faces US–Japan Trade Frictions

Trade frictions between the two countries entered their final period of tension during the early-to-mid 1990s. The Clinton administration made an attempt to expand the share of American products in the Japanese market by setting numerical import targets, an approach that was contrary to the principle of free trade espoused by the United States. Prime Minister Miyazawa discussed the issue with Clinton during his visit to America in April 1993, but failed to reach an agreement.

In July 1993, Japan hosted the nineteenth G7 Summit amid domestic political upheaval. Just weeks before the summit, the Lower House had been dissolved for a general election after it had passed a vote of no-confidence against the Miyazawa cabinet—with a significant number of LDP members refusing to support their party because they shared the opposition members' frustration with the lack of progress in political reform. In the general election held in the aftermath of the summit, the LDP was soundly defeated and in August the Miyazawa cabinet resigned *en masse*, marking an end to 38 years of the LDP in government. At the same time, Miyazawa made a final push during the summit, rejecting Clinton's numerical targets at the US–Japan summit meeting and instead proposing a compromise to establish "objective standards" with separate criteria for each area. In the end the leaders reached an agreement to work together in a wide range of areas by establishing the Common Agenda, a framework for cooperation in fields such as the environment, health, AIDS, population, and anti-terrorism measures.

Miyazawa thereby averted the collapse of US–Japan trade negotiations, but after the 1955 System came to an end, Japanese politics entered the age of coalition governments. In August 1993, Ozawa Ichirō formed the first non-LDP coalition government with the Japan New Party (*Nihon Shintō*) and Hosokawa Morihiro as prime minister. Hoping that the advent of a non-LDP coalition government would relax the "iron triangle" between the LDP, bureaucrats, and business, Clinton once again called for the introduction of specific numerical targets at a US–Japan summit in February 1994. However, his demands were steadfastly rejected by Hosokawa. Given the anti-American sentiment in Japan at the time, there was widespread support for his decision; this was the first time that Japan had said "No" to the United States since World War II. Hosokawa tended to cater to public opinion in this way; he had a weak support base within the government, and saw approval ratings as his chance of hanging on to power.

Japanese leadership underwent further upheaval the following year. In April 1994, Hata Tsutomu succeeded Hosokawa as the head of the non-LDP coalition government. A mere two months later, the LDP returned to power when it formed a coalition with the SDPJ and the New Party Sakigake (*Shintō Sakigake*) by agreeing to support SDPJ chairman Murayama Tomiichi as prime minister of the new government.

Prime Minister Murayama and the North Korean Nuclear Crisis

Following the collapse of Japan's economic bubble, trade frictions between the United States and Japan were intensifying again, and Tokyo's political leadership had lapsed into utter confusion. Moreover, a serious security issue was developing in Northeast Asia as the nuclear challenge from North Korea emerged in a number of events between 1993 and 1994. The International Atomic Energy Agency (IAEA) demanded North Korea's submission to special inspections to investigate claims that it was pursuing nuclear development, to which North Korea responded by both rejecting the inspections and declaring its withdrawal from the Non-Proliferation Treaty (NPT) in March 1993. In May 1993, North Korea conducted a test launch of the intermediate-range ballistic missile Rodong-1 toward an area just offshore of the Noto Peninsula in Ishikawa Prefecture. The tensions reached their peak during working-level talks between North and South Korea in March 1994, when the North Korean representative threatened to turn Seoul into a "sea of fire" if war were to ensue.

Prior to this crisis, Clinton had failed in his handling of the regional crises in Bosnia and Somalia. However, North Korea's actions posed a serious challenge to the entire NPT system. The Clinton administration launched economic sanctions against North Korea, and the US forces in South Korea prepared for large-scale hostilities under Operations Plan 5027, a scenario for an all-out war of aggression against North Korea. The Pentagon predicted that if it came to a full-scale war, US casualties would exceed 50,000 and South Korean casualties would exceed 490,000 in the first 90 days of conflict alone.

In June 1994, at the height of the crisis, former President Jimmy Carter was sent to North Korea as a special envoy. Carter succeeded in securing North Korean President Kim Il-sung's commitment to freezing the nuclear program, a commitment that was formalized in an agreement between the two governments entitled the Agreed Framework Talks. In exchange for North Korea's agreement to freeze the operation and construction of nuclear reactors suspected to be part of nuclear weapons development, the United States established the Korean Peninsula Energy Development Organization (KEDO) in March 1995 and began to supply energy to North Korea. Carter's efforts averted crisis for the time being, and Washington overoptimistically predicted that the North Korean leader would eventually lose his grip on power just as was hoped for Hussein's regime in Iraq. However, the North Korean regime not only remained in power (it still is as of this writing) but it also continued with its nuclear program, which led to frustration and criticism among Americans, particularly conservatives, toward Clinton's policies.

The North Korean nuclear crisis also had a serious impact on US–Japan relations, because it revealed that Japan, America's staunch ally in Asia, was barely capable of providing logistical support if a crisis were to occur in Northeast Asia. In spring 1994, Washington sounded out Tokyo on the potential for Japan to fulfill 1,059 cooperation requirements in the event of conflict on the peninsula. However, Ishihara Nobuo, the deputy chief cabinet secretary at the time, admitted that Japan was far from sufficiently prepared in such matters regarding the application of the US–Japan Security Treaty, and thus he suggested a manual be drafted to contemplate any possible crises (Mikuriya and Watanabe 2002).

Concerns over an "Alliance Adrift"

The North Korean nuclear crisis prompted developments in Japan's defense policy. In February 1994, the Hosokawa cabinet set up the Advisory Group on Defense Issues (*Boei Mondai Kondankai*), headed by Higuchi Hirotarō, chairman of Asahi Breweries, as the prime minister's private advisory body for a comprehensive review of Japan's post–Cold War defense policy. Although Hosokawa intended to reduce defense expenditure, equipment, and personnel, the advisory group's report—the Higuchi Report, submitted to the Murayama cabinet in August 1994—called for active measures to foster multilateral security cooperation, improve the function of the US–Japan security relationship, and maintain efficient defense capabilities. This report contributed to a significant shift in the stance of the SDPJ, which had adjusted course and decided to accept the maintenance of the US–Japan Security Treaty and approve of the existence of the JSDF.

However, a number of American government experts on Japan were concerned that the Higuchi Report focused too heavily on multilateral security cooperation and overlooked the US–Japan alliance itself. These Japan experts were also increasingly concerned about America's domestic status quo under the Clinton administration as it became even more inward-looking following the Democratic defeat in the 1994 midterm elections. Assistant Secretary of Defense Joseph S. Nye, Jr., among others, voiced these concerns to the administration and put together the East Asia Strategy Report—the Nye Report—in February 1995. This report called for America to station 100,000 US troops in East Asia and redefine the security relationship between the two nations. In November of the same year, Japan pursued the recommendations of the Higuchi Report and responded to America's East Asia Strategy Report by revising the National Defense Program Outline (*Bōei keikaku no taikō*) for the first time in nearly two decades.

However, the efforts to revise Japan's defense policy were eclipsed in 1995—the fiftieth anniversary of the end of the Second World War—by more rapid and dramatic shifts affecting Japan's security both overseas and at home. The first shift was China's missile tests in the waters offshore of Taiwan in July and August, which demonstrated that classic games of power were still being played in Northeast Asia even after the Cold War. This tension between China and Taiwan flared up again the following March in the run-up to Taiwan's first direct election for the president of the Republic of China. America assuaged tensions by sending two aircraft carriers through the Taiwan Strait. At the root of the tension was China's rapid economic growth that allowed for the modernization of the military and the surge of nationalism.

Second, strong opposition toward the United States and its bases among the Okinawan public was reignited in September 1995 following the brutal rape of a 12-year-old Japanese girl by three US servicemen. The public outrage toward the incident was further fueled by the slow response from the Murayama cabinet. The incident, which Assistant Secretary of Defense Nye described as "a typhoon-like shock," highlighted the limits of the Cold War strategy of forward deployment and posed a huge risk to America's use of bases across Japan, the core aspect of the US–Japan security relationship. Of particular concern were the bases in Okinawa Prefecture, which accounted for 75% of the land area occupied by the US military in Japan, and was also of considerable strategic importance. Therefore, both governments embarked on reexamining the bases issue and established the Special Action Committee on Okinawa (SACO; *Okinawa ni kansuru Tokubetsu Kōdō Iinkai*) to devise recommendations that would alleviate tensions.

A succession of unforeseeable domestic crises occurred in 1995 in Japan, including the Great Hanshin-Awaji Earthquake Disaster in January and the sarin gas attacks on the Tokyo subway carried out by the Aum Shinrikyō cult in March. The Murayama cabinet had great difficulty tackling these crises. On top of these challenges, the friction between the United States and Japan over automobiles and automobile parts became increasingly tense as Washington proceeded to apply 100% punitive tariffs on Japanese luxury cars. Japan responded promptly by lodging a formal complaint with the World Trade Organization (WTO). The US–Japan automobile negotiations were wrapped up in late June when the Clinton administration finally yielded to the lack of international support for its proposed numerical targets. This marked the final stage of trade friction between the two countries.

While the United States and Japan were tackling such crises and friction, a number of security experts in both nations became deeply concerned that the US–Japan alliance was "drifting." Secretary of Defense William J. Perry was particularly keen to achieve a prompt resolution of the issues surrounding US base in Okinawa. He was supported by Assistant Secretary Nye, who had called for the redefinition of relations based on the East Asia Strategy Report. Akiyama Masahiro, the then head of the Bureau of Defense Policy (*Bōeikyoku*) at the Defense Agency (*Bōeichō*), remarked that while Japanese bureaucrats were still able to practice "silent leadership" over defense policy this would probably be the last time they could do so. Japanese bureaucrats were still compensating for the weakness of Japan's political leadership and were the primary responders to the approaches made by the United States (Akiyama 2002).

Both governments hastily prepared for a US–Japan summit, but Clinton had to postpone his participation in the APEC meeting held in Osaka in November 1995 due to clashes with the Republican-led Congress over the budget bill. Shortly thereafter, Murayama resigned as prime minister in January 1996, having lost the will to continue in the position.

Prime Minister Hashimoto and "Redefinition" of the Alliance

Murayama was succeeded by the LDP leader Hashimoto Ryūtarō, in the first cabinet in several years to be headed by a leader from the LDP. Prime Minister Hashimoto was keen to resolve the Okinawa issue, with which his support base within the LDP, the Keiseikai (formerly the Takeshita faction), had been involved in for some time. In April 1996 President Clinton visited Japan and issued a joint declaration on security entitled the "Alliance for the Twenty-First Century" with Prime Minister Hashimoto, marking the beginning of the "redefinition" of the US–Japan security alliance.

In the declaration, both leaders reaffirmed their commitment to the "profound common values" guiding Japan and America's national policies: the maintenance of freedom, the pursuit of democracy, and respect for human rights, and confirmed the Japan–US security relationship as the cornerstone for achieving common security objectives and for maintaining a stable and prosperous environment for the Asia-Pacific region. The declaration ensured that the main points of the Nye Report were carried out and that the United States maintained a forward deployment of 100,000 troops in the region. Furthermore, the United States and Japan began the process of revising the Guidelines for Japan–US Defense Cooperation (*Nichibei bōei kyōryoku no tame no shishin*) that had originally been formulated in 1978 during the Cold War.

At the same time, the SACO process led to an agreement on ways to "realign, consolidate, and reduce" the facilities and areas used by the US forces, with the aim of tackling the ongoing issue of Okinawa. It is particularly significant that the reversion and relocation of the Futenma base was decided prior to the Clinton–Hashimoto summit. Some Japanese felt that the political risk of demanding the reversion of Futenma was too high, but Washington acquiesced due to Hashimoto's tenacity and the efforts of such figures as Walter Mondale, the American ambassador to Japan.

If the Miyazawa cabinet's enactment of the PKO Cooperation Act was an indirect response to the setback that Japanese diplomacy had encountered in the aftermath of the Gulf War, the redefinition of the US–Japan alliance was an ambitious attempt both to respond to the demands for greater regional security—raised by the North Korean and Taiwan Strait crises—and also to reduce the local burden of having US troops based in their communities. Furthermore, the redefinition also expanded the security cooperation between the two nations on a global scale. As Japan's economic strength waned, it had become necessary for Japan to approach diplomacy more prudently and in cooperation with the United States. Such changes were combined with the fact that the Ministry of Foreign Affairs released its monopoly on the management of the US–Japan alliance, allowing the Defense Agency to also become a key player.

Because the redefinition of the alliance was declared just weeks after the Taiwan Strait crisis in March 1996, it made Beijing suspicious that it was actually a move toward containing China. There were in fact a few American participants involved in the redefinition process who perceived China as a threat (Akiyama 2002). A new paradigm was emerging between Japan, America, and China in regards to security and economic issues as well as political values.

THE SHIFT FROM "JAPAN BASHING" TO "JAPAN PASSING"

Once the United States and Japan had committed to reviewing the Guidelines for US–Japan Defense Cooperation under the Joint Declaration on Security, proposals were further developed at the working level until a final proposal was completed in September 1997. The guidelines divided US–Japan defense cooperation into three categories: (i) cooperation under normal circumstances; (ii) response to armed attack against Japan; and (iii) cooperation in situations in areas surrounding Japan. While the former guidelines had focused on a response to direct military attacks on Japan, the key focus of the new guidelines was upon cooperation in areas *surrounding* Japan. Particularly with regard to cooperation in surrounding areas, an annex to the guidelines set out 40 items covering cooperation in a broad range of fields, including humanitarian relief, evacuation of noncombatants, use of facilities by the American military, local logistical support, and cooperation between the JSDF and the US forces.

Concurrently, due to the concerns of China with its ongoing problems with Taiwan, and in consideration of the fears in Japan that the security alliance could drag Japan into conflict involving the United States (*makikomare-ron*), the guidelines defined the concept of "situations in areas surrounding Japan" as "not geographic but situational" and stated that the United States and Japan would "make every effort, including diplomatic efforts, to prevent such situations from occurring." As relations between Japan and China were relatively stable at the time, it was in fact the United States that had stronger concerns regarding China's rapid military modernization and diplomatic offensive, while such concerns were not yet widely shared among the Japanese public.

The redefinition of the US–Japan alliance set forth in the Joint Declaration on Security also needed to be reflected in concrete measures at the working level. However, when the 1996 presidential election saw Clinton return to office for his second term, the momentum toward strengthening the alliance was temporarily lost. Secretary of Defense Perry, a key proponent of the redefinition of the alliance, had left the administration, and in his place Secretary of the Treasury Robert E. Rubin and Deputy Secretary of the Treasury Lawrence H. Summers began to guide the US policies toward Japan and shifted the focus more toward fixing the Japanese economy as it continued to struggle after the collapse of the bubble economy. In Clinton's second term, US diplomacy in Asia made improving relations with China a top priority. This is clearly reflected by the fact that there is absolutely no reference to the redefinition of the US–Japan security relationship in Clinton's voluminous post-presidency memoirs.

Hashimoto steadfastly pursued administrative and financial reforms and made efforts to maintain and strengthen the US–Japan alliance while simultaneously seeking to diversify Japan's diplomacy through forging stronger relations with Russia, France, and other European nations. His efforts came to fruition in the following century with the substantial bolstering of the US–Japan alliance and the strengthening of the functions of the prime minister's office under the leadership of political rival Koizumi Junichirō. Hashimoto was also keen to address security issues; he oversaw the partial revision of the PKO Cooperation Act so that the use of firearms would be permitted under the orders of a commanding officer on the ground, rather than on the individual judgment of the soldier. He also contributed to creating legal and systematic frameworks for security policy, including a system for efforts to rescue Japanese people overseas in times of crises such as those witnessed in Cambodia and Indonesia.

However, while Hashimoto was a known as "policy expert," he also made a succession of poor policy decisions. His cabinet suffered key failures at home and overseas, and it prevented domestic economic recovery, as seen by his decision to implement tax increases. Moreover, his coveted proposal for a coordinated multilateral effort to tackle the 1997 Asian currency crisis was soundly rejected by America because he had proceeded without first consulting with Washington. While his cabinet was preparing a bill to create the domestic legal framework to support the new guidelines, he was forced to resign following the LDP defeat in the July 1998 elections for the House of Councilors.

This was also a time when economic globalization was progressing at a rapid pace, as reflected by the 1994 GATT agreement during the Uruguay Round, which led to the establishment of the World Trade Organization in January of the following year. Japan provided strong backing for China's entry into the WTO, which was eventually agreed upon in 1999 and implemented in December 2001. China's accession to the WTO along with the experience of the 1997 Asian financial crisis no doubt accelerated the economic integration of Asia.

China became committed to improving relations with the United States as it sought to recover from the diplomatic setbacks of the 1995–96 Taiwan Strait crisis and the redefinition of the US–Japan alliance. At the same time, it was also seeking to target Japan. When Chinese President Jiang Zemin visited America in October 1997, before meeting with President Clinton in Washington he started his visit in Hawaii, where he proudly spoke about both countries being the victors of World War II. In summer that year, Iris Chang's account of the 1937 Nanking Massacre, *The Rape of Nanking*, had become a bestseller in America. The following year, in June 1998, shortly before the resignation of the Hashimoto cabinet, Clinton visited China, where he affirmed the "three NOs" position on the Taiwan question (No recognition of Taiwanese independence, No support for two Chinas, and No support for Taiwan's entry into international organizations), and also joined Jiang Zemin in criticizing Japanese economic policy. Furthermore, Clinton did not even call on Japan during his visit to Asia.

During the peak of its economic prosperity Japan had been the constant target of "Japan bashing," but ever since its economy had begun to weaken in the early 1990s it had increasingly been bypassed or even completely ignored in favor of other nations, prompting the Japanese media to coin the phrases "Japan passing" and "Japan nothing." By this point, America and China had become "strategic partners" and Japanese diplomacy was being harshly criticized from both sides. This was also partially due to a powerful diplomatic offensive by China that led to a significant increase in anti-Chinese sentiment in Japan.

Obuchi Keizō, who succeeded Hashimoto as prime minister in July 1998, faced a difficult challenge. On top of the growing rivalry with China, in August North Korea had launched a Taepodong missile that had flown over Japan. Although North Korea had already conducted such a launch when it had tested the Rodong-1 missile in May 1993, its significant progress in missile technology had shaken Japanese public opinion. Following on the heels of the missile launch was a succession of acts of provocation, such as the encroachment of North Korean vessels into Japanese waters. Ironically, this helped to shore up a public consensus regarding Japan's need to boost its security. When Obuchi ordered the maritime patrol to take action against unidentified boats off the Noto Peninsula in March 1999, the Japanese public did not oppose the decision as it might have done in the past.

The prime minister was able to take firm action because he had been able to stabilize his domestic authority base by forming a coalition with the Liberal Party (*Jiyutō*) led by Ozawa in January 1999. Given increased threats abroad, and with Obuchi firmly in control, in May the cabinet was able to pass legislation regarding the revised Guidelines for the US–Japan Defense Cooperation, which had been under review for quite some time. However, even after the guideline revisions, North Korea's movements continued to have significant influence on Japanese security policy. Meanwhile, former Secretary of Defense Perry was appointed to conduct a review of policy toward North Korea, and in October 1999 the Review of US Policy toward North Korea—the so-called Perry Review—a report setting out guidelines for "dialogue and deterrence" was made public in response to North Korean aggression. The report argued for closer cooperation between the trilateral powers of the United States, Japan, and South Korea.

The Final Years of Clinton's Presidency

Clinton tackled new challenges through diplomacy and anti-terror measures, alliance revision, new foreign policy toward China, and humanitarian intervention, but ultimately he failed to establish a "new world order," a goal that had been set forth by the previous Bush administration. While one problem of Bush's diplomacy had been its lack of a clear vision, Clinton struggled with a lack of experience and interest in his first term, and a lack of a clear order of priorities in his second. But Clinton was res-

cued by luck; America's pioneering role in globalization and the development of an information-based society helped its economy to surge ahead
once again. This recovery of America's global competitiveness became a
significant asset for his administration.

The US economic globalization under Clinton also aroused concerns
in China about American hegemony. This was further reinforced when
American planes inadvertently bombed the Chinese Embassy in Belgrade
during the bombing of Yugoslavia in May 1999, an incident which provoked a strong emotional backlash from China. Such incidents prevented
the development of a "strategic partnership" between Washington and
Beijing and in the end the United States was forced to recognize that it
needed to depend on its allies such as Japan.

But there remained the thorny question of the bases on Okinawa; plans
for relocating the Futenma base had reached an impasse due to local opposition. In his commitment to resolve the issue, Obuchi selected Okinawa
and Kyushu as the sites of the 26th G8 Summit, which Japan would host
in 2000. In doing so, he sought to provide support for the development
of the Okinawan economy as well as to allow Clinton to directly witness
and appreciate the severity of the bases issue.

However, Obuchi suddenly passed away in May 2000, a mere few
months shy of the summit. The senior leaders of the LDP hastily chose
Mori Yoshirō, the LDP secretary general, as his successor. For his part,
Clinton visited Okinawa in July to attend the G8 Summit and delivered a
solemn apology to the citizens of Okinawa in which he called for the need
of greater understanding and cooperation. Clinton was also nearing the
end of his second term, and he had neither the time nor the capacity to
solve such a complex issue. In his final months in the presidency, Clinton
was consumed with dealing with the renewed tensions in the ongoing
Israeli-Palestinian conflict, a much more pressing issue for America.

Keen on leaving a legacy in the arena of diplomacy, Clinton attempted
a significant breakthrough in relations with North Korea by dispatching
Secretary of State Madeleine K. Albright to North Korea in October, marking a shift toward the "dialogue" aspect of the "dialogue and deterrence"
course that had been set out by the Perry Review. South Korean President
Kim Dae-jung also visited Pyongyang in June 2000 for a summit meeting
with the North Korean leader Kim Jong-il as part of his "Sunshine Policy,"
a foreign policy that sought to appease North Korea. These developments
put Japan at risk of becoming isolated, but ultimately such concerns proved
unfounded as the United States and South Korea failed to bring about any
meaningful change of course in North Korea's nuclear policy.

BIBLIOGRAPHY

Akiyama, Masahiro. 2002. *Nichibei no senryaku taiwa ga hajimatta* [The Japan–US Strategic Dialogue]. Tokyo: Aki Shobō.

Iokibe, Makoto, Itō Motoshige, and Yakushiji Katsuyuki, ed. 2007. *Gaikō gekihen: Moto-gaimushō jimujikan Yanai Shunji* [Revolution in Diplomacy: Former Vice-Minister of Foreign Affairs Yanai Shunji]. Tokyo: Asahi Shimbunsha.

Mikuriya, Takashi, and Takafusa Nakamura, ed. 2005. *Kikigaki Miyazawa Kiichi kaikoroku* [Oral History: The Memoir of Miyazawa Kiichi]. Tokyo: Iwanami Shoten.

Mikuriya, Takashi, and Akio Watanabe, ed. 2002. *Shushō kantei no ketsudan* [Decisions of the Office of the Prime Minister]. Tokyo: Chūōkōron-shinsha.

CHAPTER 12

US–Japan Leadership in the Post–9/11 World

Makoto Iokibe and Fumiaki Kubo

AMERICAN AND JAPANESE LEADERSHIP IN THE PRESENT CENTURY

While acknowledging Clinton's role in building a healthy economy, the George W. Bush camp saw inherent weakness in the previous administration's approach to diplomacy and security, particularly as it dealt with China. Bush therefore quickly declared his intent to pursue a foreign policy that would take a more critical view of China while also placing greater emphasis on its allies who shared common core values with the United States, and this was reflected in the implementation of a more pro-Japanese approach.

Prior to the presidential election, a bipartisan project led by experts on US foreign policy toward Japan, published its policy recommendations in the form of the first "Armitage–Nye Report," advocating for the development of a closer relationship between two nations modeled on the one that the United States had fostered with Britain. These experts sought to reorient American policies through working much closer with Japan, a nation

M. Iokibe
Prefectural University of Kumamoto, Kumamoto, Japan

Hyogo Earthquake Memorial 21st Century Research Institute, Kobe, Japan

F. Kubo
Graduate Schools for Law and Politics, University of Tokyo, Tokyo, Japan

© The Author(s) 2017
M. Iokibe (ed.), T. Minohara (trans. ed.), *The History of US–Japan Relations*, DOI 10.1007/978-981-10-3184-7_12

with which it had fierce trade disputes as recently as 1995. The importance that the Bush administration attached to Japan manifested itself in the appointment of Richard L. Armitage, then deputy secretary of state, as well as other policy experts who possessed an extensive knowledge of Japan including Michael J. Green and James A. Kelly.

When forming his administration, President Bush appointed a few moderates as well as realists who were cautious about using force as a policy tool; these included Colin L. Powell, who became secretary of state in January 2001. However, it was conservative hardliners such as Secretary of Defense Donald H. Rumsfeld and neoconservatives such as Deputy Secretary of Defense Paul Wolfowitz who would come to dominate the foreign policy scene in the first term. But by far, the conservative hardliner Vice President Dick Cheney had the greatest influence in both domestic and foreign politics within the administration. The neoconservatives were adamant that the United States had a moral obligation to ward off any threat posed by its enemies, which justified the use of force in spreading democracy and other liberal values (Kubo 2007; Gellman 2008).

Consequently, in its initial stages Bush's diplomacy was focused on unilateral action rather than the international cooperation favored by Clinton. For instance, the Bush administration aggressively tackled its concerns regarding China not only by condemning its human rights abuses, but also by proceeding with a large weapons sale to Taiwan. However, Bush's confrontational stance toward China made an abrupt shift to a more business-like approach amid the Hainan Island incident of April 2001 in which a US naval reconnaissance plane and a Chinese fighter plane had a midair collision off the shores of Hainan.

Other notable examples were the US unilateral secession from the Anti-Ballistic Missile (ABM) Treaty with Russia in December 2001, pointing to Bush's firm resolve to pursue missile defense, and withdrawal from the Kyoto Protocol that aimed to reduce global warming, thus inviting criticism from the Europeans. US–Japan relations also took an unexpected turn when in February 2001, the nuclear submarine USS *Greeneville* collided offshore Hawaii with the *Ehime-maru*, a training ship from a Japanese fishery high school, killing nine of those aboard the *Ehime-maru*, including four students. But the Bush administration prevented the issue from boiling over by promptly issuing a heartfelt apology.

Prime Minister Koizumi at the Helm

After the sudden death of Prime Minister Obuchi Keizō in April 2000, his successor, Mori Yoshirō, was selected behind closed doors by the leading figures within the Liberal Democratic Party (LDP). The nature in which Mori was appointed tainted his administration from the outset as it was viewed as not only lacking legitimacy, but also being out of touch with the times. His tenure was fraught with difficulties as he needed to shoulder the blame for the many problems faced by Japan—continuing recession, lack of progress with reform, issues in crisis management—and even the most trivial statements he made and actions he took became targets of severe criticism. The Japanese were losing patience as the nation stagnated and still continued to struggle in overcoming its "lost decade" as it entered a new century.

In contrast, Koizumi Junichirō successfully capitalized on this feeling of impatience and anxiety. Unlike Mori, Koizumi gained power by garnering overwhelming support from local party members and the general public. He won the support of the public by demonstrating his passionate commitment to intensive reform, pledging to "destroy" the style of politicking that the LDP had cultivated for many years, such as catering solely to the vested interests of its supporters and relying on "pork-barrel" spending. Coupled with the increased authority of the prime minister's office that had been established through administrative reforms by the Hashimoto Ryūtarō cabinet, Koizumi was able to show strong leadership upon taking office in April 2001.

The tasks that the Koizumi government sought to tackle were predominantly focused on domestic structural reform, and diplomacy was not given a particularly high priority until, as seen above, the chance to reestablish solid diplomatic relations with the United States had manifested itself under the new Bush government. While visiting the United States in June 2001, a casual and friendly Koizumi formed a close personal relationship with the new president, and as a result he was able to bring attention to the importance of the US–Japan alliance.

THE BUSH–KOIZUMI RELATIONSHIP AND 9/11

Bush defined the 9/11 attacks as an act of war, and he made it his personal mission to prevent further attacks upon American soil. The threat of terrorism posed a very different difficulty for America in comparison with the Soviet menace during the Cold War. While in terms of total military capacity the Soviet Union was clearly a much greater threat to America than Al Qaeda; additionally, during the Cold War the relationship between the two superpowers had been surprisingly stable due to the possession of nuclear weapons on both sides. In contrast, suicide bombings and other typical terrorist attacks were more difficult to deter and preempt. In this sense, the events of 9/11 instilled in America a far greater sense of fear than what had existed during the Cold War.

The Bush administration's first step was to order the Afghanistan government to hand over Bin Laden and other senior members of the Al Qaeda network. When this demand was rejected outright, Bush resorted to a military invasion of Afghanistan in October 2001 with the objective to dismantle terrorist groups and destroy its bases by removing the Islamic fundamentalist Taliban government from power, and quickly brought down the Afghanistan government (Woodward 2002). In January 2002, President Bush declared Iraq, Iran, and North Korea the "Axis of Evil," and two months later implied the development of a global-scale anti-terrorist strategy when he stated that the "second stage" of the war on terror was underway. At the same time the so-called "Bush doctrine" was laid out, asserting that the United States would not hesitate in exerting its right to self-defense by conducting preemptive strikes on terrorists or nations sponsoring terrorism that were likely to use weapons of mass destruction (WMD).

Just two weeks after 9/11, Prime Minister Koizumi visited the site of the attacks in New York and stated that Japan was ready to "stand by America" and assist in the new war against terrorism. True to his words, Koizumi promptly agreed to provide logistical support as well as financial assistance to the United States.

With the outbreak of hostilities in Afghanistan in 2001, the Koizumi cabinet implemented the Anti-Terrorism Special Measures Law and launched logistical support activities, including sending a Maritime Self-Defense Force (JMSDF) vessel to the Indian Ocean in order to help with the refueling operations of coalition warships. While this was mere logistical support, it was groundbreaking in that it was the first time under Japan's postwar constitution that the JSDF had ventured this far from Japan in order to cooperate in a military operation. This was not overlooked by the United States, and as a consequence the Bush administration praised Japan's actions.

Another notable aspect of Japan's response to the war was the proactive role that it played in supporting the reconstruction of Afghanistan. At the

International Conference on Reconstruction Assistance to Afghanistan held in Tokyo in January 2002 (co-chaired by Ogata Sadako), a total of more than US $4.5 billion in aid was pledged from international donors. Learning from the lessons of the Gulf War, Japan was now playing a proactive role in supporting the United States.

America and the Iraq War

A key issue during the 2002 midterm elections was whether or not the United States should go to war against Iraq. The situation in Iraq had been an ongoing concern for America since the Gulf War, especially since the Iraqi government had begun to ignore the UN Security Council Resolution 687 that prohibited possessing WMD and had obstructed the mandated inspections by the UN and the International Atomic Energy Agency (IAEA), with which it ceased all forms of cooperation in 1998. Based on the testimonies of the parties involved, it is now believed that the Bush administration had settled on the use of military force toward Iraq as its basic policy by mid-2002. The resolution on the authorization for the use of military force against Iraq passed by the Senate and House of Representatives in October 2002 was approved by an overwhelming majority, due to the fact that a large number of Democrats in Congress also voted in favor of the resolution because it was just before the midterm elections.

US Secretary of State Powell, British Prime Minister Tony Blair, and Japanese Prime Minister Koizumi all advised President Bush to seek international cooperation with any action against Iraq. President Bush heeded this advice and acted to obtain a consensus at the UN. As a result, on November 8, 2002, the UN Security Council proclaimed Security Council Resolution 1441, which declared that Iraq had repeatedly been in material breach of various UN resolutions, and on this basis demanded that Iraq agree to "unconditional and unrestricted" inspection and warned that the failure to comply would bring about "serious consequences." Faced with this threat, Iraq complied with the resolution, and inspections once again resumed from late November. As these developments were transpiring, America and Britain proceeded with a large-scale mobilization of troops in the regions surrounding Iraq.

America pressed for war with Iraq for two reasons. First, Washington was convinced that Iraq possessed WMD and had strong ties to Al Qaeda and that it was necessary to launch a preemptive attack to mitigate the risk of WMD being turned over to terrorist groups. Second, there were also significant calls for America to go to war with the aim of democratizing not only Iraq but the entire Middle Eastern region as a path to its stability. However, the US and Britain's draft resolution paving the way for the use of military force in Iraq was strongly opposed by the other UNSC members. Despite this, three days later, the United States and the United Kingdom launched their attack: the Iraq War had begun.

During the conflict, the American government received support in various forms from 44 countries, including Japan. Iraq was rapidly defeated, but the true struggle only began with the occupation, as the whole security apparatus for maintaining public order was removed. This prompted a strong sentiment of resistance to the US and British forces and led to frequent terrorist attacks, including suicide bombings.

The Iraq War and Koizumi's Diplomacy

Prime Minister Koizumi steadfastly supported America's policies, considering them to be part of Japan's own anti-terrorism measures. In July 2003, the Koizumi administration enacted the Act on Special Measures concerning Humanitarian Relief and Reconstruction Work and Security Assistance in Iraq, and in February 2004 it dispatched the Japan Ground Self-Defense Force (JGSDF) to Samawah in the Muthanna Governorate of southern Iraq. Thus began the humanitarian relief work in addition to reconstruction support activities such as restoring and maintaining public facilities that included hospitals, water supply facilities, and schools. These projects were intended to help the people as well as to cultivate a friendly working relationship with the population. The JGSDF completed its 30-month mission in July 2006 without having to fire a single shot and without a single fatality. The Japan Air Self-Defense Force (JASDF) also participated in airlift support operations in Iraq for nearly five years until late 2008.

Koizumi effectively responded to the international crises that followed 9/11 by establishing close cooperative relations with Washington while also demonstrating his capacity for leadership. This in turn expanded Japan's role in international security. Koizumi was keen to strengthen the Japan–US alliance given that in Northeast Asia Japan faced threats that it could not handle alone, such as the North Korean nuclear and missile issues and the rise of China. These concerns were clearly evident in his decision in December 2003 to implement a ballistic missile defense

(BMD) system. He also enhanced the US–Japan Security Consultative Committee (2+2) meetings and expanded the US–Japan alliance into a more comprehensive and cooperative relationship in 2005 by outlining common goals that covered both military and public welfare issues. This strong alliance, initiated by Koizumi, would form the foundation of Operation Tomodachi.

By dispatching its JSDF to Iraq, Japan also provided symbolic international support to American war effort against terrorism. During the 2004 election campaign, when the Democrats challenged Bush by suggesting that America was "isolated," he was able to respond by highlighting the contributions the United States had received from several key countries such as Japan.

Koizumi's Asian Diplomacy

When standing for election as president of the LDP in April 2001, Koizumi had stated that if he became prime minister he would visit Yasukuni Shrine on August 15, the anniversary of Japan's surrender declaration in the Second World War. During his time in office, Koizumi did in fact visit Yasukuni Shrine every year, explaining that he did so to pray for peace, rather than to justify Japan's war of aggression. However, China interpreted Koizumi's visit to the shrine as implying Japanese government's exoneration of war guilt and thus retaliated by avoiding summit meetings that were normally held alternating between Beijing and Tokyo. As a result, constructive dialogue between Japan and China subsequently came to a standstill and the latter vehemently opposed Japan's proposal for UN reform with the intent of obtaining a permanent seat on the UN Security Council. Matters became worse when in 2005 violent anti-Japanese demonstrations broke out in various cities across China. This souring of relations with China also contributed to a setback in relations with South Korea.

Meanwhile, in September 2002, Koizumi's sudden visit to North Korea—a nation with which Japan had no diplomatic ties—was met with tremendous surprise, not least because Koizumi was believed to have limited interest toward Asia. During his visit, Koizumi met with General Secretary Kim Jong-il and issued the Japan–North Korea Pyongyang Declaration that proclaimed the resumption of normalization talks. The visit had been arranged through secret preliminary negotiations conducted by Tanaka Hitoshi, Director General at the Asian and Oceanian Affairs Bureau at the Ministry of Foreign Affairs (MOFA).

Contrasting strongly with the cautious Japanese politicians who had preceded him, Koizumi was a new type of leader who was prepared to take action despite the risks involved. The task of bringing North Korea back into international society and thereby stabilizing it was a significant challenge that Northeast Asia needed to tackle, but bilateral talks stumbled over two key issues. First, difficulties soon emerged over how to deal with the issue of the past abduction of Japanese citizens by North Korean operatives. While North Korea acknowledged 13 abductions and allowed five of the abductees to return to Japan, Tokyo rejected outright the claim that the remaining eight were already dead. Second, negotiations faltered due to a US revelation that North Korea had been developing a clandestine nuclear weapons program in contravention of the 1994 Agreed Framework. Amid this situation, it was China that took a leading role in the handling of North Korean issue.

At the behest of the the United States, China was successful in nudging North Korea to attend the Six-Party Talks involving America, China, Japan, North Korea, South Korea, and Russia in August 2003. The talks, which were conducted on six occasions over the following four years, led to such announcements as the September 2005 agreement between North Korea and America: in return for the disposal of North Korea's nuclear weapons the United States would support the construction of light-water reactors. However, the Six-Party Talks ultimately failed in the objective of ceasing North Korea's nuclear weapons development and testing.

One issue that must not be overlooked is that by playing a key role in the talks China reflected its desire to once again be a key player in the arena of international politics after a long hiatus. It was three decades since Deng Xiaoping had introduced a policy of reform and opening China to the outside world which, in turn, set in motion the nation's rapid economic development. By the turn of the century, China had finally achieved economic success as "the world's factory" and it used this new economic power as the tool for returning to the center stage of Asia for the first time since the Opium War in the mid-nineteenth century.

Bush's Diplomacy During his Second Term

When Bush sought reelection in 2004, the ensuing campaign became highly charged due to increased instability in Iraq and the rapidly growing number of casualties suffered by US troops. The fact that WMD were never found in Iraq delivered a serious blow to Bush and he faced a tough contest with the Democratic Party nominee, John F. Kerry, who finally lost to Bush due to his lack of a clear position on the Iraq War.

In Iraq, the election for the National Assembly that took place on January 30, 2005 went on rather peacefully despite initial worries. A new government was formed under Prime Minister Ibrāhim al-Ja'fari, the first time the government was led by an Iraqi national after the war. Despite this, there was no end in sight of attacks by the militant opposition forces on American troops, the Iraqi government, and the Iraqi people. Furthermore, during Bush's second term, tensions resurfaced between Washington and Beijing, chiefly over the issue of the cheap manufactured products from China that were flooding the American domestic market. Bush was critical of the artificially low exchange rate of the Chinese yuan, which was pegged to a fixed exchange rate against the US dollar.

By this time, China had already surpassed Japan in becoming the country with which America had the largest trade deficit. Harsh criticism of China arose in the United States and this economic and trade friction also became entangled with various other issues such as human rights, intimidation of Taiwan, restrictions on workers' rights to organize and assemble, lack of freedom of religious beliefs, and a pronounced increase in its military expenditures (Mann 2004). Washington also had hopes that China would apply pressure on North Korea in cooperating with the Six-Party Talks, but these were quickly dashed.

The poor handling of the Hurricane Katrina disaster in late August 2005, combined with its failure to control the situation in Iraq, as well as a number of scandals involving Republican politicians, led to a Republican defeat in the 2006 midterm elections and the loss of their position as the majority party in both the Senate and the House. Faced with this predicament, the president made the decision to increase the number of troop deployments to Iraq at a time when the conflict was already extremely unpopular with the American public. No doubt this was a political gamble, but in the end it succeeded in bringing Iraq back on the path to normalcy.

In his second term, Bush removed the strong neoconservative influence that had characterized his first term and began placing more emphasis on realism, not only in the area of policy implementation, but also in terms of personnel, as reflected by Condoleezza Rice's appointment as secretary of state, and the appointment of Robert M. Gates as secretary of defense in the aftermath of the 2006 midterm elections. This was also evident in the restarted negotiations with North Korea, which were conducted under the insistence of Secretary of State Rice and which resulted in North Korea making concessions, including publicly demolishing the cooling tower of an old graphite reactor at Yongbyon in June 2008 as way to demonstrate its commitment in getting rid of nuclear weapons. Washington reciprocated this gesture four months later by lifting North Korea's designation as a nation that sponsored terrorism.

The Japanese government was consistently skeptical about these developments, believing that, in the end, North Korea would renege on its part of the bargain. Subsequent events showed that Japan was correct in its assessment as Secretary of State Rice's initiatives did not prevent North Korea from developing nuclear weapons (Rice 2011). The 2008 presidential elections, taking place during the severest economic recession since the Great Depression, ended with Barack Obama's victory. The mutual friendship between the two conservative politicians, Koizumi and Bush, helped to nurture a strong alliance that had not existed since the time of Nakasone and Reagan during the 1980s. Thus there was a strong sense of apprehension on part of Japan over how US–Japan relations would be altered under a more progressive American leadership.

Japan's Diplomacy in the Post-Koizumi Period

In September 2005, Koizumi called for a snap election in response to a vote of no-confidence in his bill for privatization of the Japanese postal service. The so-called "postal reform election" ended in a landslide victory for Koizumi, and the LDP succeeded in controlling two-thirds of the seats in the House of Representatives by forming a coalition government with the Kōmeitō. Attaining a powerful mandate from the Japanese people, Koizumi stepped down in 2006 at zenith of his popularity. He had been prime minister for five years, quite an impressive feat considering that in recent years Japanese prime ministers had served only short stints. However, Koizumi's departure did have an impact on US–Japan relations as Bush's personal ties with Koizumi's successors, Abe Shinzō, Fukuda Yasuo, and Asō Tarō, who were each prime minister for around a year, never really developed beyond a polite, businesslike relationship.

Nevertheless, Prime Minister Abe Shinzō, who followed on the heels of Koizumi, inherited a solid power base when he took office in September 2006. In the following month, Abe restarted the summit meetings with China and South Korea that had been put on hold. The summit meeting with China produced an agreement that espoused "strategic reciprocal relations," and the highlight was that it led to President Hu Jintao's praise of the "peaceful development of postwar Japan." While China had always made Japan's wartime aggression a core issue, at this juncture it instead opted to turn its attention to the positive aspects of postwar Japan in order to seek a common ground that could lead to improved relations. In regards to North Korea, the Abe government took a harsher position and was unwilling to budge on both the abduction and nuclear weapons development issues.

At the same time, the Abe government also took steps in boosting Japan's security, upgrading the Defense Agency (Bōeichō) to the Ministry of Defense (Bōeishō), for example, and finalizing the Japan–Australia Joint Declaration on Security Cooperation, which was a "quasi-alliance" with Australia. Despite these significant developments, domestic support for the LDP government and the bureaucracy declined due to successive scandals that involved ministers of his cabinet. The biggest blow came in February 2007 when it was revealed that the Social Benefits Agency had somehow lost the pensions records of a great number of Japanese. As a result of these unexpected events, in the House of Councillors election in July that year the LDP government was punished at the polls and lost control of the Upper House to the opposition. The defeat was so severe that the LDP was unable to secure even half of the seats in coalition with the Kōmeitō. The significant challenges posed by a divided Diet, along with Abe's own health problems, led to the resignation en masse of Abe's cabinet just two months later. In September 2007, Fukuda Yasuo formed the succeeding government.

Fukuda made inroads in Japan's relations with China and other Asian countries. During his visit to Japan in May 2008, President Hu Jintao reversed China's earlier position and now expressed his support for an "even greater constructive role" for Japan within the United Nations. The following month, China also acquiesced to Japan's request for it to participate in joint development of the Chunxiao gas field that lies across the median line between China and Japan in the East China Sea. Although Prime Minister Fukuda made progress in the area of foreign policy, he struggled in dealing with a divided Diet when pushing forward domestic political agendas. At one point, Fukuda pursued talks with the DPJ leader Ozawa Ichirō with the goal of establishing a "grand coalition," but when this collapsed, the Fukuda cabinet resigned en bloc after just a year.

Asō Tarō, who succeeded Fukuda as prime minister in September 2008, tackled economic reforms in order to cope with the global economic disorder amid the Great Recession. However, in such a crisis, ordinary fiscal and monetary policies did not adequately reinvigorate the economy.

However, Asō undertook notable diplomatic initiatives, including the dispatch of JMSDF warships to the Gulf of Aden in order to participate in the international initiative to combat maritime piracy, and the hosting of the inaugural summit meeting of the three major northeast Asian nations, China, South Korea, and Japan. But in the end, the three successive LDP prime ministers who came after Koizumi struggled to build upon his diplomatic gains as they were all in office for too short of a time to bring about any substantial changes.

PRESIDENT OBAMA'S DIPLOMACY AND JAPAN

The 2008 US elections saw the return of a Democratic administration. The Democrats also maintained the majorities that they had secured two years earlier in both houses of the Congress, and the US government was completely controlled by the Democrats for the first time since 1993–94.

By appointing Hillary Rodham Clinton as his secretary of state, Obama made significant progress in areas of diplomacy and security policy, especially during his first term. He initiated the New Strategic Arms Reduction Treaty (New START) with Russia which placed tighter upper limits on the nuclear arsenals of both countries. In 2011, Obama successfully completed the withdrawal of American troops from Iraq, and in the same year a US Navy special forces team assassinated Osama Bin Laden. President Obama also sent troop reinforcements to Afghanistan on two occasions, but he later made an abrupt reversal in his policy and announced plans for the complete withdrawal of US troops from Afghanistan by the end of 2016.

The relentless focus on the war on terror had effectively prevented the United States from devoting sufficient time and energy to other vital issues such as China. Obama had initially declared that he would actively pursue dialogue and enhance cooperation with China (Bader 2012). This was seen as a pragmatic approach because the United States needed China to boost its economy, tackle global environmental issues, form a coalition against terrorism, and address the North Korea issue. Simultaneously, however, there were also a great many points of contention between the two countries, such as China's enhancement of its military capabilities, foreign exchange manipulation, violation of intellectual property rights, and the issue of the Great Firewall, in addition to other outstanding issues.

The United States also kept a watchful eye on the territorial issues in the South China Sea, where China was taking increasingly aggressive actions to unilaterally change the existing status quo. In July 2010, Secretary of State Clinton announced that although America possessed no territorial ambitions in the area, it had an interest in preserving the freedom of navigation in the seas and therefore would be quite willing to mediate in territorial disputes. In November the following year, Obama officially declared that Asia was a "top priority" for American diplomacy—a policy which became widely known as the "pivot to Asia"—and announced America's plans to station a small number of Marines in Darwin, Australia. In his response to China's rapid rise, the president had made a fundamental directional change in his approach to China, shifting from one that was based on cooperation to one that was less willing to accommodate Chinese desires (Bader 2012; Clinton 2014). This policy shift was embraced in Japan as China was becoming a larger threat to its national security.

During the 2010 midterm elections, the Democrats lost their majority in the House. The Republicans who now gained control of the House used their new political power to demand significant cuts to government spending. The fact that Republicans supported a large reduction in defense expenditure reflected the enormity of the debt that the United States had accumulated during the conflict in the Middle East.

Change of Government in Japan

In the May 2005 elections the LDP had suffered a massive defeat, tumbling from 296 to 119 seats. As a result, it lost its position as the majority party in the lower house for the first time since the party was formed in 1955. The gradual path of LDP decline reached its lowest moment during the August 2009 general election of the House of Representatives when a historic change of government took place in Japan. The DPJ gained a landslide victory, leaping from 113 to a whopping 308 seats—amounting to 64% of the total seats—and became the majority party outright. As a result, the new government was formed under Hatoyama Yukio in September 2009. However, because the DPJ did not control a majority in the upper house, they formed a coalition with the Social Democratic Party and the *Kokumin Shintō* (People's New Party).

Before the general election, then-DPJ President Hatoyama declared in a rally in Okinawa that the Marine Corps Air Station at Futenma should be relocated "outside of the prefecture at a minimum." Subsequently, this statement and his obstinate desire to materialize relocation would have substantial repercussions on Japanese diplomacy and Japan's security relations with its most vital ally. His calls for relocation outside of Okinawa came just as years of earnest preparation to move the air station to Henoko Bay in Nago City were about to reach fruition. This was first agreed in April 1996, planned in May 2006, and reconfirmed in February 2009, along with the transfer of 8,000 US Marines from Okinawa to Guam. Given the history of the fierce fighting that took place on Okinawa in the final months of the Second World War, Okinawans possessed a keen desire for peace and a general wariness toward the military bases. Despite this, however, the Okinawa Prefectural Governor Nakaima Hirokazu had reached the conclusion that the relocation of the base within the prefecture was unavoidable.

Hatoyama had a tendency to be vague in his policies, but it was clear that he wished to lessen Japan's reliance on Washington and establish a more equal footing with the United States. In making this move, Hatoyama also sought to develop a new identity for Japan that was rooted in Asia, and thus advocated the establishment of an East Asian Community. However, achieving this would require Japan to commit itself to a number of initiatives, including securing an alternative ally that could replace the United States, and seeking out an amicable partner in Asia, as well as supporting further change in the international environment in East Asia. This also meant that Japan needed to boost its capacity—as had been proposed by Hatoyama's grandfather, Hatoyama Ichirō, who had proposed constitutional revision and rearmament.

Of course, Prime Minister Hatoyama did not actually take on any of these tasks, but he did play down the reality that relations with the United States should remain the cornerstone of Japanese diplomacy. At a summit meeting in November, Prime Minister Hatoyama asked for President Obama's trust, but in the end his words were not followed by proper actions. Although Washington had initially planned to cut Hatoyama some slack, it soon became concerned by the lack of any real progress and began to view the new Japanese government more dimly.

Eight months had elapsed and there were still no concrete options for an alternate location for the base that made the government return to the initial plan of relocating it to Henoko. While Hatoyama issued an official apology, he justified his actions by saying that he had realized the base needed to be in Okinawa as a "deterrent." Being an inept leader, Hatoyama finally resigned as prime minister in June after leaving a scar on US–Japan relations and the feeling of the Okinawans. Ultimately, the Hatoyama government was unable to benefit from the historical election victory and came out as a loser in both domestic and foreign politics.

Hatoyama's successor, Kan Naoto, took office in early June 2010. The following month, the DPJ suffered a decisive blow in the 2010 House of Councillors elections. The LDP boosted its presence, winning 51 of the seats up for re-election, while the DPJ secured 44. This effectively increased the division between the House of Representatives (controlled by the DPJ) and House of Councillors (controlled by the LDP). Two months later, on September 7, 2010, a Chinese fishing trawler rammed a Japan Coast Guard patrol boat in the waters near the Senkaku Islands. Beijing protested fiercely at Japan's decision to arrest and detain the Chinese trawler captain and took a number of retaliatory measures, including an embargo on the export of rare earth metals to Japan.

Tokyo was initially reluctant to escalate tensions and therefore refrained from appealing to international public opinion and releasing the video footage of the incident that was shot by members of the Japanese crew. It also released the captain of the trawler without filing any charges on September 24 by applying pressure on the local prosecutor's office. In contrast, US Secretary of State Hillary Clinton was quick to criticize China's attempt to unilaterally revise the status quo, and asserted that Article Five of the US–Japan Treaty—the article prescribing America's obligation to defend Japan—also applies to the Senkaku Islands. This had been the basic posture since the Bush administration, but it was the first time that a senior government official had defined the scope of the treaty.

Beijing soon realized that it was being perceived as a bully in the eyes of the world and thus, in September 2010, Hu Jintao reversed his hardline stance and renewed efforts toward establishing a more conciliatory diplomacy as a way to patch up relations with Japan. However, just two years later the Senkaku issue flared up once again, during the transition to the new Xi Jinping government. The rationale behind Beijing's return to a hardline position was that the governor of Tokyo, Ishihara Shintarō, had announced his intention that the metropolitan government would purchase three of the rocky islands from their private owners. Concerned that this would be an unnecessary provocation of China, the DPJ prime minister at the time, Noda Yoshihiko, nationalized the islands in an attempt to assuage China.

This move unexpectedly backfired, and purchase of the islands by the Japanese government became a significant point of contention with

Beijing, which was undergoing a domestic power struggle at the time. As such, the new Chinese leader Xi needed to take a staunch position on the issue and therefore it announced a stern protest. Anti-Japanese demonstrations erupted in many of China's major cities, and bilateral relations deteriorated quickly. Furthermore, China also began to openly challenge Japan's control of the Senkaku Islands by repeatedly encroaching upon its territorial waters with government ships. As this was a time when Xi was in the process of establishing political control and influence, Beijing flexed its muscles and moved rapidly to expand its control not only in the waters around the Senkakus in the East China Sea, but also in the South China Sea.

China was not the only headache for Tokyo. Japan's lack of firm resolve on the territorial issues and the ensuing decline in its international standing encouraged bolder moves by other nations that challenged Japan's existing territorial claims; in November 2010 Russian President Dmitry Medvedev visited the disputed Northern Territories (referred to as the Southern Kuril Islands by Russia), and in August 2012 South Korean President Lee Myung-Bak made a sudden visit to Takeshima (referred to as Dokdo by South Korea).

The 3/11 Disaster and Operation Tomodachi

On March 11, 2011, a powerful magnitude 9.0 earthquake struck northeastern Japan, which triggered, in turn, a massive tsunami that wrought havoc upon a huge portion of the Pacific coast. The tsunami also contributed indirectly to the nuclear meltdown of reactor units one, two, and three at the Fukushima Daiichi Nuclear Power Station as a result of a malfunctioned cooling system, which led to a hydrogen explosion. As Japan reeled from the enormity of the disaster, the SDF acted bravely in an attempt to avert further nuclear disaster by dropping water from the air onto reactor units. In the end, the disaster led to 20,000 deaths, mostly resulting from the tsunami. Countless others lost their homes and were in need of assistance.

A massive relief effort, known as Operation Tomodachi, was quickly put into action by US armed forces. This was a large-scale operation that involved more than 24,500 service members, 24 naval ships, and 189 aircraft during the peak of the operation, as well as nearly $80 million in US government aid. Donations from the American private sector—individuals, companies, and private organizations, etc.—totaled US $736.9 million and is believed to be America's fifth-largest private donation in history, as well as the third largest to a foreign country, and also the largest to a developed nation (JCIE 2014). This figure clearly demonstrated that the US–Japan relationship was not supported merely by national security concerns. The enthusiastic support and cooperation shown by America at the time of the disaster further strengthened US–Japan relations and was able to reverse most of the damage inflicted by Hatoyama's policies.

In sum, the six cabinets following the Koizumi government—three LDP cabinets and three DPJ cabinets—were each in government for only a brief period of no more than one year at most, and they also struggled in dealing with a divided Diet. Following the failure of the Hatoyama government, the subsequent DPJ governments under Kan and Noda began to pursue a more pragmatic course of action. For example, agreements were quickly secured between the DPJ and the opposition parties regarding the reconstruction efforts in the aftermath of the Great East Japan earthquake, as well as the implementation of reforms in the tax and social security systems. Under Noda, the DPJ returned to governing in a more logical manner, but its failures early on were too serious for the party to regain the public's trust. Thus, it was soundly defeated in the December 2012 general election, holding on to a mere 57 seats versus 294 seats for the LDP. This landslide victory led to another change in government and the second Abe Shinzō administration was formed.

Diplomacy in Obama's Second Term

During his second term in office, President Obama encountered many challenges in foreign affairs, a number of which were the result of the domestic political restrictions that he faced. Although he had secured his reelection in 2012, the Congress still remained divided due to the Republican majority in the House of Representatives. Moreover, following the 2014 midterm elections, the Republicans were able to regain a majority in both Houses. The rise in prominence of Tea Party Republicans in Congress made many of its Republican members lean toward isolationism.

Obama's diplomacy was also at the mercy of a number of sudden changes on the international stage: a chemical weapons attack by the Syrian government under President Bashār al-Assad against his own people in August 2013; the annexation of Crimea by Russia in 2014; and the rise of the "Islamic State in Syria (ISIS)," which expanded its military control deep into Iraqi territory and threatened to topple the Iraqi government. In all of these cases, Obama was quick to declare that the United States would not send ground forces, which was perceived globally as attesting to the president's ineffectiveness as a world leader; it appeared to signal that America was in retreat. It should also be noted that because the Obama administration had decreased US defense spending in its second term, it became increasingly imperative that it strengthened ties with Japan and its other allies.

Washington also took a more conciliatory approach toward Beijing, although aggressive Chinese actions in expanding its influence in Asia still remained a sticking point. John Kerry, the secretary of state in Obama's second term, sought to emphasize that America's "pivot to Asia" had not been designed with the aim of curbing China's growing dominance. Thus, the phrase was reworded as a "rebalance to Asia." Obama engaged in long discussions with China's President Xi Jinping in June 2013 as well as November 2014, impressing upon the world that the spirit of cooperation was still being maintained between the two nations. This was met with great indignation from Japan and the Philippines, two nations struggling to cope with increased military pressure from China.

It would not be long, however, before President Obama changed course. In 2015, China began to step up its unilateral artificial island construction in the Spratly Islands, which were also claimed also by both the Philippines and Vietnam. Faced with this transgression, Obama now spoke about the necessity of forming a Trans-Pacific Strategic Economic Partnership Agreement (commonly referred to as the Trans-Pacific Partnership, or TPP). The president also delivered a strong message to China in which he stressed that rewriting the rules would not be permitted. In essence, the US strategy was to use a trade agreement as a vehicle for supporting and collaborating further with Japan, the Philippines, and Vietnam.

The Second Abe Cabinet and the Resurgence of Japan

A staunch conservative with nationalistic leanings, Abe did not immediately create a good rapport with the more liberal Obama, especially after Abe's controversial visit to Yasukuni Shrine—where Japan's war dead, including Class A war criminals, are commemorated—which provoked fierce criticism and disappointment on the US side. Given Japan's difficult relationship with China and Korea at that time, any tension with Washington was a serious cause for concern, which made Abe break away from his ideological inclinations and instead redirect his focus on pursuing diplomacy that was based firmly upon national interests. He also made a concerted effort to improve Tokyo's relations with neighboring nations in Asia by pledging to uphold past statements made by Japan's leaders in recognizing the country's responsibility for Japanese aggressions in the Pacific War.

The second Abe cabinet brought Japan a long-awaited surge of energy by learning from the LDP's three years away from power as well as from Abe's first term. His primary task was to free Japan from the protracted economic slump and deflation that had extended itself from a "lost decade" to "two lost decades." Abe pursued a package of measures which consisted of three elements (or "arrows," as he called them) which has been dubbed "Abenomics": quantitative monetary easing to shake off deflation and aim for a 2% inflation rate; the flexible mobilization of public finances in order to pursue revitalization measures in each area of society and stimulate the economy; and, finally, the promotion of reform and capital investment aimed at maintaining growth by increasing the competitiveness of Japanese industry.

This approach devalued the yen, which led, in turn, to an upsurge in stock prices. The Abe cabinet also paved the way for Japanese entry into the TPP, which previous prime ministers had recognized as necessary but could not accomplish due to opposition from the political interests in the agricultural sector. The signs of economic recovery were well received by the general public and Abe was rewarded by a victory in the July 2013 election of the House of Councillors. This allowed the LDP to unify a divided Diet for the first time in several years and also to stabilize the government that presently enjoys a majority in both the lower and upper houses.

The Abe government also set out to enhance its alliance with the United States. In order to do this, Abe worked to increase the defense capabilities of Japan by tackling various initiatives such as establishing the National Security Council, relaxing the Three Principles on Arms Exports, and enacting the Act on the Protection of Specially Designated Secrets. He also increased Japan's defense expenditure, mustered all his political capital to revise the interpretation of the constitution so that it would allow Japan the right to collective self-defense (approved by the cabinet in July 2014), and modified other related security legislation. Further, Abe visited around 50 countries in a span of two years; this was part of his pro-active effort to not only strengthen relations with these nations but also to demonstrate to the world that "Japan is back."

Obama welcomed Abe's proactive initiatives, but nevertheless still made it clear that he was "disappointed" by his right-wing tendencies, as highlighted by the visit to Yasukuni Shrine in late 2013. The visit not only led to numerous headaches for Japan in sustaining cordial relations with China, but was also frowned upon by the United States given the increased risk of confrontation between its key allies in East Asia, Japan and South Korea, which could compromise the security of Asia. But Abe eventually came around to understanding the importance of improving relations with China, and personally met with President Xi Jinping in November 2014 and April 2015.

Other key events around this time were Obama's visit to Japan in April 2014, and Abe's reciprocal visit to the United States in April 2015. During his official visit to Tokyo, Obama strove to further enhance the US–Japan alliance in order to stem the tide of Chinese unilateral actions in both the East China and South China Sea. In this process, he became the first sitting American president to declare that Article Five of the Japan-US Security Treaty encompassed the Senkaku Islands.

In return, Tokyo made meticulous preparations for Abe's visit to the United States in 2015 and ensured that he would have something substantial to present to Obama. This came in the form of finalizing the revision of the Guidelines for US–Japan Defense Cooperation that was made possible due to the recent changes made in interpreting the constitution that permitted the right to collective self-defense under certain circumstances.

The ensuing talks in Washington allowed both Abe and Obama to make unprecedented progress in defining when the US–Japan alliance would be put into force. In addition, both leaders took this opportunity to reaffirm their commitment to the TPP. However, the highlight of Abe's visit was that he became the first Japanese prime minister to address a joint session of Congress. In his address, which was, by and large, well received in the United States, he traced the path of reconciliation that the United States and Japan had embarked on after the Pacific War, pointing out the level of cooperation that had developed between the two nations during the subsequent 70 years. He wrapped up his speech by calling for further strengthening of the alliance in the future.

***

The violent surge of Islamic radicalism, such as seen in the grip of "Islamic State (ISIS)" in western Eurasia, in conjunction with China's rise as a great power and the expansion of its influence in the East are two primary global phenomena that pose a menace to the world today. In hindsight, it was America that brought peace and stability in the aftermath of the two world wars in the twentieth century. If we look specifically at East Asia, the United States was able to check the establishment of a Russian sphere of influence by supporting Japan against Russia's southward expansion in the early twentieth century. On the other hand, when Japan tried to obtain exclusive control of mainland China during the 1930s, the America supported China with the aim of defeating Japan. After World War II, the United States acted resolutely in standing up to the North Koreans when they breached the 38th Parallel in June 1950 with the intent of forcibly unifying the peninsula. Furthermore, the United States also responded to the southward expansion of North Vietnam as well as the invasion of Kuwait by Saddam Hussein's Iraq. In other words, in all these cases America intervened in order to maintain the status quo by refusing to accept any unilateral changes brought out by the use of force.

However, will America be able to continue playing this role as China becomes increasingly more aggressive in its expansionist policies? Surely this will be difficult, as America's bitter experiences in the Iraq and Afghanistan wars has made the public increasingly wary of overseas interventions. Moreover, the United States no longer possesses the overwhelming international dominance that it once had; China is simply too powerful. The United States could not intervene when Russia, a smaller power compared to China, invaded Ukraine and annexed Crimea by force.

But it still is important to keep things in perspective. America's military capability is still the greatest in the world, and it will take many years—if not decades—for China to catch up. Besides its military strength, the United States also maintains a tremendous "soft" power in the form of many allies and friends across the globe. The same cannot be said about China, and surely it will face increased international criticism as it continues to pursue an expansionist policy that is based on flexing its military might.

Of course, the best scenario is to avoid a military showdown with China. Neither the United States nor Japan are necessarily opposed to China growing in power, but they do want China to develop into a responsible global player. This may be difficult to expect, however, as even now China is refusing to comply with decisions handed down by the Permanent Court of Arbitration. If China persists in following its present course of action by aggressively expanding its sphere of control, then the United States and Japan should cooperate with other nations and stand up to such actions because accepting them would signify the collapse of the postwar international order.

In this way, the US–Japan alliance is facing an immense challenge from China. Moreover, as North Korea attains complete nuclear missile capability, the true meaning of the relationship between America and Japan will be tested, for it will need to overcome these challenges if they are unwilling to fade into history. In this way, the challenges to the US–Japan relationship are not so much about the past, but rather about what kind of future they will create.

However tragic, no assurances can be given that the United States will never face another terrorist attack of the magnitude of 9/11. On the other hand, Japan too may encounter a national crisis, such as defending the Senkaku Islands, which will require American military support. In an era in which Japan possesses the right to collective self-defense, both the United States and Japan will have to constantly reexamine and reaffirm their mutual obligations and expectations so that peace and stability will define this region into the foreseeable future. The history of America and Japan shows us that two nations which had once fought a bitter war against each other can indeed reconcile and create a strong and lasting friendship with the mutual goal of making the world a safer and better place.

Bibliography

Bader, Jeffrey A. 2012. *Obama and China's Rise*. Washington, DC: Brookings Institution Press.

Clinton, Hillary Rodham. 2014. *Hard Choices*. New York: Simon and Schuster.

Gellman, Barton. 2008. *Angler*. New York: Penguin Press.

Japan Center for International Exchange (JCIE/USA). 2014. US Giving for Japan Disaster Reaches $730 Million. *Civil Society Monitor*, JCIE Special Report (March 2014). http://www.jcie.org/311recovery/usgiving4.html.

Kubo, Fumiaki, ed. 2007. *Amerika gaikō no shochōryū* [Various Currents of American Diplomacy]. Tokyo: Japan Institute of International Affairs.

Mann, James. 2004. *Rise of the Vulcans*. New York: Viking Press.

Rice, Condoleezza. 2011. *No Higher Honor*. New York: Crown Publishers.

Woodward, Bob. 2002. *Bush at War*. New York: Simon and Schuster.

Afterword of the English Translation Edition

It was a tremendous honor when I was personally asked by Professor Makoto Iokibe to become the English translation editor of *Nichibei kankei shi*, which was a very important book for both of us. The origins of the Japanese edition can be traced back to when I had just begun my academic career at Kobe University. As one of the senior students among the Iokibe *monka*, or cohort, I had arranged a graduate student workshop at a ryokan in Arima onsen, in northern Kobe. The purpose of the gathering was to discuss an ambitious new project that I had in mind; a research collaboration that would examine the history of US–Japan relations in its entirety. Having arrived in Japan as a foreign student from America, it had quickly come to my attention that despite the importance of US–Japan relations, there was a lacuna in the studies that examined the bilateral relationship of the two nations from the perspective of diplomacy and politics. The existing literature was either outdated, focused on a specific issue, or only covered the postwar era. Thus, I felt a strong need for an easily accessible and readable textbook—for students as well as the general public—that could fill this lacuna and contribute in its own way in furthering the understanding between America and Japan. Everyone at the Arima conference was highly enthusiastic about this endeavor and we were soon able to sketch a basic outline. Although I did not realize it at that time, this was the genesis of a project that would eventually culminate in a book, published in 2008, that would be widely read throughout universities across Japan.

© The Author(s) 2017
M. Iokibe (ed.), T. Minohara (trans. ed.), *The History of US–Japan Relations*, DOI 10.1007/978-981-10-3184-7

But the single individual who helped turn my aspirations into reality was my mentor, Professor Iokibe. When I had brought the idea to him after the conference, he wholeheartedly embraced the project and provided a few suggestions of his own. Initially, I had envisioned the contributors of the book to be comprised primarily of former Iokibe students. However, as many of us were still early in our careers, in hindsight this was clearly a very naïve idea as it exceeded our individual abilities at that time. Therefore, Professor Iokibe took it upon himself to invite several leading scholars of the field to participate in the project. Unfortunately, this meant that not all of the original intended members could remain as contributors. Ultimately, however, Professor Iokibe's decision not only added more credibility to the undertaking, but it also led to an enormous boost in the overall quality of the book. Furthermore, the inclusion of these senior scholars allowed us—that is, the younger scholars—the precious opportunity to interact and learn from these sages as numerous seminars were held during the preparation of the manuscript. This invaluable experience has undoubtedly helped us to mature as scholars.

The Japanese edition was well received, as attested by the fact that it is now in its tenth printing. However, because the main theme of the book was "US–Japan relations," it did make sense for the book to be read by Americans as well as the larger English-reading population who have an interest in the subject. As a book only available in Japanese, the limitation to the readership was all too obvious. Thus, when I was asked by Professor Iokibe to take the lead role in creating and editing an English edition, I jumped at the opportunity as it would be a fulfillment of my original aspiration.

My initial jubilation soon turned to anxiety as I realized the magnitude of the project that I had taken on. Although I had edited volumes in the past, such as *Tumultuous Decade: Empire, Society, and Diplomacy in 1930s Japan* (University of Toronto Press, 2013) and *The Decade of the Great War: Japan and the Wider World in the 1910s* (Brill, 2014)—I recommend both books as companion volumes to this one—this was a very different endeavor due to the sheer number of contributors involved as well as the tight deadlines. In fact, looking back, this has definitely been the most grueling project that I have ever accomplished to date. Therefore, it is with a great sense of relief that I am penning these last few words, but at the same time it is my hope that the readers of this book will come away with some new knowledge or insight into the deep and rich relationship between these two great nations that have experienced both the best of times, as good friends, and the worst of times, as bitter foes.

ACKNOWLEDGEMENTS

First and foremost, I would like to extend my greatest appreciation to Professor Makoto Iokibe, for without his wisdom and support this book would never have seen the light of day. This project, generously supported by the Japan Publishing Industry Foundation for Culture (JPIC), was fortunate in that a well-established publisher, Palgrave Macmillan, realized the significance of the project early on and showed great enthusiasm for publishing the book. Of course, this also meant that this project now had a firm deadline which immensely increased the stress level of the editor. In this regard, however, I was truly blessed by the highly competent cadre of 17 fellow contributors who were not only cooperative at all times, but who also, despite their hectic schedules, set aside the time to carefully read through the edited chapters and did not spare any effort in providing many insightful comments. In this way, the editor was never left alone in the herculean task of producing this volume; in every sense of the word, it was truly a collaborative team effort.

Many people have read the manuscript either in whole or in part, offering helpful critiques and suggestions along the way. An anonymous reader read the entire manuscript with minute attention and gave a review that was not only positive on the whole, but also provided several key constructive comments on how to better shape the volume. I am grateful for this, as these helpful suggestions have undeniably vastly improved the final quality of the book.

One of my first tasks as editor was to find a professional translator who could convert the Japanese text into a workable English manuscript. In

© The Author(s) 2017   259
M. Iokibe (ed.), T. Minohara (trans. ed.), *The History of US–Japan Relations*, DOI 10.1007/978-981-10-3184-7

this regard, I was very fortunate to have been able to secure the services of Ms Helen Kenyon who did a magnificent job in her translations. Always prompt and responsive, she also kindly assisted in proofreading the final manuscripts after my extensive edits as each chapter had to be shortened by nearly 40% on average. I also would like to mention my two bright graduate students (both ABDs) who helped with the volume: Ms Aleksandra Babovich thoroughly read over the entire manuscript with great attention to catch any inadvertent errors that still remained, and the research for the chronology of events was undertaken by Mr Tomoaki Hagito.

Gratitude needs to be extended to the publishing editor of the original Japanese edition, Mr Yasushi Seikai of Yuhikaku, for nagging me constantly about the deadline. His pressure was definitely frustrating at times, but I will be the first to admit that it did keep me adhered to the schedule, which is an impressive feat. He also undertook the burdensome task of acting as the go-between with other contributors and the editor. As he applied the same heat to them about strictly observing the deadline in returning the manuscripts, we were able to avoid any serious delays that would have otherwise pushed back the publication date.

In addition, I would like to personally thank the Director of JPIC, Mr Kiyoshi Nakaizumi, for his kind words of encouragement and support from the beginning to the end, a span of nearly three years. We overcame many hurdles together and along the way, and through this project, I have developed a strong sense of respect and friendship toward him. His staff member, Ms Ayako Akaogi, did a superb job of liaising with both Yuhikaku and Palgrave Macmillan to resolve the technical and legal issues of the project. Of course, no book is complete without an index, and in this regard I would like to thank Ms Christine A. Retz for doing an excellent job in her task. In this way, this final book is the result of a collective effort by many individuals.

Lastly, a few words of explanation are warranted regarding the rendering of the text of the volume. As is true in most cases, the use of non-English (in this case Japanese) sources requires the adoption of an established standard of conventions. For purposes of this volume, as editor, I have incorporated Romanized transliterations of non-Western names, words, phrases, and titles, rather than utilize Japanese, Chinese, and Korean characters. I have also observed the traditional Japanese, Chinese, and Korean practice of putting family or surnames first, with the exception of instances where the particular individuals regularly use the conventional Western format for writing their names or are individuals who are well-known by the

Western rendition of their names. As a general rule, all Chinese people and place names appear in Pinyin except for when the name is widely recognized and accepted in Wades-Giles. For instance, this volume uses Chiang Kai-shek rather than Jiang Jieshi. Also, for the sake of reducing ambiguity, all non-English sources have been referenced with their Romanized versions of the original titles followed by an approximate English title. As the Romanization of Japanese can sometimes lead to confusion among even the most advanced readers of Japanese, it is hoped that this addition will allow for more clarity.

I will conclude with the standard disclaimer that the content within this volume, and any errors that may remain, are the sole responsibility of the authors, and not those of any organizations or individuals who have supported this work. I do speak for all the contributors, however, in saying that I hope the readers of this volume will gain a deeper understanding of the dynamics and complexities of the diplomatic and political interaction between America and Japan spanning nearly two centuries.

Tosh Minohara
English translation editor
January 2017

CHRONOLOGY OF EVENTS

1825
February 18   Proclamation of the Order for the Repelling of Foreign
               Ships by the Tokugawa Shōgunate (*Muninen uchiharairei*)

1829
March 4   **Andrew Jackson (Democrat) is inaugurated as the sev-
               enth president** (to March 4, 1833)

1833
March 4   **Jackson (Democrat) is inaugurated for his second term
               as president** (to March 4, 1837)

1837
March 4   **Martin Van Buren (Democrat) is inaugurated as the
               eighth president** (to March 4, 1841)
June 28   Morrison Incident occurs

1840
April   Opium War (to August 29, 1842)

1841
March 4   **William Henry Harrison (Whig) is inaugurated as the
               ninth president** (to April 4, 1841)

© The Author(s) 2017   263
M. Iokibe (ed.), T. Minohara (trans. ed.), *The History of US–Japan
Relations*, DOI 10.1007/978-981-10-3184-7

April 6	**Vice President John Tyler (Whig) is sworn in as the tenth president** (to March 4, 1845)

1842

July	Order for the Provision of Firewood and Water is promulgated by the Tokugawa Shōgunate (*Shinsui kyūyorei*)

1845

March 1	Tyler approves a joint resolution for the annexation of Texas
March 4	**James K. Polk (Democrat) is inaugurated as the 11th president** (to March 4, 1849)
July	Term "Manifest Destiny" first appears in a US magazine

1846

May 13	Mexican–American War (to February 2, 1848)
June 15	Oregon boundary established by treaty with Britain
July	Commodore James Biddle brings his East India Squadron to Uraga to open Japan for trade with the US; his request is denied by the Tokugawa Shōgunate

1848

January 24	Gold discovered in California
February 2	US obtains California, Nevada, Arizona, Utah, New Mexico, and Colorado through a treaty with Mexico

1849

March 4	**Zachary Taylor (Whig) is inaugurated as the 12th president** (to July 9, 1850)

1850

July 9	**Vice President Millard Fillmore (Whig) is sworn in as the 13th president** (to March 4, 1853)

1853

March 4	**Franklin Pierce (Democrat) is inaugurated as the 14th president** (to March 4, 1857)

July 8	Commodore Matthew C. Perry, Commander of the East India Squadron, visits Uraga as the US envoy to Japan
October 4	Crimean War (to March 30, 1856)

1854

February 13	Commodore Perry returns with his squadron to Kanagawa, Japan
March 31	Treaty of Peace, Amity and Commerce is signed in Kanagawa between Japan and the US (Treaty of Kanagawa)

1856

August 21	US Consul General Townshend Harris arrives in Shimoda, Japan
October 23	Arrow War [Second Opium War] (to October 25, 1860)

1857

March 4	**James Buchanan (Democrat) is inaugurated as the 15th president** (to March 4, 1861)
June 17	Tokugawa Shōgunate signs the Treaty of Shimoda with the US

1858

July 29	Japan signs the trade regulations conforming the Treaty of Peace with the US
October 13	Suppression of extremists by the Tokugawa Shōgunate begins (*Ansei no taigoku*)

1860

February 9	Japanese Embassy staff, including Shinmi Masaoki, departs for the US
March 24	Sakurada Gate incident (*Sakuradamongai no hen*)

1861

January 15	Dutch-American interpreter Henry C. Heusken is assassinated by anti-foreign samurais from the Satsuma clan
March 4	**Abraham Lincoln (Republican) is inaugurated as the 16th president** (to March 4, 1865)
April 12	American Civil War (to April 9, 1865)

1863

August 15   Anglo–Satsuma War

1864

September 5   Chōshū clan clashes at Shimonoseki with four nations: Britain, France, the Netherlands and the US

1865

March 4   **Lincoln (Republican) is inaugurated for his second term as president** (to April 15)

April 14   Lincoln shot by John Wilkes Booth in Washington

April 15   **Vice President Andrew Johnson (Democrat) is sworn in as the 17th president** (to March 4, 1869)

1866

June 25   Conclusion of amended tariff treaty (*Kaizei yakusho*)

1867

March 30   US purchases Alaska from Russia

November 9   15th Shōgun Tokugawa Yoshinobu reverts political power to Emperor of Japan (*Taisei hōkan*)

1868

January 3   Emperor declares the restoration of Imperial Rule

January 27   Japanese civil war between Imperial and Shōgunate forces breaks out (Boshin War)

October 23   Era name is changed from Keiō to Meiji and the system of naming to periods of Japanese emperor's reign is revised

1869

March 4   **Ulysses S. Grant (Republican) is inaugurated as the 18th president** (to March 4, 1873)

May 10   First US transcontinental railroad is opened for business

1871

August 29   Abolition of Japanese feudal domains and the establishment of prefectures is introduced by the Meiji Emperor (*Haihan Chiken*)

November 20	Japan dispatches the Iwakura Tomomi Mission to Europe and the US

1873

March 4	**Grant (Republican) is inaugurated for his second term as president** (to March 4, 1877)

1874

April 9	Japan sends troops to Taiwan (Seitai Campaign)

1877

February 15	Satsuma Rebellion [Seinan War] (to September 24)
March 4	**Rutherford B. Hayes (Republican) is inaugurated as the 19th president** (to March 4, 1881)

1878

July 25	Treaty for the recovery of tariff rights is concluded (Evarts–Yoshida Treaty)

1881

March 4	**James A. Garfield (Democrat) is inaugurated as the 20th president** (to September 19, 1881)
July 2	Garfield is assassinated in Washington
September 20	**Vice President Chester A. Arthur (Republican) is sworn in as the 21st president** (to March 4, 1885)

1882

January 25	Preliminary conference for Japan's Treaty Revision begins (to July 27)

1885

March 4	**Grover Cleveland (Democrat) is inaugurated as the 22nd president** (to March 4, 1889)
December 22	Cabinet system is established in Japan and **the first Itō Hirobumi cabinet is formed** (to April 30, 1888)

1886

May 1	Inoue Kaoru convenes a treaty revision conference (agreement reached on April 22, 1887)

1888

February 1	Ōkuma Shigenobu becomes Foreign Minister of Japan
April 30	**Kuroda Kiyotaka cabinet is formed** (to October 25, 1889)

1889

February 11	Constitution of the Empire of Japan is promulgated
March 4	**Benjamin Harrison (Republican) is inaugurated as the 23rd president** (to March 4, 1893)
December 24	**First Yamagata Aritomo cabinet is formed** (to May 6, 1891)

1891

May 6	**First Matsukata Masayoshi cabinet is formed** (to August 8, 1892)

1892

August 8	**Second Itō Hirobumi cabinet is formed** (to August 31, 1896)

1893

March 4	**Grover Cleveland (Democrat) is inaugurated as the 24th president** (to March 4, 1897)

1894

July 16	Anglo–Japanese Treaty of Commerce and Navigation is concluded (abolishes consular jurisdictions and also reduces tariff rates)
July 25	Imperial Japanese Navy attacks Chinese warships (*Hōtōoki kaisen*)
August 1	Sino–Japanese War
November 22	Japan signs the Treaty of Commerce and Navigation with the US in Washington (promulgated March 24, 1895 and effective July 17, 1899)

1895

April 17	Sino–Japanese Peace Treaty is concluded at Shimonoseki, Japan

| April 23 | Germany, France, and Russia pressure Japan to return Liaodong Peninsula to China (Tripartite Intervention) |

1896

| September 18 | **Second Matsukata Masayoshi cabinet is formed** (to January 12, 1898) |

1897

| March 4 | **William McKinley (Republican) is inaugurated as the 25th president** (to March 4, 1901) |

1898

January 12	**Third Itō Hirobumi cabinet is formed** (to June 30)
April 18	Spanish–American War breaks out (to December 10)
June 30	**First Ōkuma Shigenobu cabinet is formed** (to November 8)
July 7	US annexes Hawaii
November 8	**Second Yamagata Aritomo cabinet is formed** (to October 19, 1900)
December 10	US acquires sovereignty over the Philippines by the Treaty of Peace with Spain

1899

| September 6 | Secretary of State John Hay proclaims his Open Door policy notes with China |

1900

June 20	Boxer Rebellion (to August 14)
July 3	Secretary of State Hay proclaims the second Open Door policy notes with China
October 19	**Fourth Itō Hirobumi cabinet is formed** (to May 10, 1901)

1901

March 4	**McKinley (Republican) is inaugurated for his second term as president** (to September 14)
June 2	**First Katsura Tarō cabinet is formed** (to January 7, 1906)
September 6	McKinley is assassinated by an anarchist and dies on September 14, 1902
September 14	**Vice President Theodore Roosevelt (Republican) is sworn in as the 26th president** (to March 4, 1905)

1902
January 30   Anglo–Japanese Alliance is concluded in London

1904
February 10   Russo–Japanese War
December 6   Roosevelt announces the Corollary to the Monroe Doctrine

1905
March 4   **Roosevelt (Democrat) is inaugurated for his second term as president** (to March 4, 1909)
July 29   Taft–Katsura agreement (in exchange for supporting the US interests in the Philippines, Japan is given unchallenged control over the Korean Peninsula)
August 12   Second Anglo–Japanese Alliance is concluded in London
September 4   Japan signs the Peace Treaty in Portsmouth with Russia, leading to the Hibiya Incendiary Incident of September 5
October 12   Harriman–Katsura Note is exchanged (but is rejected on October 23)
December 22   Japan signs the Sino–Japanese Treaty concerning Manchuria with China

1906
January 7   **First Saionji Kinmochi cabinet is formed** (to July 14, 1908)
October 11   San Francisco Board of Education adopts a resolution to allow public schools to refuse admission to Japanese children
November 26   South Manchurian Railway Company is founded (*Mantetsu*)

1907
April 19   Imperial Defense Policy is resolved
July 30   Japan signs the first Russo–Japanese Agreement with Russia

1908
March 25   Japan–US Gentleman's Agreement is concluded
July 14   **Second Katsura Tarō cabinet is formed** (to August 30, 1911)
October 18   US Navy's Great White Fleet, on a tour circumnavigating the globe, calls at the Port of Yokohama

November 30	Japan and the US reach agreement on Pacific Ocean affairs (Root–Takahira Agreement)

1909

March 4	**William H. Taft (Republican) is inaugurated as the 27th president** (to March 4, 1913)

1910

July 4	Japan signs the Second Russo–Japanese Agreement
August 22	Japan signs the Treaty of Annexation with Korea
November 10	US forms a Loan Consortium with Britain, Germany and France to bolster China's currency reserves

1911

February 21	Japan signs the New Treaty of Commerce and Navigation between with the US (Japan recovers tariff autonomy; signed on July 17)
August 30	**Second Saionji Kinmochi cabinet is formed** (to December 21, 1912)
October 10	Xinhai Revolution

1912

January 1	Sun Yat-sen officially declares the establishment of the Republic of China (ROC)
July 8	Japan signs the Third Russo–Japanese Agreement
August 5	Former President Theodore Roosevelt forms the Progressive Party (to 1916)
December 19	First movement for the defense of the Constitution causes Taisho Political Crisis (to February 11, 1913)
December 21	**Third Katsura Tarō cabinet is formed** (to February 20, 1913)

1913

February 20	**First Yamamoto Gonnohyōe cabinet is formed** (to April 16, 1914)
March 4	**Woodrow Wilson (Democrat) is inaugurated as the 28th president** (to March 4, 1917)
May 2	California State Legislature passes the anti-Japanese 1913 Alien Land Law

1914

April 16	**Second Ōkuma Shigenobu cabinet is formed** (to October 9, 1916)
July 28	First World War (to November 11, 1918)
August 23	Japan declares war on Germany (enters WWI on the allied side along with the UK)
November 7	Imperial Japanese Army takes over Qingdao, China

1915

January 18	Japan submits the Twenty-One Demands to China
March 13	First Bryan Note accepting Japan's special interests in South Manchuria and Eastern inner Mongolia is issued
May 7	Japan delivers an ultimatum to China (China accepts demands on May 9)
May 11	Second Bryan Note condemning Japan's violation of Chinese sovereignty is issued

1916

July 3	Fourth Russo–Japanese Agreement
October 9	**Terauchi Masatake cabinet is formed** (to September 29, 1918)

1917

January 9	Germany begins unrestricted submarine warfare (notice given to the US on January 31)
January 22	Wilson's speech in the Senate, "Peace Without Victory"
March 4	**Wilson (Democrat) is inaugurated for his second term as president** (to March 4, 1921)
April 6	US declares war on Germany
November 2	Ishii–Lansing Agreement
November 7	October Revolution in Russia

1918

January 8	Wilson presents Fourteen Points program for world peace to the Senate
August 2	Japan and the US dispatch troops to Siberia (to October 25, 1922)
August 3	"Rice Riots" in Japan
September 29	**Hara Takashi cabinet is formed** (to November 4, 1921)

1919

January 18	Versailles Peace Conference (to June 28)
March 1	Anti-Japanese independence movement breaks out at Gyeongseong, Pyongyang and elsewhere (March First Movement in Korea)
May 4	May Fourth Movement in Beijing
June 28	Signing of the Versailles Peace Treaty

1920

January 10	League of Nations is founded
March 19	US Senate rejects ratification of the Versailles Peace Treaty once again
September	Morris–Shidehara Talks (to January, 1921)
October	US forms a new loan consortium with Britain, Japan, and France to bolster China's currency reserves
November 2	California passes the 1920 Alien Land Law as a ballot measure ("Second Anti-Japanese Land Law")

1921

March 4	**Warren G. Harding (Republican) is inaugurated as the 29th president** (to August 2, 1923)
November 4	Hara Takashi is stabbed to death by Nakaoka Konichi at Tokyo station
November 12	Harding opens the Washington Conference on Limitation of Armaments (to February 6, 1922)
November 13	**Takahashi Korekiyo cabinet is formed** (to June 12, 1922)
November 19	US delegate Elihu Root enunciates the Four Principles
December 13	Japan signs the Four-Power Treaty that maintains the status quo in the Pacific for ten years (abrogation of the Anglo–Japanese Alliance) with the US, Britain, and France

1922

February 6	Five-Power Treaty for naval disarmament, and the Nine-Power Treaty eliminating internal customs in China and adopting a Chinese Tariff Commission are signed
June 12	**Katō Tomosaburō cabinet is formed** (to August 25, 1923)

1923

August 2	Harding dies suddenly of a stroke in San Francisco
August 3	**Vice President Calvin Coolidge (Republican) is sworn in as the 30th president** (to March 4, 1925)
September 2	**Second Yamamoto Gonnohyōe cabinet is formed** (to January 7, 1924)

1924

January 7	**Kiyoura Keigo cabinet is formed** (to June 11)
January 10	Second movement for the defense of the Constitution begins
May 26	1924 Immigrant Act, which includes the Japanese exclusion provision, is signed by President Coolidge
June 11	**First Katō Takaaki cabinet is formed** (to August 2, 1925) and Shidehara Kijūrō is appointed Foreign Minister

1925

March 4	**Coolidge (Republican) is inaugurated for his second term as president** (to March 4, 1929)
August 2	**Second Katō Takaaki cabinet is formed** (to January 28, 1926)

1926

January 30	**First Wakatsuki Reijirō cabinet is formed** (to April 20, 1927)
July 9	Generalissimo Chiang Kai-shek carries out the Northern Expedition in China

1927

March 15	Financial crisis occurs in Japan
March 24	Nanking Incident
April 20	**Tanaka Giichi cabinet is formed** (to July 2, 1929)
May 28	Imperial Japanese Army marches to Shandong
June 20	Geneva Naval Conference (ends a failure on August 4)

1928

April 19	Second Shandong Expedition
May 3	Jinan Incident
May 9	Third Shandong Expedition

| June 4 | Zhang Zuolin is assassinated |
| August 27 | Representatives of the US, Britain, France, Germany, Belgium, Italy, Japan, Canada, India, Australia, New Zealand, Poland, Czechoslovakia, the Irish Free State, and South Africa sign the Kellogg–Briand Pact (General Treaty for Renunciation of War as an Instrument of National Policy) in Paris. |

1929

March 4	**Herbert C. Hoover (Republican) is inaugurated as the 31st president** (to March 4, 1933)
July 2	**Hamaguchi Osachi cabinet is formed** (to April 14, 1931), Shidehara Kijūrō is once again appointed Foreign Minister
October 24	New York Stock Exchange crash leads to the Great Depression (Black Tuesday)
November 21	Ministry of Finance promulgates a ministerial ordinance removing the embargo on the export of gold (Implemented on January 11, 1930)

1930

January 21	US, France, Britain, Italy, and Japan convene the Five-Power Naval Conference (to April 22)
April 22	The Five Powers affix their signatures to the London Conference Treaty, which limits and reduces the navies of the US, Britain, and Japan, and restricts the naval forces of France and Italy.
April 25	Opposition party *Seiyūkai* leaders, Inukai Tsuyoshi and Hatoyama Ichirō, accuse the Hamaguchi cabinet of a violation of supreme command rights by signing the London Conference Treaty
June 17	Smoot–Hawley Tariff Act is enacted in the US
November 14	Hamaguchi Osachi is nearly assassinated by Sagoya Tomeo

1931

April 14	**Second Wakatsuki Reijirō cabinet is formed** (to December 13)
September 18	Liutiaohu Lake Incident occurs in Manchuria, also known as the Manchurian Incident
October 8	Kwantung Army Fighter Squadron bombs Jinzhou

December 13	**Inukai Tsuyoshi cabinet is formed** (to May 16, 1932); Finance Minister Takahashi Korekiyo orders a gold re-embargo at the first cabinet meeting

1932

January 7	Secretary of State Henry L. Stimson announces the Stimson Doctrine
January 28	First Shanghai Incident occurs
February 29	League of Nations Commission called Lytton Commission visits Japan to investigate Zhang Zuolin's assassination
March 1	Declaration of the establishment of Manchukuo
May 15	May 15 Incident, Junior naval officers attempt a coup
May 26	**Saitō Makoto cabinet is formed** (to July 8, 1934)
September 15	Japan signs the Japan–Manchukuo Protocol (confirms the recognition of Manchukuo; (*Nichiman Giteisho*))

1933

February 24	Head of the Japanese delegation, Matsuoka Yōsuke, walks out of Geneva Assembly. Japan gives formal notice of its withdrawal from the League of Nations on March 27
March 4	**Franklin D. Roosevelt (Democrat) is inaugurated as the 32nd president** (to January 20, 1937)
May 31	Japan signs the Tanggu Truce Agreement with China
June 12	London Monetary and Economic Conference convenes (ends in failure on July 27)

1934

April 17	The public information chief of the Gaimushō, Amō Eiji, states that Japan objects multinational co-operation in China by the Western powers at a press conference (The Amō Statement)
June 12	Reciprocal Trade Agreement is established in the US
July 8	**Okada Keisuke cabinet is formed** (to March 9, 1936)
December 29	Japan gives advance notice of its intention to abrogate the 1922 Washington Conference Treaty to the US

1935

June 10	Japan signs the Umezu–He Agreement
June 27	Japan signs the Doihara–Qin Agreement
August 31	US Congress passes the Neutrality Act

1936

February 26	Young extremists of the Imperial Way faction (Kōdō-ha) of the Imperial Japanese Army attempt a coup
March 9	**Hirota Kōki cabinet is formed** (to February 2, 1937)
November 25	Japan signs the Anti-Comintern Pact with Germany
December 12	Zhang Xueliang confines Chiang Kai-shek at Xi'an

1937

January 20	**Roosevelt (Democrat) is inaugurated for his second term as president** (to January 20, 1941)
February 2	**Hayashi Senjūrō cabinet is formed** (to June 4)
June 4	**First Konoye Fumimaro cabinet is formed** (to January 5, 1939)
July 7	Marco Polo Bridge Incident occurs (Sino–Japanese War breaks out)
August 13	Second Shanghai Incident occurs
October 5	Quarantine Speech is given by Roosevelt in Chicago
December 12	USS *Panay* Incident occurs
December 13	Imperial Japanese Army occupies Nanjing

1938

January 16	Konoye cabinet declares, "We will never again deal with the Chinese Nationalist Government," and gives notice of discontinuation of a peace overture to China (First Konoye Statement)
September 29	Signing of agreement at Munich Conference held by Germany, Britain, France and Italy allowing German expansion, September 30, 1938
November 3	"New Order for Greater East Asia" is expanded by Konoye (Second Konoye Statement)

1939

January 5	**Hiranuma Kiichirō cabinet is formed** (to August 30, 1939)
May 12	Soviet–Japanese conflict along the Manchurian–Mongolian frontier at Nomonhan (to September 15)
July 15	Arita–Cragie Agreement is formulated
July 26	US gives notice of abrogation of Treaty of Commerce and Navigation between Japan and the US (effective January 26, 1940)

August 23	Germany signs the Treaty of Non-Aggression with the USSR
August 30	**Abe Nobuyuki cabinet is formed** (to January 16, 1940)
September 3	Britain and France declare war on Germany (Second World War breaks out; to August 15, 1945)

1940

January 16	**Yonai Mitsumasa cabinet is formed** (to July 22)
March 30	Wang Jingwei establishes the Republic of China government in Nanjing
July 22	**Second Konoye Fumimaro cabinet is formed** (to July 18, 1941)
September 3	US Congress signs agreement with Britain exchanging destroyers for bases
September 16	US enacts Selective Training and Service Act
September 23	Imperial Japanese Army moves to seize Northern French Indochina
September 27	Japan signs the Tripartite Pact with Germany and Italy in Berlin
December 29	Roosevelt uses the term "Arsenal of Democracy" in his fireside chat

1941

January 6	Roosevelt speaks of Four Freedoms in State of the Union Address
January 20	**Roosevelt (Democrat) is inaugurated for his third term as president** (to January 20, 1945)
March 11	Lend-Lease Act is established by the US
April 13	Matsuoka Yōsuke signs the Japan–Soviet Neutrality Pact in Moscow
April 16	Secretary of State Cordell Hull and Ambassador Nomura Kichisaburō hold negotiations based on the Draft Understanding between Japan and the US
June 22	Germany invades the USSR
July 2	"Outline of Imperial Policy following the changes in circumstances" is approved by the Imperial Council
July 18	**Third Konoye cabinet is formed** (to October 18, 1941)

July 25	Japanese assets in the US is are frozen by the US as a result of Japan's foray into Southern French Indochina (Britain follows suit on the 26th and the Netherlands on the 27th)
July 28	Imperial Japanese Army moves to seize Southern French Indochina
August 1	US implements an embargo on all types of oil to Japan
August 14	Roosevelt and British Prime Minister Winston Churchill announce the Atlantic Charter
August 28	Konoye proposes s summit meeting with Roosevelt but is rebuffed
September 6	"Guideline for the execution of Imperial Policy" is approved by the Imperial Council
October 2	US hands a memorandum of four principles to Japan
October 18	**Tōjō Hideki cabinet is formed** (to July 22, 1944)
November 26	US submits a new proposal of "Hull Note" to Ambassador Nomura
December 1	Imperial Council decides on war against the US, Britain, and the Dutch
December 7	Imperial Japanese Army lands on the Malay Peninsula and bombs Pearl Harbor in Hawaii (Japan announces an Imperial edict of a declaration of war on the US and Britain on December 8; the US and Britain also declare war on Japan)

1942

January 1	United Nations Declaration is signed by 26 Allied powers and the US and Britain against the Axis Powers
May 29	Roosevelt presents plans for the "Four Policeman" at a conference with the USSR Foreign Minister Vyacheslav Molotov
June 4	Battle of Midway

1943

January 14	Casablanca Conference between Roosevelt and Churchill (to January 25)
November 3	Greater East Asia Conference is held (Joint Declaration on the 6th)
November 22	US, Britain, and China meet at the Cairo Conference (to November 26)

November 27	Cairo Declaration is signed by Roosevelt, Churchill, and Chiang (announced December 1)
November 28	Tehran Conference (to December 1)

1944

June 15	US Army lands on Saipan in the Mariana Islands
June 19	Naval Battle of the Philippine Sea
July 1	United Nations Monetary and Financial Conference is held at Breton Woods (to July 22)
July 22	**Koiso Kuniaki cabinet is formed** (to April 7, 1945)
August 21	Dumbarton Oaks conference on the foundation of the UN convenes (UN Proposal is officially unveiled on October 9, 1944)

1945

January 20	**Roosevelt (Democrat) is inaugurated for his fourth term as president** (to April 12)
February 4	Roosevelt, Churchill, and Stalin meet at the Yalta Conference (to April 11)
March 9	Tokyo is devastated by the bombs of more than 300 B-29s (to March 10)
April 1	US forces land on Okinawa
April 5	USSR refuses to extend the Neutrality Pact with Japan
April 7	**Suzuki Kantarō cabinet is formed** (to August 17)
April 12	Roosevelt dies, **Vice President Harry S. Truman (Democrat) is sworn in as the 33rd president** (to January 20, 1949)
April 25	San Francisco Conference convenes (to June 26)
May 7	Germany unconditionally surrenders to the Allied Powers
June 26	Signing of the UN Charter in San Francisco
July 16	First Atomic Bomb is successfully tested in the US
July 26	The US, Britain, and China announce the Potsdam Declaration on July 26
July 28	Suzuki announces to the press that he will disregard the Potsdam Declaration (*mokusatsu*) and push forward with the war effort
August 6	US drops an atomic bomb on Hiroshima
August 8	USSR declares war on Japan (entry into battle at dawn on August 9)

August 9	US drops an atomic bomb on Nagasaki
August 14	Japan accepts to the Potsdam Declaration
August 15	Imperial Rescript declaring the end of the war broadcast at noon (WWII ends)
August 17	**Higashikuni Naruhiko cabinet is formed** (to October 9)
August 30	General Douglas MacArthur arrives at Atsugi air base as Supreme Commander of the Allied Powers
September 2	On behalf of Japan, Shigemitsu Mamoru and Umezu Yoshijirō sign the Instrument of Surrender on the deck of USS *Missouri*
September 6	Truman approves the "US Initial Post-Surrender Policy for Japan," and orders MacArthur to implement it (announced September 22)
September 17	General Headquarters (GHQ) moves its headquarters to the Dai Ichi Seimei Building in Hibiya, Tokyo. MacArthur proclaims the occupation of Japan a success
September 27	Emperor Hirohito meets MacArthur for the first time at the US Embassy in Tokyo
October 4	GHQ issues the Civil Liberties Directive (Memorandum on Removal of Restrictions on Political, Civil, and Religious Liberties) and MacArthur suggests Konoye proceed with constitutional revisions
October 9	**Shidehara Kijūrō cabinet is formed** (to May 22, 1946)
October 11	MacArthur meets with Shidehara and demands "Five Great Reforms on Democratization"
October 13	Japan begins the process of revising the Constitution under the leadership of Matsumoto Jōji
October 25	GHQ issues orders to cease the operations and transfer of property and archives of all Japanese diplomatic institutions (all overseas diplomatic missions shut down on October 31); Constitutional Problems Investigation Committee established with Matsumoto Jōji as chairman
November 1	GHQ issues a statement repudiating any connection with Konoye regarding the revision of the constitution of Japan
November 6	GHQ issues "Memorandum on the Dissolution of Business Conglomerates" (*Zaibatsu Kaitai*)

November 21	Ministry of Foreign Affairs (MOFA) establishes the "Peace Treaty Problems Research Executive Committee"
December 17	House of Representatives Election Revision Law is promulgated (Japanese women gain suffrage)
December 22	Trade Union Law is promulgated (effective March 1, 1946)
December 27	Moscow Conference of Foreign Ministers announces the Far Eastern Commission and Allied Council for Japan
December 29	Amendments to Agricultural Land Adjustment Law are promulgated

1946

January 1	Emperor Hirohito issues an Imperial Rescript denying his divinity (Declaration of Humanity)
January 4	GHQ issues a directive ordering the removal and exclusion of militarists from public office and the dissolution of ultra-nationalist societies to comply
January 11	State–War–Navy Coordinating Committee (SWNCC) sends a notice to MacArthur regarding the revision of the Constitution (SWNCC 228)
January 24	Shidehara consults with MacArthur (agreement on continuing reign of the Emperor system and renunciation of war)
January 25	MacArthur sends a telegram to Washington reporting that there is no evidence of the Emperor having committed any war crimes
February 1	Japanese newspaper *Mainichi Shimbun* runs a scoop on "Constitutional Problems Investigation Committee Draft Proposal"
February 3	MacArthur orders the Government Section (GS) to draft a proposal for constitutional revision (GHQ draft)
February 13	GHQ hands over the draft to Japan
February 21	Shidehara meets with MacArthur to confirm the intentions of the GHQ draft
February 22	Cabinet decides to accept the GHQ draft
March 5	Winston Churchill gives the "Iron Curtain Speech" in Fulton, Missouri
March 6	Japan announces "Outline of the Draft for a Revised Constitution"
April 10	22nd general election of the House of Representatives (Japan Liberal Party (JLP) 140, Japan Progressive Party

	94, Socialist Party (SP) 93, Cooperative Party 14, Japan Communist Party (JCP) 5, Minors 38, Independent 80)
April 17	Japan announces "Draft for a Revised Constitution," which is presented to the Privy Council
May 3	International Military Tribunal of the Far East begins its proceedings (25 defendants indicted for Class A War Crimes
May 4	GHQ orders the removal of Hatoyama from public office
May 21	MacArthur promises Yoshida, "I will not allow one Japanese to die of starvation."
May 22	**First Yoshida Shigeru cabinet is formed** (to May 24, 1947)
October 21	Amendments to the Agricultural Land Adjustment Law are promulgated (effective November 22); Owner-Farmer Establishment Special Measures Law is promulgated (effective December 29); Second Land Reform
November 3	Constitution of Japan is promulgated (effective May 3, 1947)

1947

March 12	Truman announces the Truman Doctrine
March 17	MacArthur makes a statement accelerating the establishment of peace with Japan
April 14	Antimonopoly Law is promulgated (effective on July 20)
April 17	Local Autonomy Law is promulgated (effective May 3)
April 25	3rd general election of the House of Representatives (SP 143, JLP 131, Democratic Party 126, People's Cooperative Party 31, JCP 4, Minors 17, Independent 12)
May 3	Constitution of Japan comes into force
May 6	Fourth Meeting between Emperor Hirohito and MacArthur
May 24	**Katayama Tetsu cabinet is formed** (to May 10, 1948)
June 5	US announces the European Recovery Program known as the Marshall Plan
July 26	Ashida consults with Chief of the Diplomatic Section George Atcheson Jr., the GS chief Whitney on July 28, and British Commonwealth representative in Japan W. McMahon Ball on August 11. General Robert L. Eichelberger, commander of the 8th Army in Yokohama, receives a document suggesting the Japan–US Security Arrangement on September 13

August 5	Bureau of Far Eastern Affairs, the US State Department, reveals to Japan the Draft Treaty of Peace and Tariffs with Japan
September 20	"Emperor's Message" is relayed to Atcheson's successor William J. Sebald by Terasaki Hidenari
December 31	Abolition of Ministry of Home Affairs

1948

January 6	Secretary of the Army Kenneth C. Royall makes a speech on the US policy for modifying the occupation policy of Japan (Reassessment of Demilitarization toward Japan)
March 1	Head of the US State Department Policy Planning Staff, George F. Kennan, visits Japan and suggests development of new policies on Japan after return on March 25
March 10	**Ashida Hitoshi cabinet is formed** (to October 19)
April 1	USSR begins the blockade of Berlin
June 11	US Senate passes the Vandenberg Resolution that permits the right of collective self-defense
August 15	Republic of Korea (ROK) is established
September 9	Democratic People's Republic of Korea (DPRK) is established
October 9	National Security Council (NSC) approves NSC13/2 and shifts its policy toward Japan
October 14	Attempt to form an anti-Yoshida cabinet led by Democratic Liberal Party (*Minshu Jiyūtō*) Secretary General Yamazaki Takeshi is unsuccessful
October 19	**Second Yoshida Shigeru cabinet is formed** (to February 16, 1949)
December 18	GHQ announces Nine Principles for Economic Stability

1949

January 1	MacArthur announces in his New Year message that the US policy toward Japan shifts the major concern from political reform to the economic rehabilitation of Japan
January 20	**Truman (Democrat) is inaugurated for second term as president** (to January 20, 1953)
January 23	24th general election of the House of Representatives (Democratic Liberal Party 264, DP 69, SP 48, JCP, 35, PCP 14, Labor Farmer Party 7, New Farmers Party 6,

	Social Reform Party 5, New Liberal Party 2, Japan Farmers Party 1, Minors 3, Independent 12)
February 1	General Royall and Joseph M. Dodge with the personal rank of Minister (GHQ economic adviser) visit Japan
February 16	**Third Yoshida cabinet is formed** (to October 30, 1949)
March 7	Dodge, who is sent to Japan to advise on economic policy, requests a resolution for the stabilization of Japanese economy through a fiscal retrenchment policy, known as the Dodge Line
March 22	Dodge unofficially informs Ikeda Hayato of a "super balanced budget plan" featuring a surplus of 156.9 million yen
April 4	Signing of the North Atlantic Treaty (effective August 24)
April 23	GHQ sets the single foreign exchange rate of 360 yen to US$1 (implemented April 25)
September 13	US Secretary of State Dean Acheson and British Foreign Secretary Ernest Bevin agree to initiate a peace treaty with Japan without the Soviet Union's assent
September 25	TASS news agency announces the USSR has tested an atomic bomb
October 1	People's Republic of China (PRC) is established

1950

February 14	Signing of Treaty of Friendship, Alliance, and Mutual Assistance between the USSR and the PRC
April 6	John Foster Dulles is appointed as advisor. Truman assigns Dulles with a special responsibility to negotiate Japanese Treaty on May 18
April 25	Yoshida dispatches Ikeda Hayato to Washington (to May 22); Ikeda holds talks with Dodge and brings up the offer to the US government of continued use of bases in Japan after signing of the Peace Treaty
June 21	Consultant to the Secretary, Dulles visits Japan (to June 27) and holds talks with Yoshida on June 22
June 25	Korean War (to July 27, 1953)
July 8	MacArthur orders Yoshida to establish a National Police Reserve (*Keisatsu Yobitai*) and strengthen the Maritime Safety Agency (*Kaijō Hoanchō*)

August 10	National Police Reserve Law is promulgated and becomes effective
September 14	Truman accepts the policy document initiating preliminary discussions on Japanese Peace Treaty (NSC60/1)
October 25	Chinese forces cross the Yalu River and enter Northern Korea
November 24	Seven Principles on Japanese Peace Treaty set in motion by the US

1951

January 4	UN troops retreat to Seoul in Korea
January 25	Dulles visits Japan to conclude the peace treaty (to February 11)
April 11	Truman dismisses MacArthur as SCAP for making statements critical of the government's military and foreign policies and appoints Lieutenant General Matthew. B. Ridgway as his successor
April 16	Dulles visits Japan and holds talks with Yoshida and General Ridgway on the 18th
September 4	San Francisco Peace Conference convenes (to September 8)
September 8	Japan signs the San Francisco Peace Treaty and the Japan–US Security Treaty
December 24	Yoshida informs Dulles that Japan will enter into a treaty with the ROC in Formosa (Yoshida Letter)

1952

January 18	ROK sets the boundary of water in which the activities of Japanese fishing boats are prohibited, called the Rhee Syngman Line
February 15	First Japan–Korea Formal Conference convenes
February 28	Japan signs the Administrative Agreement with the US (regulation regarding the status of the US armed forces in Japan based on the Japan–US Security Treaty)
April 28	Occupation formally ends and the Japan–US Security Treaty takes effect; Japan signs a peace treaty with ROC (effective August 5, 1952)
October 1	25th general election of the House of Representatives (Liberal Party 240, Reform Party 85, Right Wing

Socialist Party 57, Left Wing Socialist Party 54, LFP 4, Minors 4, Independent 19)

October 30   **Fourth Yoshida cabinet is formed** (to May 21, 1953)

1953

January 20   **Dwight D. Eisenhower (Republican) is inaugurated as the 34th president** (to January 20, 1957); Dulles becomes Secretary of State on January 21

April 19   26th general election of the House of Representatives (LP 199, RP 76, LWSP 72, RWSP 66, Separatists Liberal Party 35, LFP 5, JCP 1, Minors 1, Independent 11)

May 21   **Fifth Yoshida cabinet is formed** (to December 10, 1954)

October 2   Ikeda Hayato visits the US and holds talks with Assistant Secretary Walter Robertson in Washington (to October 30)

December 24   Japan and the US sign an agreement on the restoration of the Amami Islands to Japan (effective December 25)

1954

March 1   Fukuryū Maru fishing boat is contaminated by radioactive fallout from a US thermonuclear bomb test in the Bikini Atoll (Lucky Dragon Incident)

March 8   Mutual Defense Assistance Agreement between Japan and the US (the MSA Agreement) is signed (effective May 1)

June 9   Defense Agency Act and Self-Defense Forces Act are promulgated (effective July 1)

July 21   Geneva Agreement regarding end of the French Indochina War is signed (dated July 20)

September 3   China begins shelling Quemoy, along with Matsu

September 26   Yoshida makes a tour of seven Western nations (to November 17). Yoshida–Eisenhower Joint Declaration announced on November 10

November 5   Japan signs the Japan–Burma Peace Treaty and the Agreement on Reparations and Economic Cooperation (effective April 16, 1954)

December 10   **First Hatoyama Ichirō cabinet is formed** (to March 19, 1955)

1955

January 25	Soviet representative—and former acting head of Permanent Delegate of the USSR—Andrei Domnitsky makes an secret overture toward normalization of ties with Japan
February 27	27th general election of the House of Representatives (Japan Democratic Party 185, LP 112, LWSP 89, RWSP 67, LFP 4, Minors 2, Independent 6, JCP 2)
March 19	**Second Hatoyama cabinet is formed** (to November 22)
April 9	US National Security Council adopts NSC5516/1
April 18	Conference of Asian and African Nations is held in Bandung (to April 24)
May 8	Large rally against expansion of Tachikawa US air base is held
May 10	US forces conduct an artillery training at North Fuji Maneuver Camp (heats up the struggle against US military bases in Japan)
June 1	Peace negotiations between Japan and the USSR held in London
June 7	Japan joins the General Agreement on Tariffs and Trade (GATT; effective September 10)
July 18	Leaders of the US, Britain, France, and the USSR convene for the Geneva Summit meeting (to July 23)
August 29	Shigemitsu visits the US to propose revision of the Security Treaty to Dulles but is rebuffed (to August 31); announcement on the Japan–US communiqué on August 31
October 13	Meeting to unify the two Japan Socialist Party factions (Left Faction Chairman Suzuki Masaburō and Asanuma Inejirō representing the Right Faction)
November 15	Two conservative parties—the Liberal Party and the Japan Democratic Party—merge to form the Liberal Democratic Party (so-called "unification of the the conservative parties, or *hoshu gōdō*)
November 22	**Third Hatoyama cabinet is formed** (to December 23, 1956)

1956

January 17	Peace negotiations between Japan and the USSR held again in London (indefinitely adjourned on March 20)

April 29	Kōno Ichirō holds fishery talks between Japan and the USSR in Moscow
May 9	Japan–Philippines Reparations Agreement (payment of US $550 million over 20 years) is signed (effective July 23)
July 17	Economic White Paper by the Economic Planning Agency declares: "Japan is no longer in the post-war period"
July 31	Shigemitsu resumes negotiations of the normalization of Japan–Soviet diplomatic relations
August 24	Shigemitsu meets with Dulles in London to discuss the Japanese negotiations with the USSR
October 19	Hatoyama signs the Japan–Soviet Joint Declaration in Moscow (effective December 12)
December 18	UN General Assembly decides unanimously to admit Japan into the UN
December 23	**Ishibashi Tanzan cabinet is formed** (to February 25, 1957)

1957

January 20	**Eisenhower (Republican) is inaugurated for his 2nd term as president** (to January 20, 1961)
January 30	US soldier kills a Japanese woman at US Sōmagahara Camp in Gunma, Japan (Girard Incident)
February 25	**First Kishi Nobusuke cabinet is formed** (to June 12, 1958)
May 20	Kishi visits six Southeast Asian nations (to June 4); Kishi talks in Taipei to support the "recapture" of the Mainland attempted by ROC on June 3
June 16	Kishi visits the US (to July 1) and holds talks with Eisenhower on June 19
August 1	US Department of Defense announces withdrawal of American ground combat forces in Japan (withdrawal completed on February 8, 1958)
September 28	MOFA publishes Diplomatic Bluebook presenting an overview of Japan's diplomatic performance
October 4	Successful launch of satellite Sputnik by the USSR
November 18	Kishi visits nine Southeast Asian nations (to December 8)

1958

January 20	Japan signs the Japan–Indonesia Peace Treaty and the Agreement on Reparations and Economic Cooperation (Payment US $223 million in 12 years)
March 5	Japan signs the 4th private trade agreement with the PRC. On the 14th, the ROC threatens Japan to terminate the ongoing trade negotiations in protest
May 2	A right-wing youth pulls down a Chinese flag at the trade fair in Nagasaki
May 22	28th general election of the House of Representatives (Liberal Democratic Party 287, Japan Socialist Party 166, JCP 1, Minors 1, Independent 12)
June 12	**Second Kishi cabinet is formed** (to July 19, 1960)
July 19	Japan proposes a draft resolution under the UN Security Council (UNSC) considering the dispatch of US forces to Lebanon; proposal is vetoed by the USSR on July 22
August 23	PRC opens fire on the offshore islands of Quemoy controlled by the ROC; the US sends the 7th Fleet into the Taiwan Straits and remains on a high alert until the 24th
October 4	Negotiation for a revision of the Japan–US Security Treaty is held in Tokyo
October 8	Japan presents a bill to revise Police Official Duties Execution Act to Diet

1959

March 9	Head of the Japan Socialist Party delegation, Asanuma Inejirō, proclaims in China that "American imperialism is a common enemy for both the Chinese and Japanese people"
May 13	Japan signs agreements with South Vietnam to pay reparations (US $39 million in five years) and provide yen loans (US $7.5 million in three years; effective January 12, 1960)
September 25	Eisenhower and Khrushchev meet for talks at Camp David

1960

January 19	Japan signs the New Japan–US Security Treaty in Washington; the Japan–US Joint Communiqué issued
May 5	USSR announces that an American U-2 spy plane was shot down while flying through Soviet airspace on May 1
June 10	White House Press Secretary James Haggerty escapes aboard a US military helicopter after demonstrators surrounded his car at Haneda Airport in Japan
June 15	Storming of Diet building by mainstream faction of the All-Japan Federation of Students' Self-Governing Associations and subsequent clash with riot police results in death of one University of Tokyo student, Kanba Michiko
June 16	Extraordinary Meeting of the cabinet is convened in order to request the postponement of Eisenhower's visit to Japan
June 19	New Security Treaty and Agreements are automatically ratified at midnight
June 22	US Senate approves ratifying the Japan–US Security Treaty
June 23	Exchange of ratification instruments for the new Japan–US Security Treaty and entering into force of the new treaty; Kishi announces his resignation
July 19	**First Ikeda Hayato cabinet is formed** (to December 8)
November 20	29th general election of the House of Representatives (LDP 296, JSP 145, Democratic Socialist Party 17, JCP 3, Minors 1, Independent 5)
December 8	**Second Ikeda cabinet is formed** (to December 9, 1963)
December 27	Second Ikeda cabinet unveils the Income Doubling Plan

1961

January 20	**John F. Kennedy (Democrat) is inaugurated as the 35th president** (to November 22, 1963)
February 21	Japan's ambassador to the UN Matsudaira Kōtō states, "It is fundamental for the development of the UN to dispatch Japanese troops to aid UN military police."
April 19	Edwin O. Reischauer, the new US ambassador, arrives in Japan.

June 19	Ikeda visits the US and Canada (to June 30) and holds talks with Kennedy on June 20 (to June 22)
August 13	GDR constructs a wall dividing East and West Germany (Berlin Wall)
November 16	Ikeda visits four Southeast Asian nations (to November 30)

1962

September 19	LDP Advisor Matsumura Kenzō holds talks with Chinese Premier Zhou Enlai in Beijing; agreement on working toward normalization of Japan–China diplomatic relations
October 22	Kennedy announces the blockade of Cuba (Cuban Missile Crisis)
November 4	Ikeda visits seven European nations (to November 25)
November 9	Takasaki Tatsunosuke and Liao Chengzhi sign a memorandum regarding an unofficial Long-Term Trade Agreement between Japan and China (LT trade begins)
November 12	Ōhira Masayoshi and Kim Jong Pil, Director of the KCIA, agree to a compromise of US $300 million in grants and a yen loan of US $100 million to South Korea in lieu of war reparations

1963

February 20	Japan gains GATT Article 11 nations status
August 5	US, Britain and the USSR sign the Partial Nuclear Test Ban Treaty (PTBT; effective October 10)
September 23	Ikeda visits the Philippines, Indonesia, Australia, and New Zealand (to October 6)
November 21	30th general election of the House of Representatives (LDP 283, JSP 144, DSP 23, JCP 5, Independent 12)
November 22	Kennedy is assassinated in Dallas, Texas; **Vice President Lyndon B. Johnson is sworn in as the 36th president** (to January 20, 1965)
December 9	**Third Ikeda cabinet is formed** (to November 9, 1964)

1964

March 23	UNCTAD is held at Geneva (to June 16); 1,500 members of 121 nations participate

April 1	Japan accepts International Monetary Fund (IMF) Article VIII Obligations
April 28	Japan joins the OECD
August 2	Gulf of Tonkin incident in Vietnam
October 10	Tokyo Olympics begin (to October 24)
October 16	PRC conducts first atomic bomb test
November 9	**First Satō Eisaku cabinet is formed** (to February 17, 1967)

1965

January 20	**Johnson (Democrat) is inaugurated for his second term as president** (to January 20, 1969)
February 7	US commences bombing of North Vietnam
February 17	Shiina Etsusaburō visits South Korea (to February 20); Japan–ROK Treaty on Basic Relations is agreed upon in Seoul on February 20
April 20	Japan Overseas Cooperation Volunteers is founded
April 24	First Demonstrations are held by peace group Beheiren in Japan
June 22	Japan–ROK Treaty on Basic Relations is signed in Seoul (effective December 18)
August 19	Satō visits Okinawa (first prime minister to visit since WWII)

1966

| May 16 | Central Committee of the Chinese Communist Party withdraws the "February Outline" written by Peng Zheng group, and the Cultural Revolution begins |
| November 24 | Asian Development Bank founded (headquarters based in Manila) |

1967

January 29	31st general election of the House of Representatives (LDP 277, JSP 140, DSP 30, Clean Government Party 25, JCP 5, Independent 9)
February 17	**Second Satō cabinet is formed** (to January 14, 1970)
May 15	Kennedy Round of the General Agreement of Tariffs and Trade (GATT) is concluded (signed June 30)

June 6	Cabinet approves the Basic Policy for the Liberalization of Capital Transactions
July 1	Merger Treaty comes into force, combining the European Coal and Steel Community (ECSC), European Economic Community (EEC), and European Atomic Energy Community (Euratom) into the European Communities
August 8	Founding of ASEAN (Association of Southeast Asian Nations)
September 20	Satō visits Southeast Asian nations (to September 30)
October 8	Satō second visit to Southeast Asia, and Oceania (to October 21)
November 12	Satō visits the US (to November 20); announces the Japan–US Joint Declaration on the 15th (agreement for the restoration of Bonin Islands and Okinawa within three years)

1968

January 27	Satō announces three non-nuclear principles at the administrative policy speech, and announces the four nuclear principles in the Lower House plenary session on January 30
July 1	Non-Proliferation Treaty (NPT) is signed (Japan signs February 3, 1970)
August 20	USSR intervenes in Czechoslovakia (Prague Spring)
November 10	Unified opposition candidate Yara Chobyō is elected as Chief Executive of the Ryukyu Islands (Okinawa)

1969

January 20	**Richard M. Nixon (Republican) is inaugurated as the 37th president** (to January 20, 1973)
July 25	Nixon announces the Guam Doctrine (later known as the Nixon Doctrine)
November 17	Satō visits the US (to November 26); first summit meeting with Nixon on November 19; announcement of Joint Communiqué on the 21st (promise of return administrative rights of Okinawa to Japan in 1972)
December 27	32nd general election of the House of Representatives (LDP 288, JSP 90, CGP 47, DSP 31, JCP 14, Independent 16)

1970

January 14	**Third Satō cabinet is formed** (to July 7, 1972)
March 14	1970 World Exposition is held in Osaka (to September 13)
June 23	Japan–US Security Treaty extended automatically per stipulation
October 20	Japan publishes the first Defense White Paper

1971

March 27	US 7th Infantry Division (20,000) completes pullout from Korea
June 17	Japan and the United States sign an agreement for the reversion of Okinawa
July 15	Nixon announces a visit to the People's Republic of China in 1972, creating "Nixon Shock"
August 15	Nixon announces new economic policy, a temporary abandonment of the gold standard and an introduction of an import surcharge of 10%—leads to the "Dollar Shock"
October 25	United Nations General Assembly (UNGA) invites the PRC's membership
November 24	Lower House of Japan resolves to approve the Japan–US agreements concerning the Ryukyu Islands and the Daito Islands, the three non-nuclear principles, and the reduction of US military bases in Okinawa
December 18	Ministerial Meeting of Group of Ten agrees to a multilateral monetary realignment; on the 19th, the exchange rate is set at 308 yen per dollar (Smithsonian Agreement)

1972

January 5	Satō and Fukuda visit the US and hold talks with Nixon on January 6; Joint Communiqué announced on January 7
January 22	UK signs European Community Act (effective January 1, 1973)
February 21	Nixon visits the PRC; joint declaration between the US and the PRC called the Shanghai Communiqué announced on the 27th
May 15	Administrative authority of Okinawa reverts to Japan; Okinawa Prefecture founded
May 26	Nixon visits the USSR; SALT I agreement is signed

June 17	Watergate scandal breaks
July 7	**First Tanaka Kakuei cabinet is formed** (to December 22)
September 25	Tanaka visits the PRC and signs a Joint Communiqué on the 29th (diplomatic relations normalized)
December 10	33rd general election of the House of Representatives (LDP 271, JSP 118, JCP 38, CGP 29, DSP 19, Minors 2, Independent 14)
December 22	**Second Tanaka cabinet is formed** (to December 9, 1974)

1973

January 20	**Nixon (Republican) is inaugurated for his second term as president** (to August 9, 1974)
January 27	Vietnam peace treaty signed in Paris (effective January 28)
February 1	Chief of War Defense Agency, Masuhara Keikichi, outlines "The Limitation of Defense Capacity in Peacetime"
February 14	Japan shifts to a floating exchange rate system along with six other nations at the Economic and Financial Affairs Council (ECOFIN) meeting on March 11 (effective March 19)
August 8	Korean opposition politician, Kim Dae Jung (later president) is kidnapped from Tokyo
September 14	Tokyo Round of GATT begins
September 21	Japan and North Vietnam normalize diplomatic relations; sign the Exchange of Notes in Paris.
October 6	Fourth Arab–Israeli War
October 17	Six Persian Gulf countries declare a 21% increase in oil prices, and the 30% increase notified by Royal Dutch Shell and US Exxon Mobil on October 23 (First Oil Crisis)
November 5	OAPEC announces a cut in crude oil production.
November 14	Kissinger visits Japan; talks with Tanaka and Ōhira about the oil crisis in Middle East
December 25	OAPEC announces Japan as a "friendly nation" and supplies the required oil

1974

January 7	Tanaka visits five Southeast Asian nations and encounters anti-Japanese student demonstrations on January 15 in Bangkok and anti-Japanese riots on January 17 in Jakarta.

February 11	Oil-importing countries convene the Washington Energy Conference (to February 13)
August 8	Nixon announces his resignation from the Presidency in a televised broadcast from the White House
August 9	**Vice President Gerald R. Ford is sworn in as the 38th president** (to January 20, 1977)
October 10	Tachibana Takashi's article entitled "A Study of Tanaka Kakuei: His Gold Vein and Human Vein" is published in the November 1974 issue of the magazine *Bungei Shunju* leads to his resignation
November 18	Ford visits Japan (the first visit by a sitting US president)
November 26	Tanaka makes public his resignation as Prime Minister
December 9	**Miki Takeo cabinet is formed** (to December 24, 1976)

1975

January 16	Miyazawa Kiichi holds talks with Andrei Gromyko in Moscow and announces a joint communiqué on January 18
April 30	Saigon falls to North Vietnam, bringing an end to the Vietnam War.
July 30	Conference on Security and Cooperation in Europe (CSCE) convenes and the Declaration of Helsinki is signed on August 1
August 2	Miki visits the United States for a summit meeting with Ford on August 5; the Japan–US Joint Declaration including new Korea Clause is announced on August 6
November 15	First summit meeting convenes in Rambouillet (to November 17, 1975)

1976

January 9	Gromyko visits Japan
February 23	First ASEAN Summit meeting convenes (to February 24)
February 24	Miki requests Ford to provide details regarding the Lockheed scandal
September 6	Pilot of an MIG-25 lands his plane at Hakodate airport in Hokkaidō with the hope of defecting to the US
October 29	Japan establishes National Defense Program Outline (NDPO; *Bōei Keikaku no Taikō*)

November 5	Japan introduces a 1% ceiling of GNP for future defense spending
December 5	34th general election of the House of Representatives (LDP 249, JSP 123, CGP 55, DSP 29, JCP 17, New Liberal Club 17, Independent 21)
December 24	**Fukuda Takeo cabinet is formed** (to December 7, 1978)

1977

January 20	**Jimmy Carter (Democrat) is inaugurated as the 39th president** (to January 20, 1981)
May 7	London Summit meeting convenes (to May 8); Fukuda promises a growth rate of 6.7% for fiscal year 1977
July 10	11th general election of the House of Councilors (LDP 63, JSP 27, CGP 14, DSP 6, JCP 5, NLC 3, Socialist Citizen's Federation 1, United Progressive Liberals 1, Minors 1, Independent 5)
August 6	Fukuda visits six Southeast Asian nations, and announces three new diplomatic principles for enhanced cooperation between them on August 18 in Manila (Fukuda Doctrine)

1978

April 12	108 Chinese fishing boats take aggressive action over the Senkaku Islands
May 3	Fukuda visits the US and holds talks with Carter
May 11	JDA Director General Kanemaru Shin announces the sharing of financial cost for the US forces based in Japan (*Omoiyari yosan*)
July 16	Bonn Summit meeting convenes (to July 17); Fukuda pledges a reduction in the current account surplus and the achievement of a GDP rate of 7%
August 12	Sonoda visits the PRC and signs Japan–PRC Treaty of Peace and Friendship
October 23	Deng Xiaoping states, "It's natural for Japan to maintain the Japan–US Security Treaty and build up defenses"
November 26	Secretary General of LDP Ōhira Masayoshi wins a landslide victory to become party president. Fukuda withdraws his candidacy for the election on the 27th

November 27	Guidelines for the Japan–US Defense Cooperation are established
December 7	**First Ōhira Masayoshi cabinet is formed** (to November 9, 1979)

1979

January 1	US establishes full diplomatic relationship with the PRC
January 16	Shah Pahlavi leaves for Egypt; Ayatollah Khomeini returns to Iran and leads the Iranian Revolution on February 1 (Second Oil Crisis occurs)
February 17	Sino-Vietnamese War (to March 16)
April 30	Ōhira visits the US and holds talks with Carter on May 2
June 18	US and the USSR sign the SALT II agreement in Vienna which limits the number of missile launching facilities
June 28	Tokyo Summit meeting convenes (to June 29); participating nations agree to control imports of petroleum products
July 27	Japan signs the Geneva Protocol of GATT for the Tokyo Round (effective January 1, 1980)
October 7	35th general election of the House of Representatives (LDP 248, JSP 107, CGP 57, JCP 39, DSP 35, NLC 4, Socialist Democratic Federation 2, Independent 19)
November 4	Iranian radicals seize the US Embassy in Teheran
November 9	**Second Ōhira cabinet is formed** (to July 17, 1980)
December 5	Ōhira visits the PRC and holds talks with Chinese Premier Hua Guofeng; Ōhira promises to provide a five billion yen loan at the second meeting on December 6
December 27	Soviet military forces advance into Afghanistan (to February 15, 1989)

1980

January 23	Carter announces the Carter Doctrine for security in the Middle East
February 26	Japan's Self-Defense Forces (JSDF) participate in the multilateral Rim of the Pacific "RIMPAC 80" exercises for the first time (to March 18)
April 25	Japan announces intention to boycott the Summer Olympics in Moscow; the US attempts to rescue its staff from the embassy in Teheran, Iran but fails

April 30	Ōhira visits the US and Canada, meets Carter on May 1 in Washington and announces the concept of "shared existence, shared sacrifice" (*Kyōzon kyōku*)
June 22	36th general election of the House of Representatives (LDP 284, JSP 107, CGP 33, DSP 32, JCP 29, NLC 12, SDF 3, Independent 11); 12th general election of the House of Councilors (LDP 69, JSP 22, CGP 12, JCP 7, DSP 6, Minors 2, Independent 8); simultaneous elections for both houses of the Diet for the first time
July 17	**Suzuki Zenkō cabinet is formed** (to November 27, 1982)
September 1	Chun Doo Hwan becomes president of South Korea
September 9	Iran-Iraq War (to August 20, 1988)
September 15	Pacific Community Seminar convenes in Canberra, Australia (to September 19); the Pacific Economic Cooperation Council (PECC) is founded

1981

January 20	**Ronald W. Reagan (Republican) is inaugurated as the 40th president** (to January 20, 1985)
May 4	Suzuki visits the US and holds talks with Reagan on May 7; joint declaration is announced on May 8 (Suzuki agrees at press conference to defend the sea lanes to a distance of 1,000 nautical miles)

1982

November 27	**First Nakasone Yasuhiro cabinet is formed** (to December 27, 1983)

1983

January 11	Nakasone visits South Korea and holds talks with Chun; agreement is reached where by Japan would provide a loan of US $4 billion
January 17	Nakasone visits the US and holds talks with Reagan on the 18th
January 19	*Washington Post* reports that Nakasone likened the Japanese archipelago to an "unsinkable aircraft carrier"
March 23	Reagan announces the SDI initiative
May 28	Williamsburg Summit meeting convenes (to May 30)

September 1	Soviet aircraft shoots down a Korean Air flight over the southern Sakhalin Island
November 23	General Secretary of the Communist Party of China Hu Yaobang visits Japan and holds talks with Nakasone on November 24; agreement reached on the establishment of the 21st Century Committee for Japan–China Friendship
December 18	37th general election of the House of Representatives (LDP 250, JSP 112, CGP 58, DSP 38, JCP 26, NLC 8, SDF 3, Independent 16)
December 27	**Second Nakasone cabinet is formed** (to July 22, 1986)

1984

| March 23 | Nakasone visits the PRC and holds talks with Chinese Premier Zhao Ziyang; agreement reached on providing a second loan to China of 470 billion yen |
| September 6 | South Korean President Chun Doo Hwan visits Japan; during a reception at the Imperial Palace, Emperor Hirohito states that he "regrets" the unfortunate history |

1985

January 20	**Reagan (Republican) is inaugurated for his second term as president** (to January 20, 1989)
March 11	Mikhail Gorbachev is appointed General Secretary of the Communist Party of the USSR
August 15	Nakasone officially visits the Yasukuni Shrine
September 22	G5 conference of the financial ministers and central bank governors; the group settles on the need for coordination of macroeconomic policies known as the Plaza Accords
October 15	Gorbachev unveils his policy of perestroika

1986

| April 7 | Advisory Group on Economic Structural Adjustment for International Harmony (*Kokusai Kyōchō no Tame no Keizai Kōzō Chōsei Kenkyūkai*) releases what becomes known as the Maekawa Report |
| May 4 | Tokyo Summit meeting convenes (to May 6); the need for surveillance of macro-policy coordination is discussed |

July 6	38th general election of the House of Representatives (LDP 300, JSP 85, CGP 56, DSP 26, JCP 26, NLC 6, SDF 4, Independent 9); 14th general election of the House of Councilors (LDP 72, JSP 20, CGP 10, JCP 9, DSP 5, NLC 1, Second Chamber Club 1, Salaryman New Party 1, Tax Party 1, Independent 6); simultaneous elections for both houses of the Diet
July 22	**Third Nakasone cabinet is formed** (to November 6, 1987)
December 30	Japan decides fiscal year 1987 budget and approves a defense budget that surpasses 1% of the GNP for the first time

1987

May 15	Toshiba Electronics is punished for breaking COCOM restrictions
June 8	Venice Summit meeting convenes (to June 10)
October 2	US and Japanese Defense Officials Meeting decides on the joint development of the FSX support fighter
October 19	New York Stock Exchange crashes (Black Monday)
November 6	**Takeshita Noboru cabinet is formed** (to June 2, 1989)
December 8	US and the USSR sign the Intermediate-Range Nuclear Force (INF) Treaty, leading nuclear arsenal reductions for the first time
December 16	South Korea's ruling Democratic Justice Party candidate, Roh Tae Woo, is elected as president

1988

June 19	Toronto Summit meeting convenes (to June 21)
July 5	Recruit stocks-for-favor scandal
August 25	Takeshita visits the PRC and holds talks with Chinese Premier Li Peng; agreement on providing a third yen loan to China, which amounts to 810 billion yen with a six-year grace period

1989

January 7	Emperor Hirohito dies; the Rites of the Imperial Funeral (Taisō no rei) held at Shinjuku Gyoen

January 20	**George H. W. Bush(Republican) is inaugurated as the 41st president** (to January 20, 1993)
April 28	FSX joint development project is settled between Japan and the US
June 2	**Uno Sōsuke cabinet is formed** (to August 9)
June 4	PRC government uses force to suppress groups of students calling for democratization in the heart of the capital (Tiananmen Square incident)
July 14	Arche Summit meeting convenes (to July 16)
July 23	15th general election of the House of Councilors (JSP 46, LDP 36, Japanese Trade Union Confederation Association 11, CGP 10, JCP 5, DSP 3, SCC 2, TP 2, Sports Peace Party 1, Independent 10)
August 9	**First Kaifu Toshiki cabinet is formed** (to February 28, 1990)
September 4	Japan–US Structural Impediments Initiative (SII) Talks commence; interim report published on April 6, 1990
November 6	Inaugural meeting of APEC (Asia-Pacific Economic Cooperation) in Canberra, Australia (to November 7)
November 9	GDR permits free travel to West, initiates a process leading to the fall of the Berlin Wall on November 10
December 2	Bush and Gorbachev hold a summit meeting in Malta

1990

February 18	39th general election of the House of Representatives (LDP 275, JSP 136, CGP 45, JCP 16, DSP 14, SDF 4, Progressive Party 1, Independent 21)
February 28	**Second Kaifu cabinet is formed** (to November 5, 1991)
July 9	Houston Summit meeting convenes (to July 11)
August 2	Iraqi forces invade Kuwait and the Gulf crisis erupts
October 3	German unification
November 21	CSCE summit meeting convenes; signing of the Paris Charter

1991

January 17	International coalition begins its liberation of Kuwait, leading to the beginning of the Gulf War (to February 27)
January 24	Japan provides an additional US$9 billion to the international coalition

April 25	Japan dispatches four minesweepers to the Persian Gulf (to October 30, 1991)
November 5	**Miyazawa Kiichi cabinet is formed** (to August 6, 1993)
December 11	EC drafts Maastricht Treaty at summit meeting (signed February 7, 1992)
December 26	Supreme Soviet of the Soviet Union convenes and formally dissolves the USSR

1992

March 15	United Nations Transitional Authority in Cambodia (UNTAC) is established
June 15	PKO Cooperation Bill is passed
July 6	Munich Summit meeting convenes (to July 8)
September 17	JSDF participates in UN peacekeeping operations (PKO) in Cambodia
September 30	US returns Naval Base Subic Bay to the Philippines

1993

January 1	EC Common Market is formed
January 20	**William J. Clinton (Democrat) is inaugurated as the 42nd president** (to January 20, 1997)
April 16	Miyazawa–Clinton summit meeting to bring agreement on a plan to lower trade imbalance
June 21	Sakigake (Pioneer) Party is set up by Takemura Masayoshi and another defector from the LDP (Shintō Sakigake); Ozawa Ichirō and Hata Tsutomu factions, having left the LDP, form the Japan Renewal Party (Shinseitō) on June 23
July 6	Miyazawa–Clinton summit meeting reaches agreement on a "framework" for the Japan–US trade talks but bicker over "numerical targets" on specific sectors
July 7	Tokyo Summit meeting convenes (to July 9)
July 18	40th general election of the House of Representatives (LDP 223, JSP 70, Japan Renewal Party 55, CGP 51, Japan New Party 35, JCP 15, DSP 15, New Party Sakigake 13, SDF 4, Independent 30)
August 9	**Hosokawa Morihiro non-LDP coalition cabinet is formed** (to April 25, 1994); the 1955 system comes to a close
November 20	Congress passes the North American Free Trade Agreement known as NAFTA (effective January 1, 1994)
December 15	Uruguay Round of GATT is adopted

1994

January 29	Package of four bills for political reforms is approved by the Diet
February 11	Hosokawa–Clinton summit meeting leads to a breakdown of the framework trade talks in five key areas
February 23	Prime Minister's Advisory Group on Defense Issues (Bōei Mondai Kondankai) is established, headed by Higuchi Hirotarō
March 15	IAEA (International Atomic Energy Agency) inspectors are forced to leave North Korea
March 19	Working-level talks between North and South Korea break down; North Korea walks out, threatening to turn Seoul into "a sea of fire"
April 25	**Hata Tsutomu cabinet is formed** (to June 29)
June 17	Former President Carter holds talks with North Korean President Kim Il-sung and receives commitment from North Korea to abandon ongoing nuclear development and permit IAEA inspectors in remain
June 29	Coalition cabinet is established, including the Socialist Party, the LDP, and the Sakigake Party, and is headed by Murayama Tomiichi, chairman of the Socialist Party (to January 11, 1996)
July 1	Murayama expresses his support for the Japan–US security arrangements in a telephone conversation with Clinton
July 8	Naples Summit meeting convenes (to July 10)
July 20	Murayama states at the House of Representatives, "the JSDF is constitutional, and the Japan–US Security Treaty is necessary"
August 12	Prime Minister's Advisory Group on Defense Issues reports to Murayama
September 3	JSP approves the JSDF as a constitutional entity and the firm maintenance of the Japan–US Security Treaty
October 1	Japan–US Framework Talks reach agreement on two sectors (telecommunications equipment, medical products/insurance) to avert the US imposition of trade sanctions, but dispute over auto parts remains unresolved
October 21	US and North Korea sign an "Agreed Framework" on North Korean nuclear weapons development

| November 15 | APEC heads of state meeting adopts "Bogor Declaration" on economic liberalization |

1995

January 1	WTO (World Trade Organization) is founded in Geneva
January 17	Hanshin-Awaji Great Earthquake strikes
March 20	Tokyo subway Sarin gas attack by the Aum Supreme Truth (Aum Shinrikyō)
May 11	NPT (Non-Proliferation Treaty) is extended indefinitely
May 16	US announces plans to implement a 100% tax on Japanese luxury cars; on the 17th, Japan contends that the sanctions violate arrangements and that it will bring action against the United States at the WTO
June 28	Japan–US compromise agreement regarding automobiles and bilateral trade
July 21	China conducts missile tests near Taiwan
August 15	Statement by Murayama on the 50th Anniversary of the end of WWII
September 4	Rape incident of an Okinawan schoolgirl by three American servicemen
November 19	APEC heads of state meeting in Osaka; adopts "The Osaka Action Agenda" (Clinton is absent)

1996

January 11	LDP cabinet is revived with **Hashimoto Ryūtarō as Prime Minister** (to November 7)
February 23	Hashimoto raises the reversion of Futenma base at his first summit meeting with Clinton; the return of the base to Japan is agreed on April 12
March 1	ASEM (Asia–Europe Meeting) is founded
March 8	China conducts missile tests near Taiwan (to March 25; Taiwan Strait crisis)
March 23	Lee Tenghui wins Taiwan's first direct presidential election
April 16	Clinton visits Japan, and signs the Japan–US Joint Declaration on Security Cooperation at Hashimoto–Clinton summit meeting on the 17th
September 10	UNGA adopts CTBT (Comprehensive Nuclear-Test-Ban Treaty)

| October 20 | 41st general election of the House of Representatives under the new election system combining single-seat constituencies with proportional representation (LDP 239, New Frontier Party 156, Democratic Party of Japan 52, JCP 26, Socialist Democratic Party 15, NPS 2, Democratic Reform Party 1, Independent 9) |
| November 7 | **Second Hashimoto cabinet is formed** (to July 30, 1998) |

1997

January 20	**Clinton (Democrat) is inaugurated for his second term as president** (to January 20, 2001)
April 25	Hashimoto and Clinton reach agreement to draft New Guidelines for the Japan–US Defense Cooperation at the summit meeting
June 20	Denver Summit meeting convenes (to June 22); Russia is officially included in the G7 meeting, which becomes the G8
July 2	Thai baht allowed to float, leading to the East Asian financial crisis
September 23	Japan–US agree on the revised Guidelines for the Defense Cooperation
November 28	Financial Structural Reform Law is approved by the Diet

1998

May 15	Birmingham Summit meeting convenes (to May 17)
May 29	Act on Special Measures concerning Promotion of Fiscal Structural Reform is enacted
June 25	Clinton visits the PRC and holds talks with Jiang Zemin on June 27
July 12	18th general election of the House of Councilors (LDP 44, DPJ 27, JCP 15, CGP 9, Liberal Party 6, SDP 5, Independent 20)
July 30	**Obuchi Keizō cabinet is formed** (to April 4, 2000)
August 31	North Korea test-fires suspected Taepodong-1 ballistic missile over the Japanese archipelago
October 3	Miyazawa announces US$30 billion, "New Miyazawa Initiative" for aid to Asian nations at the G7 meeting
October 7	Kim Dae-jung visits Japan (to October 10); Kim seeds a new relationship between Japan and South Korea with emphasis on the future in a joint declaration on October 8

November 13	Obuchi visits Russia and reaches an agreement with Boris Yeltsin to create a National Borders Demarcation Committee (Kokkyō kakutei iinkai); signs the Moscow Declaration
November 19	Clinton visits Japan
November 25	Jiang Zemin visits Japan (to November 30) and raises the issues of history and Taiwan as a issues in the bilateral relations
December 6	Obuchi expresses his commitment to "revitalize Asia" in Hanoi, Vietnam
December 11	Financial Structural Reform Law is suspended by the Diet

1999

January 1	EU's single currency is introduced
March 24	North Atlantic Treaty Organization (NATO) involvement in the Kosovo crisis leads to air strikes against Yugoslavia (to June 10)
April 29	Obuchi visits the US (to May 4) and holds talks with Clinton on May 3
May 24	Diet passes legislation to implement revised Guidelines for the Japan–US Defense Cooperation, revised ACSA, and revised JSDF law
June 18	Cologne Summit meeting convenes (to July 29): The Kosovo issue is discussed
July 8	Diet approves, "Package of bills for reforms of central ministries and agencies," and "Package Promoting Decentralization bill;" Obuchi visits China (to July 10); agreement is reached on easing of restrictions on foreign investment in business activities to help China's drive for membership in the WTO on July 9
November 28	ASEAN+3 Summit meeting adopts a resolution to convene every other year

2000

March 18	Former mayor of Taipei Chen Shuibian (Taiwan's largest opposition party, the Democratic Progressive Party) wins the presidential election
April 2	Obuchi is hospitalized with a massive stroke; his cabinet resign on April 2 (Obuchi dies on May 14)

April 5	**First Mori Yoshirō cabinet is formed** (to July 4)
June 13	Kim Dae-jung visits North Korea and holds First Inter-Korean Summit meeting with Kim Jong-il (to June 14)
June 25	Forty-second general election of the House of Representatives (LDP 233, DPJ 127, CGP 31, LP 22, JCP 20, SDP 19, Conservative Party 7, Independent's Club 5, Liberal League 1, Independent 15)
July 4	**Second Mori cabinet is formed** (to April 26, 2001)
July 21	Kyushu–Okinawa Summit meeting convenes (to April 23)
October 11	First Armitage–Nye Report is issued

2001

January 20	**George W. Bush (Republican) is inaugurated as the 43rd president** (to January 20, 2005)
February 9	Japanese fisheries high school training vessel, the *Ehime Maru*, sinks after collision with a US nuclear submarine off the coast of Oahu, Hawaii
March 28	Bush administration withdraws from the Kyoto Protocol for reducing the ongoing problem of global warming
April 23	Koizumi Junichirō wins a landslide victory for the LDP presidency
April 26	**First Koizumi Junichirō cabinet is formed** (to November 19, 2003)
June 29	Koizumi visits the US (to July 1) and holds talks with Bush at Camp David on June 30
July 20	Genoa Summit meeting convenes (to July 22)
July 29	19th general election of the House of Councilors (LDP 64, DPJ 26, CGP 13, LP 6, JCP 5, SDP 3, Minors 1, Independent 3)
August 13	Koizumi officially visits the Yasukuni Shrine
October 7	US and British forces begin airstrike of Afghanistan
October 29	Enactment of three new laws related to anti-terrorism, including Anti-Terrorism Special Measures Law
November 9	JSDF's three vessels leave for the Indian Ocean to provide support for US forces
December 7	Collapse of the Taliban regime in Afghanistan
December 11	China officially becomes a member of the WTO
December 22	Establishment of the Afghanistan Interim Authority

2002

January 1	Euro notes and coins come into circulation in 12 EU countries
January 21	Afghanistan Reconstruction Conference convenes (to January 22)
January 29	Bush describes Iran, Iraq, and North Korea as belonging to an "Axis of Evil" in his State of Union address
May 28	Russia becomes an associate member of NATO
June 13	Bush administration withdraws from the Anti-Ballistic Missile (ABM) Treaty, leading to its termination
September 9	Koizumi visits the US (to September 14) and holds talks with Bush to seek international support
September 17	Koizumi visits North Korea and holds the first summit meeting with Kim Jong-il, leading to the Pyongyang Declaration
September 20	Bush Doctrine is announced which claims the right to utilize preemptive strikes for self-defense
November 8	UNSC unanimously passes a resolution demanding that Iraq fully cooperate with inspectors looking for weapons of mass destruction (WMD); Iraq accepts on November 13

2003

January 10	North Korea declares intent to withdraw from the NPT
March 15	National People's Congress elects Hu Jintao as the PRC president
March 20	Outbreak of the Iraq War
April 9	Baghdad falls; Hussein regime collapses
April 30	North Korea makes a statement on its possession of nuclear weapons
May 1	Bush declares an end to the Iraq War
June 1	Evian Summit meeting convenes (to June 3)
June 6	Enactment of three new laws related for contingencies, including Armed Attack Situations Response Act
July 26	Enactment of an Iraq Reconstruction Special Measures Law (Iraku Fukkō Shien Tokubetsu Sochihō)

August 27	First Round of Six-Party Talks concerning North Korea's nuclear weapons problem convenes in Beijing (to August 29)
October 16	UNSC passes a resolution for an increase in troops and financial contributions to help with the reconstruction of Iraq
November 9	43rd general election of the House of Representatives (LDP 237, DPJ 177, CGP 34, JCP 9, SDP 6, New Conservative Party 4, IC 1, LL 1, Independent 11)
November 19	**Second Koizumi cabinet is formed** (to September 21, 2005)
December 8	Koizumi announces the dispatch of the JSDF to Iraq
December 13	US troops capture former Iraqi President Saddam Hussein
December 19	Libya announces the abandonment of its WMD program
December 24	Japan imposes ban on US beef imports due to BSE

2004

February 8	JSDF arrives in Iraq's southern city of Samawah and begins non-combat humanitarian reconstruction mission from the end of March
May 1	EU membership grows from 15 to 25 countries
May 22	Koizumi revisits North Korea and holds talks with Kim Jong-il, which leads to the five families of the abductees returning to Japan
June 18	EU Constitution is unanimously adopted at the EU summit meeting
June 28	Establishment of the Iraqi Interim government
July 11	20th general election of the House of Councilors (DPJ 50, LDP 49, CGP 11, JCP 4, SDP 2, Independent 5)
October 6	US–Iraq Survey Group announces final report that Iraq had neither weapons of mass destruction nor significant WMD production programs at the time of the invasion
November 3	George W. Bush is reelected as president
November 5	Russia ratifies the Kyoto Protocol for reducing greenhouse gasses (effective as of February, 2005)
December 26	Indonesia earthquake and tsunami

2005

January 6	Special ASEAN Leaders' Meeting on the Aftermath of Earthquake and Tsunami convenes in Indonesia; Koizumi announces Japan will provide US$500 million in aid
January 20	**George W. Bush. (Republican) is inaugurated for his second term as president** (January 20, 2009)
January 30	National elections are held in Iraq
April 9	Anti-Japanese riots occur in Beijing; tens of thousands of protesters participate in cities including Shanghai on the 16th to 17th
August 8	Bills related to the privatization of the postal service are defeated by the Diet; Koizumi dissolves the House of Representatives
August 15	Cabinet approves the address by Koizumi at the 60th Memorial ceremony for the War Dead, following the Murayama Statement
September 11	44th general election of the House of Representatives (LDP 296, DPJ 113, CGP 31, JCP 9, SDP 7, People's New Party 4, Minors 2, Independent 18); landslide for the Koizumi government due to the victory of postal privatization scheme
September 14	UN summit meeting to commemorate the 60th anniversary of the founding of the UN (to September 16); UN reform to consider Japan as a permanent member of the UNSC
September 19	North Korea pledges to abandon all nuclear weapons and existing nuclear programs in Fourth Round of Six-Party Talks
September 21	**Third Koizumi cabinet is formed** (to September 26, 2006)
November 15	Bush visits Japan and holds talks with Koizumi in Kyoto on November 16
December 8	Koizumi cabinet makes a decision to extend the dispatch of the JSDF troops in Iraq until December 14, 2006
December 12	Japan resumes import of US and Canadian beef
December 14	Inaugural East Asia Summit meeting convenes in Kuala Lumpur

2006

January 20	Japan halts US beef imports completely due to the discovery of BSE
March 16	White House announces the Bush administration's second release of the National Security Strategy (NSS)
April 21	Japan decides to revise the Basic Plan until November 1 in order to dispatch the JSDF vessels to the Indian Ocean for refueling operations
May 1	Finalization on realignment of US force in Japan at the Security Consultative Committee between Japan and the US in Washington
June 20	Koizumi announces plans to withdraw the JSDF from Iraq (withdrawal accomplished on July 17)
June 29	Koizumi visits the US and holds talks with Bush; the two leaders announce a joint document, the "Japan–US Alliance of the New Century"
July 5	North Korea test launch of the "Taepodong-II"
July 15	UNSC unanimously passes resolution to prevent materials from being transferred to North Korea
July 27	Japan decides to reopen US beef imports
September 26	**First Abe Shinzō cabinet is formed** (to September 26, 2007)
October 6	Japan decides a proposed amendment to extend the expiration date of ATSML for one year; enacted at Upper House plenary session on the 27th
October 8	Abe holds talks with Hu Jintao in Beijing and holds talks with Roh Moo Hyun on October 9
October 9	North Korea announces it has conducted successful nuclear tests
October 14	UNSC unanimously passes resolution condemning North Korea
December 23	UNSC unanimously passes final resolution condemning Iran to permanently relinquish uranium enrichment, and all UN member states to prevent the transfer of materials to Iran that could be used for nuclear program

2007

January 10	Bush announces a plan to send more than 20,000 troops to Iraq in a temporary surge
January 15	Second East Asia Summit meeting convenes in Cebu Island, the Philippines
February 8	Six-Party Talks conclude with an agreement on the shutdown of North Korea's nuclear facilities at Yongbyon and allowing IAEA inspections in return for an shipment of 50,000 tons of heavy-fuel oil
February 16	Second Armitage-Nye Report is issued
March 24	UNSC unanimously passes resolution to impose additional sanctions to Iran, regarding its uranium enrichment program
April 11	Chinese Premier Wen Jiabao visits Japan, and has a meeting with Abe
April 27	Abe visits the US and holds a summit meeting with Bush
July 18	Sixth Round of Six-Party Talks in Beijing (to July 20)
July 29	21st general election of the House of Councilors (LDP 37, DPJ 60, CGP 9, JCP 3, SDP 2, PNP 2, Minors 1, Independent 7); ruling party loses in a landslide
July 30	US House passes a resolution demanding that Japan should formally apologize for the coercion of young women into sexual slavery, known as "comfort women"
September 26	**Fukuda Yasuo cabinet is formed** (to September 24, 2008)
November 1	ATSML expires, and the JSDF cease refueling operations in the Indian Ocean
November 16	Fukuda visits the US and holds a summit meeting with Bush
November 21	Third East Asia Summit meeting convenes in Singapore
December 28	Fukuda visits the PRC and holds talks with Chinese leader including Hu Jintao (to December 30)

2008

January 11	Replenishment Support Special Measures is passed by the Diet. The JSDF's refueling operations in the Indian Ocean resume
May 7	Chinese President Hu Jintao visits Japan

June 24	Council on Reconstruction of a Legal Basis for Security (Anpohōseikon) issues a report
July 1	Japan makes a decision to extend the dispatch of the JSDF vessels for six months to the Indian Ocean for refueling operations
July 7	Hokkaidō-Tōyako Summit meeting convenes (to July 9)
September 15	Lehman Brothers files for bankruptcy initiating worldwide financial crisis
September 24	**Asō Tarō cabinet is formed** (to September 16, 2009)

2009

January 20	**Barack Obama (Democrat) is inaugurated as the 44th president** (to January 20, 2013)
February 17	Agreement between Japan and the US concerning the implementation of the relocation of three marine expeditionary force personnel and their dependents from Okinawa to Guam (effective on May 13, 2009)
February 24	Asō visits the US and holds talks with Obama
March 14	JSDF's two vessels leave for the coast of Somalia to participate in an anti-piracy mission
April 5	North Korea announces plans to conduct missile test as artificial satellite launch
June 16	Japan decides on additional sanctions on North Korea at the cabinet meeting
July 8	L'Aquila Summit meeting convenes (to July 10, 2009)
August 30	45th general election of the House of Representatives (DPJ 308, LDP 119, CGP 21, JCP 9, SDP 7, Your Party 5, PNP 3, Minors 2, Independent 6); landslide for the DPJ
September 16	**Hatoyama Yukio cabinet is formed** (June 8, 2010)
October 13	Defense Minister Kitazawa Toshimi states that the Indian Ocean refueling mission will not be extended beyond January 2010
October 16	Hatoyama suggests he may postpone a decision on whether to accept the existing bilateral agreement on the relocation of the US forces on Okinawa
November 13	Hatoyama holds talks with Obama in Tokyo to discuss bilateral security relations, Afghanistan, Pakistan, North Korea, nonproliferation, and energy and climate

December 26	Hatoyama announces at a press conference that the Futenma base decision will be made by the end of May 2010 (ruling out relocating Futenma to Guam)

2010

January 19	Obama and Hatoyama each issue statements to commemorate the 50th anniversary of the signing of the Japan–US Security Treaty; the "2+2" bilateral Security Consultative Committee (SCC) also reaffirms the importance of the Japan–US alliance
February 1	US Department of Defense publishes the Quadrennial Defense Review
April 6	US releases the Nuclear Posture Review (NPR); the MOFA issues its annual Bluebook on foreign policy
April 12	Hatoyama holds talks with Obama during a working dinner at the Nuclear Security Summit in Washington
May 28	SCC issues a joint statement reiterating a commitment to relocate Marine Corps Air Station (MCAS) Futenma
June 5	Japan hosts the APEC forum trade minister's meeting in Sapporo, Hokkaidō (to June 6, 2010)
June 8	**Kan Naoto cabinet is formed** (September 2, 2011)
June 25	Muskoka Summit meeting convenes (to June 26)
June 27	Kan and Obama meet during the G20 Summit in Toronto; discussions include the Futenma issue
July 11	22nd general election of the House of Councilors (LDP 51, DPJ 44, YP 10, CGP 9, JCP 3, SDP 2, Minors 2)
July 16	Japan decides to extend JSDF participation in an anti-piracy mission off the coast of Somalia for one year
July 23	Secretary of State Hillary R. Clinton and Foreign Minister Okada Katsuya discuss Futenma relocation and the upcoming APEC forum in a meeting on the sidelines of the ASEAN Regional Forum (ARF) in Hanoi, Vietnam
August 6	US Ambassador to Japan John Roos represents the US at the Hiroshima Peace Memorial Ceremony; Japan decides to extend the JSDF participation in the UN peacekeeping mission in the Golan Heights until March 2011
September 3	Japan approves fresh sanctions on Iran over its nuclear enrichment program

September 7	Chinese fishing boat collides with a Japanese Coast Guard ship in waters around the Senkaku Islands; captain, crew, and ship are detained
September 23	Kan visits the US and holds talks with Obama in New York on the sidelines of the UNGA
October 25	US and Japan sign Open Skies memorandum of understanding on air transportation
October 28	Clinton reasserts the U position that the Senkaku Islands are covered by Article 5 of the Japan–US Security Treaty
November 12	Obama visits Japan (to November 14) and holds talks with Kan in Yokohama on November 13, 2010
November 14	APEC leaders adopt a joint declaration entitled "Yokohama Vision: Bogor and Beyond" outlining steps toward a Free Trade Area of the Asia-Pacific (FTAAP)
November 23	North Korea fires approximately 100 artillery rounds on and around Yeonpyeong island in the Yellow Sea; Obama denounces North Korea for the attack, consults with Lee, and agrees that a first response will be to hold joint military exercises
December 3	US military personnel and the JSDF participate in a bilateral training exercise titled Keen Sword 2011 (to December 10, 2010)
December 17	Japan releases the NDPG and Midterm Defense Plan

2011

February 14	Japan confirms that China has surpassed Japan as the world's second-largest economy in 2010
March 11	Magnitude-9.0 earthquake strikes off the northeast coast of Japan, generating a tsunami that devastates coastal areas and damages the Fukushima Daiichi nuclear power plant in Fukushima; Obama issues a statement sending condolences to the people of Japan and pledging US assistance
March 13	White House issues a press statement on the US response to the earthquake and tsunami in Japan including the dispatch by the US Agency for the International Development of a Disaster Assistance Team to Japan including nuclear experts from the Nuclear Regulatory Commission (NRC) and the positioning of the USS *Ronald Reagan* Carrier Strike Group off the coast of Japan to support the SDF in search-and-rescue and refueling efforts

April 1	Approximately 18,000 JSDF and 7,000 US military personnel begin a three-day joint operation to find people missing since the March 11 disaster
April 17	Secretary Clinton visits Japan, holds talks with Kan, Foreign Minister Matsumoto Takeaki, and meets the Emperor and Empress of Japan
May 1	Ministry of Defense announces that US military has mostly concluded earthquake relief efforts under the rubric of Operation Tomodachi but will continue to airlift personnel and supplies as needed
May 26	Deauville Summit meeting convenes (to May 27)
July 9	US, Japan, and Australia hold a joint naval exercise in the South China Sea
July 27	JSDF officially opens its own base in Djibouti in support of anti-piracy operations in the Gulf of Aden
August 2	Japan approves the annual defense white paper, which makes specific reference to Chinese maritime activities in the East and South China Seas
September 2	**Noda Yoshihiko cabinet is formed** (to December 26, 2012)
September 21	Noda visits the US and holds talks with Obama on the sidelines of the UNGA
November 12	Noda holds talks with Obama during the APEC forum in Honolulu, Hawaii
December 17	Kim Jong-il dies, and is succeeded by his son Kim Jong-un

2012

January 5	US releases a new strategic guidance for the Department of Defense emphasizing the centrality of the Asia-Pacific region to US defense strategy
April 26	"2+2" SCC meeting issues a joint statement detailing an agreement on the relocation of USMC from Okinawa to Guam
April 30	Noda holds talks with Obama and the two leaders issue a joint statement on the Japan–US alliance
May 14	40th anniversary of the reversion of Okinawa
May 18	Camp David Summit meeting convenes (to May 19)
May 21	Gemba and Hillary hold talks at the NATO Summit meeting in Chicago

June 18	Noda holds talks with Obama on the sidelines of the G20 Summit meeting in Mexico; they agree to proceed with consultations aimed at Japan's entry into the Trans-Pacific Partnership (TPP) free trade talks
June 29	US confirms that it will go ahead with the deployment of 12 MV-22 Osprey aircraft to American bases in Japan
July 7	Tokyo Conference on Afghanistan (to July 9, 2012)
August 10	Korean President Lee visits Takeshima Island, heightening tensions between Japan and Korea
September 11	Japan nationalizes three of the Senkaku Islands by purchasing them from a private owner; widespread anti-Japanese demonstrations follow in China
September 19	US and Japan agree on safety measures for the deployment of the MV-22 Osprey aircraft to Japan
October 16	Okinawa prefectural police arrest two US servicemen in the alleged rape of a Japanese woman
November 5	US military and JSDF begin biennial exercises near Okinawa
December 16	46th general election of the House of Representatives (LDP 294, DPJ 57, Japan Restoration Party 54, CGP 31, YP 18, Tomorrow Party of Japan 9, JCP 8, SDP 2, Minors 1, Independent 5); LDP returns to power with a landslide victory
December 26	**Second Abe Shinzō cabinet is formed** (to December 24, 2014)

2013

January 18	Foreign Minister Kishida Fumio visits the US, and holds talks with Clinton; reiterates that the islands are protected by the Japan–US security treaty and that the US "would oppose any unilateral actions that would seek to undermine Japanese administration"
January 20	**Obama (Democrat) is inaugurated for his second term as president** (to January 20, 2017)
January 30	Chinese warships locked fire-control radars on a Japanese helicopter and destroyer in the East China Sea
February 22	Abe and Obama hold a summit meeting
March 1	Japan decides to allow exports of parts produced by Japanese firms for the F-35 stealth fighter jet as an exception to Japan's ban on weapons exports

March 11	First Japan–US Comprehensive Dialogue on Space is held in Tokyo
March 15	Abe announces Japan's intention to enter the TPP negotiations and references bilateral consultations on market access in Japan
April 9	US and Japanese officials convene in Washington state for a bilateral extended deterrence dialogue (to April 11, 2013)
April 14	Secretary of State John Kerry visits Japan and holds talks with Kishida; goes even further during a press conference in Tokyo, stating that the US would "oppose any unilateral or coercive action that would somehow aim at changing the status quo" (to April 15, 2013)
April 29	Defense Minister Onodera Itsunori visits the US to discuss bilateral and regional defense issues with Secretary of Defense Chuck Hagel; reiterates that the Senkaku Islands fall under the US treaty obligations
June 10	JSDF participate in the amphibious exercise Dawn Blitz hosted by the US Navy and Marine Corps at Camp Pendleton, California (to June 26, 2013)
July 9	Japan releases its annual defense white paper expressing concern about China's military buildup
July 21	23rd general election of the House of Councilors (LDP 65, DPJ 17, CGP 11, JRP 8, JCP 8, YP 8, SDP 1, Minors 1, Independent 2)
July 23	US and the other parties to the TPP trade talks welcome Japan as the 12th member country at the 18th round of negotiations held in Malaysia
July 24	Obama nominates Caroline Kennedy to succeed John Roos as US ambassador to Japan
August 5	US military helicopter crashes on the grounds of Camp Hansen in Okinawa
September 5	Abe and Obama discuss security issues including Syria and North Korea, TPP trade negotiations, and other issues in a meeting on the margins of the G20 summit in St. Petersburg, Russia
September 7	International Olympic Committee selects Tokyo to host the 2020 Olympic Games

October 1	Abe announces a decision to increase the consumption tax from 5 to 8% beginning in April 2014
October 2	Kerry and Hagel visit Japan for the "2+2" SCC meeting in Tokyo; they sign a protocol amending the 2009 Guam International Agreement regarding the realignment of US forces in Japan (to October 3, 2013)
October 4	Kerry, Kishida, and Australian Foreign Minister Julie Bishop convene for a ministerial meeting of the US–Japan–Australia Trilateral Strategic Dialogue on the margins of the APEC summit in Bali, Indonesia
November 23	China announces plans for "East China Sea Air Defense Identification Zone" that includes the Senkaku Islands in its proper territory
November 26	US sends two B-52 bombers into China's ADIZ to demonstrate freedom of navigation in international airspace
December 17	Japan approves the country's first National Security Strategy as well as new NDPG and Midterm Defense Plan
December 26	Abe officially visits the Yasukuni Shrine

2014

January 24	Japan formally declares that Japan has ratified the Hague Convention on the Civil Aspects of International Child Abduction
March 18	Russia annexes Ukrainian territory of Crimea; Japan suspends bilateral talks on an investment pact with Russia to protest and to underscore its recognition of Crimea as an independent state
March 30	Department of State issues a statement commemorating the 160th anniversary of the establishment of diplomatic relations between the US and Japan
April 1	Japan increases the consumption tax from 5 to 8%; Abe cabinet approves new principles on the transfer of defense equipment, previously dubbed the three arms export principles; Hague Convention enters into force between the US and Japan
April 23	Obama visits Japan; the two governments issue a joint statement and fact sheet outlining priorities for bilateral cooperation on regional and global issues on April 25, 2014

May 15	Government advisory panel submits a report to Abe recommending changes in defense policy to exercise the right of collective self-defense
June 4	Brussels Summit meeting convenes (to June 5)
June 26	RIMPAC, the world's largest international maritime exercise, is hosted by the US Pacific Fleet in Hawaii; JSDF conducts an amphibious landing exercise with US counterparts on the margins of RIMPAC
July 1	Japan issues a decision on defense policy reforms including measures that would allow the JSDF to exercise the right of collective self-defense; the US welcomes and supports efforts made by Japan in the security field
July 9	North Korea launches multiple ballistic missiles toward the Sea of Japan
July 15	USMC begins relocating KC-130 refueling aircraft from MCAS Futenma in Okinawa to MCAS Iwakuni in Yamaguchi Prefecture
August 5	Japan imposes sanctions against Russia, restricting imports from Crimea and freezing assets in Japan of individuals and organizations associated with Russia's involvement in Ukraine
September 25	Abe visits the US and addresses the UNGA in New York
November 10	Prime Minister Abe and President Xi hold Japan–China summit at Beijing APEC
December 14	47th general election of the House of Representatives (LDP 291, DPJ 73, JRP 41, CGP 35, JCP 21, SDP 2, Minors 4, Independent 8); the ruling LDP and CGP prevail in the Lower House election, securing a two-thirds majority in the chamber
December 22	Obama signs the 2015 National Defense Authorization Act including partial funding for the transfer of USMC from Okinawa to Guam
December 24	**Third Abe cabinet is formed**

2015

January 26	Members of the US Marines and JSDF begin the annual bilateral training exercise Iron Fist, to include amphibious operations, at Camp Pendleton in Southern California

February 10	Japan revises official development assistance charter to allow funding on a case-by-case basis for non-military activities of another nation's armed forces such as disaster relief
February 17	The US think tank, the Center for Strategic and International Studies, publishes satellite imagery of construction of a man-made island in the South China Sea
March 9	US hosts a meeting in Hawaii among chief negotiators of the TPP (to March 15, 2015)
April 22	Prime Minister Abe and President Xi hold second Japan–China summit at the 60th anniversary ceremony marking the Asian–African Conference held in Bandung
April 26	Abe visits the US (to May 3) and holds summit meeting with Obama on April 28; addresses a joint session of Congress (to April 29, 2015)
April 27	"2+2" SCC meeting convenes in New York and issues new guidelines for bilateral defense cooperation and a joint statement on the Japan–US alliance
June 7	Schloss Elmau Summit meeting convenes (to June 8)
July 1	Abe cabinet enacts cabinet decision reinterpreting the constitution to enable a limited exercise of the right of collective self-defense
August 6	Prime Minister Abe's private "Advisory Panel on the History of the Twentieth Century and on Japan's Role and World Order in the Twenty-First Century" issues report
August 14	Abe issues a statement for 70th anniversary of the end of the Pacific War
October 27	United States conducts "freedom of navigation" operations, concerned by China's unilateral change in the status quo of the South China Sea

BIBLIOGRAPHY

Acheson, Dean. 1987. *Present at the Creation.* New York: Norton.

Adler, Selig. 1957. *The Isolationist Impulse.* New York: Abelard-Schuman.

Akami, Tomoko. 2002. *Internationalizing the Pacific.* London and New York: Routledge.

Akashi, Yasushi. 1995. *Nintai to kibō* [Hope and Perserverance]. Tokyo: Asahi Shimbunsha.

Amaya, Naohiro, Kyōgoku Junichi, and Kōsaka Masataka. 1984. Shinpojium: Kokkai kaikau e no teigen [Symposium: Opinions on Reforming the Diet]. *Chūōkōron.*

Amemiya, Shōichi. 1997. *Kindai Nihon no sensō shidō* [War Leadership of Modern Japan]. Tokyo: Yoshikawa-kōbunkan.

Andō, Yoshio, ed. 1979. *Kindai Nihon keizai-shi yōran* [Handbook of Modern Japanese Economic History]. 2nd ed. Tokyo: University of Tokyo Press.

Armacost, Michael H. 1996. *Friends or Rivals?* New York: Columbia University Press.

Asakawa, Kanichi. 1987. *Nihon no kaki* [Japan's Possible Calamities]. Annotated by Yura Kimiyoshi. Tokyo: Kōdansha (reprint).

Auslin, Michael R. 2004. *Negotiating with Imperialism.* Cambridge, MA and London: Harvard University Press.

Bailey, Thomas A. 1964. *Theodore Roosevelt and the Japanese American Crises.* Gloucester, MA: Peter Smith (reprint).

Beale, Howard K. 1956. *Theodore Roosevelt and the Rise of America to World Power.* Baltimore: Johns Hopkins University Press.

Bemis, Samuel Flagg. 1965. *A Diplomatic History of the United States.* 5th ed. New York: Holt, Rinehart and Winston.

© The Author(s) 2017   325
M. Iokibe (ed.), T. Minohara (trans. ed.), *The History of US–Japan Relations*, DOI 10.1007/978-981-10-3184-7

Bōeichō, Bōeikenshūjo Senshishitsu, ed. 1973–74. *Senshi sōsho: Daitōa sensō kaisen keii* [Official War History: Developments Leading Up to the Outbreak of the Greater East Asian War]. 5 Vols. Tokyo: Asagumo Shimbunsha.

Borton, Hugh. 1970. *Japan's Modern Century.* 2nd ed. New York: Ronald Press.

Brzezinski, Zbigniew. 1983. *Power and Principle.* New York: Farrar, Straus, and Giroux.

———. 2007. *Second Chance.* New York: Basic Books.

Burns, James MacGregor. 1970. *Roosevelt.* New York: Harcourt Brace Javanovich.

Bush, George W. 2010. *Decision Points.* New York: Crown Publishers.

Bush, George, and Brent Scowcroft. 1998. *A World Transformed.* New York: Knopf.

Chiba, Isao. 2005. 'Jiritsusei' kakutoku kateiki (1889–1919) no Nihon gaimushō [The Japanese Ministry of Foreign Affairs During the Period toward Attaining Autonomy (1889–1919)]. *Rekishigaku kenkyū* 806, 1–18, 43. Rekishgaku Kenkyūkai.

Clinton, Bill. 2004. *My Life.* New York: Alfred A. Knopf.

Cole, Wayne S. 1962. *Senator Gerald P. Nye and American Foreign Relations.* Minneapolis: University of Minnesota Press.

———. 1983. *Roosevelt and the Isolationists, 1932–1945.* Lincoln: University of Nebraska Press.

Coletta, Paolo E. 1973. *The Presidency of William Howard Taft.* Lawrence: University Press of Kansas.

Daalder, Ivo H., and James M. Lindsay. 2003. *America Unbound.* Washington, DC: Brookings Institution.

Dallek, Robert. 1995 [1979]. *Franklin D. Roosevelt and American Foreign Policy, 1932–1945.* New York: Oxford University Press. 1995 (2nd ed.).

Daniels, Roger. 1962. *The Politics of Prejudice.* Berkeley: University of California Press.

Davis, Kenneth S. 1986. *FDR: The New Deal Years 1933–1937.* New York: Random House.

———. 1993. *FDR: Into the Storm, 1937–1940.* New York: Random House.

———. 2000. *FDR: The War President, 1940–1943.* New York: Random House.

Dennett, Tyler. 1933. *John Hay.* New York: Dodd, Mead & Company.

———. 1959. *Roosevelt and the Russo-Japanese War.* Gloucester, MA: Peter Smith (reprint).

———. 1963. *Americans in Eastern Asia.* New York: Barnes & Noble.

Dumbrell, John. 1996. *American Foreign Policy.* New York: St. Martin's Press.

Eldridge, Robert D. 2003. *Okinawa mondai no kigen* [The Origins of the Bilateral Okinawa Problem]. Nagoya: Nagoya University Press.

———. 2014. *The Origins of US Policy in the East China Sea Islands Dispute.* London: Routledge.

Engelbrecht, H.C., and F.C. Hanighen. 1934. *Merchants of Death.* New York: Dodd, Mead & Co.

Esthus, Raymond A. 1966. *Theodore Roosevelt and Japan*. Seattle: University of Washington Press.

Feinman, Ronald L. 1981. *Twilight of Progressivism*. Baltimore: Johns Hopkins University Press.

Friedberg, Aaron L. 2011. *A Contest for Supremacy*. New York: W. W. Norton & Co.

Fujimoto, Kazumi, and Kazuhiro Asano. 1994. *Nichibei shunō kaidan to seiji katei* [Japan–US Summit Meetings and Political Processes]. Tokyo: Ryūkeishosha.

Fukuda, Shigeo. 1967. *Amerika no tainichi sansen* [America's Entry to the War Against Japan]. Kyōto: Minerva Shobō.

Fukunaga, Fumio. 1997. *Senryōka chūdō seiken no keisei to hōkai* [The Rise and Fall of the Centrist Administration in the Occupation Period]. Tokyo: Iwanami Shoten.

Funabashi, Yōichi. 1997. *Dōmei hyōryū* [Alliance Adrift]. Tokyo: Iwanami Shoten.

———. 2006. *Za peninshura kuesuchon* [The Peninsula Question]. Tokyo: Asahi Shimbunsha.

———. 2012. *Kauntodaun merutodaun* [Countdown to Meltdown]. Tokyo: Bungeishunjū.

Gaddis, John Lewis. 2005. *The Cold War*. New York: Penguin Press.

Gaimushō, ed. 1952. *Shūsen shiroku* [History of Events Leading to Japan's Surrender]. Tokyo: Shimbun Gekkansha.

———, ed. 2001–02. *Nihon gaikō monjo* [Documents on Japanese Foreign Policy]. Vol. 1–5. Tokyo: Gaimushō.

Gaimushō, Chōsa-bu, ed. 1992. *Nichibei gaikō-shi* [History of US–Japan Diplomacy]. Tokyo: Kress Publishing, (copy).

Gaimushō hyakunen-shi hensan iinkai. 1969. *Gaimushō no hyakunen* [A Hundred Years of the Ministry of Foreign Affairs]. Vol. 1. Tokyo: Hara Shobō.

Gallicchio, Marc S. 1988. *The Cold War Begins in Asia*. New York: Columbia University Press.

Gardner, Lloyd C. 1993. *Spheres of Influence*. Chicago: Elephant Paperback.

Gotō-Shibata, Harumi. 1995. *Japan and Britain in Shanghai, 1925–31*. Basingstoke: Macmillan Press.

Griswold, A. Whitney. 1966. *The Far Eastern Policy of the United States*. New Haven: Yale University Press (reprint).

Hammersmith, Jack L. 1998. *Spoilsmen in a "Flowery Fairyland."* Kent: Kent State University Press.

Harris, Townsend. 1959. *The Complete Journal of Townsend Harris*. Revised edition. Rutland: C.E. Tuttle.

Hata, Ikuhiko. 1972. *Taiheiyo kokusai kankei-shi* [History of the International Relations of the Pacific Area]. Tokyo: Fukumura Shuppan.

Hatano, Sumio. 1988. *Daitōa sensō no jidai* [The Era of the Greater East Asia War]. Tokyo: Asahi Shuppansha.

———. 1991. *Bakuryō tachi no Shinjuwan* [The Role of Military Officials in the Decision Making Process for Pearl Harbor]. Tokyo: Asahi Shimbunsha.

Henning, Joseph M. 2000. *Outposts of Civilization*. New York: New York University Press.

Hirama, Yōichi. 1998. *Daiichiji sekai taisen to Nihon kaigun* [World War I and the Japanese Navy]. Tokyo: Keio University Press.

Hirobe, Izumi. 2001. *Japanese Pride, American Prejudice*. Palo Alto: Stanford University Press.

Hodgson, James D. 1995. *US Ambassador to Japan*. Beverly Hills: Private Publisher.

Hosokawa, Morisada. 2002. *Hosokawa nikki* [The Hosokawa Diary]. 2 Vols. Tokyo: Chūōkōron-shinsha.

Hosoya, Chihiro, ed. 1982. *Nichiei kankei-shi* [Anglo–Japanese Relations]. Tokyo: University of Tokyo Press.

———. 1984. *San Furanshisuko kōwa e no michi* [Road to the San Francisco Peace Treaty]. Tokyo: Chūōkōronsha.

———. 1988. *Ryō taisenkan no Nihon gaikō* [Japanese Diplomacy between the Wars]. Tokyo: Iwanami Shoten.

———. 2005. *Shiberia shuppei no shiteki kenkyū* [A Historical Study of the Siberian Intervention]. Tokyo: Iwanami Shoten.

Hosoya, Chihiro, and Homma Nagayo, ed. 1991. *Nichibei kankei-shi* [History of US–Japan Relations]. 2nd ed. Tokyo: Yūhikaku Publishing.

Hubbard, Richard B. 1899. *The United States in the Far East, or, Modern Japan and the Orient*. Richmond: B.F. Johnson Publishing.

Hull, Cordell. 1948. *The Memoirs of Cordell Hull*. 2 Vols. New York: Macmillan.

Igarashi, Takeshi. 1995. *Sengo Nichibei kankei no keisei* [The Formation of Postwar US–Japan Relations]. Tokyo: Kōdansha.

Ikeda, Tadashi. 1996. *Kanbojia wahei e no Michi* [Toward a Peace Settlement in Cambodia]. Tokyo: Toshi Shuppan.

Ikenberry, G. John. 2001. *After Victory*. Princeton: Princeton University Press.

Imagawa, Yukio. 2000. *Kanbojia to Nihon* [Cambodia and Japan]. Tokyo: Rengō Shuppan.

Inoki, Masamichi. 1981. *Hyōden Yoshida Shigeru* [Yoshida Shigeru]. 4 Vols. Tokyo: Yomiuri Shimbunsha (Popular edition).

Inoue, Katsuo. 2002. *Kaikoku to Bakumatsu henkaku* [The Opening of the Country and Changes during the Late Bakufu Period]. Tokyo: Kōdansha.

Inoue, Toshikazu. 1994. *Kiki no naka no kyōchō gaikō* [Cooperative Diplomacy in a Period of Crisis]. Tokyo: Yamakawa Shuppansha.

Iokibe, Makoto. 2005. *Nichibei sensō to sengo Nihon* [The US–Japan War and Postwar Japan]. Tokyo: Kōdansha.

———, ed. 2008. *90-nendai no shōgen: Okamoto Yukio* [Testimony from the 1990s: Okamoto Yukio]. Tokyo: Asahi Shimbun Publications.

————, ed. 2014. *Sengo Nihon gaikō-shi* [The Diplomatic History of Postwar Japan]. 3rd Revised and Enlarged edition. Tokyo: Yuhikaku Publishing.

Iokibe, Makoto, and Miyagi Taizō, ed. 2013. *Hashimoto Ryūtarō gaikō kaikoroku* [Memoir of Hashimoto Ryūtarō's Foreign Policy]. Tokyo: Iwanami Shoten.

Iokibe, Makoto, Itō Motoshige, and Yakushiji Katsuyuki, ed. 2006. *90-nendai no shōgen: Miyazawa Kiichi* [Testimony from the 1990s: Miyazawa Kiichi]. Tokyo: Asahi Shimbunsha.

Iriye, Akira. 1972. *Pacific Estrangement*. Cambridge: Harvard University Press.

————. 1987. *The Origins of the Second World War in Asia and the Pacific*. London and New York: Longman.

Ishii, Takashi. 1972. *Nihonkaikoku-shi* [History of the Opening of Japan]. Tokyo: Yoshikawa-kōbunkan.

————. 1982. *Meiji shoki no Nihon to Higashi-Ajia* [Japan and East Asia in Early Meiji]. Tokyo: Yūrindō.

Japanese Political Science Association, ed. 1997. *Nenpō seijigaku 1997: Kiki no Nihon gaikō* [Annual Report on Political Science 1997: Japanese Diplomacy in Crisis]. Tokyo: Iwanami Shoten.

Johnson, U. Alexis, and Jeff O. McAllister. 1984. *The Right Hand of Power*. Englewood Cliffs, NJ: Prentice Hall.

Kaikoku Hyakunen Kinen Bunka Jigyōkai, ed. 1956. *Nichibei bunka kōshō-shi* [A History of US–Japan Cultural Relations], ed. Kamikawa Hiromatsu. Vol. 1. Tokyo: Yōyōsha.

Kajima, Morinosuke. 1958. *Nihon gaikō seisaku no shiteki kōsatsu* [Historical Examination of Japanese Diplomatic Policy]. Tokyo: Kajima Kenkyūjo.

————. 1970. *Nihon gaikō-shi Dai-8 kan.* [History of Japanese Diplomacy]. Vol. 8. Tokyo: Kajima Kenkyūjo Shuppankai.

Katagiri, Yasuo. 2003. *Taiheiyō mondai chōsakai no kenkyū* [Study on the Institute of Pacific Relations]. Tokyo: Keio University Press.

Katō, Yūzō. 1994. *Kurofune zengo no sekai* [The World at the Time of the Black Ships]. Tokyo: Chikuma Shobō.

Kennan, George F. 1983. *Memoirs 1925–1950*. New York: Pantheon (reprint).

Kimball, Warren F. 1984. *Churchill and Roosevelt, the Complete Correspondence: I, II, III*. Princeton, NJ: Princeton University Press.

————. 1991. *The Juggler*. Princeton: Princeton University Press.

Kimura, Masato. 1997. *Zaikai nettowāku to Nichi-Bei gaikō* [Businessmen's Networks and US–Japanese Relations]. Tokyo: Yamakawa Shuppansha.

Kissinger, Henry. 1982. *Years of Upheaval*. Boston, MA: Little, Brown.

Kitaoka, Shinichi. 1978. *Nihon rikugun to tairiku seisaku* [The Japanese Army and Its Continental Policy]. Tokyo: University of Tokyo Press.

Kitasaki, Susumu. 1909. *Nichibei kōshō gojū-nen-shi* [50 Years of US–Japan Negotiations]. Tokyo: Dainihon Bunmei Kyōkai.

Kōsaka, Masataka. 1996. *Fushigi no Nichi-Bei kankei-shi* [A Peculiar Affair: Japan and the US]. Tokyo: PHP Kenkyūjo.

Kubo, Fumiaki, ed. 2003. *G.W. Busshu seiken to Amerika no hoshu seiryoku* [The G.W. Bush Administration and the Conservative Forces in the United States]. Tokyo: Japan Institute of International Affairs, 2003.

Kubo, Fumiaki, Nakayama Toshihiro, and Watanabe Masahito. 2012. *Obama, Amerika, sekai* [America and the World in the Age of Obama]. Tokyo: NTT Publishing.

Kubo, Fumiaki, Takahata Akio, and The Tokyo Foundation, ed. 2013. *Gendai Amerika purojekuto*. Ajia kaiki suru Amerika [America's Rebalancing to Asia]. Tokyo: NTT Publishing.

Kuriyama, Takakazu. 1997. *Nichibei dōmei hyōryū kara no dakkyaku* [The Japan–US Alliance: From Drift to Revitalization]. Tokyo: Nihon Keizai Shimbunsha.

Kuroki, Yūkichi. 1968. *Komura Jutarō* [Komura Jutarō]. Tokyo: Kōdansha.

Kurosaki, Akira. 2006. *Kakuheiki to nichibei kankei* [Nuclear Weapons and Japan–US Relations]. Tokyo: Yūshisha.

Kusunoki, Ayako. 2006. Yoshida Shigeru no anzen-hoshō seisaku [Yoshida Shigeru's National Security Policy]. *Kokusai Seiji* 144, 99–115.

———. 2009. *Yoshida Shigeru to Anzen Hosho Seisaku no Keisei: Nichibei no Anzen Hosho Koso to sono Sogo Sayo, 1943–1952* [Yoshida Shigeru and the Making of Japan's Postwar Security Policy: The Interaction of Ideas for Peace and Stability between the US and Japan, 1943–1952]. Minerva Shobō.

LaFeber, Walter. 1993. *The American Search for Opportunity, 1865–1913*. Cambridge: Cambridge University Press.

———. 1997. *The Clash*. New York: W.W. Norton & Company.

Leopold, Richard W. 1954. *Elihu Root and the Conservative Tradition*. Boston: Little Brown and Co.

Link, Arthur S. 1979. *Woodrow Wilson*. Arlington Heights: Harlan Davidson.

MacMillan, Margaret. 2002. *Peacemakers*. London: John Murray.

Mann, James. 1999. *About Face*. New York: Knopf.

———. 2007. *The China Fantasy*. New York: Viking Press.

Masuda, Hiroshi. 1996. *Kōshoku tsuihō* [The Purging of Public Officials]. Tokyo: University of Tokyo Press.

Masumi, Junnosuke. 1966/67. *Nihon seitō shiron* [On the History of Japanese Political Parties]. Vol. 2–3. Tokyo: University of Tokyo Press.

———. 1983. *Sengo seiji* [Postwar Politics]. 2 Vols. Tokyo: University of Tokyo Press.

Matsuoka, Yōsuke. 1931. *Ugoku manmō* [Moving Manchuria-Mongolia]. Tokyo: Senshinsha.

Minohara, Toshihiro. 2002. *Hai-Nichi iminhō to nichibeikankei* [The 1924 Immigration Act and US–Japan Relations]. Tokyo: Iwanami Shoten.

———. 2006. *Kaliforunia shū no hai-Nichi undō to Nichibei kankei* [The Anti-Japanese Movement in California and US–Japan Relations]. Tokyo: Yūhikaku Publishing.

Mitani, Hiroshi. 2003. *Perri raikō* [Commodore Perry's Delegation]. Tokyo: Yoshikawa-kōbunkan (new format).

Mitani, Taichirō. 1995. *Zōho Nihon seitō seiji no keisei* [The State of Japanese Party Politics]. Extended edition. Tokyo: University of Tokyo Press.

Miyagi, Taizō. 2001. *Bandon kaigi to Nihon no Ajia fukki* [The Bandung Conference and Japan's Return to Asia]. Tokyo: Sōshisha.

Miyazato, Seigen. 2000. *Nichibei kankei to Okinawa 1945–1972* [Japan–US Relations and Okinawa 1945–1972]. Tokyo: Iwanami Shoten.

Miyazawa, Kiichi. 1999. *Tōkyō–Washinton No Mitsudan* [The Tokyo–Washington Secret Talks]. Chūōkōronsha.

Mōri, Kazuko, and Mōri Kōzaburō, trans. 2001. *Nikuson hōchū kimitsu kaidan-roku* [Confidential Meeting Transcripts from Nixon's Visit to China]. Nagoya: University of Nagoya Press.

Mōri, Toshihiko. 2002. *Meiji ishin seiji gaikō-shi kenkyū* [Research on Political Diplomacy of the Meiji Restoration]. Tokyo: Yoshikawa-kōbunkan.

Morison, Elting E., ed. 1951, 1954. *The Letters of Theodore Roosevelt*. Vol. 3, 4, 7. Cambridge, MA: Harvard University Press.

Morison, Samuel Elliot. 1967. *Old Bruin*. Boston: Little, Brown and Company.

Motohashi, Tadashi. 1986. *Nichibei kankei-shi kenkyū* [Research on the History of US–Japan Relations]. Tokyo: Gakushūin University.

Murai, Ryōta. 2005. *Seitō naikakusei no seiritsu 1918–1927* [The Establishment of the Party Cabinet System, 1918–1927]. Tokyo: Yūhikaku Publishing.

Murata, Kōji. 1998. *Daitōryō no zasetsu* [The President Fails]. Tokyo: Yuhikaku Publishing.

Mutsu, Munemitsu. 1983. *Shintei Kenkenroku* [New Revision Diplomatic Records]. Annotated by Nakatsuka Akira. Tokyo: Iwanami Shoten.

Naganuma, Hideyo. 2000. Reexamining the "American Century." *The Japanese Journal of American Studies* 11, 13.

Nakano, Hirofumi. 1990. Dainiji FDR seikenki ni okeru kakushinha gurūpu [The progressives in the second FDR administration]. *Seijigakuronshū* [Journal of the Gakushuin University Graduate School of Political Studies], 3, 1–39.

Naraoka, Sōchi. 2006. *Katō Takaaki to seitō seiji* [Katō Takaaki and Party Politics]. Tokyo: Yamakawa Shuppansha.

Neu, Charles E. 1967. *An Uncertain Friendship*. Cambridge: Harvard University Press.

———. 1975. *The Troubled Encounter*. New York: John Wiley and Sons.

Neumann, William L. 1963. *America Encounters Japan*. Baltimore: Johns Hopkins Press.

Nichibei sentetsu kōkan dōmeikai, ed. 1920. *Nichibei sentetsu kōkan dōmei-shi* [History of the US–Japan Steel and Ships Exchange Alliance]. Tokyo: Nichibei sentetsu kōkan dōmeikai.

Nihon Kokusai Seiji Gakkai Taiheiyō Sensō Genin Kenkyūbu, ed. 1987–88. *Taiheiyō sensō e no michi* [The Road to the Pacific War]. Vols. 1–7. Tokyo: Asahi Shirnbunsha (new format).

Nishimura, Kumao. 1971. *Nihon gaikō-shi 27: San Furanshisuko heiwa jōyaku* [A Diplomatic History of Japan Vol. 27: The San Francisco Peace Treaty]. Tokyo: Kajima Kenkyūjo.

Nishizaki, Fumiko. 1992. *Amerika reisen seisaku to kokuren 1945–1950* [American Cold War Policy and the United Nations, 1945–1950]. Tokyo: University of Tokyo Press.

Oberdorfer, Don. 1997. *The Two Koreas*. New York: Basic Books.

Ogura, Kazuo. 2003. *Yoshida Shigeru no jimon* [Yoshida Shigeru's Reflections]. Tokyo: Fujiwara Shoten.

Okamoto, Shumpei. 1970. *The Japanese Oligarchy and the Russo-Japanese War*. New York: Columbia University Press.

Patterson, James T. 2005. *Restless Giant*. New York: Oxford University Press.

Paulson, Henry. 2010. *On the Brink*. New York: Business Plus.

Perkins, Bradford. 1993. *The Creation of a Republican Empire, 1776–1865*. Cambridge: Cambridge University Press.

Perry, Matthew C. 1954. *Narrative of the Expedition of an American Squadron to the China Seas and Japan, performed in the years 1852, 1853, and 1854*. London: MacDonald.

Plischke, Elmer. 1999. *US Department of State*. Westport: Greenwood Press.

Pringle, Henry F. 1939. *The Life and Times of William Howard Taft*. 2 Vols. New York: Farrar and Rinehart.

———. 1956. *Theodore Roosevelt*. New York: Harcourt.

Reagan, Ronald. 1990. *An American Life*. New York: Simon and Schuster.

Safford, Jeffrey J. 1970. Experiment in Containment. *Pacific Historical Review* 39. Berkeley: University of California Press.

Sakai, Tetsuya. 1992. *Taisho demokurashi taisei no hōkai* [The Collapse of Taisho Democracy]. Tokyo: University of Tokyo Press.

Sakamoto, Kazuya. 2000. *Nichibei dōmei no kizuna* [The Bond of the Japan–US Alliance]. Tokyo: Yūhikaku Publishing.

Sanbō, Honbu, ed. 1967. *Haisen no kiroku* [A Record of the Defeat]. Tokyo: Hara Shobō.

Sasaki, Takuya. 1993. *Fūjikome no keisei to henyō* [The Development and Shift of Containment]. Tokyo: Sanrei Shobō.

Satō, Hideo. 1991. *Nichibei keizai masatsu 1945–1990-nen* [Economic Friction between Japan and the US, 1945–1990]. Tokyo: Heibonsha.

Satō, Tatsuo. 1994. *Nihonkoku kenpō seiritsushi* [Making the Japanese Constitution: A History]. Annotated by Satō Isao. Vol. 3–4. Tokyo: Yūhikaku Publishing.

Schaller, Michael. 1997. *Altered States.* New York: Oxford University Press.

Sears, Louis Martin. 1938. *A History of American Foreign Relations.* 3rd ed. New York: Thomas Y. Crowell.

Seki, Shizuo. 2007. *Rondon kaigun jōyaku seiritsushi* [History of the Establishment of the London Naval Treaty]. Kyōto: Minerva Shobō.

Shibayama, Futoshi. 2010. *Nihon Saigunbi he no Michi, 1945–1950 Nen* [Road to Japanese Rearmament, 1945–1950]. Minerva Shobō.

Shigemitsu, Mamoru. 1952. *Shōwa no dōran* [The Showa Era: Years of Upheaval]. 2 Vols. Tokyo: Chūōkōronsha.

Shimada, Yōichi. 1997. Taika nijūikkajō mondai [The Problem of the Twenty-One Demands to China]. In *Nihon rekishi taikei fukyūban 16* [Outline of Japanese History Popular Edition], ed. Inoue Mitsusada, Nagahara Keiji, Kodama Kōta, and Ōkubo Toshiaki, 45–58. Tokyo: Yamakawa Shuppansha.

Shimizu, Hajime, ed. 1986. *Ryō taisen kanki Nihon Tōnan Ajia kankei no shosō* [The History of Japan and Southeast Asia during the Two World Wars]. Tokyo: Ajia Keizai Kenkyūjo.

Shimazu, Naoko. 1998. *Japan, Race, and Equality.* London: Routledge.

Shinobu, Seizaburō, and Nakayama Jiichi, ed. 1972. *Nichiro Sensō-shi no kenkyū* [Research on the Russo-Japanese War]. Revised publication. Tokyo: Kawade Shobō-shinsha.

Shinoda, Tomohito. 2006. *Reisengo no Nihon gaikō* [Post–Cold War Japanese Foreign Policy]. Kyōto: Minerva Shobō.

Shiozaki, Hiroaki. 1984. *Nichi-bei-ei sensō no kiro* [The Crossroads of War Between Japan, America, and Britain]. Tokyo: Yamakawa Shuppansha.

Shōda, Tatsuo. 1981. *Jūshin-tachi no Shōwa-shi.* Vol. 2 [History of the Senior Statesmen in the Showa Period]. Tokyo: Bungeishunjū.

Shōji, Takayuki. 2015. *Jieitai kaigai haken to Nihon gaikō* [Overseas Dispatch of the Self-Defense Forces and Japan's Foreign Policy]. Tokyo: Nihon Keizai Hyōronsha.

Slavinsky, Boris N. 1995. *The USSR–Japan Treaty and Stalin's Diplomacy.* Moscow: TOO Novina.

———. 1999. *USSR–Japan: On the Way to War.* Moscow: ZAO Iaponiia segodnia.

Soeya, Yoshihide. 2005. *Nihon no 'midoru pawā' gaikō* [Japan's Middle Power Diplomacy]. Tokyo: Chikuma Shobō.

Steinberg, James B., and Michael E. O'Hanlon. 2014. *Strategic Reassurance and Resolve.* Princeton: Princeton University Press.

Stoler, Mark A. 2000. *Allies and Adversaries.* Chapel Hill: University of North Carolina Press.

Sudō, Shinji. 1986. *Nichibei kaisen gaikō no kenkyū* [Study on the Diplomacy Leading Up to War Between Japan and America]. Tokyo: Keiō Tsūshin.

Sugiyama, Shinya, and Ian Brown, ed. 1990. *Senkanki Tonan Ajia no keizai masatsu* [International Commercial Rivalry in Southeast Asia in the Interwar Period]. Tokyo: Dōbunkan.

Suzuki, Akinori. 1995. *Nihonkoku kenpō o unda misshitsu no kokonokakan* [The Nine Days Behind Closed Doors that Led to the Establishment of the Japanese Constitution]. Osaka: Sōgensha.

Tabohashi, Kiyoshi. 1976. *Zōtei: Kindai nihon gaikoku kankei-shi* [A History of Modern Japanese Foreign Relations]. Revised edition. Hara Shobo.

Tadokoro, Masayuki. 2001. *Amerika o koeta doru* [The Dollar that Goes beyond the United States]. Tokyo: Chūōkōron-shinsha.

Takagi, Yasaka. 1971. *Takagi Yasaka chosaku shū dai-san kan* [Collection of the Writings of Takagi Yasaka], ed. Tōkyō Daigaku Amerika Kenkyū Sentā. Vol. 3. Tokyo: University of Tokyo Press.

Takahara, Shūsuke. 2006. *Uiruson gaikō to nihon* [Wilson Diplomacy and Japan]. Tokyo: Sōbunsha.

Takemae, Eiji. 1992. *Senryō sengo-shi* [History of the Postwar Occupation Period]. Tokyo: Iwanami Shoten.

Tanaka, Akihiko. 1997. *Anzen hoshō* [Military Security]. Tokyo: Yomiuri Shimbunsha.

Tanaka, Takahiko. 1993. *Nisso kokkō kaifuku no shiteki kenkyū* [Historical Research on the Restoration of Relations between Japan and the Soviet Union]. Tokyo: Yuhikaku Publishing.

Teramoto, Yasutoshi. 1999. *Nichiro sensō igo no Nihon gaikō* [Japan's Diplomacy after the Russo–Japanese War]. Tokyo: Shinzansha Shuppan.

Terasaki, Osamu. 1980. Meiji Nijū-nen, Ikeshima jiken no ikkōsatsu [An Inquiry Into the Ikeshima Incident, 1887]. *Keio Gijuku Daigaku hōgaku kenkyū* 53 (6 and 7). Tokyo: Keio University.

Teshima, Ryūichi. 1996. *1991-nen Nihon no haiboku* [Japan's Defeat in 1991]. Tokyo: Shinchōsha.

Thomson, James C. Jr., Peter W.I. Stanley, and John Curtis Perry. 1985. *Sentimental Imperialists.* New York: Harper and Row (reprint).

Tōgō, Shigenori. 1985. *Jidai no ichimen* [An Aspect of the Showa Period]. Tokyo: Hara Shobō.

Tōmatsu, Haruo. 1999. Nanyō guntō inintōchi keizoku o meguru kokusai kankyō 1931–35 [The International Environment Around the Renewal of the Mandate of the Pacific Islands 1931–35]. *Kokusai Seiji* 122, 101–115.

Trani, Eugene P. 1969. *The Treaty of Portsmouth.* Lexington: University of Kentucky Press.

Treat, Payson Jackson. 1921. *Japan and the United States, 1853–1921.* Boston: Houghton Mifflin.

————. 1963. *Diplomatic Relations Between the United States and Japan.* Gloucester, MA: Peter Smith (reprint).

Tsunoda, Jun. 1967. *Manshū mondai to kokubō hōshin* (The Manchuria Problem and the Basic Plan of National Defense). Tokyo: Hara Shobō.

United States Congress, Senate, 74th Congress, 2nd Session, Special Committee to Investigate the Munitions Industry. 1936. *Munitions Industry (The Nye Report).* Washington, DC.

United States Department of State. 1977. *Foreign Relations of the United States (FRUS)* 1951. Vol. 6, Asia and the Pacific, part 1. Washington, DC: US Government Printing Office.

Usui, Katsumi. 1972. *Nihon to Chūgoku* [Japan and China]. Tokyo: Hara Shobō.

————. 2000. *Nitchū sensō* [The Second Sino–Japanese War]. 2nd ed. Tokyo: Chūōkōron-shinsha.

Utley, Jonathan G. 1985. *Going to War with Japan, 1937–1941.* Knoxville: University of Tennessee Press.

Watanabe, Akio, and Miyazato Seigen, ed. 1986. *San Furanshisuko kōwa* [The San Francisco Peace Treaty]. Tokyo: University of Tokyo Press.

Williams, Samuel Wells, ed. 1973. *A Journal of the Perry Expedition to Japan, 1853–1854.* Wilmington: Scholarly Resources (reprint).

Williams, William J. 1993. American Steel and Japanese Ships. *Prologue: The Journal of the National Archives* 25 (3). Washington, DC: National Archives and Records Service.

Woods, Randall Bennett. 1990. *A Changing of the Guard.* Chapel Hill: University of North Carolina Press.

Woodward, Bob. 2004. *Plan of Attack.* New York: Simon and Schuster.

————. 2006. *State of Denial.* New York: Simon and Schuster.

————. 2010. *Obama's Wars.* New York: Simon and Schuster.

Yakushiji, Katsuyuki. 2014. *Gendai nihon seijishi* [Political History of Contemporary Japan]. Tokyo: Yūhikaku Publishing.

Yamaoka, Michio. 1997. *"Taiheiyō mondai chōsakai" kenkyū* [Study on the Institute of Pacific Relations]. Tokyo: Ryūkeishosha.

Yoshii, Hiroshi. 1987. *Zōho: Nichi-Doku-I sangoku dōmei to Nichi-Bei kankei* [The Tripartite Pact and US–Japan Relations]. Enlarged edition. Tokyo: Nansōsha.

Yoshino, Sakuzō. 1996. *Yoshino Sakuzō senshū 8* [Collected Works of Yoshino Sakuzō, vol. 8]. Tokyo: Iwanami Shoten.

Yui, Daizaburō. 1989. *Mikan no senryō kaikaku* [Unfinished Reforms in Occupied Japan]. Tokyo: University of Tokyo Press.

INDEX

© The Author(s) 2017

M. Iokibe (ed.), T. Minohara (trans. ed.), *The History of US–Japan Relations*, DOI 10.1007/978-981-10-3184-7